Michael Draxlbauer, Astrid M. Fellner, Thomas Fröschl (Eds.)

# (Anti-)Americanisms

# American Studies in Austria

edited by

Astrid M. Fellner
(University of Vienna)

Klaus Rieser
(University of Graz)

Hanna Wallinger
(University of Salzburg)

Volume 2

LIT

Michael Draxlbauer, Astrid M. Fellner,
Thomas Fröschl (Eds.)

# (Anti-)Americanisms

LIT

Gedruckt mit Förderung des Bundesministeriums für Bildung, Wissenschaft und Kultur in Wien.

**Bibliographic information published by Die Deutsche Bibliothek**
Die Deutsche Bibliothek lists this publication in the Deutsche Nationalbibliografie; detailed bibliographic data are available in the Internet at http://dnb.ddb.de.

ISBN 3-8258-6763-3

© LIT VERLAG Wien 2004
Krotenthallergasse. 10  A-1080 Wien
Tel. +43 (0) 1 / 409 56 61   Fax +43 (0) 1 / 409 56 97
e-Mail: wien@lit-verlag.at    http://www.lit-verlag.at

# Table of Contents

In Memoriam Kurt Albert Mayer     8

*Michael Draxlbauer, Astrid M. Fellner and Thomas Fröschl*
Introduction     11

*Paul Lauter*
Is American Studies Anti-American?     18

**Part I: (Anti-)Americanisms since the Mid-18th Century**

*Timothy Conley*
Ante-Americanisms: Friendly Critiques of the Emerging Nation     33

*Thomas Fröschl*
Historical Roots of European Anti-Americanism in the 18th
and 19th Centuries     59

*Paul Crumbley*
The "Purple Democrat": Emily Dickinson and the Sovereignty
of Democratic Consent     74

*Markus Heide*
Ambivalent Vistas: José Martí's "Our America," Nineteenth-
Century Pan-Americanism and Hemispheric American Studies     89

*Louis J. Kern*
'The Biologic Aspects of Immigration,' 'Racial Crime,' and
the Looming Threat of Cacocracy: Eugenics, Immigration
Restriction, and the Reconstruction of Americanism in the 1920s     106

*Roman Puff*
Three-Quarter Enemies: Anti-Americanism in Austria-Hungary

during World War I                                                    130

*Günter Bischof*
Austrian Anti-Americanism after World War II              140

## Part II: (Anti-)Americanisms in Some 20th-Century Literary Texts

*Vincent Kling*
Surrounding Johann Breitwieser: A Comparative Literary Study
in Representation                                                     173

*Verena Klein*
Anti-Americanisms in Contemporary Canadian Fiction       208

*Sylvia Schiefer*
Americanisms under the Critical Eye of African-American
Poet, Writer, Singer and Musician Gil Scott-Heron: the
"Movie" Poems                                                        224

## Part III: (Anti-)Americanisms in Popular Culture, Sport and the Media

*Greta Olson*
Inarticulate, Violent White American Men                      233

*Carmen Birkle*
Barbie's (American) Success Story                                252

*Duco van Oostrum*
The Black Athlete's Battle Royal of the 1960s: Anti-American
Protests in American Sports                                       268

*Monika Messner*
"On Behalf of a Proud, Determined, and Grateful Nation . . .":
Americanism in Sports                                              285

*Andreas Weissenbäck*
Advertising and the 'Americanization' of Western Europe   295

*Claudia Schwarz*
Spin-ning Wheel America: Americanism and Anti-Americanism
Constructed by the Media   307

*Markus Rheindorf*
Civilization(s): Rewriting History in Interactive Media   323

Contributors   340

# In Memoriam Kurt Albert Mayer
## (1955–2002)

### AAAS President 2001/02

Kurt Albert Mayer passed away tragically and unexpectedly on July 19, 2002. He was 47 years old. As President of the Austrian Association for American Studies he had been in charge of organizing the 29th annual conference in November 2002 and had begun planning the conference proceedings.

At his death, Kurt Mayer was Professor of American Studies at the Department of English and American Studies at the University of Vienna, where he had taught since 1986. From 1980 to 1982 he had held a Fulbright scholarship at the English Department at SUNY/Buffalo, where he studied with Marcus Klein and received an M.A. Upon his return to Vienna he began work on his doctoral thesis entitled "Jack Kerouac, Ken Kesey, and Richard Brautigan: Popular Culture and Literary Aspirations." After receiving his Ph.D. in 1986, he became Assistant Professor in the Department. In 1999 he was appointed Associate Professor after having completed his "Habilitation" on the topic of "Henry Adams and the German-speaking World."

Kurt Mayer was an excellent scholar and teacher, whose work will continue to inspire young colleagues and students. His scholarship went deeper than research, for he brought to his intellectual projects a great depth of experience and enthusiasm. His knowledge of Austrian and American cultures was impressive, ranging from Ambrose Bierce to Wolfgang Ambros, from Reconstruction to road movies, from Longstreet to Little Feat. To his students, he was unique as he considered them partners in the project of critical inquiry. He will be fondly remembered for his outstanding scholarship, his pivotal position as an organizer of scholarly groups and excursions, and his prolific production of pioneering academic websites. The "Easy Rider" web anthology (at <http://www.univie.ac.at/Anglistik/easyrider/welcome.htm>) remains a living presence of Kurt's spirit.

Kurt was a compassionate intellectual, and his aspirations seemed boundless. It is tragic that his many projects were cut short by his death at such an early age. The editors hope that this volume of papers from the conference Kurt had envisioned, reflects his multi-faceted ideas and ideals.

Selected Publications:

"Some German Chapters of Henry Adams's Education: 'Berlin (1858-1859),' Heine, and Goethe." *Arbeiten aus Anglistik und Amerikanistik* 19.1 (1994): 3-25.

"Henry Adams: 'And I've Retouched My Austria.'" *Images of Central Europe in Travelogues and Fictions by North American Writers.* Ed. Waldemar Zacharasiewicz. Tübingen: Stauffenburg, 1995. 104-18.

*Die Wienbilder der amerikanischen Delegierten John Hay und Charles Francis Adams jr.* Wien: n.p., 1995.

"Henry Adams and the Race for Race." *Amerikastudien/American Studies* 41 (1996): 83-111.

"'*We Are On the Borderline of Civilzation*': John Hay als Bevollmächtigter Gesandter der Vereinigten Staaten in Wien (1867/68)." *Mitteilungen des Österreichischen Staatsarchivs* 44 (1996): 194-234.

"Henry Adams and the Education of Henry Cabot Lodge." *Multiculturalism and the American Self.* Ed. William Boelhower and Alfred Hornung. Heidelberg: Universitätsverlag C. Winter, 2000. 177-99.

"A Massachusetts Yankee at Emperor Franz Josef's Court. Charles Francis Adams, Jr., Sojourning in Vienna, 1873." *Die österreichische Nordamerikaforschung (Wiener Beiträge zur Geschichte der Neuzeit* vol. 24). Ed. Thomas Fröschl et al. Wien: Verlag für Geschichte und Politik, 2000. 174-91.

"Augustan Nostalgia and Patrician Disdain in Longstreet's Georgia Scenes." *The Humor of the Old South.* Ed. M. Thomas Inge and Edward J. Piacentino. Lexington: UP of Kentucky, 2001. 101-12.

# Introduction

The contributions to this volume are the result of the 29th annual Austrian Association for American Studies conference organized at the University of Vienna in November 2002. This conference, on the topic of "(Anti-)Americanisms," was conceived by Kurt Albert Mayer, who wanted his colleagues to, on the one hand, inquire into the roots of European – and especially Austrian – anti-Americanism, and, on the other hand, address the many aspects of "Americanism."

"(Anti-)Americanisms" was the first truly interdisciplinary AAAS conference. Co-organizer Thomas Fröschl and his colleagues from the History Department of the University of Vienna contributed a number of historical discussions, drawing attention to the varied attitudes Austrian governments and the public have displayed toward the United States of America in the last 225 years. (More often than not these were less than friendly – John Adams remarked already in 1779 that the House of Austria "will be one of the last Powers to acknowledge our Independence.") The interplay of historical, literary and cultural approaches to the conference topic resulted in a mosaic of analyses, most of which are collected in this volume.

The title "(Anti-)Americanisms" is itself a mosaic, combining the polysemous notion of "Americanism" with its equally multi-faceted antonym. "Americanism," the standard dictionaries tell us, is variously defined as "a characteristic feature of American English esp. as contrasted with British English," "an attachment or allegiance to the traditions, interests, and ideals of the U.S.," "a custom or trait peculiar to America," "the political principles and practices essential to American culture," as "devotion to or preference for the U.S. and its institutions," "adoption or display of American ideas, habits, etc.," and even as "love of America." In a lexical sense, the word "Americanism" itself is quite likely an Americanism, first used in "America," or more precisely, within the limits of what now constitutes the USA. Thus the London-born Robert Bolling (1646-1709), after having moved to Virginia (marrying there the great-granddaughter of Pocahontas), describes, in his memoirs, a linguistic peculiarity of the early transatlantic settlers:

> The Colonists brought over the vocabulary of King James' day, . . . preserved in its purity. As we had no accessions of population from any other quarter than England, and were engaged in agriculture that required no new words for its processes, it happened, in the progress of years, that we retained words that became obsolete in the parent country, and have been denounced subsequently as *Americanisms*, though a portion of the legacy brought over by our fathers. (22)

Yet it was the later, though by no means secondary meanings of the term that engaged the conference participants. In the expansive spirit of American Studies, the focus was on the various propagations of "Americanism" in literature, music, film, "the new media," society, and politics. The discussions of this concept prepared the logical basis for the papers dealing with its semantic opposite. "Anti-Americanism" means "opposition" or "hostility" to the United States, its people, its principles, or its politics – yet this seemingly straightforward definition masks a crucial indeterminacy of the term. One can, for instance, be "anti-American" by opposing the right-wing crusade mentality of the George W. Bush administration (inside and outside the USA), yet one can be equally "anti-American" by being hostile to the country's blatantly secular materialism and liberalism (inside and outside the USA). The concept thus demands a semantic and a historical contextualization. Similarly, "anti-Americanism" carries different meanings in different parts of the world, referring to U.S. imperialism or U.S. capitalism, or generally criticizing "Western decadence."

"Anti-Americanism" and "Americanism" are thus two distinct yet interdependent notions. Both terms are used as convenient vehicles to transport ideology and propaganda. The present volume questions the stability of these concepts, drawing attention to the multiplicity of meanings inherent in them.

In an international context, the topic of the 2002 conference was certainly timely, as demonstrations of pro-Americanism in the aftermath of the 9/11 attacks gave way to sentiments of anti-Americanism fueled by the divisive role of United States politics in Iraq. Many of the papers referred to the "present political crisis," which, at the time they were written, was the impending war in Iraq. When the conference took place, the threat of an American(-led) invasion was for most participants predictable; by the time their papers were submitted, it had become a reality. The speakers, in presenting their various analyses, thus also repeatedly described their personal position vis-à-vis the U.S. – which led to the basic question of how to define, as an American Studies scholar, one's enchantment, or disenchantment, with specific "customs or traits peculiar to America."

The global impact of the United States as the leading economic, military, political, and cultural power is one of those contemporary truisms one is tempted not to repeat at the beginning of a volume on "(Anti-)Americanisms." But this very impact is one of the reasons for the complaint about the power and influence of U.S. hegemony and *hyperpuissance*. Though political and cultural influences are difficult to measure, the "Americanization" of the globe is taken as a given. "Cocacolonization," "McDonaldization" or "Hollywoodization" are global catch phrases. Yet the basic phenomenon of extensive "influence" itself represents nothing specific nor unique in world history. Counter-reformation Spain once had a tremendous cultural impact reaching far beyond the Catholic part of 16th-century Europe, and France exercised an even greater (cultural) influence, a truly global one, during the 19th century. But hardly anyone today would refer with disdain to a "Hispanization" of Europe (the case is different regarding South America), or would speak of a destructive impact of the French and their civilization on European (or global) cultures.

The American influence, however, is judged quite differently, and negative perceptions prevail – on all continents. A common stereotype holds that, at best, the United States have only very little, if anything, to contribute to world culture and that, at worst, America threatens to destroy other national (and regional) cultures. To the French writer Henry de Montherlant (1896-1972) the United States is unique as being the only country able "to lower intelligence, morality, human quality on nearly all the surface of the earth," and such a thing "has never been seen before in the existence of the planet" (Ceasar 2). Critiques of the United States are often irrational, impressionistic, not the result of impartial analysis. To differentiate continues to be the scholar's moral duty. Part of such an obligation is to value pluralism, to cherish the variety of human ways of life – and to question the intellectual and psychological coordinates of one's criticisms.

There may be different anti-Americanisms in Germany, Austria, France, or Greece. Yet there is a perception they all have in common: the United States of America may have begun as an ideal, but now is perceived as a failure; at the beginning there may have been a grand promise, a universal experiment in liberty and democracy, but over time the country metamorphosed into an oppressor, with the great promises broken, the hopes of the past shattered. The "American Creed" (Gunnar Myrdal), a set of principles deeply rooted in the European Enlightenment and Christian tradition, while it is still addressed to mankind, has no longer a global audience. America's standing in the rest of the world has taken a dramatic beating over the first years of the 21st century. The percentage of the population with a favorable view of the United States has plunged to (often much) less than 50% in European countries (traditional allies most of them), and to much less than even that in the Islamic world. Anti-Americanism is more widespread, and more militant, than ever before.

For many Europeans, in particular in those countries which discovered and/or later colonized the Americas, the United States remains, psychologically, a colonial extension of the Old World. Americans are therefore expected to still pay respect to the various "mother countries," and to acknowledge that Europe is the powerhouse of civilization and the hotbed of high culture. Eurocentrism may no longer be the predominant strand in the European treatment of Asia, Africa, or Latin America. Yet Eurocentrism still dominates Europe's perception of the United States.

Already four decades ago the American scholar Richard Hofstadter contended that every American author writing critically about the United States had to keep in mind the risk of "encouraging the canting and self-righteous anti-Americanism that in Europe today so commonly masquerades as well-informed criticism of this country." And he immediately defended his country:

> For all their bragging and their hypersensitivity, Americans are, if not the most self-critical, at least the most anxiously self-conscious people in the world, forever concerned about the inadequacy of something or

other – their national morality, their national culture, their national purpose. This very uncertainty has given their intellectuals a critical function of special interest. The appropriation of some of this self-criticism by foreign ideologues for purposes that go beyond its original scope or intention is an inevitable hazard. (vii)

The present volume – combining articles by authors from the United States, Germany, the United Kingdom, and Austria – wants to contribute to the polyphonic debate of such national and international criticism and self-criticism by providing scholarly evaluations of historical, political, literary, and cultural instances of "Americanisms" and "anti-Americanisms." It is introduced by the keynote lecture. Drawing on his rich experience as a political activist, Paul Lauter explores the perhaps essential connections between the discipline of American Studies and anti-Americanism, "an oxymoron" that "presumes a settled definition of . . . the meaning of 'American' or 'America'".

Part I (organized largely along chronological lines) opens the discussion of the conference theme in the mid-18th century. While Timothy Conley analyzes the "ante-Americanisms" in a number of colonial and Revolutionary texts dealing with individual and communal characteristics of the emerging nation, Thomas Fröschl describes the historical roots of European anti-Americanism, stressing the fact that this phenomenon reached a first culmination point already in the late 18th century. Paul Crumbley discusses the highly political notion of sovereignty, and of the relationship between individualism and democracy, in some poems by the famously reclusive Emily Dickinson, while Markus Heide takes us into the last decades of the 19th century, widening the perspective to include both the Americas, as addressed in the "Pan-American" writings of José Martí. Louis J. Kern documents how peculiarly narrow and reactionary racialist and eugenicist movements attempted to redefine the notion of true Americanness (and of who would be allowed to immigrate into the United States) in the first third of the 20th century. Two historical papers on Austria conclude this part of the book: Roman Puff describes aspects of anti-Americanism during the last years of the Habsburg Empire, and Günter Bischof presents a wealth of information on the political and cultural shifts of that concept in Austria from 1945 to the present day, with echoes of the Third Reich still audible in the agendas of the New Right and Left.

Part II deals with various representations of "(Anti-)Americanism" in a handful of 20th-century literary texts. Vincent Kling describes the fascination "America" and American technological models held for a number of Austrian modernist writers, Verena Klein looks at the critical attitudes towards the United States inherent in Canadian literature, and Sylvia Schiefer focuses on Gil Scott-Heron and the critical view on various American clichés evinced in his lyrics.

Part III addresses the dissemination of various Americanisms in popular culture. Both Greta Olson and Carmen Birkle write on contested sexualized American cultural icons: while Olson focuses on issues of masculinity in her analysis of the figure of the inarticulate, white American man, Birkle elaborates on the Barbie doll as an American success story, which promotes ideals of traditional femininity and beauty. The next two articles stress the importance of the category of "race" and ethnicity in the conception of "Americanism." Duco van Oostrum investigates the stories of black athletes in the Civil Rights movements of the 1960s, demonstrating how sports was at the center of debate about American freedom, becoming a potential for protest. Monika Messner highlights the relation between sports and the construction of national identity, with sports serving as a unifying force of national pride that often diverts the attention from the political reality of the nation. The last three articles focus on the role of the media in the construction of "Americanisms." Andreas Weissenbäck examines the process of Americanization of European culture through advertising. Claudia Schwarz, in turn, focuses on the role of the media in creating "reality." Analyzing the coverage of the 9/11 attacks and the ensuing "War on Terrorism," she delineates the media's active role in the creation of "Americanism" and "anti-Americanism." Markus Rheindorf explores a popular computer game, showing how interactive media rewrite history, contributing to an ever-increasing American global dominance.

The editors hope that the papers collected in this volume will help shed light, from a variety of angles, on a productive conceptual antagonism that is arguably as old as the New World. Issues of

"Americanism" and of "anti-Americanism" – since the November 2002 conference prevalent in increasingly stark and disturbing manifestations – continue to shape not only the richly controversial field of American Studies, but the discourses of the global forum.
   It is tragic that Kurt Albert Mayer did not live to see the conference and the present book – which is dedicated to him.

*Michael Draxlbauer, Astrid M. Fellner and Thomas Fröschl*

**Works Cited**

*A Dictionary of American English on Historical Principles*. Ed. Sir William A. Craigie and James R. Hulbert. 4 vols. Chicago: U of Chicago P, 1938.

Bolling, Robert. *A Memoir of a Portion of the Bolling Family in England and Virginia*. Richmond, VA: W. H. Wade & Co., 1868.

Ceaser, James W. *Reconstructing America. The Symbol of America in Modern Thought*. New Haven: Yale UP, 1997.

Hofstadter, Richard, *Anti-Intellectualism in American Life*. New York: Alfred A. Knopf, 1963.

*Merriam-Webster's Collegiate Dictionary*. 10th ed. Springfield, MA: Merriam-Webster, Inc., 1995.

*Random House Dictionary of the English Language*. 2nd ed. New York: Random House, 1987.

# Is American Studies Anti-American?

## Paul Lauter

I want to begin with a quotation peculiarly relevant to our subject. The speaker is commenting on possible reactions to what he has been saying about U.S. policies in Vietnam, Rhodesia (as it was then called), the South Africa of apartheid, Watts, and Mississippi. "What do you make of it?" he asks: "Some will make of it that I overdraw the matter. . . . And others will make of it that I sound mighty anti-American. To these I say: Don't blame *me* for *that*! Blame those who mouthed my liberal values and broke my American heart."[1]

The speaker is Carl Oglesby, then president of Students for a Democratic Society (SDS). The occasion is the March on Washington to End the War in Vietnam of 27 November, 1965. It is the second major demonstration against the Vietnam war. The first had taken place seven months before, on April 17. The then president of SDS, Paul Potter, had given the main speech at that rally; he had said that we must "name the system" that had created and maintained the war in Vietnam, and the crowd, one far larger than we had expected or that the press—typically—had reported, took up his refrain as a kind of chant: "name the system, name the system." Now, in November, Oglesby is doing so.

Or is he? The name he evokes, not exactly one to fit a ringing slogan, is "corporate liberalism." The central fact about corporate liberalism, he insists, is this: "With about five percent of the world's people, we consume about half the world's goods" (318). In the face of this addiction to a "stolen and maybe surplus luxury" it is the task of humane liberals not only to name the system but to "describe it, analyze it, understand it, and change it" (312). I think it is fair to say that that states the agenda pursued now by more than three generations of progressive Americans, including many whose work goes by the name of "American Studies."

What I wish to talk about here is the process that has produced today's American Studies, or, as some would have it, "Anti-American Studies." At the center of that process are the larger historical movements that have made Oglesby's evocation of "humane liberalism"—his term—seem to us as quaint as the Gilbert and Sullivan lines about how "every boy and every girl/ That's born into the world alive,/ Is either a little Liberal,/ Or else a little Conservative. . ." One might indeed argue that Oglesby's speech and the death of Paul Wellstone can be taken to stand as signposts marking, as the 2000 and 2002 elections so painfully demonstrated, the increasingly marginal status of liberalism as a political player in the 20th, much less the 21st, century. However that might be, my own subject is the movement of a set of ideas, an analytic framework, from the streets of Washington in the mid-sixties to the books, classrooms, and conferences that define our field of inquiry, American Studies. In particular, I want to look at the ideas that cohere around the term "imperialism," for when we speak of anti-Americanism today we are, on the whole, speaking primarily of the reactions to whatever it is that word names.

You would, if you reread Oglesby's speech, notice one vivid fact: that heavy word, "imperialism," the name now so familiar and easily spoken about U.S. policy, overseas and domestic, never appears. "Liberalism" does, of course, "corporatism," "radical," "revolution," "Communism," "anti-communism," even "humanism." But never that word, now so familiar, so resonant, so daunting, the word "imperialism."

That is a curious fact, and what it names, I think, is the point in American intellectual history at which Oglesby, and with him a generation of activists and intellectuals, stands. It is not, of course, that "imperialism" had not before been named in America, nor that specific opposition to it, anti-imperialism, had not existed. We can recollect the opposition of Thoreau, Fuller, and even Emerson to the Mexican war and the annexation through the Treaty of Guadalupe Hidalgo of what now constitutes the "American," that is, the Norteamericano, southwest. We might recite the once-famous lines of James Russell Lowell attacking the Mexican war:

> Ez fer war, I call it murder,—
> There you hev it plain an' flat;
> I don't want to go no furder
> Than my Testyment fer that.

Or we might evoke the bitter late writings of Mark Twain, like "To the Person Sitting in Darkness," and other works by intellectuals and politicians active in the "Anti-Imperialist League" of the late 19th and early 20th centuries. But it remained the case, nevertheless, that right into the 1960s "imperialism" was largely the language of the organized Left, the language at least in the U.S. of Lenin pamphlets and obscure journals. The language reflects the culture, the notion, that is, that America had been and remained different from the imperial powers resident between the Irish Sea and the Caucasus. Bernard de Voto had put it this way in 1952: "One of the facts which define the United States is that its national and its imperial boundaries are the same."[2] Later still, in 1968, Oscar Handlin in his classroom text was arguing that "The experiment in imperialism at the turn of the century had been confusing, because it made the United States party to a kind of domination most Americans did not wish to exercise. After 1900, therefore, they had attempted to withdraw from colonialism, but they still hoped to play an important role in world affairs."[3] As late as 1973, Ernest N. Paolino in his book on William Henry Seward[4] feels constrained to argue against Samuel Flagg Bemis' contention that the Spanish-American War was a "Great Aberration" in American politics. Even the continued enthusiasm of people around the world for American ideals, so ironically reflected in Ho Chi Minh's decision to model the Vietnamese Declaration of Independence on that of the United States, seemed to bolster this pillar of American exceptionalism. But by 1965, that had begun to change.

I want to point to two factors central to that process of change. First, a factor embodied in Oglesby's rhetoric, there is a growing perception that American policy abroad can be read in its policies at home, and vice versa. Oglesby connects them, for example, by complaining that the country can "send 200,000 young men to Vietnam to kill and die in the most dubious of wars, but it cannot get 100 voter registrars to go into Mississippi" (315). And, he argues, American overseas polices are directed by individuals—like Kermit Roosevelt of Gulf Oil and Walter Bedell Smith of the United Fruit Company—who in various ways profit from those policies . . . by (strange thought) controlling oil and pipelines, banana plantations, and the like (318). Now these are not in many respects tightly-drawn associations. And, in fact, the connections between domestic and foreign policies were widely resisted in the mid-Sixties, even by progressive people. In June of 1965, to take a personal example, I was involved in organizing a "Faculty Committee to Support the Mississippi Freedom Democratic Party Challenge" to the seating of the five "regular" Democratic Mississippi congressmen, elected in significant measure because most blacks had been systematically disenfranchised. I wrote to a number of academics opposed to the increasing American involvement in the Vietnam war. Many joined the committee. But some saw the step as, at best, a diversion of resources and attention, at worst, an imposition of Old Left ideology upon a New Left movement. Indeed, I received a letter from a well-known practitioner of American Studies explaining why he could not sign our statement. He said he was on the whole opposed to U.S. policy in Vietnam and in favor of the MFDP challenge. "But," he wrote,

> the connection between the two implicit in this letter is forced and dubious; and it defeats the very aims of your program to have academics seeming to submit themselves to synthetic ideological arguments. By that I mean that only on the basis of a priori ideological assumptions could anyone possibly believe that the Negroes of Mississippi, if granted the vote, necessarily would be any more opposed to the U.S. policy in Vietnam than the rest of the electorate.

Of course, that was not an argument we were making, but the real burden of his complaint came a moment later: "as a veteran of the Thirties, when again and again I saw good causes dissipated by just this sort of imposition of ideology upon perfectly straight-forward political issues, I find this disheartening." In other words, we were repeating the mistakes of the Old Left and would thus isolate ourselves from the mainstream of American politics.

Meantime, however, SNCC field staff and young people with whom they worked were themselves insisting upon those connections. In July, word had arrived in McComb, Mississippi, one of the most dangerous venues in that violent state, that a young black draftee of 23, John D. Shaw, who had participated in 1961 civil rights demonstrations there, had been killed in action in Vietnam. A group of his classmates, with Joe Martin of McComb and Clint Hopson, a law student from New Jersey, had written and passed out a leaflet titled "The War on Viet Nam." This is what it said:

> Here are five reasons why Negroes should not be in any War fighting for America:
> 1. No Mississippi Negroes should be fighting in Viet Nam for the White Mans freedom, until all the Negro People are free in Mississippi.
> 2. Negro boys should not honor the draft here in Mississippi. Mothers should encourage their sons not to go.
> 3. We will gain respect and dignity as a race only by forcing the United States Government and the Mississippi Government to come with guns, dogs and trucks to take our sons away to fight and be killed protecting Miss, Ala, Ga, and La.
> 4. No one has a right to ask us to risk our lives and kill other Colored People in Santo Domingo and Viet Nam, so that the White American can get richer. We will be looked upon as traitors by all the Colored People of the world if the Negro people continue to fight and die without a cause.
> 5. Last week a white soldier from New Jersey was discharged from the Army because he refused to fight in Viet Nam he went on a hunger strike. Negro boys can do the same thing. We can write and ask our sons if they know what they are fighting for. If he answers Freedom, tell him thats what we are fighting for here in Mississippi. And if he says Democracy tell him the truth—we don't know anything about Communism, Socialism, and all that, but we do know that Negroes have caught hell here under this American Democracy.[5]

The leaflet was reprinted, with a brief story about its distribution, in the MFDP's Newsletter, and there ensued precisely the kind of patriotic storm that my academic friend had implicitly predicted. Every

Mississippi newspaper and politicians across the South chimed in to deplore this supposedly unpatriotic stand by the organization—which had not in fact endorsed the position of the leaflet, but simply reported on its existence. And there were many in the black community who were unhappy with its circulation, if not necessarily with its contents. But the leaflet's contents in fact reflected an increasingly widely-held view among black Southerners. We found it on a raggedy porch in McComb, talking with Joe Martin's mother, who had been visited by the FBI. We found it in New Orleans, as part of a response to a film I had been showing, called "The Magician." We found it in a poem written by Mrs. Ida Lawrence, of Rosedale, a small Delta town near Greenville. She wrote:

> We say we love our country
> We say other people love their country
> We said that all men are brothers.
> What would we call the war
> in Vietnam
> Would we call that brotherly love
> Does the word freedom have a meaning
> Why do the history books say
> America is the Land of Liberty a Free Country,
> Then why do all mens Negro and White fight
> the Vietnam and Korea why cant we be Americans
> as North and South regardless of color
> What does we have against
> the Vietnams?
> Why are we fighting them?
> Who are really the enemy?
> Are Vietnam the enemy or we
> Americans enemies to ourselves,
> If we are the same as Vietnams
> Why should we fight them?
> They are poor too.
> They wants freedom.
> They wants to redster to vote.
> Maybe the people in the Vietnam
> can't redster to vote
> Just like us.

By the end of the summer, this growing anti-war sentiment among black Americans had been summed up in one leaflet by the phrase "No Viet Cong Never Called Me Nigger." Draft resistance and opposition to the war was in this way and others made into a function of American domestic policy.

Nor was this kind of connection quite as marginal as it might have appeared. Even Drew Pearson had been writing columns that summer about Lyndon Johnson's problem in explaining to leaders of African decolonization America's politics of race. His article for Sept. 20, 1965, mourns that while Johnson is remembered fondly in Senegal, "his policy of massing military might in Viet Nam is undoing part of his earlier friendship. Furthermore it plays directly into the hands of the Chinese Communists in their campaign to penetrate this wealthy and relatively empty continent."

Now one might argue that these instances point not so much to general connections between American foreign and domestic policies, much less to their union in a critique of imperialism, but only to an insistent relationship between war abroad and racism at home. Indeed, that is my point: Oglesby's speech stands right at the cusp of the transformation of what is still a rhetorical union into a more thoroughgoing anti-imperialist analysis.

It stands at another cusp as well, that which would transform the academy. I cannot here line out all of the changes in the American academy that have taken place during the last quarter century. Some, like what I would call its Enronization, are disastrously ugly and undermine any conception of traditional ideas about education, especially of the liberal arts variety. But that's another story, one that I and others have written about elsewhere. Here I want to point to two more positive qualities that were largely set into motion during the 1960s. One has to do with the vast expansion of American higher education, and coincident with that its opening up to new student constituencies—its democratization, in short. The other has to do with the parallel opening up of the curriculum, the development of black and women's studies, as well as other ethnic and minority studies programs, and especially here how this process, however limited and incomplete, has affected American Studies as an institutional form.

First, growth: in 1940, there were about 1,500,000 students attending U.S. colleges and universities. By 1960, that number had climbed to 3,600,000; by 1980, 11,600,000, and by 2000, 14,400,000. (I might mention that while the United States contains about 5 percent of the world's population, its higher education system enrolls about 22 percent of all "tertiary" students; in fact, the U.S. economy gains over $7 billion per year from foreign student tuition and costs, no negligible amount.)[6] As you can see, the period of greatest growth was during the 1960s and 1970s, a phenomenal spurt that has since slowed down. But while it was going on, faculties, budgets, programs, departments, indeed new institutions expanded wildly—spending, for example, went up from about $5.6 billion in 1960 to about $57 billion in 1980.

In the context of such enormous expansion, it was not hard for university administrators to accommodate the demands, increasingly raised by the social movements of the Sixties, to open admissions to non-traditional college students, those we called at Old Westbury during the 1970s, the "historically by-passed." These included older women returning from suburban homes and offices to the college opportunities they had missed; working-class women and men, for the first time sensing that college perhaps included them; and most visibly members of minority groups, who raised the same demand for access that they had claimed with respect to the ballot box, the front of the bus, public accommodations, and even the Democratic National Convention. Nor was it difficult either for administrators to respond positively to the demands that such new students and their supporters raised for access to the curriculum as well as to the dorm. While they were, and are, hardly well-established, black studies, ethnic studies, women's studies were certainly a meaningful presence on many, and probably most campuses, by the mid-1970s. American Studies, relatively well-established even by 1965, itself underwent a transition from the more or less promotional paradigms of the early Salzburg Seminar days to what might be represented by the 1993 volume called *Cultures of United States Imperialism*, edited by Amy Kaplan, president-elect of the American Studies Association in the U.S., and Donald Pease of Dartmouth

College.[7] The outlook of this volume and something of its character can usefully be gathered from a few passages from Pease's introductory essay. In characterizing Kaplan's companion piece, he writes: "In 'Left Alone With America,' Amy Kaplan uncovered as a cognitive gap in the inaugural moment of American Studies the ideological disjuncture separating the diplomatic history of U.S. imperialism from academic study of the national culture and enabling imperialism to go unrecognized as an American way of life" (23). Later, he writes of the "recent changes in the understanding of U.S. diplomatic history and the emergent interest in the importance of imperialism to cultural constructions in general and for critical multiculturalism's understanding of race, class, and gender" (26). Writing of Gauri Viswanathan's essay "The Naming of Yale College," he suggests that the author's "association of a Yale education with its namesake's imperialism is startling partly because the imperial origins of his patrimony have been all but erased" (29). One last citation: "In the complex interaction it . . . effects among race, nation, and empire, U.S. foreign policy becomes a medium . . . for the policing of domestic racial tensions" (31). In other words, imperialism as an analytic framework and as a description of everyday American practice has come to be critical to understanding multiculturalism, gender, race, Yale, the American Museum of Natural History . . . in short, the American way of life. We are, indeed, many steps from Oglesby's unmentionable word, much less from *Virgin Land* or even *The Machine in the Garden*.

Let me make clear at once that, as an activist and as a scholar, I am largely in sympathy with the approach articulated in these passages, though I might be inclined to argue with some of the contributions to the book. But that's obviously not my object in this project. It is, rather, twofold: I want to track out, if only fragmentarily, the processes by which, I would argue, the sometimes inarticulate values of the anti-war movement of the 1960s and 1970s were translated over a quarter century into a central analytic category and a fundamental outlook of the profession in which we participate. And I want to explore briefly the convergence of this intellectual practice with what has been tagged Anti-Americanism.

As the war on Vietnam expanded, dragged on through the Nixon years, corrupted everything it touched, and was rationalized by a generation of people who could in no sense of the term be called "liberal," the focus of academic work shifted significantly. As I have suggested, a major component of that shift had to do with the well-known categories of identity and analysis, race, gender, and class. But it was also the case, perhaps most among white academics, that the war itself established a fundamental divide. Donald Pease has described the divide in intellectual terms by casting the "new Americanists" against the ideology of such founding figures of American Studies as Lionel Trilling. The "liberal imagination," Pease writes, "discloses itself as ideological when it produces an *imaginary separation* between the cultural and the public spheres."[8] One result of "Trilling's ideological usage," he argues, "was the construction of an American Studies movement for which the end of ideology consensus became the dominant ideology" (9). To be sure. But that notion had been undermined by at least three factors. First, we had experienced directly the power of culture in the public sphere, as, for example, in the anti-war poetry readings during 1967 and 1968 conducted by writers like Robert Bly, Denise Levertov, and Galway Kinnell. How could we take seriously strictures like those of the Trillings and others about the immaturity of politically-centered writing when we had before us the instances of "Life at War" or "The Teeth-Mother Naked at Last"? How could we, moreover, take seriously people who in practice, if they did not support the war makers, certainly did not stand in their way? The slogan of the time, for better and for worse, was "if you're not part of the solution, you're part of the problem." Clearly, to us, those who stood aside as the cops busted students or our colleagues, were no part of the solution. What, then, did they have to say to us? And if they argued that the realm of culture and of politics met, if they met at all, at a bloody crossroads (to use Irving Howe's wonderful metaphor), well then, let us stake out that crossroads and see what we could learn at it. We were led, that is, toward a very different conception of our work, toward an effort as we put it at the time, to bring together our politics and our classroom practice.

It wasn't that we wished to indoctrinate our students. That would not only have been impractical, but the culture of the Sixties movements was too fixed on freedom to sustain such an enterprise. Rather, we asked—as in the volume Louis Kampf and I edited in 1972, *The Politics of Literature*[9]—what did it mean in the study of literature, culture, or of the United States to maintain the claim to being a socialist, a feminist, or a citizen committed to an equitable non-racist future? In answering such questions, we found little help in the classic texts of the American Studies movement. It was, rather, people like Raymond Williams, Edward Thompson, and Stuart Hall who turned us on. Indeed, because we had come to question the actions and thus the values and motives of people like Trilling and even that good-hearted soul, Henry Nash Smith, we came to doubt the Cold War intellectual work they had come to represent.

What I am arguing here can in some measure be symbolized by the events at the 1968 MLA meeting in New York. I have described it in some detail elsewhere, but I want here to call particular attention to one event, a talk by Noam Chomsky in an enormously crowded room at the New York Hilton. Chomsky, as is his wont, laid out in stunning detail a systematic analysis of the policies underlying the American war on Vietnam. And, yes, he probably used the language of imperialism. But what seems to me central here are two things: first, his talk emerged from an activist anti-war campaign that included a variety of political actors—from those who were campaigning against holding the 1969 MLA meeting in Chicago because of the police riot at the 1968 Democratic National Convention, to those of us who had recently organized the New University Conference, a kind of "adult" SDS, and who styled ourselves the "radical caucus" (a formation still alive and active, by the way). Second, his talk brought into the very center of our professional lives, the big annual convention, a systematic analysis of American policies—in Vietnam, in Chicago, and on many of our campuses.

It would, of course, be a decade and more before this union of political analysis and cultural work would begin to take on the character I have symbolized by the Kaplan and Pease collection. There were many notable stations along the way, like Alan Trachtenberg's *The*

*Incorporation of America*[10] and Michael Denning's important article "'The Special American Conditions': Marxism and American Studies,"[11] wherein he argues that American Studies had itself "served as a substitute for a developed marxist culture" (357). I could name many other texts significant to the transformation of the field from the dominance of myth and symbol to the emergence of the "new Americanists." But a survey is not my intent.

It is, rather, to ask whether, or in what ways, this newly-defined form of American Studies constitutes in its nature an attack on as much as an analysis of its subject. To say that the last election has heightened the relevance of that question is to put the case mildly. The problem resides, however, in any definition of what we mean by "anti-American" and how we approach it. The term has always struck me as something of a contradiction, an oxymoron. It presumes a settled definition of what seems to me always at contest—i.e., the meaning of "American" or "America." Consider, for example, the poem of that name by Claude McKay, of 1921:

> Although she feeds me bread of bitterness,
> And sinks into my throat her tiger's tooth,
> Stealing my breath of life, I will confess
> I love this cultured hell that tests my youth!
> Her vigor flows like tides into my blood,
> Giving me strength erect against her hate.
> Her bigness sweeps my being like a flood.
> Yet as a rebel fronts a king in state,
> I stand within her walls with not a shred
> Of terror, malice, not a word of jeer.
> Darkly I gaze into the days ahead,
> And see her might and granite wonders there,
> Beneath the touch of Time's unerring hand,
> Like priceless treasures sinking in the sand.

Is this an anti-American poem or, rather, one that richly engages the contradictions of America? If we teach about the U.S., is this perhaps—especially after September 11, 2001—a more useful poem than McKay's more familiar but more one-dimensional "If we must die"?

Similarly, we may wish to think about Allen Ginsberg's poem by the same title, "America." In this poem, it seems to me, Ginsberg captures the contradictory impulses that have defined the experiences of ethnically-marked Americans. Drawn and repulsed, we are never at rest, forever caught up in a struggle that is at once a process of self-definition and an effort to shape the culture in which we are enmeshed.

But is that not the underlying definition both of Americanism and anti-Americanism itself: drawn and repulsed? What could be more repulsive than the oil-slicked rationalizations of imperial power coming with ever-increasing volume and speed from the White House, regardless of party? Or the casual banality with which current administration spokespeople dismiss years of carefully-built international structures, like the World Court or the Kyoto protocol? Nevertheless, are we not drawn to the pulse and power of New York, precisely in its contradictory status as victim and aggressor? Or to the contradictory, dangerous and therefore compelling work of Ginsberg, Toni Morrison, or . . . who would you prefer to add?

So it is not enough to denounce the arrogant and corrupt politics of one American administration after another. Or to point to the ways in which the charge of anti-Americanism has been deployed to marginalize and disarm legitimate criticism of current U.S. policies, and its (or our) war-like practices. Or to claim, hopefully, that hegemony based on the impoverishment of half the world's people cannot, should not last. These are all useful, no doubt, for us and for you. But it is also essential that we—and that you—likewise acknowledge the pleasures both of America and of anti-Americanism. It is as much the pleasure as the critique and the bravado that is startling about McKay's poem. The pleasures are not the same, of course. What the new Americanist scholarship has helped uncover are the guilty pleasures of people like ourselves, who necessarily share the imperial loot, however much we despise and deplore it—and stand against it.

But what I would emphasize, rather, are the pleasures of opposition. That powerfully engaged us in 1965, as it may well today. In 1965, as Oglesby suggested, we faced—indeed embraced—the charge of anti-Americanism by opposing the war on Vietnam. To be sure, we were not anti-, much less un-American; we were beginning, only beginning, to see the policies of Johnson, Kennedy, McNamara and the others for what they were: arrogant, delusional, destructive and—as we came in time to recognize—imperial. Those actions, I am arguing, propelled the insights, the understandings of America, that have come to mark our profession, American Studies. It may be that the present crisis—so different and yet so much the same, only just beginning—will also engage us not only in new perceptions about the "cultured hell that tests our youth" or our age, but will generate a new movement that will, to reprise Oglesby's words, "describe it, analyze it, understand it, and change it."

**Notes**

[1] Carl Oglesby, "Let Us Shape the Future," *The New Student Left*, ed. Mitchell Cohen and Dennis Hale (Boston: Beacon P, 1966) 316.
[2] Bernard De Voto, *The Course of Empire* (Boston: Houghton Mifflin, 1952) xiii.
[3] Oscar Handlin, *The History of the U.S.* vol. 2 (New York: Holt, Rinehart, Winston, 1968) 353.
[4] Ernest N. Paolino, *The Foundations of the American Empire* (Ithaca: Cornell UP, 1973).
[5] This leaflet and other materials from Mississippi Summer in 1964 are in my personal files.
[6] These and the succeeding figures are drawn from the presentation of Vice-President Charles Muscoplat to the University of Minnesota Senate Committee on Finance and Planning, 28 Aug., 2001 <http//www.1.umn.edu/usenate/scfp/01-08-28pt2.html>.
[7] *Cultures of United States Imperialism*, ed. Amy Kaplan and Donald E. Pease (Durham: Duke UP, 1993).
[8] Donald E. Pease, "New Americanists: Revisionist Interventions into the Canon," *Revisionary Interventions into the Americanist Canon*, ed. Donald E. Pease (Durham: Duke UP, 1994) 8.
[9] *The Politics of Literature: Dissenting Essays on the Teaching of English*, ed. Louis Kampf and Paul Lauter (New York: Pantheon Books, 1972).
[10] Alan Trachtenberg, *The Incorporation of America: Culture and Society in the Gilded Age* (New York: Hill and Wang, 1982).
[11] Michael Denning, "'The Special American Conditions': Marxism and American Studies," *American Quarterly* 38 (1986): 356-80.

# Part I: (Anti-)Americanisms since the Mid-18th Century

# Ante-Americanisms: Friendly Critiques of the Emerging Nation

## Timothy Conley

Sarah Kemble Knight's journal of her 1704 horseback trip from Boston to New York and back offers explicit critiques of excesses in drinking and smoking, rude treatment by those she finds beneath her, the poverty of rural America, indulgent treatment of African American slaves, religious independence and the lack of education in New Haven, the presence of "the most salvage of all the salvages" (qtd. in Martin 65), who have land of their own and are governed by their own laws, and the difficulties and dangers of traveling through thickets and across threatening rivers.

William Byrd's account of the expedition in 1728 to determine the boundary between Virginia and North Carolina appears in both a private *Secret History* and a work intended for publication, the *History of the Dividing Line*. Although the *Secret History* includes far more explicit and biting criticism of the North Carolina commissioners than does the *History*, both works find fault with some of the same aspects of colonial American life as did Knight: lazy, impoverished settlers of the countryside, excessive drinking, felonious Indians lurking on the fringes of settlements, a lack of serious religious sentiment, and an often intimidating landscape. However, Byrd also condemns the unjust treatment of native peoples (speaking in favor of intermarriage as a solution to "the Indian question"), and he impugns "those 3 great Scourges of Mankind, Priests, Lawyers, and Physicians" (*History* 9).

In his account of a 1744 journey from Maryland to New England and up-state New York, Alexander Hamilton, himself a physician, apparently did not encounter the scourge of lawyers, but he does condemn incompetent physicians (that is, those who did not share his Edinburgh training), "New Light" ministers and religious enthusiasts of any brand—"hair brained fanatics" (183), as he called them. Like Knight, Hamilton finds fault with Connecticut and its "surfeit of ragged money, rough roads, and enthusiastick people" (304). Like both Knight and Byrd, Hamilton decries drunken country revelers (although like Byrd, he drinks and revels during his travels), what he considers lazy and uncivilized Indians, and the poor conditions of many inns. Hamilton adds a particularly Anglophile critique of recent immigrants—clumsy Dutchmen, "slovenly and dirty . . . att best, rustick and unpolished" (230), stinking Irishmen, and loquacious Frenchmen whose discourse is "interlaced with oaths and smutt" (257). Hamilton does, however, find time to praise a French landlady, who had "much of the humour of that nation, a deal of talk, and a deal of action" (255)—a most pleasing combination, particularly in contrast with the Dutch, whose "women in general, both old and young, are the hardest favoured ever I beheld. Their old women wear a comical head dress, large pendants, short petticoats, and they stare upon one like witches" (230-31).

Hamilton's male-centered observations on the women of the colonies suggests another critique which marks his commentary as somewhat different from those by Knight and Byrd—the extreme parochial aspect of most communities through which he travels. Time and again he finds himself stared at as a stranger: they "stared att me like sheep" in rural Pennsylvania (185) and in Greenwich, Connecticut (216). In New Haven, the public house keepers "gape and stare when you speak as if they were quite astonished" (300). Travel is difficult for strangers, both because of unfamiliar terrain and unmarked highways (243), and because of the constant threat of mis-identification: Hamilton is mistaken for a peddler in Bristol (254), an Indian king in Boston (281), a peddler once again in Newport (288). In New York, Hamilton himself carefully guards against staring "for fear of being remarked for a stranger, gaping and staring being the true criterion or proof of rustick strangers in all places" (208).

Hamilton also differs from Knight and Byrd in his continuing attacks on what he perceives as either "lumpish and heavy" conversation (181) or annoying pedantry. He criticizes Quakers, in whose conversation, he notes, "zeal wanted fervency" (191), his own participation in a conversation in Brunswick which was "such a confused medley that I could make nothing of it" (203), "clumsy wit" (209) and "some confused topsy-turvy conversation" (237) in New York, and "rude and clamorous" conversation in Schenectady (226). In Boston, however, Hamilton encounters "a very agreeable lady [whose] conversation was lively, entertaining, and solid, neither tainted with false or trifling wit nor ill natured satire or reflexion" (281); likewise, in Philadelphia Hamilton participates in "agreeable and instructing" conversation (319). In Whitehall, he promenades with "the ladies" and "enjoyed all the pleasures of gallantry without transgressing the rules of modesty or good manners" (292).

These models of conversation contrast sharply with those for whom Hamilton reserves much of his harshest criticism. Captain Lyon of Norwalk "wore an affected air of wisdom in his phiz and pretended to be a very knowing man" (303); Dr. McGraa of New York speaks knowingly of the effect the moon has upon all fluids, but "understood as much as a goose" (240). Men such as Lyon and McGraa speak with "a puff of clownish pedantry" (325). Such a pedantic disposition, states Hamilton after another disputatious evening in New York, "may arise from the naturall perverseness of human nature, which is always most absurd and unreasonable when free from curb or restraint" (307). "These dons" of New York, Hamilton concludes, "held their heads higher than the rest of mankind. . . . But this I found always proceeded from their narrow notions, ignorance of the world, and low extraction, which indeed is the case with most of our aggrandized upstarts in these infant countrys of America" (316). Hamilton's reference to a plural "countrys of America" suggests one of the key points in understanding 18th-century critiques. The many differences among (and within) the colonies (including population, economy, religion, and currency) argue against any notion of essential and manifest national destiny. 18th-century America was the site of multiple conflicts and negotiations; to understand "America," it is necessary to identify the terms and resolutions of these struggles—and to uncover the forgotten or suppressed struggles. When we turn to three accounts written by or about Quaker communities, we encounter representations of conflicting power relationships. These texts do not fully resolve the conflict, but they establish the basis for critiques of both pre- and post-Revolutionary America.

John Woolman's argument against slavery clearly is among the struggles highlighted in our reconstructions of early America, and yet the terms by which he constructed his argument do not emerge from the liberal revolutionary sentiment so often cited by apologists for American essentialism. As Fritz Oehlschlager very rightly notes, "Woolman is not a libertarian individualist seeking to maximize autonomy over against collective institutions dedicated to imposing conformity" (206). Rather, Woolman's Christian critique of what he terms "a dark gloominess hanging over the land" (22) emerges from a moral and highly spiritual indictment of "degeneracy":

> It appeared to me that through the prevailing of the spirit of this world the minds of many were brought to an inward desolation, and instead of the spirit of meekness, gentleness, and heavenly wisdom, which are the necessary companions of the sheep of Christ, a spirit of fierceness and the love of dominion too greatly prevailed. (58)

When he travels to Native American settlements in Pennsylvania, Woolman considers the plight of both Indians and African slaves as signs of impending doom: "And here luxury and covetousness, with the numerous oppressions and other evils attending them, appeared very afflicting to me, and I felt in that which is immutable that the seeds of great calamity and desolation are sown and growing fast on this continent" (145). This spirit of fierce domination and greed stems from self-interest, which, like the individual's will, must be governed by submission to the Divine Will. Only then, Woolman argues, may "the pure peaceable government of Christ . . . spread and prevail among mankind" (200).[1]

Woolman's spiritual invocation of peaceable government suggests a model of political relationships different from those implicit in earlier narratives by Knight, Byrd, and Hamilton—a Quaker model of "Americanism" which is both "anti-American" and, in some respects, revolutionary. As Margaret Stewart notes, Woolman provides an alternative definition of American culture.[2] Knight, Byrd, and Hamilton accept the terms and social manifestations of Anglo-sovereign culture: order must be imposed on marginal peoples and communities by visible representatives of a political-cultural authority. External "curbs and restraints," as Hamilton says, are necessary to maintain civility in conversation and to civilize the peoples both in rural New England and along the dividing line between Virginia and North Carolina. In this regard, the "anti-American" critique accepts the political relationships characteristic of monarchies, albeit with a decidedly capitalist spirit.

Woolman's model, however, relies on an inward discipline of will, not on external imposition of control; those who "profess the truth," he says, must be "inwardly acquainted with it" and must behave "as becomes our peaceable profession" (34). This "peaceable profession" demands that individuals be "inwardly acquainted" with the truth, unlike the models of sovereign power which depend upon obeisance to external authority, whether or not that authority is royal or colonial. "Quakers substituted the notion of consensus and the practice of censorship by the meeting," writes Michael Heller, "for the Puritan reliance on clerical and scriptural authority" (12)[3]. In Woolman's model, Indians, African slaves, or rural farmers may all bear witness to the Inner Light; in the model assumed by Knight, Byrd, and Hamilton, such figures are suspect until they are externally supervised.

Such reliance on internal disciplinary power, rather than external coercive authority, likewise characterizes the model of "Americanism" represented in William Bartram's *Travels*. Like Woolman, Bartram was raised in a Quaker family, albeit a rather atypical Quaker family[4]; like Woolman, Bartram traveled throughout Indian country and found much to praise in Native American cultures, as well as much to condemn in contemporary American settlements. Bartram's "anti-American" critique does not focus on the presence of slavery, as does Woolman's; rather, Bartram finds fault with Euro-American environmental and Indian policies. Ramona Ralston notes, "the majority of his text frustrated or discouraged the inclination towards an exploitive capitalist appropriation of the territories which would become the southern United States" (24). As he tours the American southeast, Bartram also notes the ruins of many failed communities and, like Woolman, suggests an alternative model for relationships of power within culture. Bartram, like Woolman, had little use for what Robert Sayre calls "'modernity' . . . a fully commercial, capitalistic economy with all the civilisational attributes associated with it" (29).[5]

Unlike Woolman's response to Nature, Bartram's model is not based upon the complete resignation of will to God. Within Nature, however, Bartram does encounter and carefully describe many of the harsh conditions which Knight and Byrd had detailed. Bartram does not underestimate the dangers of being lost in the swamp or isolated during a thunderstorm (e.g., 38-39) or the "harsh treatment from thorny thickets, and prickly vines" (76). Such observations suggest that the wilderness awaits transformation to useable fields and friendlier terrain. Yet Bartram's travels typically alternate between moments of careful observation, moments of travail and moments of sublime pleasure: "After getting through this morass," notes Bartram, "we arrived on a delightful, level, green meadow" (175-76).[6] Journeys through such delightful meadows then carry Bartram back to the swamp and the plagues of mosquitoes and the warfare of alligators: young broods of teal "were frequently surprised by the voracious trout; and he, in turn, as often by the subtle greedy alligator" (115). In fact, this state of war seems to characterize the natural world: "Behold the watery nations, in numerous bands roving to and fro, amidst each other; here they seem all at peace, though, incredible to relate! but a few yards off, near the verge of the green mantled shore there is eternal war, or rather slaughter" (195).

Such slaughter troubles Bartram even more when it is the result of human action, as when his companions destroy a herd of deer (174) or when British colonists "indiscreetly" devastate native orange groves (213). This environmental degradation emerges in part from the failure of hunters to heed Bartram's philosophy of internal discipline and in part from the plantation economy of the colonists. The hunters are skillful but not disciplined; the plantations owners, like those along the Georgia coast whom Bartram similarly indicts (77), are wealthy but not moral.

In contrast to these versions of Americanism, it may appear as if Bartram favors natural scenes "secure and tranquil . . . as yet unmodified by the hand of man" (65). However, as noted above, he does not discover an ideal pre-lapsarian garden in the American wilderness. Rather, he finds scenes of violence and destruction alternating with scenes of beauty and peace. So too when he observes Native American cultures, he can paint an idyllic portrait of a noble savage who "reclines and reposes under the odoriferous shades of Zanthoxylon, his verdant couch guarded by the Deity; Liberty, and the Muses, inspiring him with wisdom and valour, whilst the balmy zephyrs fan him to sleep" (107). He also states that "we see that war or the exercise of arms originates from the same motives, and operates in the spirits of the wild red men of America, as it formerly did with the renowned Greeks and Romans, or modern civilized nations" (315). Bartram, like Woolman, finds much to praise in native cultures; he says of the Muscogulges, "As moral men, they certainly stand in no need of European civilization" (385). However, Indian cultures do not present models of ideal human relationships.

Neither do most European-American communities present such models. Bartram particularly indicts the introduction of alcohol among Indian peoples (214) and the "dishonesty and violence" of white traders (286), "the ill, immoral conduct of too many white people" (386). As Joshua Bellin states, Bartram makes such observations in "a period of acute racial conflict" (2), and, through his travels, "registers doubts about the absoluteness of Euro-American conceptions of, and claims to, the continent" (3).[7] Bartram likewise sees ample evidence of failed communities of European colonists: an abandoned English fortress (73), "vestiges of the old Spanish plantation and dwelling" (198), vacant and ruined houses in Mobile (323-24), and the ruins of deserted French plantations (326). Such recurring scenes of failure in the New World are not always explained by Bartram, but when he visits East Florida and encounters the ruins of another deserted settlement, he offers one analysis:

> But it seems, from an ill-conceived plan in its infant establishment, negligence, or extreme parsimony in sending proper recruits and other necessaries, together with a bad choice of citizens, the settlement grew weaker, and at length totally fell to the ground. (97)

Such a critique points to the significance of a disciplined, "correct" population of individual citizens. Lacking such governance, American communities will fail.[8]

Bartram's "anti-Americanism" is thus both a particular indictment of European attitudes toward the environment and Native American peoples and a more general critique of ways of organizing society. At the same time, he does find some alternative models for the organization of relationships. Bartram and his white companion seem to realize such a relationship when they are "far removed from the seats of strife": "Our situation was like that of the primitive state of man, peaceable, contented, and sociable. The simple and necessary calls of nature being satisfied, we were altogether as brethren of one family, strangers to envy, malice, and rapine" (110). The "primitive state" is thus enshrined because familial relations, not commercial or monarchal, establish the right order of human governance.

Bartram likewise praises French planters who "live easily and plentifully, and are far more regular and commendable in the enjoyment of their earnings than their neighbors the English" (346). They manifest the right order of living in their "easy, moral and entertaining" conversation (346). The Hon. B. Andrews, a Carolina planter, similarly offers Bartram a "hearty welcome, plain but plentiful board, free conversation and liberality of sentiment" (37). It is possible then to establish "American" communities which conform to Bartram's peaceable philosophy. It is even possible in Bartram's view to establish such communities which also depend upon slave labor. When he travels in rural Georgia, Bartram "was kindly saluted by my host and his wife, who I found were superintending a number of slaves" (255). Whereas Woolman condemns the entire slave system, Bartram may praise such a gentleman as his Georgia host because his rule is based upon internal discipline, not external coercion: "almost every object in our progress contributed to demonstrate this good man's system of economy to be not only practicable but eligible; and the slaves appeared on all sides as a crowd of witnesses to justify his industry, humanity, and liberal spirit" (256-57). Such an industrious, human community is thus governed by benevolent and paternal leaders—who inculcate codes of discipline in a willing population, a form of governance which Michel Foucault calls "pastoral."[9]

Bartram finds an Indian model of such relationships among the Muscogulges, a people for whom, "the same moral duties which with us form the amiable, virtuous character, so difficult to maintain there, without compulsion or visible restraint, operates like instinct, with a surprising harmony and natural ease" (182). As Sayre notes, according to Bartram, "Indian lifeways create the necessary social conditions for the generalization of virtue" (45).[10] Bartram later commends the Muscogulges' "excellent policy in civil government" which "cannot derive its influence from coercive laws, for they have no such artificial system" (387). The Muscogulges follow

> the simple dictates of natural reason, plain to every one, yet recommended to them by their wise and virtuous elders as divine, because necessary for securing mutual happiness: equally binding and effectual, as being proposed and assented to in the general combination: every one's conscience being a sufficient conviction . . . instantly presents to view, and produces a society of peace and love, which in effect better maintains human happiness, than the flaws, enforced by coercive means. (388)

"The constitution or system of their police," says Bartram, "is simply natural, and as little complicated as that which is supposed to direct or rule the approved economy of the ant and the bee" (388). Like the beehive, the Muscogulge community—and rightly disciplined European-American communities—are not governed by coercion or visible external authority. Rather, they represent a model of organization and relationships which is both anti-American in its rejection of prevailing authority and American in its acceptance of new (at least for Europeans) modes of governance.

Such a community of disciplined individuals and mild government forms the basis for J. Hector St. John de Crèvecoeur's analysis of the possibilities offered in American culture. In *Letters from an American Farmer* and *Sketches of Eighteenth-Century America*, Crèvecoeur describes the emergence of American communities governed by benevolent pastoral authority and by an emerging discipline of a particular population. He also documents the disruption of that community by the Revolution. After the Revolution, Crèvecoeur served as French consul in New York, 1783-1790, when he returned to France. Between 1794 and 1800, Crèvecoeur recorded his observations on the newly-independent United States of America in *Journey into Northern Pennsylvania and the State of New York* (1801)—a collection of personal notes, recollections of travelers throughout the East coast, and unacknowledged borrowings from many other writers, including Jefferson, Imlay, and Bartram. Crèvecoeur also pays homage to Bartram's father: *Letters from an American Farmer* includes the account of a Russian gentleman's visit to the home of Mr. John Bertram, "the celebrated Pennsylvania botanist" and William's father.

According to Letter XI's narrator, "Mr. Iw__n A__Z, A Russian Gentleman," John Bartram governs his farm, his family, and his freed slaves according to the principles of willing subordination which William Bartram had identified in Quaker and Muscogulge communities: "I observed in all the operations of his farm, as well as in the mutual correspondence between the master and the inferior members of his family, the greatest ease and decorum; not a word like command seemed to exceed the tone of a simple wish" (195). Bartram tells his visitor that he learned that "good example, gentle admonition, and religious principles could lead them [his former slaves] to subordination and sobriety" (196). Thus, Bartram's Pennsylvania farm provides a fitting model for the possibilities of governance in the Anglo-American colonies.[11]

Crèvecoeur finds other such possibilities in "that excellent government" of beehives (*Letters* 58; *Sketches* 244), in the Quaker settlement on Nantucket Island, and in the Indian community to which his alter ego, Farmer James, and his family flee when the discord of the American Revolution threatens the tranquility of their New York farm. Crèvecoeur devotes one-third of the *Letters* to a description of the customs, economy, and political networks of the Quakers of Nantucket. This society is characterized by the industry and harmony of the colonists and the absence of "coercive powers" (124) of intrusive government: "Here, happily, unoppressed with any civil bondage, this society of fishermen and merchants live without any military establishments, without governors or any masters but the laws; and their civil code is so light that it is never felt" (152). Such a system of governance is possible because early in life Quaker children are "inured to a principle of subordination, arising neither from sudden passions nor inconsiderate pleasure; they are gently holden by an uniform silk cord, which unites softness and strength" (127). "The manners of the Friends," notes Crèvecoeur, "are entirely founded on that simplicity which is their boast and their most distinguished characteristic, and those manners have acquired the authority of laws" (155). Individuals in such communities have internalized codes of conduct and subordinated their own interests to the interests of the group, knowing well that in so doing they themselves will flourish. Thus discipline, not the pastoral rule of John Bartram's farm community, governs the Quakers of Nantucket.[12]

As much as Farmer James, Crèvecoeur's authorial voice throughout the *Letters*, admires both the pastoral and disciplinary modes of governance, he cannot prevent the chaos of the American Revolution. In response to the violent actions of both Revolutionaries and Loyalists, Farmer James proposes removing his family to an Indian settlement "where, far removed from the accursed neighborhood of Europeans its inhabitants live with more ease, decency, and peace than you imagine; who, though governed by no laws, yet find in uncontaminated simple manners all that laws can afford" (211). Crèvecoeur again identifies the key elements in this community as simple manners and the lack of visible, external authority: "Without temples, without priests, without kings, and without laws, they are in many instances superior to us" (215). Like the industrious bees, the subordinated Quakers of Nantucket, and disciplined family and servants at Bartram's farm, these Native Americans provide a model of governance which is at once typically American and critically anti-American.

Within these communities, we find at times conflicting modes of governance, populations, and pastoral leaders. At the same time, these communities are also threatened by changes in the economic order and by abuses of authority. When Farmer James explains the potential of the American community, he cites the lack of aristocracy and the rule of "mild government, all respecting the laws without dreading their power" (*Letters* 67), a description Crèvecoeur repeats in "Reflections on the Manners of the American" in the *Sketches* (253, 259). Such a government establishes a network of rational laws and, as Crèvecoeur notes of the Canadians before the Revolution, "a state of perfect subordination; their government pervaded everything, and yet could not change their opinions" (*Sketches* 337-38).

Such a state of willing subordination is possible in pre-Revolutionary America, according to Crèvecoeur, because the colonies are composed of independent, landowning farmers. "The instant I enter on my own land," says Farmer James in Letter II, "the bright idea of property, of exclusive right, of independence, exalt my mind. . . . What should we American farmers be without the distinct possession of that soil?" (54). Possession of that soil, according to Farmer James, is possible because "There is room for everybody in America" (Letter III, 81). This extensive terrain likewise discourages the religious discords of Europe: "The great and immense room in which they expand themselves prevents them from producing those evil consequences which opposition and contracted limits formerly occasioned" (*Sketches*, "Liberty of Worship," 324; see also Letter III, 74-76). Diverse religions and diverse national origins "are melted into a new race of men" (70), whose success depends upon the American landscape, ownership of land, and the leadership of paternal shepherds who govern by example and gentle persuasion.

Farmer James embodies this pastoral form of governance in his relationships in his household and in his stable: "there my well-known voice has immediate influence and soon restores peace and tranquility. Thus, by superior knowledge I govern all my cattle, as wise men are obliged to govern fools and the ignorant" (57). This governor is familiar to his subjects, speaks softly, and seeks peace and tranquility for the benefit of the entire community. In the first of the sketches, "A Snow-Storm as it Affects the American Farmer," we find a similar figure: "The farmer's vigilant eye has seen every operation performed; has numbered every head; and, as a good master, provided for the good welfare of all" (234). The good master oversees all details of life for the good of all who live within his domain. Similarly, the good master and his flock are self-sufficient: the farmer is "a universal fabricator like Crusoe" (*Sketches* 258). Unlike Crusoe, however, the American farmer stands not only for himself but for the entire community. "I have been the pastor of my family," says Farmer James, "and the teacher of many of my neighbors" (212), like S. K., the American Belisarius of Chapter XI of the *Sketches*: "a father to the poor of this wilderness. . . . At home he was hospitable and kind, an indulgent father, a tender husband, a good master" (411).[13]

Such leadership, however, is not sufficient to ward off the disruption of the Revolution nor to eliminate the many threats to both pastoral order and disciplinary governance in the emerging nation. When Farmer James is confronted with the horrors of slavery, he despairs of the condition of humanity throughout history: "everything is submitted to the power of the strongest. . . . Such is the ascendancy of power. . . . Such is the perverseness of human nature" (174). "Man is a huge monster," Crèvecoeur writes in the *Sketches*, "who devours everything and will suffer nothing to live in peace in his neighborhood" (294). Pastoral governance amid rural retreats may mitigate the perversity of human nature, but in urban, mercantile society mankind manifests the very worst of relations. "How I hate to dwell in these accumulated and crowded cities! They are but the confined theatre of cupidity!" (*Sketches* 243). In such an emerging capitalist society, the exemplary figure is not the caring shepherd but rather the "land-merchant, who, like all other merchants, has no other rule than to get what he can" (*Sketches* 256). Urban acquisitiveness and self-interest form the eastern moral boundary for the ideal American farmer; at the western edge of pastoral society we find the "indolence, indifference" (*Sketches* 376) of the Euro-American frontiersman, an insidious threat to the integrity of the model American community.[14]

These threats stem from human nature and human occupation. They also reveal relationships of power and authority which run counter to the pastoral and disciplinary systems which Crèvecoeur so admires in Native American culture and which apparently dominate the emerging American nation. In "Landscapes," the series of dramatic scenes which conclude the *Sketches*, Crèvecoeur charts the rise of "The hypocrisy, slyness, cupidity, inhumanity, and abuses of power in these petty country despots" (427).[15] Such petty despots, like Aaron Blue-Skin, attempt to speak for the Revolution and, by extension, all "Americans": "I am the very soul and quintessence of a committee-man . . . we are the appointed guardians, the watch-towers of this country" (456). Blue-Skin thus attempts to embody visible, coercive authority, rising above and dominating the countryside. Colonel Templeman stands as the military presence of this authority; his very name manifests the type of authority Farmer James had earlier decried. Templeman is confronted by Martha Corwin, who laments that "The malice and power of our great ones have overtaken us" (485). Templeman responds with a lesson in Revolutionary politics: "There is the precinct; there is the county; there are the united committees of the county. You must apply to them; they replace all other authorities" (485). In Templeman's vision, the shepherd is replaced by the bureaucrat, and thus ante-American pastoral order yields to an emerging American national political organization.[16]

Crèvecoeur's critique of America similarly includes warnings about the appearance of religious demagogues (*Sketches* 373), who attempt to govern by rhetorical force, and petty political officials who claim to be "the voice of the people" (*Sketches* 432): "'Aye, aye,'" as Mrs. Marston laments, "'popularity' is the word. 'Tis the God to whom you must sacrifice the dictates of your conscience" (*Sketches* 480). These minor local officials attempt to rule by democratic force, not moral or pastoral authority; they are what Crèvecoeur calls "inferior satellites who crush, who dispel" and who "from religious hypocrites are become political tyrants" (*Sketches* 422). "This delegation of power ad infinitum from the imperial Congress to these low-lived rulers," says the sympathetic and eloquent American gentleman, Mr. Ecclestone, "is intolerable" (*Sketches* 447). Ecclestone's critique reveals what Crèvecoeur saw as an "intolerable" continuation of sovereign rule in a supposedly-democratic America. "Imperial Congress" has simply re-imposed the rule of coercion on communities who had attempted to govern by the pastoral model of internal discipline. "Ante-America" has in fact emerged as "Anti-America."

Even prior to the Revolution, Crèvecoeur had noted the presence of authoritarian religious figures (*Sketches* 331) and, even more ominous, lawyers: "Lawyers are so numerous in all our populous towns . . . they are plants that will grow in any soil that is cultivated by the hands of others; and when once they have taken root, they will extinguish every other vegetable that grows around them" (*Letters* 151). Lawyers are troublesome because their presence encourages a contentious atmosphere, which in turn disrupts the harmony of the pastoral community and yields profit to one group only: "the county of ___ is famous for the litigious spirit of its inhabitants. There the lawyers will have it all" (*Sketches* 276). However, the economic gain of lawyers does not represent their primary threat. Even more significantly, they, like the petty officials, re-inscribe sovereign relations of power on the emerging American culture: "These men are more properly lawgivers than interpreters of the law and have united here, as well as in most other provinces, the skill and dexterity of the scribe with the power and ambition of the prince" (*Letters* 168). Rule by law could signal the emergence of disciplinary culture, but only if members of that community internalize the conduct which the laws seek to regulate. By the beginning of the Revolution, lawyers, clergy, merchants, and minor political officials seem to Crèvecoeur to be dominating the emerging America. Agrarian communities disciplined by pastoral figures who govern by mild example and whose members willingly subordinate themselves to such leadership, like the Indian nations of the Eastern coast, are fast disappearing.

Crèvecoeur himself was forced to leave his family and upstate New York farm during the Revolution, was suspected by both British and American forces, and finally fled to France. Upon his return in 1783, he found his wife dead, his family scattered, and his estate in ruins. We might then assume that his portrait of post-Revolutionary America in the *Journey to Northern Pennsylvania and the State of New York* would be highly critical, especially of the political networks which governed the new nation. However, if we look to the model communities which Crèvecoeur had identified in the *Letters* and *Sketches* and if we review the characteristic relationships within and leadership of these communities, we find both affirmations and critiques of the emerging America.[17]

Post-revolutionary America remains the home for Quaker and Indian communities, those models of pastoral and disciplinary order cited by Crèvecoeur in the *Letters*. However, these communities have not extended their political organization throughout the emerging nation. The *Journey* does include one extensive commentary on Quakers of southeastern Pennsylvania, in the form of comments to the narrator by a Mr. Hazen, who recuperated from a serious fall with the aid of "fine and saintly hospitality" (447) of the Society of Friends. Hazen finds much to praise in this Quaker community: "Content with their lot, they do not know, like so many others, that fever of anxiety, that eternal desire to do better, which so often prevents one's ever considering himself good. Each one follows his profession or cultivates his land, with order, intelligence, and industry" (447). In his notes to this section, Crèvecoeur adds: "Such is the happy effect of a good example, which, if it were better known, would serve to convince those who, in their crazy pride, have believed that the teaching of religious precepts was useless; how much, on the contrary, these very precepts serve to make men more industrious, happier, more submissive to laws and better citizens" (574).

The disciplinary model of industrious submission and internal mechanisms of control enables the Quaker community to thrive. However, such a community appears to be an isolated instance, not a general rule of post-Revolutionary America.

So too, the Indian community to which Farmer James had fled to escape the chaos of the Revolution no longer offers a thriving alternative to either sovereign or capitalist models of political organization. Native America is disappearing from America, in part because of inter-tribal warfare (389) and failure to rely on farming (60), but more so because of the debilitating effects of alcohol (266) and disease (157)—both introduced by European colonists. Crèvecoeur also blames the greed typical of the emerging American economy for the decline of Indian cultures: "we know too well," he states, "the arrogance, so indigenous of the Europeans, to believe that this harmony can last long. The more land and woods they gave the white men, the more they demanded" (609). Neither the Indian nor the Quaker communities serve as models of power relationships in the emerging United States.

Crèvecoeur, however, does find several new institutional models which incorporate measures of restrained authority and internal discipline. The newly-constructed prison in Philadelphia, "built according to the plan suggested to the legislature by various members of the Society of Friends" (530), focuses on internal discipline of the criminal: "the wisdom of the legislature has achieved the aim it set for itself: of reforming rather than punishing the guilty" (530). "Everywhere silence and decency reign," he continues, under mild but continual supervision: "This prison is governed, or rather administered, by directors chosen annually from among the citizens of the town; and it is always on the most respectable that the choice falls" (531). "What happy results," he concludes, "emanate daily from this effective discipline!" (531).

Institutions such as the prison—as well as the hospital and "Bettering House" which Crèvecoeur similarly praises (393-94)—are based upon architectural designs which foster reformation and internal discipline and upon a communal-pastoral agreement legally codified in a charter. Crèvecoeur writes extensively of the significance of such charters, which manifest the subordination of private interests to communal good and which enable communal authority to express itself indirectly and, apparently, to the benefit of all:

> Public prosperity, being nothing more than the total of family and individual prosperity, these charters which unite and concentrate the efforts, the means, and the interests of a great number of persons, and direct them toward a common end, which sanction pious and praiseworthy views, or useful projects of these associations, these charters, I say, have contributed substantially in this young land to the development, progress, and perfection; and to cap the good fortune, the spirit of the Government, even in colonial times, has always been more kindly disposed toward protecting than governing. (524)

Charters thus disseminate the mechanisms of protection and the "interests of a great number of persons" throughout the emerging nation, and, apparently, they enable Crèvecoeur to forget the despair of Farmer James and the victims of Revolutionary violence depicted in his earlier sketches.

Crèvecoeur's antipathy to the mechanisms of external authority of Revolutionary America seems largely absent in his observations in the *Journey*. Quaker and Indian communities do not form the basis for political organization, as he had hoped, but new institutions and charters seem to embody familial relations, rather than sovereign authority. "The inhabitants of this state [Connecticut] are like one big family, wisely and well governed, among whose members one finds the same attitudes and the same inclinations" (376). Such governance, which Crèvecoeur finds throughout the nation, is characterized by mild and just laws (35), peace (98), lightness of taxes (502), and lack of interference with religious beliefs (550). The population governed in such manner is dramatically increasing in size and, like the new settlements in Kentucky, benefits from "a melting pot of individuals" (202)—an image which Crèvecoeur resurrects from the essay written before the violence of the Revolution.

Crèvecoeur likewise returns to an analogy he had employed in the *Sketches* to describe the model American farmer: "Like Robinson Crusoe," we are told of a farmer in the *Journey*, "he is sufficient unto himself and is never idle" (340). Such self-sufficiency, but not self-aggrandizement, had also characterized the ancient Indian peoples, who had enjoyed "security without the oppressive succor of laws and of independence and liberty which are restricted, without hurting anyone" (314). The self-sufficient Indian, however, is fast disappearing, and so the emerging nation must look to other figures to embody the ideals of discipline.

Crèvecoeur finds such models in "the patriarch of Orange County" (324), who, "like the patriarchs of ancient times," abandoned his homeland during war and sought refuge for his family in the mountains. Colonel Williamson, "the owner of an immense grant" in upstate New York (491), similarly governs a larger community according to patriarchal discipline: "He thinks of everything and foresees everything. . . . We respect him like a father; he loves us as his children. Consequently, the price of his land goes up every day" (491-92). The national model for such patriarchal rule—a system of governance which embodies benevolence, detailed supervision, and exemplary behavior—is found in George Washington, who "unites the qualities and virtues which honor man, citizen, and great magistrate: wisdom and moderation, enlightenment, humanity, modesty": "he had the good fortune to silence slander, to mollify exhibitions of jealousy, to unite the opinions of his fellow countrymen; and through the confidence he inspired in them, he knew how to direct their efforts toward a single, united aim in freeing his country" (544).

Individuals such as Washington, Williamson, and the South Carolina patriarch disperse internal discipline throughout the population, and, at its best, the emerging national political order similarly operates with "paternal vigilance" (46) so that citizens are "living under the most paternal Government in the land, in the shelter from burdensome and arbitrary impositions" (309). For such governance to succeed, children must be educated according to religious principles which impress "on all minds respect for the laws, gratitude toward the most paternal Government in the world, and that subordination of desires that foster order, peace and industry" (76). Laws and subordination are necessary, argues Crèvecoeur, because of the frailty of human nature, the conditions of life in both the city and the frontier, and new dangers posed by both American democracy and European decadence.

As in both the *Letters* and the *Sketches*, Crèvecoeur in the *Journey* is skeptical of the innate goodness of human nature. As he had asked in Letter IX, he asks in the *Journey*, "Placed between these different points which surround and escape him relentlessly, what is man?" (567). The answer does not depend upon what Crèvecoeur terms "the dangerous mania of ideal perfection" (507); rather, "it seems evident that we on earth are toys of chance, others fate" (428). "That is typical of man," says the narrator of the *Journey*, "circumstances alone decide their relationships" (245). The invocation of the power of circumstance suggests a fatalism that at times dominates Crèvecoeur's narratives and his critique of America. He is especially critical, as he was in the *Letters* and *Sketches*, of the circumstances of urban-mercantile America, what he calls "the tumult and squalor of the towns" (83), "the chaos and worries of business and trade" (541). As in the *Letters* and the *Sketches*, the circumstances of frontier life prove as problematic as those of the city. Removed from the pastoral-patriarchal discipline of agrarian America, we find "the baseness and vice of most of the inhabitants of the frontier" (316).

The abuses of both urban and frontier circumstances stem in part from the absence of discipline and the mechanisms of patriarchal governance. In the *Letters*, Crèvecoeur found the most egregious example of such abuse in the conditions of slavery in the American South. In the *Journey*, however, he includes only one brief commentary on slavery, even though the narratives he includes extend to observations on conditions throughout the United States (not merely New York and Pennsylvania, as the title suggests). In fact, he includes more commentary on the abuses of authority stemming from freedom of speech and freedom of the press (e.g., 366ff.) than he does on those stemming from slavery.

Crèvecoeur's critique of Americanism in the *Journey*, based upon his belief in the need for subordination and discipline, focuses on the dangers of American democracy and European ideas and immigrants rather than the enslavement of Africans. He does cite the difficulties resulting from the high cost of labor, the solitude of life in rural America, and the lack of an internal system of communication and travel. However, he also suggests that these problems will be rather easily and rather quickly solved. Far more threatening are the "craze and fury of political parties" (545) and the "far too democratic" (179) government of Rhode Island with its "exaggerated form of its democracy" (503). Gustave Herman, the narrator's traveling companion, concludes his commentary with this admonition:

> If the too democratic form of government, if the reaction of the new principles which have just missed upsetting Europe have given birth to parties, those fermentations which one sees especially in the towns have no influence on the progress of the clearings of the inland colonies or on those of trade. (570)

Herman's critique points both to the internal dangers of democratic, rather than pastoral-patriarchal, government and to the external dangers of "European" thought. These "new opinions from Europe" threaten to "plunge us into the horrors of chaos and the bloody furies of anarchy" (46)—a striking instance of the optimistic endorsement of "new" ideas in Crèvecoeur's Letter III. The political and religious philosophy of revolutionary France now "like a volcano, has just manifested itself in such a violent manner. . . . Can the moment be far away when these convulsions crossing the Ocean will come to shake this Government"? (314). "We are not far enough from Europe," states Mr. Finley, one of Crèvecoeur's numerous reporters, "to prevent a volcanic explosion of new opinions which are spreading from there." To prevent such chaos, the emerging American nation must be ever-vigilant:

> The arrival in this country of so great a number of foreigners of all shades of political opinion, the secret and treacherous intrigues of our enemies, as well as those who are jealous of our good fortune, the political parties that have arisen among us; such are in part the dangers in the midst of which we find ourselves in the twentieth year of our political existence." (239)

The increase in population and prosperity in America is not due to "the arrival among us of a crowd of foreigners of all castes and kinds" (554), but rather to the industry and discipline of native-born citizens. Crèvecoeur's ante-American vision of an asylum for the oppressed of Europe has in the *Journey* been transformed into an anti-immigrant, anti-democratic critique of the emerging United States.

In *Democracy in America*, Tocqueville reports that the American democratic state of society "has destroyed or modified the old relations of men to one another and has established new ones" (Author's Preface to the Second Part, xi).[18] I have attempted in this essay to describe the terms in which three texts represented these shifting relationships of power, networks which protect and produce, as well as discipline and punish. Eighteenth-century America was yet the site of sovereign and pastoral communities, tactics, and relationships. However, it was also witnessing the emergence of disciplinary order and American capitalism, which would, in the second half of the nineteenth century, triumph.

## Notes

[1] Oehlschlager quite rightly argues that we should abandon the "paradigm of individualism" when reading Woolman's journal and instead heed his commitment to a "radical obedience to God" (198) and his theme of "creatureliness" (206).
[2] Stewart focuses on the tension between notions of individualism and white supremacy and those of sociability and harmony. Woolman employs a particularly Quaker form of asceticism to struggles against feelings of separation from others and against the hegemony of white supremacy. He also works within the eighteenth-century sensibility of "sympathy," although he does so, argues Stewart, via "an impersonal union with entire groups" (270).
[3] Heller also includes a valuable discussion of Woolman's Quaker rhetoric of "attractive plainness" and the Inner Light (11), the privileging of silence over speech (11-13), and the relationship between social reform and Quaker "ethical mysticism" (15).
[4] Larry Clarke ascribes much of Bartram's natural philosophy to the influence of Quakerism; Bruce Silver believes that his views were not uniquely Quaker, citing a similarity to Crèvecoeur's attitudes toward Indians in the *Letters*.
[5] Sayre's account of Bartram's encounters with Native peoples is compelling; however, this reference to the emerging "modernity" too easily reduces the complexity of the emerging nation and its competing systems of power and authority.
[6] Pamela Regis provides the most thorough account of Bartram's *Travels* as a work of science with a methodology based upon Linnaeus' system of description and classification and a world view founded upon botany and the Chain of Being. The difficulty with such an approach, Regis argues, is that it leaves no room for history, as Bartram's account denies Native Americans any historical identity. Regis is persuasive, but her focus on natural history does not, I believe, invalidate a consideration of the political significance of Bartram's

work. According to Regis, both Bartram and Crèvecoeur "lacked a political context for their works, situating them instead within the . . . universal, scientific framework of natural history" (136). However, even such a "universal" framework has a political context and, in the case of Bartram's and Crèvecoeur's works, natural history is situated within human relationships of power.

[7] Bellin also notes the critical response of Bartram's contemporaries to what they perceived as his "unseemly relativism" (12), and he quite perceptively notes two prevailing myths in Bartram's text: the myth of the "feminized wilderness" and the "Creek myth of the proper relationship to the land" (14-15). In some ways, these myths offer ecological parallels to the political/ governance systems. See also Mary Anne Schofield for a discussion of the interstices in women's texts, which express a "voice of liminality" (63) and must be read in context of women's network. As I argue, they must also be read in a context of pastoral-disciplinary networks.

[8] Bartram also frequently observes the ruins of ancient Indian settlements; however, he does not venture an analysis of the reasons for the disappearance of these communities. See, for example, pages 101, 259, and 306-7. Although he does suggest that the "proximity to the white people" causes one Indian community to abandon their homeland, Bartram finds more evidence of ancient nations whose history is unclear. Yet this sense of historical remains, of a New World that is in fact an Old World, dominates the narrative.

[9] According to Foucault, pastoral power is based on the model of the shepherd in Hebraic tradition, in which the shepherd 1) wields power over a flock; 2) gathers together, guides, and leads his flock; and 3) ensures the salvation of his flock through constant, individualized, and final kindness. The role of the shepherd/ pastor is slightly modified in the Christian tradition. The shepherd is now responsible for each and for all of the flock's actions; each member of the flock is individually and completely dependent on the pastor; and the pastor has a particular, individualized knowledge of each member of the group. The Middle Ages witness a further transformation of pastoral power, as critics of the Church reject its hierarchical structure and, in Foucault's words, "look for the more or less spontaneous forms of community in which the flock could find the shepherd it needed" (see "Politics and Reason"). Such an understanding of "pastoral" differs from that suggested by Patricia Medeiros' analysis of "the traditional three-part pastoral pattern of withdrawal from society, encounter with wild nature, and return" (202) which she finds in Bartram's *Travels*.

[10] Sayre quite accurately describes Bartram's generally favorable attitude toward Native culture, stemming in part from what Sayre calls his Quaker heritage of "lyrical pantheism" (41). The Quaker influence, however, was

tempered by Bartram's father's particular form of the Quaker spirit.

[11] In "Powerful Transformations: Crèvecoeur and the Emergence of Disciplinary Society," I discuss in detail Crèvecoeur's representation of power relationships in the *Letters*, basing my analysis on Foucault's notions of sovereign, pastoral, and disciplinary power.

[12] As many critics have noted, Crèvecoeur does offer some criticism of Nantucket, in particular the use of opium by the women of the island's Quaker community.

[13] Anna Carew-Miller persuasively argues that Crèvecoeur's Farmer James seems perplexed by the shift from the "Puritan patriarchal home of the seventeenth century" to the "mother-centered home of the nineteenth century" (247). According to Carew-Miller, Crèvecoeur constructs "a definition which ties an Americanness to a land gendered as feminine, to a version of manliness that requires men to perform certain types of labor, and to a family dynamic that centers all authority around the father-husband figure" (242).

[14] Christine Holbo offers another possibility: commercial humanism, understood within the context of Edmund Burke and Abbé Raynal. In her excellent analysis of the languages of eighteenth-century sensibility and imaginative association, Holbo states that "commercial humanism describes the development of the European world from religious monarchy toward a sociable republic of commercially involved citizens" (35). Holbo's essay is indispensable, I believe, to understanding the cultural-historical context in which Crèvecoeur's notion of the imagination operated. My analysis shifts attention to power, rather than the imagination, and argues that for Crèvecoeur the pastoral model afforded yet another possibility for communal organization.

[15] Jeffrey Richards provides the most complete analysis of "Landscapes." He focuses on the Whig-Tory conflict during the Revolution and that conflict's effect on domestic life—especially as embodied in the female as "icon for domestic tranquility" (288) and in black servants/slaves—and its effect on religious tolerance.

[16] Michel Huysseune places Crèvecoeur within the tradition of "the Enlightenment rhetorical tradition of naturalness" (47) and a "rhetoric of benevolence" (50). According to Huysseune, Crèvecoeur is "torn between the old patriarchal order (symbolized by the king) and the new, more plebeian rule of law (the revolutionaries)" (54). I agree that Crèvecoeur is torn and, as Huysseune concludes, that he does not mend this rupture in the text, but I argue that the split is more complex than this opposition between monarchy and democracy.

[17] Joseph Fichtelberg discusses Crèvecoeur's ambiguous views of republican ideology and very skillfully documents Crèvecoeur's indebtedness to Mon-

tesquieu and the Encyclopedists. Fichtelberg employs Clifford Geertz's understanding of ideology as cultural system to show how Crèvecoeur explores the limits of discursive authority in such republican ideology. Fichtelberg does not include either the *Sketches* or the *Journey* in his analysis.

[18] Tocqueville warned his contemporaries that "the species of oppression by which democratic nations are menaced is unlike anything that ever before existed in the world; our contemporaries will find no prototype of it in their memories" (318). Tocqueville particularly feared the unlimited authority of the majority, what he called the "omnipotence," the "despotism" of the majority (vol. 1, 254-60).

## Works Cited

Bartram, William. *Travels of William Bartram*. 1928. Ed. Mark van Doren. New York: Dover, 1955.

Bellin, Joshua David. "Wicked Instruments: William Bartram and the Dispossession of the Southern Indians." *Arizona Quarterly* 52 (1995): 1-23.

Byrd, William. *Histories of the Dividing Line betwixt Virginia and North Carolina*. Ed. William K. Boyd and Percy C. Adams. New York: Dover, 1967.

Carew-Miller, Anna. "The Language of Domesticity in Crèvecoeur's Letters from an American Farmer." *Early American Literature* 28 (1993): 242-54.

Clarke, Larry. "The Quaker Background of William Bartram's View of Nature," *The Journal of the History of Ideas* 46.3 (1985): 435-48.

Conley, Timothy K. "Powerful Transformations: Crèvecoeur and the Emergence of Disciplinary Society." *Borderlines* 1.2 (1993): 170-90.

Crèvecoeur, J. Hector St. John de. [Michel-Guillaume St. Jean de Crèvecoeur]. *Letters from an American Farmer and Sketches of Eighteenth-Century America*. Ed. with introd. Albert E. Stone. New York: Penguin, 1981.

Crèvecoeur, Michel-Guillaume St. Jean de [J. Hector St. John de Crèvecoeur]. *Journey into Northern Pennsylvania and the State of New York*. Trans. Clarissa Spencer Bostelmann. Ann Arbor: U of Michigan P, 1964.

Fichtelberg, Joseph. "Utopic Distresses: Crèvecoeur's Letters and the Revolution," *Studies in the Literary Imagination* 27.1 (1994): 85-101.

Foucault, Michel. "Politics and Reason." 1979. Rpt. in *Politics Philosophy Culture: Interviews and Other Writings 1977-1984*. Ed. Lawrence Kritzman. New York: Routledge, 1988.

Hamilton, Alexander. "The Itinerarium." *Colonial American Travel Narratives*. Ed. Wendy Martin. New York: Penguin, 1994.

Heller, Michael A. "John Woolman: The Quaker Meeting and Eighteenth-Century Social Reform." *New Jersey Folklife* 15 (1990): 10-17.

Holbo, Christine. "Imagination, Commerce, and the Politics of Associationism in Crèvecoeur's Letters from an American Farmer." *Early American Literature* 32.1 (1997): 20-65.

Huysseune, Michel. "Virtuous Citizens and Noble Savages of the New world [sic]: The Contamination, Juxtaposition, and (Mis)Representation of Cultural Models in Enlightenment France." *Images of America: Through the European Looking-Glass*. Ed. William L. Chew. Brussels: VUB Press, 1997. 47-62.

Martin, Wendy, ed. *Colonial American Travel Narratives*. New York: Penguin, 1994.

Medeiros, Patricia. "Three Travelers: Carver, Bartram, and Woolman." *American Literature 1764-1789: The Revolutionary Years*. Ed. Everett Emerson. Madison: U of Wisconsin P, 1977. 195-211.

Oehlschlager, Fritz. "Taking John Woolman's Christianity Seriously." *Renascence* 48.3 (1996): 190-207.

Ralston, Ramona. "Signs of Science and the Sublime in Bartram's Travels: Subverting the Colonialist Agenda." *Semiotics: 1998*. Ed. C. W. Spinks and John Deely. New York: Peter Lang, 1999. 291-98.

Regis, Pamela. *Describing Early America: Bartram, Jefferson, Crèvecoeur, and the Rhetoric of Natural History*. DeKalb: Northern Illinois UP, 1992.

Richards, Jeffrey. "Revolution, Domestic Life, and the End of 'Common Mercy' in Crèvecoeur's 'Landscapes'." *William and Mary Quarterly* 55.2 (1998): 281-96.

Sayre, Robert Woods. "Encounters with the 'Other': Three Eighteenth-Century, Anglo-American Travellers in Indian Territory." *Studies in Travel Writing* 4 (2000): 29-53.

Schofield, Mary Anne. "'Women's Speaking Justified': The Feminine Quaker Voice, 1662-1797." *Tulsa Studies in Women's Literature* 6.1 (1987): 61-77.

Silver, Bruce. "Clarke on the Quaker Background of William Bartram's Approach to Nature." *The Journal of the History of Ideas* 47.3 (1986): 507-10.

Stewart, Margaret E. "John Woolman's 'Kindness beyond Expression': Collective Identity vs. Individualism and White Supremacy." *Early American Literature* 26.3 (1991): 251-75.

Tocqueville, Alexis de. *Democracy in America.* Vol. 1, 1835; Vol. 2, 1840; The Henry Reeve text as rev. by Francis Bowen. Ed. Phillips Bradley. New York: Alfred Knopf, 1945.

Woolman, John. *The Journal of John Woolman* and *A Plea for the Poor.* The John Greenleaf Whittier Text (1871). Rpt. ed. Frederick B. Tolles. Secaucus, NJ: Citadel, 1961.

# Historical Roots of European Anti-Americanism in the 18th and 19th Centuries

Thomas Fröschl

**Introduction**

Early in July of 2001, just two months before the terrorist attack on America of September 11, a conference on "Anti-Americanism in the Twentieth Century" was held at the German Historical Institute in Washington, D.C. Among the lectures presented there the most disturbing by far was Robert McGeehan's contribution, entitled "European Unity and Anti-Americanism: Are They Inseparable?," which puzzled the participants and made them feel rather uneasy. This scholar from the University of London argued that if Europe actually attempted unification in order to separate herself from American dominance, the result of any such effort would not only be separation from, but opposition to the United States. And how to achieve such an ambitious goal? "The only political force strong enough to justify the economic sacrifices necessary to achieve a militarily operational Europe, he suggested, is – Anti-Americanism." And he added one more question: "Will European Anti-Americanism, liberated from the closet of the Cold War, develop sufficiently to achieve the unity which has so far been frustrated by the necessities of Atlanticism?" (Poutrus 168). I think one of the reasons why this statement was so deeply disturbing lies in the very fact that Anti-Americanism may indeed be used as a unifying force in Europe because people from all parts of Europe can quite easily find common ground – in accusing or admiring the United States, in talking about movies from Hollywood, in being worried about American military power.

It may well be that Europe needs again a common foe, a common threat, and it may be that this unifying force today and in the future will be the image or/and the reality of what is called and perceived as the image of "America." Yet why do so many Europeans "know" or pretend to "know" the U.S.A., why are so many of them convinced that – compared to Europe – this country and its people are vulgar, naive, immature, culturally inferior? Why are even those who have never been there "familiar" with America, and why do they hardly ever feel the incentive to visit the United States in order to make inquiries first and only then write or speak? This is the point where my specific interest as a historian comes in, and why I hope I can make some – modest – contributions to illuminate the phenomenon of European Anti-Americanism.

According to Paul Hollander, Anti-Americanism may be defined as: "A dark suspicion toward the United States and a readiness to believe the worst, . . . an unfocused and largely irrational, often visceral aversion toward the United States, its government, domestic institutions, foreign politics, prevailing values, culture, and people" (333-34), or: "A predisposition to hostility towards the United States and American Society, . . . an aversion to American culture in particular and its influence abroad, also contempt for the American national character (or what is presumed to be such a character) and dislike for the American people" (339). Historical investigation can discover and reveal certain aspects of the European idea of America, which from its 18th-century roots has never left the European mind and imagination. And because the idea of America to a large extent is in itself the result of a major Enlightenment debate, I am starting with this 18th-century discussion of "America as degraded and degenerated."

## 1. The 18th-Century Debate: The Degeneracy of the New World. A European Challenge and the American Response

Although the European critique of America is going back to the age of discovery, it was in the Age of Enlightenment that America was accused by many *philosophes* of being a failure. Europeans were interested not so much in what was similar but in what was different in the New World. Georges-Louis Leclerc, Comte de Buffon (1707-1788) claimed to have discovered the innate inferiority of America compared to Europe

– and this was the key for understanding most of what followed, for it was the comparison which made the difference. Things can be similar or they can be different, and if plants and animals and human beings in America are different from the ones in Europe, then the question arises about the very nature of this difference, that is to say: is it better or worse? Europe, both in her nature and her culture, was considered supreme, superior, and more civilized, because she alone was the seat of learning.

"Compared to Europe" – Buffon affirmed in his *Histoire naturelle* that America was backward, had emerged late from the flood and was still not dry. And in these "melancholy regions," he wrote in 1791, "everything languishes, corrupts, and proves abortive. The air and the earth, overloaded with humid and noxious vapors, are unable to purify themselves" (Commager 64). The Abbé Corneille De Pauw (1739-1799) in his *Recherches philosophiques sur les Américains* from 1768 had argued about the Indians: "Degeneracy had affected their senses and their organs, and their moral character had suffered to the same extent as their bodies. Nature . . . placed in America only children who have not yet become men. . . . even today there is not one who can think. . . . Superior to animals, . . . they are nevertheless truly inferior to the lowest Europeans" (Commager 93-94). And the Abbé Raynal (Guillaume Thomas Raynal, 1713-1796) underlined in his *Histoire philosophique et politique des Établissements et du Commerce des Européens dans les Deux Indes*, published in 1770, that "nature seems to have strangely neglected the New World. The men have less strength and less courage; no beard and no hair; they have less appearances of manhood; [there is] a sort of childhood in the people of America, similar to that of the people in our continent who are not yet arrived at the age of puberty. This seems to be a natural defect . . ., which is an indication of its being a new country" (Commager 130).

Worse, however, was the verdict of these Enlightenment *philosophes* on the Euro-Americans, which De Pauw, again in 1768, heavily attacked as well: "Studies made of Creoles have shown that in their early youth, just like American children, they give evidence of some acuteness of mind, which then dies out when they outgrow adolescence. They then become . . . unable to attain perfection in any art or science. Thus . . . their understanding diminishes when that of Europeans comes into its full force." And in all America, he was convinced, "the lack of success of Creoles . . . must be ascribed to a real defect and physical deterioration of constitution, in an unhealthy climate harmful to the human race" (Commager 101-02). And the Abbé Raynal stated in 1774 that "America has not yet produced one good poet, one able mathematician, one man of genius in a single art or a single science" (Jefferson 190).

In 1787, in his *Notes on the State of Virginia*, Thomas Jefferson dealt with Raynal's observation that America had not yet produced a great man. The Virginian, deeply hurt, pointed out three great Americans, Benjamin Franklin, David Rittenhouse and, above all, George Washington: "We therefore suppose," he wrote, "that this reproach is as unjust as it is unkind; and that, of the geniuses of the present age, America contributes its full share." Jefferson then compared population figures and the number of geniuses in three different countries: "The United States contain three millions of inhabitants; France twenty millions; and the British islands ten. We produce a Washington, a Franklin, a Rittenhouse. France then should have half a dozen in each of these lines, and Great Britain half the number, equally eminent." As far as France was concerned, Jefferson mentioned Voltaire, Buffon, Raynal, and the Encyclopedists, and has reason "to believe she can produce her full quota of genius" (191). Is this passage simply mechanistic, or is it more than that, a justification of an American Creole who was longing for acceptance among Europeans by demonstrating that America was not inferior, not immature, not feeble?

This Enlightenment debate on degenerate America, on degeneracy in America, posed an enormous challenge to 18th-century Euro-Americans, and they fiercely responded, pointing to the fact that the American Indian was not degenerate, and that the European settlers and their descendants were not degenerate either. Americans had to defend themselves against this European arrogance, and they did so. The following examples are but a small selection, but I think they will be better understood if one has this whole, widespread debate in mind. As French was the common language then among intellectuals and the *philosophes* of the Enlightenment, what was published in French was read by the elites throughout Europe and the Americas. Enlightenment cosmopolitanism and the capacity at least to read French thus helped powerfully to disseminate ideas and obser-vations on both sides of the Atlantic.

In Paris, in June 1785, Thomas Jefferson rejected the accusations of Count Buffon, and in a letter to the Marquis de Chastellux (1734-1788) he defended the American Indian – thus indirectly, as I would argue, defending himself as a European born in America: "And I am safe in affirming, that the proofs of genius given by the Indians of North America, place them on a level with whites in the same uncultivated state.... I believe the Indian, then, to be, in body and mind, equal to the white man" (801). And John Adams, in January 1787, stated in the preface of his *A Defense of the Constitutions of Government of the United States of America* that this country already

> exhibited, perhaps, the first example of government erected on the simple principle of nature. . . . It will never be pretended that any persons employed in this service had interviews with the gods, or were in any degree under the inspiration of Heaven, [but] it will forever be acknowledged that these governments were contrived merely by the use of reason and the senses, as Copley painted Chatham; . . . as Franklin practiced electricity; as Paine exposed the mistakes of Raynal, and Jefferson those of Buffon, so unphilosophically borrowed from the despicable dreams of De Pauw. . . . The writer has long seen with anxiety the facility with which philosophers of greatest name have undertaken to write of American affairs, without knowing anything of them, and have echoed and reechoed each other's visionary language. (117-19)

Adams, too, was proud of America's achievement, and he, too, rejected European assumptions and European arrogance.

When George Washington wrote to Marie Joseph Marquis de Lafayette in 1788, he, in a similar way, addressed what haunted Americans constantly, and the sentence I am quoting is, at least for me, deeply moving, considering the fact that Washington at that time (together with Benjamin Franklin) was the most famous of all Americans, a hero known all across Europe. But the great Washington felt the need to say this: "Although we are yet in our cradle as a nation, I think the efforts of the human mind with us are sufficient to refute (by incontestable facts) the doctrines of those who have asserted that every thing degenerates in America. Perhaps we shall be found, at this moment, not inferior to the rest of the world in the performances of our poets and painters, notwithstanding many of the incitements are wanting which operate powerfully among older nations" (298).

In spite of all these proofs, metropolitan cultures continued to reject American claims to equality. There is ample evidence from many documents written in London, Madrid, Paris, and Lisbon that suspicion and contempt did not vanish, that negative stereotypes about the Europeans born in the New World were not abandoned. Euro-Americans all over the Western hemisphere desperately tried to gain respect – unfortunately, in most cases, in vain. Therefore, I would suggest to read and to understand Thomas Jefferson's very personal sentences in the draft of the Declaration of Independence as a case in point. In words which the Continental Congress understandably refused to incorporate into the final version, the Virginian accused the English in a highly emotional manner – speaking as an injured, though at the same time proud American Creole: "Manly spirit bids us to renounce for ever these unfeeling brethren. We must endeavor to forget our former love for them . . . We might have been a free and a great people together; but a communication of grandeur & of freedom it seems is below their dignity. Be it so, since they will have it. The road to happiness & to glory is open to us too" (qtd. in Wills 378).

Alexander Hamilton was not a native of the United States, but born in 1755 in the British West Indies, probably on the Island of Nevis, and of Scottish descent. How was such a white West Indian at that time perceived from a European metropolis? In 1771, the comedy *The West Indian* by the English playwright Richard Cumberland (1732-1811) was performed in London for the first time, and it was to remain a highly successful theater production for decades. The play was translated into many European languages, and was staged in Germany as well. The plot develops around two opposing characters and places: an Englishman and a (white) West Indian, England and Jamaica, the Old World and the New. The (white) West Indian (of British descent) introduces himself to the metropolitan audience as follows: "I am an idle, dissipated, unthinking fellow, not worth your notice, in short, I am a West-Indian" (Act III, Scene V), and he is addressed by the English as a "Creolian," a white savage, degraded by a brutish slave society, rude, without culture: "His manners, passions, opinions are not assimilated to England, he is a new character, an inhabitant of the new world" (Act V, Scene III). Culture, the arts, politeness and elegance, all this belongs to England, and to England alone.

Alexander Hamilton – a "West Indian"? I do not know if Hamilton ever read the play by Richard Cumberland, yet I cannot but read the closing passage from the eleventh of the Federalist Papers, written by Hamilton in 1787, as the statement of another injured Creole, an affirmation of what America has achieved, and another repudiation of the idea of America being degenerate:

> The superiority [Europe] has long maintained, has tempted her to plume herself as the mistress of the World, and to consider the rest of mankind as created for her benefit. Men admired as profound philosophers have . . . attributed to her inhabitants a physical superiority; and have . . . asserted that all animals, and with them the human species, degenerate in America. . . . Facts have too long supported these arrogant pretensions of the European. It belongs to us to vindicate the honor of the human race, and to teach that assuming brother moderation. . . . Let Americans disdain to be the instruments of European greatness! Let the thirteen States . . . concur in erecting one great American system, superior to the control of all transatlantic force or influence, and able to dictate the terms of the connection between the old and the new world!" (72-73)

It seems to me that this cannot be understood simply as American arrogance, but as self-defense, and as a way to gain (or regain) self-respect.

## 2. The 19th-Century Debate: Democracy vs. Aristocracy. The Challenge of an American Principle and the European Response

In 1823, the prestigious Boston journal *The North American Review* remarked on a book called *The Principles of the Holy Alliance*, published in London, that the governing principle of this Alliance was "that all reformation originating with the people . . . is inconsistent with the welfare and repose of Europe, and as such, is to be put down by the combined arms of foreign powers" (Anonymous, *Principles* 341). A continuing conflict and active hostility between Europe and America, between the principles of Aristocracy and Liberalism, would be the consequence. "The natural tendency of all aristocratical and monarchical institutions is to augment the power in the hands of the rulers; and . . . the splendor of the privileged orders," the North American Review underlined, "is maintained at the expense of the laboring portion of the community, and they are not sensible to the misery of those beneath them. They . . . must be reminded that government was established for something besides the enjoyment of kings and nobles" (341). There is a "jealousy with which our republican institutions are viewed by the European courts, [which] may produce a state of feeling, that will not improbably result in direct hostility" (373). The article concludes: "With nations, advocating a system so opposite to ours, and with interests clashing with those of this republic at so many points, it will be next to impossible . . . to preserve our harmonious relations, and we should be prepared to maintain our rights in the manner in which the rights of such a people should be maintained" (374).

Would this result in a clash of civilizations, of principles, could it open an unbridgeable gap between the Old World and the New? In 1823 Johann Georg Hülsemann published *The History of Democracy in the United States of America*, a dissertation written in Göttingen (the author later became Austrian minister resident in Washington during the Civil War). The most interesting and illuminating part of Hülsemann's book is the Introduction, from where the following quotation is taken:

> The ascendancy of the democratic party in America is not to be deplored by us, chiefly because it annihilates all the hopes . . . by men like Washington and Hamilton. But this ascendancy is especially disastrous for Europe, for the firm support thereby afforded to the case of revolution. For this very reason it is highly desirable for us, that, at least in other portions of the New World, institutions should be preserved or established, more nearly in accord worth our own, to serve as a counterpoise to the prevalent policy of North America. This is the point of view, from which we ought to contemplate what is commonly called the struggle between Europe and America. (Anonymous, *Democratie* 310)

Hülsemann then attacked the liberals in Europe, was happy with the success of the Allied powers in Spain against a liberal regime, and considered the United States and the principle of Democracy as the enemies of the Old World. By the way, to counterbalance American democracy, Britain and the Austrian government strongly supported the establishment of a monarchy in Brazil in 1822 – while for the United States, this empire represented a European anomaly in the Americas until the end of monarchy in South America in 1889.

Monarchy as opposed to Democracy, power descending from above vs. power ascending from below – two antagonistic principles, expressly stated during the Conference of Verona in 1822:

> The great powers [Austria, France, Prussia, and Russia] . . ., fully convinced that a system of representational government is as incompatible with the principle of monarchy as is the idea of sovereignty of the people with the principle of divine right, formally undertake to use all the means at their disposal to destroy the representational system of government in every European state in which it now exists and to prevent its introduction into those countries where it is now unknown. As there can be no doubt that the freedom of the press is the most powerful single weapon in the armory of those who pretend to defend the rights of the people in their struggle against their kings, the great powers . . . promise . . . to suppress it, not only in their own states but also in every other European country. (Loveman 50)

And indeed, French military forces were entrusted to destroy the liberal regime in Spain, which had come to power in 1820, and the French succeeded. Therefore, to some extent the Conference of Verona set the stage for action in the Americas, where this assembly of European powers was understood as a sign of deep concern and alarm. Compare to this statement the First Amendment to the American Constitution, ratified in 1791: "Congress shall make no law . . . abridging the freedom of speech or of the press."

The Monroe Doctrine, i.e. two sections from the President's Seventh Annual Message to Congress, should be understood and interpreted as an ideological moment of the greatest significance, not as a military threat to the European powers. James Monroe's address of

December 1823 was an answer to and a rejection of the European principle of monarchy:

> It is only when our rights are invaded or seriously menaced that we resent injuries or make preparation for our defense. With the movements in this hemisphere we are . . . immediately connected. . . . The political system of the allied powers is essentially different in this respect from that of America. . . . It is impossible that the allied powers should extend their political system to any portion of either continent without endangering our peace and happiness; nor can anyone believe that our southern brethren . . . would adopt it of their own accord. (649-50)

It should be noticed how deep the gap already was between the political principles of the New World and the Old. In September of 1854, Leopold von Ranke held lectures in history to instruct the Bavarian king Maximilian II. Talking about the American Revolution, which in importance he placed above the French Revolution, Ranke described this revolution as the most important one the world had ever known, because it was a complete reversal of principles – from now on, Ranke explained to the king, the idea emerged that power had to ascend from below. And he concluded that the two Principles of Republicanism and Monarchy were opposed to one another like two different worlds, and that the history of modern time was nothing but the history of the conflict between them (Ranke 417).

## 3. A late 19th Century Debate: European Challenges, and One American Response

In 1884, a certain Sir Lepel Henry Griffin (1840-1908) published a book on America called *The Great Republic*, after having traveled extensively throughout the country. Two remarks in particular are striking: Griffin asserted that America had not yet contributed to civilization, because America had no "real" civilization. And he also maintained that "there is no country calling itself civilized where one would not rather live than in America, except Russia" (Arnold 489).

Both the eminent Victorian critic Matthew Arnold and the American author Mark Twain wrote reviews of the book. Arnold's response in his essay "Civilization in the United States," written in 1888, took Griffin's assertions as a point of departure. In reflecting upon the remark that "there is no country calling itself civilized where one would not rather live than in America, except Russia," Arnold concluded that such an observation made by an eminent Briton must have some validity. Therefore the "civilization of the United States must somehow . . . have shortcomings, in spite of the country's success and prosperity" (490). It is true, Arnold goes on to say, that a man of Sir Griffin's class "has in England everything in his favour, society appears organized expressly for his advantage. . . . On the other hand, for that immense class of people, the great bulk of the community, . . . things in America are favorable. It is easier for them there than in the Old World to rise and to make their fortune; but I am not speaking of that" (491-92).

Matthew Arnold described and explained the nature of a 'real' civilization, something America was lacking. For him a real civilization had to be "interesting," and the two great sources were "distinction" and "beauty" (496). America, unfortunately, was lacking both: it lacked distinction, basically because Americans did not cherish the discipline of awe and respect. Americans "have produced . . . very few [people] who are highly distinguished. Alexander Hamilton is indeed a man of rare distinction; Washington . . . has true distinction of style and character. But these men belong to the pre-American age. . . . Lincoln is shrewd, sagacious, humorous, honest, courageous, firm . . . but he has not distinction". Everything was against distinction in America, especially the "glorification of the 'average man' . . . is against it" (497). Therefore "a great void exists in the civilization over there: a want of what is elevated and beautiful, of what is interesting" (499).

Yet Arnold already sensed a strong American influence in Britain, the influence of Democracy, an influence beneficial in part, yet nevertheless threatening and destructive. Particularly dangerous was the leveling element in American democracy which might sweep all over England and Europe in the future. The major problem for Arnold, who, as a liberal, was in sympathy with democratic reform, was "the predominance of the average man," because this "is a malady, too. That the common and the ignoble is human nature's enemy, that . . . distinction and beauty are needs, that a civilization is insufficient where these needs are not satisfied, . . . is an instruction of which we, as well as the Americans, may greatly require to take fast hold, and not let go" (504).

Mark Twain in 1890 responded to both Sir Griffin and Matthew Arnold in the essay "On Foreign Critics." He underlines that

> Mr. Arnold granted that our whole people – including by especial mention 'that immense class, the great bulk of the community', the wage and salary-earners – have liberty, equality, plenty to eat, plenty to wear, comfortable shelter, high pay, abundance of churches, newspapers, libraries, charities, and a good education for everybody's child for nothing. He added, 'society seems organized there for their benefit' – benefit of the bulk and mass of the people. Yes, it is conceded that we furnish the greatest good to the greatest number; and so all we lack is a civilization. (944)

But Mark Twain was especially annoyed about Sir Griffin, who "won't concede that we have a civilization – a 'real' civilization, and says 'there is no country calling itself civilized where one would not rather live than in Americas, except Russia.' That settles it. That is, it settles it for Europe." For Americans, Mark Twain continued, "civilization must surely mean the humanizing of a people, not a class – there is today but one real civilization in the world, and it is not yet thirty years old . . . when we disposed of our slavery" (942). He then asked what planted the seed of Liberty in the modern world – it was the American Revolution. "When that revolution began, monarchy had been on trial some thousands of years. . . . It had never produced anything but a vast, a nearly universal savagery, with a thin skim of civilization on top . . ., slaves of an aristocracy of smirking dandies clad in unearned silk and velvet. . . . When we hoisted the banner of revolution and raised the first genuine shout for human liberty . . . what resulted in England and on the Continent? Crippled liberty took up its bed and walked. From that day to this day its march has not halted, and please God it never will." And yet: "We have contributed nothing! Nothing hurts me like ingratitude" (943-44).

Brazilian intellectuals, who during the 19th century in most cases can be considered as European intellectuals, attacked (and still attack) the United States frequently with all the familiar stereotypes. Eduardo Prado (1860-1901), the official Brazilian representative to the celebration of the Centennial of the French Revolution, published his *The American Illusion* in Rio de Janeiro in 1893. This book was the first clearly anti-American vision written by a Latin-American intellectual – prior to the many books and pamphlets published to accuse and condemn the impact of Yankee imperialism following the Spanish-American War in 1898. Prado, a convinced monarchist, asserted that the United States still remained a colony of Europe – culturally speaking, a country with plenty of *nouveaux riches*, of intellectually undemanding *parvenus*, without culture, without sophistication, a republican culture lacking traditional, aristocratic values (Oliveira 146).

## Concluding Remarks

In this article I have tried to investigate some historical roots of European Anti-Americanism, and I perceive an obvious continuity in the European rejection of America as being equal, because Americans are still seen as inferior, degenerate, immature. This characterization applies to the nature of the American people, and of the civilization of the U.S.A. in general. Of course, the Enlightenment debate on America's degeneracy is nearly forgotten, but the terms "inferior," "degenerate," "immature" persist in different contexts today.

I would argue, therefore, that at the center of contemporary anti-Americanism can be discovered a twofold heritage – one from the 18th century, portraying Americans are children, as being immature, inferior, simply not the equals of the Europeans; the other from the 19th century, portraying Americans as uncultured, materialistic, representing a vulgar mass culture which is alien to and destructive of European high culture. The anti-American "sub-text," which accompanies criticism of American politics or of America in general, and which must "not be confused with opposition to particular policies of the United States [government]" (Hollander 335), is a revealing combination of this 18th-century accusation of inferiority, immaturity, degeneracy, and of the 19th-century threat of democracy, of the common man, the people in general, the vulgar and crude masses.

**Works Cited**

Adams, John. *A Defence of the Constitutions of the United States of America*. 1786-87. *The Political Writings of John Adams*. Ed. George W. Carey. Washington, DC: Regnery Publ., 2000. 105-303.

Anonymous. "Geschichte der Democratie in den Vereinigten Staaten von Nord America, von Johann Georg Hülsemann. Göttingen 1823." *The North American Review* 23 (1826): 304-14.

Anonymous. "The Principles of the Holy Alliance; Or, Notes and Manifestoes of the Allied Powers. London 1823." *The North American Review* 17 (1823): 340-75.

Arnold, Matthew. *Civilisation in the United States*. 1888. *The Oxford Authors*. Ed. Miriam Allott and Robert H. Super. Oxford, NY: Oxford UP, 1986. 489-504.

Commager, Henry Steele, and Elmo Giordanetti. *Was America a Mistake? An Eighteenth-Century Controversy*. New York: Harper & Row, 1967.

Cumberland, Richard. *The West Indian. A Comedy*. London, 1771.

Hamilton, Alexander. *The Federalist No. 11*. Nov. 24, 1787. *The Federalist*. Ed. Jacob E. Cooke. Hanover, NH: Wesleyan UP, 1961. 65-73.

Hollander, Paul. *Anti-Americanism. Irrational & Rational*. 2nd ed. New Brunswick, NJ: Transaction Publishers, 1995.

Jefferson, Thomas. *Writings*. The Library of America. Vol. 17. Ed. Merrill D. Peterson. New York: Literary Classics of the United States, 1984.

Loveman, Brian. *The Constitution of Tyranny. Regimes of Exception in Spanish America*. Pittsburgh: U of Pittsburgh P, 1993.

Monroe, James. *Seventh Annual Message*. 1823. *The Political Writings of James Monroe*. Ed. James P. Lucier. Washington, DC: Regnery Publ., 2001. 637-651.

Oliveira, Lúcia Lippi. *Eduardo Prado. A ilusão americana*. Ed. Lourenço Dantas Mota. São Paulo: Editora Senac, 1999. 133-50.

Poutrus, Patrice G. "Anti-Americanism in the Twentieth Century." *Bulletin of the German Historical Institute, Washington, D.C.* 30 (2002): 164-68.

Ranke, Leopold. *Über die Epochen der Neueren Geschichte.* 1854. Ed. Theodor Schieder and Helmut Berding. München and Wien: Oldenbourg Verlag, 1971.

Twain, Mark. *Collected Tales, Sketches, Speeches & Essays, 1852-1890.* The Library of America. Vol. 60. Ed. Louis J. Budd. New York: Library Classics of the United States, 1992.

Washington, George. *The Papers of George Washington. Confederation Series.* Vol. 6: January–September 1788. Ed. W. W. Abbot. Charlottesville: UP of Virginia, 1997.

Wills, Garry. *Inventing America. Jefferson's Declaration of Independence.* Garden City, NY: Doubleday, 1978.

# The "Purple Democrat": Emily Dickinson and the Sovereignty of Democratic Consent

## Paul Crumbley

In "There is a flower that Bees prefer – " (Fr642), Emily Dickinson describes the preferred flower as a "Purple Democrat" that contends with the common grass, is desired by butterflies, hummingbirds and insects, and is "proclaimed" by the bee "in sovreign [sic] – Swerveless Tune." By describing the flower as both purple and a democrat, Dickinson metaphorically illuminates a central tension within the American system of constitutional democracy: that public consent appears, paradoxically, to confer the purple of royal sovereignty on exemplary individuals, whereas democratic logic militates against any attribution of absolutist distinction that by its nature threatens the sovereignty of others. Dickinson's play on the contradictory political logic of "sovereignty" constitutes a significant Americanism frequently reflected in the commonplace discourse of American writers, who regularly use language signifying political traditions antagonistic to the egalitarian ideals of popular sovereignty. The resulting "regal democrat" Americanism has in Dickinson's case contributed to striking differences in scholarly assessments of her politics. Now, at a time when the political legitimacy of canonical American writers of the nineteenth century has come under scrutiny, especially for their expression of a brand of individualism susceptible to ideological co-optation, Dickinson's work warrants close examination. Such examination reveals that the writer nineteenth-century publisher Samuel Bowles described as the "queen recluse" (Sewall 474) actively interrogates the relation of sovereignty to individualism. As I will argue, her poems in fact resist the very processes of ideological appropriation that rightfully trouble modern critics.

Dickinson's vocabulary of old-world absolutism is well established. She uses the word "purple" fifty-six times in her poems (Rosenbaum 601-02), and in doing so confirms that purple is indeed "The color of a Queen" (Fr875) and is fashionable when "a soul perceives itself / To be an Emperor" (Fr896). Other references to royalty abound in the poems and letters, including a notable poetic tribute to Elizabeth Barrett Browning, who is described as having a "Head too High – to Crown – " (Fr600).[1] Literary scholars have taken a special interest in "The Soul selects her own Society – " (Fr409A), a poem in which the soul "Choose[s] One" from among an "ample nation," then "shuts the Door – / To her divine Majority." Betsy Erkkila has written of this poem that "what Dickinson describes in a monarchical language of emperors, chariots, and divine right is a rigidly stratified social order of rank, exclusion and difference" ("Class" 8). In a similar vein, Domhnall Mitchell has argued that "the phrase 'divine Majority' inevitably echoes and recoils from its secular or democratic equivalent, the masses, while the reference to an 'Emperor' rejects the rights of that minority of the population who possess sufficient wealth and power to impose rights on others" (6). Both Erkkila and Mitchell find the use of language derived from European monarchies incompatible with a democratic sensibility. Erkkila points specifically to Dickinson's employment of "Whig political rhetoric" as evidence that her language undermines democratic values by slipping "between the old and the new, between an aristocratic language of rank, royalty, and hereditary privilege, and a Calvinist language of spiritual grace, personal sanctity and divine election" (9).

Yet there is substantial reason to believe that the very slippage in Whig rhetoric that Erkkila finds so undemocratic might conceivably be viewed as a normative pattern of democratic expression in nineteenth-century America. Political historian F. R. Ankersmit has identified an underlying political predisposition to use monarchical terminology in America's winner-take-all approach to two-party politics.[2] In Ankersmit's words, the political party in power functioned as the "successor of the absolute monarch" (101) in ways that no single party could in the coalition governments of continental democracies. Such a predisposition helps explain why many middle-class democrats appeared to have felt comfortable thinking about "the people" in terms that we find paradoxical if not flatly contradictory today. As Cathy Davidson has indicated in her study of literacy in the late eighteenth and early nineteenth centuries, many literate citizens did not acknowledge that they were surrounded by illiterate masses.[3] Such inability to recognize the presence of persons whose lives fell outside the circle of middle-class affluence was not unusual.[4] Alexis de Tocqueville is famous for his accounts of equality in America[5] and Ralph Waldo Emerson would write in 1860 that "all great men come out of the middle classes" (*Essays*, "Considerations," 1086). Sacvan Bercovitch has seen in this elevation of the middle classes a rough correspondence with monarchical traditions of Europe. "Here," he writes of nineteenth-century America, "'self-made'" performs as "a euphoric catchall that appropriated the feudal-religious rhetoric of 'kingship' on behalf of middle-class individualism" (48). In this context, Dickinson's language begins to look less like the expression of undemocratic elitist attitudes and more like the presentation of commonplace contradictions in the middle-class political logic of her day.

Pierre Bourdieu has pointed out that a major difficulty in describing the social history of literature is that "the self-evident givens of the situation . . . remained unmarked," circulating rather "in the air" writers breathed and for that reason were never part of the self-conscious record transmitted to future readers (32). Such appears to be the case with the widespread use of socially hierarchical terminology, even by writers who deliberately promoted democratic egalitarianism. Emerson refers to poets as "liberating gods" (*Selections*, "The Poet," 235), Melville writes of "genius, all over the world" standing "hand in hand" (249)[6] and even Whitman details an "I" "waiting my time to be one of the supremes" ("Song of Myself," 234, 1.1050).[7] Yet each of these writers has been approached critically as having contributed in a significant way to what F. O. Matthiessen famously described as American literature "dedicated to the possibilities of democracy" (ix).

Recent debates among literary scholars and feminist political theorists suggest that instead of treating Dickinson's monarchical language as emblematic of undemocratic elitism, her use of the "regal democrat" Americanism more accurately positions her writing within the struggle to reconcile individualism with political activism that was a central feature of nineteenth-century American culture.[8] Indeed, the degree that the Dickinson debate mirrors arguments over Emersonian individualism suggests both that Dickinson deserves the same political consideration Emerson has received and that scholarly consensus is no more likely with her than with Emerson. Emerson's famous statement that "Union is only perfect when all the Uniters are absolutely isolated" (*Essays* 216) conveys the ambiguity at the heart of individualism as he constructs it. In *Rites of Consent*, Bercovitch makes the case for political efficacy, arguing that Emerson practices a paradoxical form of dissent according to which individual "autonomy [is] preserved, precariously but decisively, . . . within the bounds of community" (344). In sharp contrast, John Carlos Rowe argues in *At Emerson's Tomb* that the "radical individualism" (22) advocated by Emerson has contributed so significantly to the flawed politics of "aesthetic dissent" (1) that the whole tradition of American literature organized around the Emersonian self has become dangerously "depoliticized" (25, 248). For Rowe, the politics of American literature must be "revaluated both in terms of its critique of ideology . . . and the discursive communities such literature helps constitute" (14). Bercovitch instead presents political content as a "distinctive type of radical thought" (345) that may remain inchoate in its outward form but nevertheless subverts the foundations of liberal thought (348). Like Rowe, Erkkila argues that "it is unclear how [Dickinson's] poetic revolution might become an agent of social change" (*Sisters* 52), while Geoffrey Sanborn resembles Bercovitch when he proposes that though "Dickinson does not participate in Marxian or postcolonial discourses, she does model a practice that is a precondition of those discourses" (1345). What these parallel interpretive impasses tell us is that contemporary scholarship can interpret the complexities of middle-class America's struggle with individual autonomy as simultaneously prime examples of American liberal politics and dangerous neutralizations of political ideology.

In Dickinson's writing, the culturally contested nature of sovereignty registers in the vocabulary of class and rank that Erkkila and Mitchell correctly link to the patriarchal tradition of divine right. For Dickinson, though, the presence of the regal democrat signals an interrogation of what feminist political theorist Kathleen Jones has described in contemporary terms as the "sovereignty trap" that draws feminists into the "same dynamics of exclusion in the struggle for sovereignty" they find so easy to criticize in the patriarchal politics they oppose (71). Dickinson was indeed blind to much of the bigotry that characterized mid-century middle-class life, and that reality has quite justifiably provoked criticism by feminists and others, but her writing also reflects an acute sensitivity to the political dynamics of sovereignty that deserves to be understood as a form of engagement with the politics of her day that resonates in important ways with contemporary feminist concerns.[9]

Viewing individual sovereignty as a contested site that surfaces frequently in Dickinson's poetry has important implications for readers, who must participate actively in the dramas of consent staged by the poems. As an alternative to readings promoted by Erkkila and Mitchell, for instance, the "divine Majority" mentioned in "The Soul selects her own Society – ," like the "divinest Sense" of "Much madness is divinest Sense – " (Fr620), may be understood as representing forms of individual sovereignty that pose difficult questions for the female citizen. In "The Soul selects her own Society – ," the speaker passively observes the conduct of the Soul who isolates herself from the speaker behind closed doors and what are described as shut valves. The exercise of "divine Majority," then, presumably takes place outside the speaker's field of vision, conveying the impression that the speaker is excluded from this highly restricted expression of female power. The social benefits of female independence are if anything even more dubious in "Much Madness is divinest Sense – ," where the speaker presents stark alternatives for the dissenting female: either pretend to conform or "Demur" and risk being "handled with a Chain." While these poems do represent selves that may be familiar to readers, and even admirable as expressions of non-conformist behavior, neither of these poems describes a politically responsible expression of democratic sovereignty.

Poems like the "Purple Democrat" demonstrate the feminism inherent in Dickinson's poetry, while also showing that Dickinson can be read just as oppositely as Emerson. She achieves this by constructing a

The "Purple Democrat"

poem that at first appears entirely familiar and predictable but turns out to contain multiple levels of meaning, each offering a different political message.

There is a flower that Bees prefer –
And Butterflies – desire –
To gain the Purple Democrat
The Humming Bird – aspire –

And Whatsoever Insect pass –
A Honey bear away
Proportioned to his several dearth
And her – capacity –

Her face be rounder than the Moon
And ruddier than the Gown
Of Orchis in the Pasture –
Or Rhododendron – worn –

She doth not wait for June –
Before the World be Green –
Her sturdy little Countenance
Against the Wind – be seen –

Contending with the Grass –
Near Kinsman to Herself –
For privilege of Sod and Sun –
Sweet Litigants for Life –

And when the Hills be full –
And newer fashions blow –
Doth not retract a single spice
For pang of jealousy –

Her Public – be the Noon –
Her Providence – the Sun –
Her Progress – by the Bee proclaimed –
In sovreign – Swerveless Tune –

The Bravest – of the Host –

> Surrendering – the last –
> Nor even of Defeat – aware –
> When cancelled by the Frost –

On the most obvious level, the poem's riddle form engages the interior thought processes of speaker and reader in what appears to be a closed game. There are many Dickinson poems that operate this way; "It sifts from Leaden Sieves" (Fr291) and "I like to see it lap the Miles – " (Fr383) are two of the best known examples. However, just as solving the riddle emerges as one facet of a far more complicated poem with the snow and train poems, so is the case with the "Purple Democrat." In the words of Cheryl Walker, the surface text conveys a "version of the self made acceptable to nineteenth-century patriarchal society" while the "deeper and less acceptable script points to a part of the self that has been violated, almost rubbed out but that speaks nevertheless" (31-32). Accordingly, the surface riddle affirms conventional American democratic practice: the female flower wins universal admiration, fearlessly confronts conventions, enjoys public affirmation and proceeds impervious to the possibilities of defeat or death.

The "deeper and less acceptable script" that Walker refers to emerges once the disjunctive power of the poem's thirty-eight dashes is combined with the clear delineation of male and female perspectives that divides the poem into two four-stanza groupings. In the first three stanzas, the flower *passively* fulfills nineteenth-century female stereotypes: as the object of universal desire, as a nurturer who has provided for each according to capacity, and as comparable to traditional symbols of female beauty, the moon and other flowers. The seventh stanza then affirms these female accomplishments with the male bee's voice that here frames the purportedly democratic and independent female with the male symbolism of "Noon" and "Sun" that together constitute the "Public" domain and "Providence" that circumscribe what is referred to ironically as the female's "Progress."[10] By contrast, the four opposing stanzas present an *active* female who rejects seasonal cycles, contends for legal property rights, disdains the demands of fashion and battles on oblivious of defeat. The resulting symmetrical structure suggests both that the bee's sovereign proclamation of the flower's purple status celebrates conformity rather than independence and that the flower's independence is too remote from collective experience to effectively challenge patriarchal politics.

Combining the riddle function of the poem with the internal divisions just described makes possible a reading that contemplates three speakers, each of which espouses a distinct political message. The first is the gender-neutral riddle speaker who seeks the confirmation of Emersonian individuality provided by the bee's sovereign male voice. This speaker communicates a vision of public consent according to which the reader joins the bee in diffusing and thereby appropriating rebellious female conduct, effectively reducing her to an acceptable reflection of reader and bee. The second speaker expresses the external male view that acknowledges as female only those outward traits that coincide with conventional patriarchal expectations. This speaker also affirms the bee's assertion of male sovereignty but does so without the riddle form's demand for reader consent. As a consequence, the supposed elevation of the sovereign female is plainly revealed as a form of patriarchal containment according to which female consent is superfluous. The third speaker conveys the internal female experience of being simultaneously alienated from the male foundations of political power and oblivious of the powerlessness that alienation entails. This speaker most emphatically embodies the sovereignty trap described by Kathleen Jones, as the speaker's obsession with personal power seals her off from the experience of others as completely as she has been sealed off from patriarchal politics. When all three speakers are considered collectively, the poem's analysis of female political subjectivity emerges with considerable force. Political complacency and ideological appropriation emerge as the outcomes of female consent to male sovereignty and the female exercise of independent sovereignty is shown as powerless to alter the patriarchal system it rejects.

By presenting conflicting assessments of the relationship between individualism and democracy, the poem, in Bercovitch's words, turns "cultural symbology against the dominant culture" (360), granting readers the opportunity to see beyond the contending social forces that prompt the flower's several refusals. When readers then imagine utopian alternatives, reading the poem itself becomes an enactment of democratic sovereignty. In Nancy Ruttenberg's words, the conversion of "negative traits into positive ones" requires "reconceptualizing democracy as a theater of verbal (symbolic) action, an experiential ground whose materializations, both historical and literary, would ultimately foster a recognizably democratic (polycentric) cultural semiotic" (15). To the extent that Dickinson's poem succeeds in provoking this sort of imaginative formation of democratic social space, the poem clearly moves beyond the private domain of isolated author and reader.

Perhaps it should come as no surprise that among the first to acknowledge Dickinson as a political writer have been women writers whose own work is openly political. At a May 15, 1986 centennial tribute to Dickinson in South Orange, New Jersey, where fifteen women poets—including Adrienne Rich, Gwendolyn Brooks and Denise Levertov—dedicated an entire day to communicating their responses to Dickinson, Sharon Olds publicly declared, "I think she's political, intensely political" (12). Olds then dedicated a poem to Dickinson titled "He Comes for the Jewish Family, 1942." At the same event, African American poet Toi Derricote expressed her desire for a more focused discussion of Dickinson's politics: "I wish we could meet, break into groups, and everybody talk about politics, poetry, and Emily Dickinson . . ." (2). Then Derricote quoted these Dickinson lines: "I took my Power in my Hand – / And went against the World –" (Fr660). Also in 1986, Chicana writer Sandra Cisneros told a group of junior high school students in Santa Barbara that Dickinson's poems gave her "inspiration and hope all the years in high school and the first two in college" (75). Writing specifically about Dickinson's political influence on Cisneros, Geoffrey Sanborn offers this conclusion: "Instead of viewing Dickinson as someone whose self-gratifying isolation is essentially at odds with democratic sociality, we should view her as someone whose 'exposure of our passionate and limitless desire to be the ideal' makes possible 'its continual deconstruction and displacement'" (1345).

That the historical record now shows Dickinson's influence on political writers does indeed strengthen the case that Dickinson can herself be read as a political writer. This achievement goes a long way toward satisfying Rowe's requirement that "the politics of American literature . . . be revaluated in terms [of] the discursive communities such literature helps constitute" (14). Facts alone are not likely to dispel uncertainties about the politics of Dickinson's writing, however. As Bourdieu has famously stated, the field of cultural production is "one of the indeterminate sites in the social structure," a site characterized by "rival principles of legitimacy" (43). A current example of the way rival principles of literary legitimacy apply directly to Dickinson, is vividly conveyed in the October 7, 2002 *New York Times* story about Laura Bush's efforts to establish a series of White House symposiums on major American writers, including Dickinson. In the piece, reporter Elizabeth Bumiller asserts in one line that "Mrs. Bush has reached out beyond ideology" and in the very next line quotes the first lady herself as stating, "There's nothing political about American literature" (*Times* A1). Here the question about politics is situated in immediate relation to American literature's power to address and potentially subvert ideology. Was the reporter implying that Mrs. Bush departed from her husband's practice by not basing her assessment of legitimacy on ideological and hence political conformity, or was she asserting that by discussing American literature the issue of ideology was no longer relevant? Mrs. Bush's response is equally ambiguous, as in her denial that American literature is political she communicates her awareness that such a statement is required, thereby acknowledging that American literature is not only political but political in a manner she is compelled to deny.

The language of the article makes it possible to conclude that like the writing of Emerson and Dickinson, American literature as a whole maintains its legitimacy precisely because it simultaneously appears to differing constituencies as either political or apolitical. As scholars concerned with the communication of democratic thought in America, we have a duty to illuminate the political dimensions of the "regal democrat" Americanism, not merely to establish that Dickinson's "Purple Democrat" can be read as ideological critique, or even a call to political action, but rather to clarify the extent that for major American writers of the nineteenth century and today democratic sovereignty continues to materialize through a delicate balancing of individualism and consent.

## Notes

I want to acknowledge the support I received from the Rothermere American Institute in Oxford, England, where I worked as a Visiting Fellow during 2002-2003, and the generous grant from the Austrian Association for American Studies.

[1] In Dickinson's poems, "royal," "royally" and "royalty" appear twenty-two times (Rosenbaum 636); "crown," "crowned" and "crowns" appear twenty-seven times (162); "queen," "queen's" and queens" appear nineteen times (605).

[2] See 99-104 in *Representational Democracy*. In these pages Ankersmit spells out what he means about the ways continental and American forms of democracy differ over the role of absolute authority. The following passage represents his general position: "In contrast to continental democracies, in Anglo-Saxon democracy the absolute monarch is still present insofar as the possession of political power and having an absolute majority in the representative body go together there" (102).

[3] Davidson writes of John Adams's "often quoted claim that America was the most literate nation on earth. 'A native American who cannot read and write,' Adams boasted, 'is as rare as a comet or an earthquake'" (56). Davidson proceeds to cite studies showing that "less than half of the population were literate." See her chapter "Literacy, Education, and the Reader" (55-79) in *Revolution and the Word*.

[4] Robert Dahl points out in *After the Revolution* that a failure to accurately associate "the people" of democratic discourse with the actual populations supposedly represented has been a familiar feature of writing about democracy. "Strange as it may seem to you," he writes, "how to decide who legitimately make up 'the people'—or rather *a* people—and hence are entitled to govern themselves in their *own* association is a problem almost totally neglected by all the great political philosophers who write about democracy" (46). See also 64-65.

[5] Tocqueville's most famous statement about equality in America comes in the opening sentence of his "Author's Introduction" to the first volume of *Democracy in America*: "No novelty in the United States struck me more vividly during my stay there than the equality of conditions" (9). Writing specifically of New England, Tocqueville states that "the colony came more and more to present the novel phenomenon of a society homogeneous in all its parts" (39). Of the United States at the time he viewed it, he notes, "the last traces of hereditary ranks and distinctions have been destroyed" (54). He concludes his commentary on equality in "Social State of the Anglo-Americans" with these words: "Men there are nearer equality in wealth and mental endowments, or, in

other words, more nearly equally powerful, than in any other country of the world or in any other age of recorded history" (56).
[6] Also in "Hawthorne and His Mosses," Melville writes of the need to create a literary supremacy that will match the global political supremacy that he anticipates for America in the near future: "While we are rapidly preparing for the political supremacy among the nations . . . in a literary point of view, we are deplorably unprepared for it" (248). There are also numerous passages where Melville expresses disdain for a public incapable of comprehending literary genius (240, 244-47, 251).
[7] Whitman also discusses the "Supremes" in his 1855 preface to *Leaves of Grass*. There he speaks for "great poets" as he invites "each man and woman" to "Come to us on equal terms" (14). He clearly promotes what might be thought of as democratic access to the sphere of the Supremes, but he persists in using hierarchical language. For instance, he urges individual recognition of "supremacy within" and mastery "of nature and passion and death, and of all terror and pain" (14-15). In language of this kind, Whitman distinguishes between the equality of access and the inequality of achievement, so that greatness is invested with qualities of the divine. The link to an aristocratic past is further established when, in the next paragraph, he writes of "American bards" who "shall not be careful of riches and privilege . . . they shall be riches and privilege" (15).
[8] Here one should bear in mind that individual consent to forms of political representation was not the exclusive province of male or female reformers. As Gillian Brown has recently argued in *The Consent of the Governed*, "Individual judgments and choices cannot occur in isolation, but always proceed in relation to existing conventions. Liberalism, as formulated by Locke, registers the connection between personal and political spheres" (9). Even though Dickinson is famous for having lived as a recluse for the last twenty years of her life, her withdrawal from public activism need not be seen as a refusal to engage in the political concerns of her day. That her grandfather, father and brother were all attorneys who also served at various times as elected officials suggests that the atmosphere in the Dickinson house reflected the political currents that swirled in the larger world.
[9] Harold Laski usefully describes what is at stake from a philosophical point of view in efforts to negotiate a consistent program of political sovereignty in a democracy. At the base of any deliberations must certainly be the observation that there is no such thing as the retention of sovereignty once it is alienated, as passing sovereign authority to another invests that other with the power to refuse to return sovereign power (50, 54). Consequently, Laski concludes,

"Those who practice the theoretic substance of sovereignty find themselves deprived of it" (48). He goes on to state the particular dilemma such circumstances create in America, where so much importance has been placed on the practice of popular sovereignty: "A peculiar historical experience has therefore devised the means of building a State from which the conception of sovereignty is absent" (49). F. R. Ankersmit argues that America "should abandon the doctrine of popular sovereignty," not because it does not exist in America but because it is maintained through representational modes controlled by political parties. He concludes, "Sovereign power exists but is in nobody's hands in a representative democracy" (118). As both Lasky and Ankersmit make clear, the dilemma posed by efforts to maintain individual sovereignty in a representative democracy was bound to provoke the sorts of anxieties reflected by nineteenth-century writers and their present-day democratic critics.

[10] The connection between sun and noon and male power has been well established in Dickinson criticism. The most famous example appears in Dickinson's June 1852 letter to Susan Huntington Gilbert where she describes married life in terms of flowers submitting to the "man of noon" and appearing "with their heads bowed in anguish before the mighty sun" (*Letters* 210). See also my discussion of this letter in *Inflections of the Pen* (25, 119-20).

**Works Cited**

Ankersmit, F. R. *Political Representation*. Stanford: Stanford UP, 2002.

Bercovitch, Sacvan. *The Rites of Assent: Transformations in the Symbolic Construction of America*. New York: Routledge, 1993.

Brown, Gillian. *The Consent of the Governed: The Lockean Legacy in Early American Culture*. Cambridge, MA: Harvard UP, 2001.

Bourdieu, Pierre. *The Field of Cultural Production: Essays on Art and Literature*. Ed. Randal Johnson. Cambridge: Polity P, 1993.

Bumiller, Elisabeth. "Quietly, the First Lady Builds a Literary Room of Her Own." *New York Times*. 7 Oct. 2002: A1+.

Cisneros, Sandra. "Notes to a Young(er) Writer." *Americas Review* 15.1 (1987): 74-76.

Crumbley, Paul. *Inflections of the Pen: Dash and Voice in Emily Dickinson.* Lexington: UP of Kentucky, 1997.

Dahl. Robert. *After the Revolution: Authority in a Good Society.* New Haven: Yale UP, 1990.

Davidson, Cathy N. *Revolution and the Word: The Rise of the Novel in America.* New York: Oxford UP, 1986.

Derricote, Toi. "We Ain't Seen Nothing Yet." *Titanic Operas: A Poet's Corner of Responses to Dickinson's Legacy.* <http://www.iath.virginia.edu/dickinson/titanic/derricote.html>.

Dickinson, Emily. *The Letters of Emily Dickinson.* 3 vols. Ed. Thomas H. Johnson and Theodora Ward. Cambridge: Belknap of Harvard UP, 1958.

– – –. *The Poems of Emily Dickinson: Variorum Edition.* 3 vols. Ed. Ralph W. Franklin. Cambridge: Belknap of Harvard UP, 1998.

Emerson, Ralph Waldo. *Essays and Lectures.* New York: Literary Classics of the United States, 1983.

– – –. *Selections from Ralph Waldo Emerson.* Ed. Stephen E. Whicher. Boston: Houghton Mifflin, 1957.

Erkkila, Betsy. "Emily Dickinson and Class." *American Literary History* 4.1 (Spring 1992): 1-27.

– – –. *The Wicked Sisters: Women Poets, Literary History & Discord.* New York: Oxford UP, 1992.

Jones, Kathleen B. *Compassionate Authority: Democracy and the Representation of Women.* New York: Routledge, 1993.

Laski, Harold. *A Grammar of Politics. Democratic Socialism in Britain.* Vol. 6. London: Pickering & Chatto, 1996.

Melville, Herman. *The Piazza Tales and Other Prose Pieces, 1839-1860.* Ed. Harrison Hayford, Alma A. MacDonald, and G. Thomas Tanselle. Chicago: Northwestern UP, 1987.

Mitchell, Domhnall. *Emily Dickinson: Monarch of Perception.* Amherst: U of Massachusetts P, 2000.

Matthiessen, F. O. *American Renaissance: Art and Expression in the Age of Emerson and Whitman*. New York: Oxford UP, 1985.

Olds, Sharon. "I think Emily Dickinson Would Have Been Political Today." *Titanic Operas: a Poet's Corner of Responses to Emily Dickinson*. 26 June 2001. <http://jefferson.village.virginia.edu/dickinson/titanic/olds.html>.

Rosenbaum, S. P. *A Concordance to the Poems of Emily Dickinson*. Ithaca: Cornell UP, 1964.

Rowe, John Carlos. *At Emerson's Tomb: the Politics of Classic American Literature*. New York: Columbia UP, 1997.

Ruttenburg, Nancy. *Democratic Personality: Popular Voice and the Trial of American Authorship*. Stanford: Stanford UP, 1998.

Sanborn, Geoffrey. "Keeping Her Distance: Cisneros, Dickinson, and the Politics of Private Enjoyment." *PMLA* 116.5 (Oct. 2001): 1334-48.

Sewall, Richard B. *The Life of Emily Dickinson*. New York: Farrar, Straus and Giroux, 1980.

Tocqueville, Alexis de. *Democracy in America*. Trans. George Lawrence. Ed. J. P. Mayer. New York: HarperCollins, 2000.

Walker, Cheryl. *The Nightingale's Burden: Women Poets and American Culture before 1900*. Bloomington: Indiana UP, 1982.

Whitman, Walt. *Walt Whitman: Complete Poetry and Collected Prose*. Ed. Justin Kaplin. New York: Literary Classics of the United States, 1982.

# Ambivalent Vistas: José Martí's "Our America," Nineteenth-Century Pan-Americanism and Hemispheric American Studies

## Markus Heide

In one of his many articles on U.S. society, politics and culture written in the 1880s and 1890s, the Cuban poet, journalist, and anti-colonial activist José Martí writes: "I feel obligated to this country, where the unprotected always find a friend. A kind hand is always outstretched to those looking for honest work. Here, a good idea always finds welcoming, soft, and fertile ground. One must be intelligent, that is all. Do something useful, and you will have everything you want" (Foner 31). In another article, however, we find a quite different assessment of "Gilded Age"-America: "What is apparent . . . is that the nature of the North American government is gradually changing its fundamental reality. Under the traditional labels of Republican and Democrat, with no innovation other than the contingent circumstances of place and character, the republic is becoming plutocratic and imperialistic" (Foner 45). Finally, in other articles the U.S. is represented as a greedy, all-devouring monster, nurturing on her hemispheric siblings. Exile in the U.S. here has turned into living *Inside the Monster* (as Philip Foner titled his collection of Martí's writings on the United States).

While the U.S. appears as a 'promised land' in the first quote from 1880, the U.S. has become infected by imperialist greed in the second, taken from an article written almost a decade later, after Martí had spent considerable time "inside the monster." As historian David W. Noble puts it: "When he came to the United States, Martí identified imperialism with Europe. When he left, he believed it was the United States that posed the greatest imperialist threat to the other American nations" (270). However, apart from the biographical and historical contexts: What do Martí's ambivalent attitudes towards the first independent nation in the Western hemisphere, as articulated in his writing, tell us about today's investigations of interamerican as well as transatlantic relations? What significance do Martí's accounts of different Americas and of various Americanisms (Anti-Americanism, Pan-Americanism, Pan-Spanish-Americanism, Latinamericanism) have for our present-day transnational and postcolonial re-conceptionalizing of American Studies? In the following I will try to give answers to these questions by reading Martí's famous and influential article "Nuestra América" ("Our America") in the historical context of its publication; I will then discuss the more recent 'Martí renaissance' that directs attention towards the transnational potential of this nationalist writer. I argue that the paradoxical quality of Martí's skeptical Pan-Americanism and his 'nationalist transnationalism' as articulated in "Our America" anticipate more recent critical investigations of national boundaries in postcolonial cultural studies and in the critical debates on globalization as put forward, e.g., in a seemingly oxymoronic phrase such as "cosmopolitan patriots" (Kwame Anthony Appiah); after all, it seems, that precisely the paradox of being a 'nationalist transnationalist' makes him such an interesting figure for present-day critical discourses on Americanisms, on "America," and on the concept of the nation.

### José Martí and "Our America"

In 1891 Martí published an article entitled "Nuestra América" almost simultaneously in the Mexican newspaper *El Partido Liberal* and in New York in *La Revista Ilustrada de Nueva York*.[1] The imagery of the article was to become most influential in future debates on Latin-American cultural identity and on interamerican relations. As the title makes explicit, "Our America" intervenes in discursive constructions of "America" and it articulates different positions in the cultural, social and political setup of the two American continents. The possessive pronoun claims specificity and marks difference by 'imagining communities.' "Our" draws a dividing line between different "Americas." The nation, an important social entity and a category with a liberating impetus in nineteenth-century popular and intellectual discourses, is alluded to here. However, although Martí's article employs the rhetoric of nationalism, it is at the same time transcending the concept of the nation. The article in many respects tries to go beyond "simplistic nineteenth-century nationalism" as the editors of a recent publication on hemispheric American Studies, Jeffrey Belnap and Raúl Fernández, put it from a critical standpoint struggling with late twentieth-century globalization (23). From such a perspective, attentive to deconstructions of national boundaries and investigating the liberating aspects of 'going beyond' national categories, Martí's article can in many respects be considered as border-crossing and transnational. With its apparently definite, yet ambivalent categories and rhetoric of "us" vs. "them" the article not only exemplifies popular Latin-American sentiments. It also establishes a discursive code for future intellectual investigations of the relations between the United States and Latin America – as the nations south of the Rio Grande were referred to since the mid-nineteenth century, just a few decades before the publication of "Our America" (Bushnell and Macaulay 3).

In romantic language Martí distinguishes between "our America" and the other America, "the America of Washington and Lincoln" as he calls it in "Madre América" ("Mother America"), another of his many interamerican articles. Interestingly, however, Martí does not merely place Latin America in a culturally divided hemisphere. Rather, he discusses the colonial and neocolonial triangular relation between Latin America, the USA and Europe. Thus, there are different lines of argument in his interamerican and transatlantic critical endeavor. The layers of political, historical and cultural analysis give this brief essay such a weight in many other examinations of interamerican relations, before and after Martí. In a most basic reading, "Our America" reminds us that at least in the English language the geographical term "America" has been successfully appropriated by the continent's most powerful nation as referring to its particular history, its values and its way of life; further refractions of this simple fact open the critical eye to conflicts, contradictions, ambivalences as well as particularities of interamerican history that cannot be reduced to antagonisms between "the monster" and the Southern dwarfs but are – as Enrico Mario Santí stresses – just as much shedding light on tensions within Latin America, within Latinamericanism as well as within singular societies south of the Rio Grande.

Much of the complex argumentation and symbolic density of "Our America" can partly be attributed to the biography of the political activist, particularly his life in exile in the Americas and in Europe. Martí's biography stands paradigmatically for the Western hemisphere's struggles with the legacies of colonialism. Colonialism and anti-colonialism, the bloody fights for national independence and the threat of neocolonial subjugation culminate in Martí's experiences as an activist, intellectual and exile. His personal history is deeply intertwined with Cuba's long fight for independence. Here it is important to note that the island gained independence from Spain much later than the other Spanish colonies in the Americas, who revolted and achieved independence between the years 1810 and 1825. Only Cuba and Puerto Rico remained under Spanish rule until the Spanish-American War of 1898. Thus Martí, unlike most of his Latin-American contemporaries, was born as a colonial subject in Cuba in 1853. His parents had immigrated from Spain. During his early education he came in contact with *criollo* intellectuals, committed to Cuba's independence and anti-slavery positions. During the Ten-Years-War (1868-1878), one of Cuba's unsuccessful wars of independence, Martí was convicted "at age sixteen for writing a letter expressing nationalist sentiment" (Belnap and Fernández 2). He spent six months of a six-year sentence in a Cuban prison and was then exiled to Spain as an alternative to imprisonment. He thereafter returned to his native land only for brief periods. Between 1881 and 1895 Martí lived almost entirely in exile in New York City. As a journalist he traveled widely in the United States and in Latin America. He participated in the first Pan-American conference, which took place in Washington for eight months in 1889 and 1890 – after this event he wrote "Our America."[2] In 1895 he returned to Cuba to take part in the militant resistance against Spanish colonial rule. Just two months after his arrival, at age 42, Martí died in a fight with Spanish troops. Although he had achieved some fame during his lifetime, he became one of the most celebrated heroes of the struggle for independence only after his death, and has been regarded as one of the major figures in Cuban intellectual and political history ever since. Particularly in socialist Cuba, after 1959, quite extraordinary attention has been given to studying his life and work. Martí is also regarded as one of Latin America's first modernist poets (Belnap and Fernández 1-3).[3]

Martí's biography and his journalistic and poetic work, I want to emphasize, illustrate Latin-American anti-colonialism and cultural decolonization. These, particularly in the late 19th century, are not only counteracting European colonialism but are just as much negotiating interamerican relations and power asymmetries. Although intellectually and politically active in the struggle against Spanish colonialism, as a Latin American Martí is at the same time observing the international interests of the economically superior northern neighbor; in his essays he anticipates the future role of U.S. imperialism in the hemisphere. During his exile in the United States he wrote for various Latin-American newspapers and magazines. As Philip S. Foner and others have emphasized, Martí's articles were read all over Latin America and "made the United States known as it was never known before" (Sturgis E. Leavitt, qtd. in Foner 30). Apart from literary topics, themes such as race relations, U.S. democracy and modernity, and particularly U.S. imperial endeavors, as well as Pan-Americanism were among his main interests.

Martí's work comments on and – at least implicitly – discusses four notions of Americanism: Latinamericanism, Pan-Americanism, Hispano-Americanism and Anti-Americanism. The first three notions of Americanism imagine (and try to establish) transnational unity in the Western hemisphere; here the history of European 'discovery,' the destruction of indigenous cultures and empires and the subsequent European colonialism figure prominently. Anti-Americanism in Martí's work is to be understood as Anti-Anglo-Americanism; such anti-American sentiments have their origins in the cultural, and specifically religious, differences between the former British colonies and the Spanish and Portuguese colonies, but are, even in Martí's time, also resulting from Latin-American experiences with U.S. foreign policies in the 19th century that established the United States' dominant hemispheric position, e.g. the history of U.S. interventions and the Monroe Doctrine (1823). Martí's work thematizes and is itself a document of what has been called Latin America's "love-hate" for the USA. While Martí and many fellow intellectuals criticize the United States for being materialistic and greedy, they at same time express admiration for its progress, democracy and modernity. In fact, Martí at various points addresses the USA as *the* anti-colonial and egalitarian nation. This ambivalence towards and love-hate for the USA has been further developed by Martí's Uruguayan contemporary José Enrique Rodó and his opposition of idealism vs. utilitarianism as categories for conceptualizing the relation between North and South in his famous essay "Ariel," first published in 1900.[4] Although "Our America" in many ways corresponds with other Latin-American assessments of interamerican relations, its ambivalences as well as its implicit references to the different notions of Americanism are displaying Martí's enthusiasm as well as his frustrations with the Pan-Americanism of his time.

## Nineteenth-Century Pan-Americanism

The first efforts to establish a forum for hemispheric exchange have been attributed to the Latin-American liberator Simón Bolívar. His ideas and his initiative briefly after the predominant part of the Spanish colonies had achieved their national independence, resulted in the first hemispheric conference, held in Panama in 1826. Although Bolívar "has been credited with the basic conception of New World separateness" that distinguishes American history and culture from Europe, and has been called the "father of Pan-Americanism" (Fagg 12), his original notion of hemispheric unity has been subject to debates among historians. Some have argued that Bolívar was mainly interested in Pan-Spanish-Americanism. Such historians, according to John Edwin Fagg's history of Pan-Americanism, maintain that Bolívar "desired only a confederacy of Spanish-American states that, with British support, would resist encroachment of the United States and Brazil" (12). Alonso Aguilar, e.g., stresses that Bolívar's "sense of continentalism . . . was one of Spanish-American continentalism" (29).[5] However, the United States and Brazil – the counterpoints in such Pan-Spanish-Americanism – were invited to the 1826 conference, initiated by Bolívar. Brazil, then still a monarchy, declined; the U.S. accepted the invitation mainly due to Secretary of State Henry Clay's support of hemispheric unity. Despite this publicly shown interest, the United States did not actually participate since one of the two delegates arrived too late, while the other, even worse, died on the way. In general, this first hemispheric conference was not regarded a success, neither in the United States nor in Latin America, neither by Clay nor by Bolívar (Aguilar 29). Conflicting regional and national interests proved to be stronger than the ambitious efforts of individuals in bringing about hemispheric unification.[6]

The inception of a transnational movement that used the term "Pan-American" and that made the term popular came about a few decades later, this time through the initiative of the United States. James G. Blaine's efforts to diminish the British influence in the American continents finally led to the First Pan-American Conference, held in Washington in 1889 and 1890. Blaine, Secretary of State in the Garfield administration, was, as Fagg notes, "an Anglophobe who deplored British expansion in the New World and who preached that rich markets there [in Latin America] awaited American exporters" (21). Already in 1881 Blaine had proposed a Pan-American conference because he felt that "things had ripened and the moment was nearing when the United States could displace Europe in trade with America" (qtd. in Aguilar 37). Except for the Dominican Republic all republics of the Americas, now including Brazil, participated. Early on it became clear that the United States claimed a powerful position, if not the leading role, in the transnational setup. Pan-Americanism, as understood at the Washington conference, aimed at unifying all American republics for enabling political and economic cooperation. It seems most significant, not just for the first Pan-American conference but also for all the following ones, that, as Fagg remarks, "the Latin Americans included prominent cultural figures in their delegations and the United States famous businessmen, such as Andrew Carnegie" (23).

Thus, the new Pan-Americanism and the obvious economic interest of the United States in the Western hemisphere have been interpreted as part of a more imperialist U.S. foreign policy in the decades after the end of the Civil War. The territorial expansion of the United States reached a halt towards the end of the 19th century while the economic upswing after the Civil War continued at accelerating speed. Thus the extension and securing of markets for U.S. goods are seen as one motive for the new expansionist and imperialist turn in U.S. politics.[7] After the Civil War the United States gradually acquired a respected position among the other colonialist powers in the world. Particularly in the Caribbean it started to claim supremacy. This most important subtext of the Pan-American movement has often been brought up as a reproach against Pan-Americanism and has led to disapproving views, as articulated, e.g., by an Argentine delegate at a later conference who remarked that "Pan-Americanism did not exist outside of Washington" (Fagg 32). In a similar manner, even more outspokenly, Aguilar concludes:

> Although it was not always easily discernible, two opposing concepts of the security, freedom, and peace of the continent frequently came into conflict: the Pan-Americanism of Jefferson, Monroe and Clay, forerunner of the system of Latin-American subordination established toward the end of the century; and the Latin-Americanism of Bolívar, San Martín, and Morelos which stood for the struggle of their people for full independence. (30)

Martí's articles on the Washington conference, and particularly his "Our America," have been read as a leading voice in the Latin-American criticism of Pan-Americanism. This criticism interprets Pan-Americanism as a cynical device by the U.S. for disguising American 'dollar diplomacy' and imperialism. In Fagg's history of Pan-Americanism Martí is represented as an influential figure in Anti-Americanism during and after the Washington conference of 1889/1890: "The Cuban refugee, José Martí, whose influence on Latin Americans was to wax greatly in the coming years, bitterly criticized the United States, which he saw as predatory and threatening" (25); and Fagg goes on, referring to the Spanish-American War: "Latin Americans were now inclined to fear United States imperialism. Martí was dead but his ideas fed anti-Americanism" (26). Fagg is certainly right when he postulates that Martí's and others' assessments of Pan-Americanism resulted in the cultivation of Pan-Hispanic and Latin-American solidarity as opposition to Pan-Americanism among intellectuals (31). However, Fagg's representation of Martí tends to overlook the nuances of Martí's criticism of Pan-Americanism, as they are characteristic of many of his articles, particularly "Our America." While some scholars stress that Martí tends to eulogize Latin-American and particularly Hispanic-American unity, others emphasize his skepticism and critique of Latin-americanism; others again concentrate on the implications of hemispheric perspectives in his writings. Susana Rotker, e.g., writes about

Martí's Latinamericanism: "the United States . . . is postulated as the empire of the practical, of cold calculation, of prosperity and corruption, opposing *Us*, or the territory of the imagination and the new" (19). However, at the same time Rotker makes clear that Martí "also attempts to reformulate the traditional "us" and "them" (18). Against her argument that Martí "generally ignores the marked differences between nations and the specificities of Latin American politics" (19) Enrico Mario Santí holds that Martí remains skeptical of too romantic notions of Latinamericanism. According to Santí, this is partly due to the history of Cuba: the island's anti-colonial resistance did not receive much support from the other Latin-American nations after they had already gained independence. These more differentiated approaches to interamerican relations have been of special interest to the recent 'Martí renaissance' that I mentioned at the beginning and that I will now focus on in the last part of this essay.

**Hemispheric American Studies**

As his writings document, Martí thoroughly studied not only the United States of his time, but also the history of the American nation-building processes. "Mother America," published two years before "Our America," also referring to Pan-Americanism and the Pan-American conference in Washington, stresses the difference between the colonial experiences of the U.S.A. and of Latin-America. In "Nuestra América," written after the Pan-American conference, Martí articulates an ambivalent perspective on what has become known as 'the promise of America.' Praising "the America of Washington and Lincoln" that gained independence earlier than most parts of the Americas, as "sacred" and "holy for humanity" (881), Martí at the same time fears that the power asymmetries between the U.S.A. and Latin America and the United States' firm determination to expand, may some day – and he fears that this might be in the near future – result in a political and cultural domination that might eventually reproduce European colonial structures and hence contradict America's democratic promise. Thus, he partly anticipates future interamerican developments and expresses the controversial status of the U.S.A. in Latin-American cultural and political theory – it is important to note that he was writing between the Mexican-American and the Spanish-American Wars, two 'contacts' between Latin America and the USA in which expansionism, imperialism and hemispheric domination came in conflict, contradicting the United States' republican and democratic ideals and traditional anti-colonialism. As Martí anticipated, the USA fought for the independence of Cuba in the Spanish-American War, but then 'colonized' the island; Martí had hoped that Cuba would achieve independence before the U.S. entered the war.

In addition to such fears of political and economic domination, "Nuestra América" directs attention to cultural and historical differences within conceptions of "America" as "ours" or "theirs." This perspective also emphasizes mutualities, or in today's terminology, interamerican transculturation and hybridity, while being aware of power asymmetries. Martí's decolonizing stance is certainly directed against the dominance of Spanish and European intellectual traditions in Latin America. While the focus on cultural matters is partly directed against "Yankee" domination, criticism of Eurocentric cultural views and the Eurocentric intellectual orientation of the elites come center stage. Referring to the intellectual culture of Latin America, Martí writes:

> How can the universities produce a governing subject, if there is not a single university in America that teaches the rudimentary basics of the art of government, to wit, the analysis of the elements peculiar to the peoples of America? Like guesswork, out in the world wearing Yankee or French spectacles, young men aspire to govern a nation they do not know. . . . To know one's country, and to govern it based on that knowledge, is the only way to free it from tyrannies. The European university must yield to the American university. The history of America, from the Incas to the present, must be taught inside out, even if the archons of Greece are not taught at all. Our Greece is preferable over the Greece that is not our own. We need it more. Nationalist politicians must replace exotic politicians. Let the world be grafted onto our republics, but the trunk must be our own. (882)

Reading Martí in today's postcolonial terms, critical of Eurocentrism and of the universalism of the European enlightenment, his statements, anchoring Latin-American nationalisms in the pre-Columbian past, emphasize cultural specificities of the countries south of the Rio Grande and particularly stress elements that do not necessarily fit into European historical parameters of teleology, universalism and progress. Such elements as, for example, *mestizaje*, creolization and religious syncretisms distinguish Latin America from Anglo-America. However, and this is characteristic of his ambivalence, the pre-Columbian history and the colonial experience, even if highly diverse, historically and culturally connect the hemisphere – and Martí wishes that these common traits would also unite the hemisphere in anti-colonialism and in the support of national self-determination. In romantic terms Martí emphasizes the importance of the pre-Columbian cultural heritage for the political emancipation as well as the aesthetic representation of the Latin-American republics and of the Americas in general: "Our Greece is to be preferred to the Greece that is not our own."[8]

Despite the distinctions between Latin America and the Anglo-Saxon United States of America, and despite his warning of U.S. dominance, Martí's writings enhance hemispheric perspectives: the connectedness of the particular histories, the community of the Americas, the overlapping of cultural identity formations. From such perspectives, Martí has lately been perceived as an "anti-Columbus" and as promoter of multicultural historiography and transnational cultural studies (Pease 54). Even more recently, his work has been used as a framework for articulating and interrogating identity formations that cross ethnic as well as national dividing lines, as, e.g., in the critical work of José David Saldívar. This approach, mostly put forward by U.S. scholars, reads Martí through the blurring of clear-cut national and cultural distinctions in the more recent Native American, Mexican-American, African American, Asian-American historical and cultural studies and their challenge of the unitary American "We." Analogously, the recent 'Martí renaissance' in 'hemispheric cultural studies' questions Eurocentric and Anglocentric notions of "America" and reads Martí as imagining postnational narratives (Pease) that redirect the narratives of the promise of America into investigating the reality of a "yet unfulfilled promise of transnational American democracy" (Belnap and Fernández 8).

In the attempts within American Studies to overcome notions of U.S. exceptionalism and to critique the traditional blindness of intellectuals towards global interconnectedness in the history of the first

American democracy, Martí's work has been re-read and has been used for redirecting American cultural studies. From a historian's perspective David W. Noble, e.g., self-critically reinvestigates such notions as "sacred nation" (266) and "innocent America" (268) through Martí's writing: "Many of us now know we need to listen to the voices who were once denied a hearing by the institutional authority of the Anglo-Protestant monopolization of 'American civilization'" (270). In general, one can say that Martí's essayistic, journalistic and poetic comments on Americanisms are particularly interesting for transnational American Studies because they are dealing with essential questions of interamerican historical, cultural and literary studies, such as: What makes the core of interamerican differences: religion, the colonial past, geography, or race relations? Comparing the USA with Latin-American colonial and post-colonial countries, Martí's work engages in examining why the American nations culturally, politically and socially developed in such different ways. Martí also asks what *the Americas* do have in common – a question that has more recently been discussed in such books as Gustavo Pérez Firmat's *Do the Americas Have a Common Literature?*. As has been argued by scholars in U.S.-Latino Studies in recent years, Martí's work is interested in, outlines and imagines cultural intersections and transculturations *avant la lettre*.[9] Saldívar refers to José Martí's essay as a "cultural deconstruction . . . of the name *America*" (*Dialectics* 43). New Americanists such as Amy Kaplan and Donald Pease, in their essay collection *The Cultures of U.S. Imperialism*, Pease in his work on "postnational narratives," and, more recently, John Carlos Rowe, in his *Post-Nationalist American Studies*, reinvestigate U.S. imperialism and *write against* the exclusion of the U.S. and of interamerican relations from the history of 19th-century colonialism. In this approach the cultures of U.S. imperialism are *writing back* to the center.[10] As Belnap and Fernandez outline in the introduction to their essay collection, Martí's "Our America" serves as the framework of a critical transnational approach to the Americas. Referring to Martí's "transnational imagery" and "antiracist nationalism" (18), they name this critical framework "Our Americanism" and emphasize the pertinence of such a critical transnationalism in contemporary debates on globalization.

The New Americanists re-imagine – in their own terms – the hemisphere's cultures as dynamic systems. However, they emphasize that transnationalism, border-crossing and cultural mobility, even hybridity, very much correspond with the discourses and desires of capitalism and of globalization. James Clifford, discussing the tropes of mobility and nomadism, has drawn attention to this point. Keeping the history of Pan-Americanism and the Latin-American criticism of this transnational endeavor in mind, George Lipsitz, e.g., discusses the changed international circumstances since Martí's time, which require new approaches to nationalism, internationalism and transnationalism. Another recent essay collection, *Performing Hybridity*, edited by May Joseph, that deals with "pan-identities," in this case West Indian, Anglophone, and Afro-Asian, reads such identity formations as "generat[ing] a political 'third space'" (4). In the introduction Joseph writes about "cultural hybridity":

> The internationalism embedded in contemporary discourses of hybridity and its mobilizing political energy open up new ways of perceiving cultural and political practices. Through historical excavation, cultural reclamation, and aesthetic appropriations across different national contexts, new forms of internationalism are articulated. (1)

In this sense, I would argue, Martí, although he did not use the term "hybridity," and although he is not much interested in cultural contact or cultural mixture, articulated "new forms of internationalism."

Connecting Martí's work with such more contemporary reorientations in American Studies and with a critical view on neoliberal globalization and "internationalism" Belnap and Fernandez write:

> Unlike a simplistic nineteenth-century nationalist, Martí strategically wielded the naturalist nationalism of his day in order to negotiate the complexities of the hemisphere's geopolitical dynamics. From twin vocations as a national activist and as transnational journalist, he learned to read national events in relation to transnational forces; he also saw Our America's nation-states as strategic actors – agents whose resources needed to be unified in a multinational consortium in order to protect their populations from the economic and political bullying of the United States. As American Studies, newly demystified, retreats from organic nationalism, it is important that the

demystification of the nation-states does not become confused with a belief that states have somehow become insignificant international actors, because the same gigantic bully still strives to push around the same countries' grandchildren and great-grandchildren. . . . those who work within the New American cultural studies, supported within the same "monster's entrails," ought to interrogate the significance of this continuity. (23)

Martí's ambivalences and contradictions, his Our-Americanism, his Pan-Americanism and his wish for hemispheric unity, his Cuban nationalism and his transnationalism, his anti-racism and his anti-imperialism, do offer a framework for re-directing the scholarly perspective on the history and cultures of the Americas.

**Notes**

[1] For further details on the publication see Belnap and Fernández 23.
[2] For details concerning Martí's positioning in the debates of the conference see Santí.
[3] Marinello emphasizes the correspondences between Martí's poetic work and political activism (9-11) and gives a detailed biographical analysis of his poetics (9-79).
[4] See also Fagg 26.
[5] For a more detailed analysis of Bolívar's position see Aguilar 23-30.
[6] Lockey gives an extensive account of the Panama conference (312-54). See also Fagg 8-20, and Aguilar 23-30.
[7] From a Mexican perspective on the Mexican-American War, Aguilar equates U.S. territorial expansionism and later U.S. imperialism (see 31-35 and 40-41).
[8] Saldívar takes up this point in his analysis of interamerican relations and transnational cultural formations (*Border Matters* 182-83).
[9] Martí, for example, translated the popular novel *Ramona* by Helen Hunt Jackson (1884) into Spanish. The novel deals with the Spanish and Mexican history of California and the Anglo-Americanization after the Mexican-American War. Marinello emphasizes that the translation received quite some attention in Latin American literary circles of the time. Referring to Martí's interest in Jackson's novel, Marinello interprets the poem "Los dos príncipes" as an example of transculturation between Anglo-American and Latin American literature (46).

[10] Concerning the 'writing back paradigm' see Bill Ashcroft, Gareth Griffiths and Helen Tiffin's *The Empire Writes Back*, by now a 'classic' in post-colonial studies. While there are certainly intellectual exchanges and parallels between transnational American Studies and post-colonial studies, Latin America has for a long time only played a minor role in postcolonial studies, while emphasis is put on the former British colonies in Asia, Africa and Oceania.

## Works Cited

Aguilar, Alonso. *Pan-Americanism from Monroe to the Present*. 1965. New York and London: MR Press, 1968.

Appiah, Kwame Anthony. "Cosmopolitan Patriots," *Critical Inquiry* 23 (1997): 114-26.

Ashcroft, Bill, Garreth Griffiths, and Helen Tiffin. *The Empire Writes Back: Theory and Practice in Post-Colonial Literatures*. London and New York: Routledge, 1989.

Belnap, Jeffrey, and Raúl Fernández, eds. *José Martí's "Our America": From National to Hemispheric Cultural Studies*. Durham and London: Duke UP, 1998.

Bushnell, David, and Neill Macaulay. *The Emergence of Latin America in the Nineteenth Century*. New York and Oxford: Oxford UP, 1988.

Clifford, James. *Routes: Travel and Translation in the Late Twentieth Century*. Cambridge, MA: Harvard UP, 1997.

Fagg, John Edwin. *Pan-Americanism. Its Meaning and History*. Malabar, FL: Robert E. Krieger Publ., 1982.

Foner, Philip S. "Introduction." *Inside the Monster: Writings on the United States and American Imperialism*. Ed. Philip S. Foner. New York and London: Monthly Review P, 1975. 15-48.

Joseph, May, et al., eds. *Performing Hybridity*. Minneapolis: U of Minnesota P, 1999.

Kaplan, Amy, and Donald E. Pease, eds. *Cultures of United States Imperialism*. Durham and London: Duke UP, 1993.

Lipsitz, George. "Their America and Ours: Intercultural Communication in the Context of 'Our America'." *José Martí's "Our America": From National to Hemispheric Cultural Studies*. Ed. Jeffrey Belnap and Raúl Fernández. Durham and London: Duke UP, 1998. 293-316.

Lockey, Joseph Byrne. *Pan-Americanism: Its Beginnings*. New York: Macmillan, 1920.

Marinello, Juan. *José Martí*. Madrid: Ediciones Júcar, 1972.

Martí, José. *Inside the Monster: Writings on the United States and American Imperialism*. Ed. Philip S. Foner. New York and London: Monthly Review P, 1975.

– – –. "Madre América." *Política de Nuestra América*. México D. F.: Siglo Veintiuno Editores, 1977. 44-52.

– – –. "Nuestra América." *Política de Nuestra América*. México D. F.: Siglo Veintiuno Editores, 1977. 37-44.

– – –. "Our America." *The Heath Anthology of American Literature*. 3rd ed. Ed. Paul Lauter. Boston and New York: Houghton Mifflin, 1998. 746-53.

– – –. *Política de Nuestra América* (prólogo de Roberto Fernández Retamar). México D. F.: Siglo Veintiuno Editores, 1977.

Noble, David W.. "The Anglo-Protestant Monopolization of 'America'." *José Martí's "Our America": From National to Hemispheric Cultural Studies*. Ed. Jeffrey Belnap and Raúl Fernández. Durham and London: Duke UP, 1998. 253-74.

Pease, Donald. "José Martí, Alexis de Tocqueville, and the Politics of Displacement." *José Martí's "Our America": From National to Hemispheric Cultural Studies*. Ed. Jeffrey Belnap and Raúl Fernández. Durham and London: Duke UP, 1998. 27-57.

Pérez Firmat, Gustavo, ed. *Do the Americas Have a Common Literature?*. Durham and London: Duke UP, 1990.

Rodó, José Enrique. "Ariel." Trans. Maria Bamberg. *Der lange Kampf Lateinamerikas*. Ed. Angel Rama. Frankfurt: Suhrkamp, 1982. 97-123.

Rotker, Susana. "José Martí and the United States: On the Margins of the Gaze." *Re-Reading José Martí (1853-1895)*. Ed. Julio Rodríguez-Luis. Albany: SUNY P, 1999. 17-34.

Rowe, John Carlos. *Post-Nationalist American Studies*. Berkeley: U of California P, 2000.

Saldívar, José David. *The Dialectics of Our America – Genealogy, Cultural Critique, and Literary History*. Durham and London: Duke UP, 1991.

– – –. *Border Matters: Remapping American Cultural Studies*. Berkeley: U of California P, 1997.

Santí, Enrico Mario. "'Our America,' the Gilded Age, and the Crisis of Latinamericanism." *José Martí's "Our America": From National to Hemispheric Cultural Studies*. Ed. Jeffrey Belnap and Raúl Fernández. Durham and London: Duke UP, 1998. 179-90.

# 'The Biologic Aspects of Immigration,' 'Racial Crime,' and the Looming Threat of Cacocracy: Eugenics, Immigration Restriction, and the Reconstruction of Americanism in the 1920s

## Louis Kern

In 1992, self-proclaimed liberal and academically-trained demographer Leon F. Bouvier, under the aegis of the Center for Immigration Studies, published *Peaceful Invasions: Immigration and Changing America,* a plea for capping immigration at 450,000 (a reduction of in-migration of about 45%). Although Bouvier maintains that "ethnic, racial, or religious background should not determine who is granted entry into the United States" (199), he concludes that

> there is growing realization that all is not well. . . . that the composition of the population is changing rapidly. . . . Should current immigration levels be maintained the future of the United States, as a twenty-first century national community, is dim. In place of a national community, the nation could consist of several ethnic communities, speaking different languages and adhering to different cultures. (204)

In the wake of the terrorist attacks of 9/11, these issues have been approached with a virulent resurgence of xenophobia and paranoiac preoccupation with the loyalty and social legitimacy of the alien within. The crisis of the "War on Terror" has raised the specter of inimical, alien forces that can utilize liberal immigration policies to infiltrate, undermine, and subvert basic American institutions, and whose ultimate goal is the destruction of the American way of life.

The current anti-immigration movement rests on the foundation of the restrictionist movement in the early twentieth century that led to the establishment of the national origins quota system, and while today open appeals to racist rationales for immigration restriction in mainline discourse are deemed socially unacceptable, the close association in today's restrictionist movement between ideologically-grounded anti-immigration groups tainted with bigotry and academic social scientists offers a chilling parallel to the coordinated efforts of racialist theorists and the pseudo-scientific eugenics movement of the early twentieth century.

Historically, popular anxiety about the rising tide of immigration and its effects on American society and culture was rooted in revived nativist sentiment. The anti-Catholic American Protective Association, organized in 1887 by H. F. Bower, became increasingly active after 1890, and by 1895, the largest of many nativist organizations, claimed a membership of two million. More directly involved in lobbying Congress and direct political action for stemming the tide of immigration was the Immigration Restriction League, established in Boston in 1894, that embodied the racist perspectives of its Brahmin membership, and that came to have especially close ties to both the central leadership of the eugenics movement and to the primary popularizers of racialist ideas.

But it was two organizational events that empowered the coalition of eugenics and Nordic racialists to become national spokesmen for a broad restrictionist movement and effectuated their impact on immigration legislation. The first, embedded in the Immigration Act of 1882, was the establishment of a national system of immigration control, the effective federalization of immigration under the aegis of the Secretary of the Treasury. Centralization allowed for maximum impact through concentration of effort rather than a laborious, piecemeal, state-by-state struggle that had characterized earlier anti-immigration activism. Within the eugenics movement itself, the foundation of the Carnegie Institution in 1902 (with a genetics division) and the American Breeders Association in 1903 marked the effective beginning of an organized biological and anthropological concern for human hereditary traits and their transmission and perpetuation via germ plasm that would form the Social Darwinian and racial foundation of the immigration restriction movement. In 1913, the ABA changed its name to the American Genetic Association, observing that "the steady growth of eugenics, and the full recognition granted to this new and important science by the association, have . . . made a change of name desirable" ("Breeders Association" 177). Recognizing further that since the rediscovery and popularization of Gregor Mendel's pioneering genetic studies cattle breeding was no longer central to its mission, the association changed the name of its official organ in the same year from *American Breeders Magazine* to the *Journal of Heredity*.

Charles Benedict Davenport (1866-1944), the leading scientific eugenicist of his time, became the director of the ABA's Eugenics Section in 1903, and in 1906 established the Association's Committee on Eugenics, with a charge to "investigate and report on heredity in the human race and emphasize the value of superior blood and the menace to society of inferior blood" (Selden 4). Tracing that menacing blood had also been the impulse behind Davenport's founding of the Station for the Experimental Study of Evolution in Cold Spring Harbor, NY in 1903 as it would be as well for the establishment of the research and propaganda agency of the eugenicist movement, the Eugenics Record Office in 1910. In 1911, as secretary of the ABA's Committee on Eugenics, Davenport appointed two founding members of the Immigration Restriction League to head up a sub-committee on immigration. So closely entwined did the eugenics movement and the immigration restriction movements become that IRL tracts were published under the scientific imprimatur of the *Journal of Heredity,* and a leading IRL member was prompted to propose renaming the anti-immigration group the Eugenics Immigration League (see Haller 64).

The early impact of the eugenics movement on immigration law can be seen in the legislation for 1903. Prior to that date, Congress had acted twice to restrict immigration, excluding criminals and prostitutes in 1875 and suspending all Chinese immigration for an initial period of ten years to protect native-born workers in the Chinese Exclusion Act of 1882. The 1903 act excluded "idiots," the insane, epileptics, those likely to become a public charge, professional beggars, persons afflicted with a loathsome or highly contagious disease, persons convicted of crimes involving moral turpitude, polygamists, anarchists and those advocating the violent overthrow of the government, prostitutes, procurers, and pimps, contract laborers, and any person whose passage had been paid by another. The exclusionary categories of this act reflected the central concerns of the family studies, often referred to as the "white trash studies," compiled by the field workers of the Eugenics Record Office under the supervision of Dr. Harry H. Laughlin.

Consider, for example, the report on his investigations of hereditary feeble-mindedness of Dr. Henry H. Goddard, director of the psychological laboratory for the Training School for Backward and Feeble-Minded Children in Vineland, NJ. On the "pedigree charts" illustrating his conclusions, the following traits are listed in close association with mental defectiveness: alcoholism, blindness, deafness, criminality, dwarfism, epilepsy, insanity, migrainosity, "grave sexual offender," syphilitic, tuberculous, illegitimacy, and wanderer, tramp, or truant (Goddard 166). Goddard's representative study neatly encoded the central concerns of eugenicists as they contemplated the biological fruits of congenital degeneracy in the years immediately following the establishment of the Eugenics Section of the ABA in 1903. In effect, the 1903 immigration act, then, designed to combat anarchism and domestic radicalism, also represented the first practical eugenical immigration act.

Concern for the elimination of the genetically deficient population came to dominate eugenical thought in the second decade of the twentieth century, and popular medical and juridical thought accepted the association of certain debilitating and sexually transmitted diseases, insanity, and a wide range of anti-social behavior with feeble-mindedness. Measures for preventing the transmission of hereditary feeble-mindedness, initially based on segregation of the afflicted population in institutions, became more radical in this period as well with the passage of state sterilization laws. The first such law was passed by Indiana in 1907; by 1917 fifteen other states had passed sterilization laws, and by 1931 twenty-seven states had such statutes on the books. Harry H. Laughlin, under the authority of the American Breeders Association's Committee to Study and Report on the Best Practical Means of Cutting Off the Defective Germ Plasm in the American Population, drafted a model sterilization law that would meet all relevant social, scientific, and legal criteria.

At the same time, management of the domestic defective population was conflated with renewed nativist and racialist concerns and immigration restriction came to rest on the association of the threat of the foreign-born with a dysgenic intrusion of a mentally deficient ("feeble-minded") and socially defective population from without.

Control of the racial and the defective threat through negative eugenics brought eugenicists and racialist ideologues together in a common cause. As early as 1911, the American Breeders Association envisioned the reconstruction of American racial stock through a program of restrictive selective breeding:

> Eugenics will ere long drive home to the human race the fact that its worst blood should be reproduced but slowly, if at all, and that it is a sacred duty of the best blood to multiply itself and people the earth. . . . Society and even the church can then place a social pressure upon, and deter from reproduction, those likely to produce weak, diseased, or criminal offspring, and the state can even restrict child bearing on the part of those most deficient. Thus the major part of the weak fibers can be eliminated from the network of human descent. . . . [Unfortunately, as a result of misguided sentimentalism] society is now rather assisting families of weaker heredity to multiply, through various forms of otherwise most beneficent charities. How to lessen the effects of thus breeding the race downward, and how to favor the production of progeny whose blood improves the network of descent of the race, are still difficult problems. ("The Field of Eugenics" 139-40)

Although the 1903 immigration law, supplemented in 1907 by a provision that excluded all persons found to be so mentally or physically defective as to materially affect their capacity to support themselves, seemed to meet eugenic criteria for reversing the degeneration of the American germ plasm, increasingly nativist critics pointed to the failure of enforcement—through corruption, political lobbying by ethnically-based immigrant assistance groups, carelessness, and insufficient funding—as a rationale for focusing eugenic attention on immigration restriction so as to check the laws' tendency "to produce an inferior rather than a superior American race; those who are eugenically unfit for race culture" (Ward, "Immigration Laws" 20). Certainly, they had a mass of evidence to sustain their Darwinist view of the menace of immigration, since Sen. William P. Dillingham's (R-VT) Immigration Commission had published its forty-two volume, statistically-laden study sustaining the racial inferiority of the new immigration in 1910.

As Robert De Courcey Ward of the Immigration Restriction League posed the resulting challenge to eugenicists:

The need is imperative for applying eugenic principles in much of our legislation. But the greatest, the most logical, the most effective step that we can take is to begin with a proper eugenic selection of the incoming alien millions. If we, in our generation, take these steps, we shall earn the gratitude of millions of those who will come after us, for we shall have begun the real conservation of the race. ("Immigration Laws" 26)

The first step towards racial conservation was taken on 30 December 1911 in Washington, DC at a meeting of the Eugenics Section of the ABA with the establishment of a permanent Committee on Immigration, empowered with "authority to cooperate with similar committees of other organizations in securing laws which will be more effective in securing immigrants which bring good health and normal and superior heredity to this country" ("First Report" 249). The second report of the Committee on Immigration of the Eugenics Section (of the now Genetic Association) noted that those concerned about the improvement of American racial stock "are turning more and more to the regulation of immigration as one of the most obvious means of accomplishing their purpose" ("Second Report" 298). In support of its position, the Committee cited Harry H. Laughlin's "Report on the Best Practical Means of Cutting Off the Defective Germ-Plasm in the American Population" (Eugenics Record Office, Bulletin No. 10B, 1914).

The scope of the Committee's cooperation with powerful mainline medical, scientific, health, and charitable organizations was clear in its support of resolutions, passed at a conference on the exclusion and deportation of insane and mentally defective aliens, sent to the President and Congress in November of 1912 by a coalition of the American Medico-Psychological Association, the National Committee for Mental Hygiene, the New York Psychiatric Society, the New York State Charities Association, the Committee of 100 on National Health, and the New York State Hospital Commission. During deliberations on the Dillingham-Burnett immigration bill (passed by Congress but vetoed by President Taft in 1913) that embodied several of the recommendations of the resolutions (most particularly a literacy test), two members of the Committee, its secretary, Robert De Courcey Ward and its chairman, Prescott F. Hall, both charter members and central figures in the

Immigration Restriction League, testified during the Congressional hearings.

United States entry into the war only intensified these fears, and by early 1919 the Committee was enthusiastically supporting House Resolution 15302, which proposed the suspension of immigration for four years following the conclusion of peace as a measure that would have "highly desirable eugenic results" ("Some Present Aspects of Immigration" 70). The U.S. Army Intelligence Tests (Alpha and Beta), administered to 1.75 million recruits in 1917 by Maj. Robert M. Yerkes, former student of Charles B. Davenport, president of the American Psychological Association and chair of the Eugenics Record Office's Committee on Inheritance of Mental Traits, seemed to provide definitive empirical evidence of the presumptive racial inferiority of non-whites and Southern Europeans.

Absolute cessation of immigration was not a realistic goal, but given successive failures to initiate a universal literacy test, Sidney L. Gulick, director of the League for Constructive Immigration Legislation, had proposed a new immigration policy based on a numerical rather than a selective standard that established a quota formula for each nation—5% of the American-born children of foreign parents plus the number of people from that nation who had become naturalized citizens. The goal of such legislation, he maintained, was that "America should admit as immigrants only so many aliens from any land as she can Americanize" (Gulick 547). As his appended hypothetical statistical tables show, if such a quota had been in effect from 1911 to 1915, Northern European immigration would have remained unaffected; the heaviest impact of such a quota would have fallen on Italy, Russia, and Eastern European countries. Similar quota proposals would dominate the consideration of a post-war immigration policy in the 1920s.

Social and political events of the wartime years at once intensified the nativist crusade for restriction and broadened the base of popular support for a eugenically-based approach to immigration law. Indeed, during these years many Progressives even came to ally themselves with the restrictionist cause, and the legislation of the 1920s marked the high-water mark for the influence of the racialist-eugenicist coalition. "We are facing," Ward wrote, "the most serious crisis which has ever arisen in the history of immigration to the United States" ("Immigration Problem" 323).

Domestically, the message that national unity could best be achieved through white racial purity was forcefully conveyed in the most widely used college textbook in eugenics (published in 1918), that in its revised fourth edition still unequivocally maintained that "if eugenic values are to be safeguarded, it is essential to prevent miscegenation between whites and blacks in the United States, so far as that is possible.... It is therefore essential that the color line be maintained for the present" (Popenoe and Johnson 302).

Earnest Sevier Cox, a prominent member of the Ku Klux Klan and protégé of racialist extraordinaire Madison Grant, published a report on the Negro repatriation movement issued jointly by the Eugenics Research Association and the Eugenics Society, U.S.A. His white supremacist tract, *White America* (1923), received a glowing review in the *Eugenical News,* the reviewer conferring heroic status on its author, noting that he "will be a greater savior of his country than George Washington. We wish him, his book, and his 'White America Society' godspeed" ("Review" 3).

But the essential links between racial theories and eugenics were forged by the two most popular proponents of Nordic racialist consciousness and white supremacy in the period 1915-35—Madison Grant (1865-1937) and T. Lothrop Stoddard (1883-1950). Together they provided an anthropological, historical, and geo-political legitimation for the racialist assumptions that underlay eugenicist science and nativist restrictionism.

Grant, vice-president of the Immigration Restriction League, president of the American Zoological Society, quondam president of the Eugenics Research Association, chairman of its Committee on Selective Immigration, and co-founder of the Galton Society, provided legitimacy and popular exposure for eugenicist ideas and directly linked scientific eugenics and restrictionist nativism. In turn, his intimate association with eugenics organizations lent scientific credence to his widely popular Nordicist racialist tract, *The Passing of the Great Race* (1916). Published in the wake of the massive report on immigration of the Dillingham commission, *Passing* was a racial history of the West, a eugenic history of mankind. It raised the specter of Nordic race suicide as a result of the dysgenic effects of World War I (considered a civil war amongst the white racial stock by Grant), played upon fears of the immigration of inferior Southern European stock to the U.S. and the decline of the native-born birthrate, and mourned the lack of racial consciousness among Nordics. As Grant saw it, unless Americans could awaken to "the menace of the impending Migration of Peoples through unrestrained freedom of entry here . . . the native American must turn the page of history and write: 'FINIS AMERICAE'" (*Passing* xxxii).

At bottom, Grant's admonitions about Nordic racial decline are grounded in his fear of differential fecundity and the perceived alien sexual threat to racial purity:

> Probably the greatest tragedy in the world today is the corrosive jealousy of the fair skin of the white races felt by those whose skin is black, yellow, or brown. . . . One of the main manifestations of this jealousy of the fair skin of the Nordics is shown in those numerous cases where members of the colored races, or even dark-skinned members of the Nordic race regard the possession of a blonde woman as an assertion of race equality. This has been true historically since the earliest times. It is more than ever in evidence at the present day. (*Conquest* 15)

Grant understood differential fecundity as the primary mechanism of Darwinian natural selection. As he put it, "the result is that one class or type in a population expands more rapidly than another and ultimately replaces it. This process of replacement of one type by another does not mean that the race changes or is transformed into another. It is a replacement pure and simple and not a transformation" (*Passing* 47). Basing his conclusions on the eugenical idea of "unit traits" as the mechanism of genetic transmission, Grant argued that racial mixture would inevitably lead to evolutionary regression:

> the result of the mixture of two races, in the long run, gives us a race reverting to the more ancient, generalized and lower type. The cross between a white man and an Indian is an Indian; the cross between a white man and a Negro is a Negro; the cross between a white man and a Hindu is a Hindu; and the cross between any of the three European races [Nordic, Alpine, and Mediterranean] and a Jew is a Jew (*Passing* 18).

The Nordic race was overwhelmed by a darkling world where unnatural conditions favored the survival of the unfittest and the degeneration of the fittest, an environmental disadvantage vastly exacerbated by the "new immigration" that brought into the country

> a large and increasing number of the weak, the broken and the mentally crippled of all races drawn from the lowest stratum of the Mediterranean basin and the Balkans, together with hordes of the wretched, submerged populations of the Polish Ghettos. Our jails, insane asylums and alms-houses are filled with this human flotsam and the whole tone of American life, social, moral and political has been lowered and vulgarized by them. (*Passing* 89-90)

Grant saw the solution in the eugenic reconstruction of Americanism. The immediate need was to cut off the unlimited influx of immigrants. As for the breeding of native American stock and race suicide, he recommended positive and negative eugenics. Like his scientific eugenicist colleagues, however, he had little faith in promoting breeding from the best native stock, and he favored the retributive application of the rigors of eugenic law to the socially undesirable and racially deficient immigrant stock. His rhetoric was uncompromising; the degenerative new immigrant germ plasm must be eliminated. "Mistaken regard," he declared,

> for what are believed to be divine laws and a sentimental belief in the sanctity of human life tend to prevent both the elimination of defective infants and the sterilization of such adults as are themselves of no value to the community. The laws of nature require the obliteration of the unfit and human life is valuable only when it is of use to the community or race. . . . As the percentage of incompetents increases, the burden of their support will become ever more onerous until, at no distant date, society will in self-defense put a stop to the supply of feeble-minded and criminal children of weaklings. (*Passing* 49)

The exaggeratedly harsh tone of this passage, which seems to recommend euthanasia as well as sterilization, remained absolutely unqualified through the first three editions of *Passing*, and was given legitimacy by citing two *Eugenics Records Bulletins* authored by Harry H. Laughlin and three issues of the *Eugenical News* from 1918. By the publication of the fourth edition, Henry H. Goddard had published the results of the intelligence tests he had administered to immigrants on Ellis Island in 1913, and given Goddard's extravagant claims that an average of 83% of all new immigrants were feeble-minded, Grant could feel confident that on the basis of mental deficiency alone the bulk of the alien population would be eligible for sterilization.

But the immigration restrictions of the 1920s, however eugenical, were insufficient to secure a Nordic, regenerated America. When Grant revisited the dual racial problem of the United States—the Negro and the alien immigrant—during the Depression years in his racial history of America, *The Conquest of a Continent* (1933), he was still concerned about the "Alien Invasion" and how it might be checked. Although the great bulk of eugenical sterilizations were performed after the Supreme Court upheld the Virginia statute in *Buck vs. Bell* (1927), there is only one passing reference to sterilization and institutionalized segregation of the unfit in this volume. Instead, Grant recommends social and political constraint—the speedy deportation of all illegal immigrants and, through a "Counsel of Perfection," universal registration of all aliens and absolute suspension of naturalization for at least a generation. "Nothing," he cried, "can be more ill-advised politically than the Americanization programs of some worthy people. An American is not made by conferring upon him the franchise, but by the alien's voluntary and genuine acceptance of our language, laws, institutions, and cultural traditions" (351).

By the 1930s, Grant was recommending the implementation of a contraceptive education program. Such a program would also address the domestic racial problem—the "immense mass of Negroes" (*Conquest* 351). Indeed, the prospects Grant envisioned for the African American population were essentially the same as those for the new immigrants—segregation and deportation. The thought of amalgamation was anathema to him, and he declared that the effect of Nordic-alien or white-Black miscegenation would be utter "racial chaos," and he recommended the passage of laws prohibiting the intermarriage of whites and Blacks. He favored the eugenical restriction of immigration from Latin America and especially from Mexico, championed the suspension of all immigration for the duration of the Depression, and ideally favored "the *absolute* suspension of all immigration from all countries" (*Conquest* 348). "Not only should European immigration be stopped," Grant argued,

> but still more, all immigration of every sort from countries to the south of us should be barred. . . . The strictest legislation at this time is necessary to prevent this impending invasion [of Negroes and Indians] before it assumes the dimensions of a flood. . . . If immigration be not absolutely prohibited, at very least, no one should be able to enter the United States . . . except white men of superior intellectual capacity distinctly capable of becoming valuable American citizens. (348-49)

Prospective Americanization was also the standard for the admissibility of aliens adopted by the other major Nordic racialist ideologue of the 1920s, T. Lothrop Stoddard (1883-1950), journalist and alarmist proponent of extreme eugenicist views, who produced two widely popular books on "the conflict of color," "the worldwide struggle between the primary races of mankind" (Stoddard, *Revolt* v)— *The Rising Tide of Color Against World Supremacy* (1920), and *The Revolt Against Civilization: The Menace of the Under Man* (1922). Writing in the aftermath of World War I, Stoddard focused his attention on global politics, arguing that "the world's race problem" was one of the burgeoning population of non-white peoples, who were consequently driven to pursue "race" expansion (*Rising* 16). Given his assumption of a racial hierarchy of intelligence and capacity for civilization—white, yellow, brown, red, black—the pervasive concern of *The Rising Tide* is the Yellow Peril. Inevitably, demographic pressure would force China and Japan to infiltrate other areas of Asia currently under white control or to invade territories colonized by whites. For Stoddard, World War I had spawned the other great dysgenic force— international, expansionist Communism, that he identified as "the archenemy of civilization and the race" (*Rising* 142). As he saw it, "The menace of Bolshevism is simply incalculable. Bolshevism is a peril in some ways unprecedented in the world's history. It is not merely a war against a social system, not merely a war against our civilization; it is a war of the hand against the brain" (218).

Stoddard deftly conflated postwar fears of alien radicalism, paranoia about race traitors, and central eugenical concerns when he observed that "Bolshevism is the renegade, the traitor within the gates, who would betray the citadel, degrade the very fibre of our being, and ultimately hurl a rebarbarized, racially impoverished world into the most debased and hopeless of mongrelizations" (*Rising* 221). Though he supported restrictions on European immigration, Stoddard felt that the "alien blood" of the colored races threatened "incalculably greater damage" to white civilization and white racial stock. "If the white immigrant can gravely disorder the national life," he wrote, "it is not too much to say that the colored immigrant would doom it to certain death." And "this doom would be all the more certain because of the enormous potential volume of colored immigration" (267-68). So, the international "rising tide of color" is translated into at once a domestic and a universal eugenic threat:

> Colored migration is a *universal* peril, menacing every part of the white world. Nowhere can the white man endure colored competition; everywhere 'the East can *underlive* the West.' The grim truth of the matter is this: The whole white world is exposed, immediately or ultimately, to the possibility of social sterilization and final replacement or absorption by the teeming colored races. (297-98)

In *The Revolt Against Civilization,* Stoddard characterizes the colored races as "stagnant or decadent peoples" (2), "congenital barbarians" (5), thus linking intellectual incapacity and the tendency to social and political radicalism. To identify the most dangerous class, inimical to civilization by virtue of incapacity and therefore eugenically undesirable, he uses the term the "Under Man," which collectively designates "the ranks of the inferior—the vast army of the unadaptable and the incapable" (22-23).

The Under Man is not a degenerative type—imbecile, feeble-minded, neurotic, or insane—but is essentially a border-line normal doomed to inferiority by his innate incapacity. Employing tabular data from the U.S. Army Intelligence tests, Stoddard finds the results, extrapolated to the entire U.S. population of 1922 (approximately 100 million), shocking. He concludes that

> the *average* mental age of Americans is only about fourteen; that forty-five millions, or nearly one-half of the whole population, will never develop mental capacity beyond the stage represented by a normal

twelve-year-old child; that only thirteen and one-half millions will ever show superior intelligence, and that only four and one-half millions can be considered "talented". (*Revolt* 69)

In sum, over forty percent of the American population are Under Men.

But "evolutionary" eugenics, for Stoddard (reflecting the prevalent opinion among eugenicists), could only effectively combat racial degeneration and Bolshevism's barbaric superordination of the proletarian Under Man through "negative" eugenics. He sought to lead reluctant public opinion towards the radical eugenical solution—involuntary sterilization of defectives. Based on the evidence of intelligence tests, he argued that

> the unsound "fringe" is so wide, the numbers of less obvious defectives above the present "commitable line" are so large, and their birth-rate tends to be so high that unless many of these grades also were debarred from having children, by either segregation or sterilization . . . society [will] continue to suffer from the burdens and dangers which widespread degeneracy involves. (*Revolt* 249)

Based on Stoddard's claims, between 35% and 45% of the general American population would qualify for eugenic sterilization, and nearly two-thirds of all Poles, Italians, and Russians (disproportionately Jews and Bolsheviks). The end result would be the creation of a "superior race," the only guarantee of the maintenance of civilization. That race would remain a work in progress, engineered by scientific eugenics and reproductive management, with the goal of nurturing the best racial qualities of the Nordic germ plasm and rearing an elite of superior men, a "*Neo-Aristocracy*" (*Revolt* 263).

The Galton Society was established in 1918 as a research and propaganda vehicle for an uncompromising eugenical science, and among its charter members were Grant, Charles B. Davenport, and Henry Fairfield Osborn, president of the American Museum of Natural History. Stoddard's name was soon added to the membership list. As Grant saw the Society, it would be staffed by Nordics and would operate for Nordics. Its membership would be "confined to native Americans, who are anthropologically, socially, and physically sound, no Bolsheviki need apply" (Selden 13).

When the Galton Society formed a Laboratory Committee under Osborn in 1919, its nominees included Robert M. Yerkes and Lothrop T. Stoddard. That Grant and Stoddard were recognized as serious students of race was clear from their official associations with the broader eugenics community. In preparation for the Second International Congress of Eugenics, held at the American Museum of Natural History in New York in 1921, Davenport wrote to Osborn, who served as president of the Congress, that he hoped that only "scientific men," like Grant and Stoddard, would be permitted to speak on race. Grant ultimately served as treasurer of the Congress (Haller 156). Indeed, both men had been part of the core eugenics group and had been intimately connected to the restrictionist movement from the early war years, and in the 1920s and early 1930s their works exerted enormous influence on behalf of racialist eugenics and Nordicism.

It was out of the 1921 Congress of Eugenics that the American Eugenics Society was born. It was originally founded as the Ad Interim Committee of the Congress, but became the Eugenics Committee of the United States of America in 1922, the Eugenics Society of the United States of America in 1923, and the American Eugenics Society in 1925. Davenport, Osborn, and Grant all assumed leadership roles in the new organization. The progress of organized eugenics, then, paralleled the immigration restriction crusade that achieved two successive selective quota limitations in the immigration acts of 1921 and 1924. Central to the success of restrictionism was Harry H. Laughlin, superintendent of the Eugenics Record Office and editor of *Eugenical News*. While the influence of Grant's and Stoddard's ideas on immigration restriction was extensive, it remained largely theoretical; the primary direct and practical influence on legislation was Laughlin, who, after his first appearance before the House Committee on Immigration and Naturalization in April of 1920, was appointed the "Expert Eugenics Agent" to the Committee by its chairman, Albert Johnson (R-WA) (Tucker 94).

Although Grant's claim in *Passing* that "one of the most far-reaching effects of the doctrines enunciated in this volume and in the discussions that followed its publication was the decision of the Congress of the United States to adopt discriminatory and restrictive measures against the immigration of undesirable races and peoples" (xxviii) was doubtless an accurate reading of the effect of the work over the long haul, it was the assiduous and indefatigable Laughlin, who testified before the House Committee on Immigration and Naturalization with some regularity between 1920 and 1931 and, as Expert Eugenics Agent, continued to provide statistical research for the Committee until 1934, who brought practical, applied eugenics most directly to bear on the question of immigration restriction. It was Laughlin who gave eugenics a public face and who translated the racial dogmas of Grant and Stoddard into graphs and tables and maps to provide a patina of scientific legitimation to their Nordic creed. Laughlin was also a tireless promoter of eugenics, who sought to make its scientific research accessible to the general public.

Consider, for example, the two exhibits he prepared for the Second International Congress of Eugenics in 1921. The first was a map display, illustrating the status of eugenic sterilization across the country, which distinguished those states in which laws were "based upon purely eugenical motives" from those whose laws were primarily therapeutic or punitive. States where sterilization laws had been declared unconstitutional or had been vetoed by their governors were also indicated. The second exhibit, "Growth of U.S. Population by Immigration and by Increase in Native Stock," was a more extensive effort, with thirteen maps, displaying the natural increase of the native population relative to total immigration on a decennial basis over the period 1800-1920. Native population was shown in white and Nordics in lighter shades, with immigrants represented by darker shades. The series of maps displays a progressive darkening of the continent until, in the 1920 map, the whole area east of the Mississippi has been overshadowed by the alien presence.

As a promoter of the eugenics cause and its front man on issues of legislative restriction of immigration, Laughlin exploited the propaganda value of the immigration maps, bringing the exhibit to Washington for a three-month run to convince Congressmen of the perils of unrestricted immigration (*Second International Exhibit*, 1923). As the sterilization exhibit suggests, Laughlin was also promoting himself as something of an expert on eugenical sterilization by the early 1920s. Laughlin initiated and served as secretary to the Committee to Study and Report on the Best Practical Means of Cutting Off the

Defective Germ Plasm in the American Population, which had been organized by the Eugenics Section of the American Breeders Association in early May 1911. The Committee on Immigration was formed in late December of that year.

Laughlin wrote a two-volume report on the status of eugenical sterilization in the U.S. for the Committee in 1914. He continued to publish on eugenic sterilization into the 1920s, his major work neatly bookending the debate over the 1924 Quota Act. Laughlin estimated that 10% of the total population of the U.S. was genetically defective, and in a radical application of eugenical principles advocated the involuntary sterilization of fifteen million people over the next two generations in order to purify the national germ plasm. So closely did Laughlin's name come to be associated with eugenic sterilization that he was consulted as an expert witness when the Virginia case of Carrie Buck came before the federal district court, where he testified, on the basis of a report by a eugenics field-worker, that the young woman was a "low-grade moron" who would perpetuate social inadequacy if allowed to breed. The Supreme Court, in its review of the case in 1927, endorsed Laughlin's view. In his report on sterilization, Laughlin also provided a model sterilization law that ultimately served as a model for the Nazi Law for the Prevention of Genetically Defective Progeny (1933) (Kevles 118). In 1928, Laughlin brought his advocacy of eugenical sterilization and immigration control together in his testimony before the House Committee on Immigration and Naturalization on the eugenical aspects of deportation.

From his earliest testimony before the Committee, Laughlin was concerned to impress on the lawmakers the fundamental racial concerns affecting immigration control and the cost to the public of supporting a substantially alien population of the socially inadequate and the genetically defective. His testimony before the Committee on 21 November 1922 provided an "Analysis of America's Melting Pot," and concluded that, based on their percentage of the total population, new immigrant groups greatly exceeded their "quota" among the institutionalized population (*Melting Pot* 325).

The Committee shared his racialist biases, and he confirmed their nativist fears; he was, after all, *their* eugenics expert. Chairman Albert Johnson had declared his personal faith in Laughlin in 1922, when he observed of the "Melting Pot" report, that "I have examined Doctor Laughlin's data and charts and find that they are both biologically and statistically thorough, and apparently sound" (Laughlin, *Melting Pot*, 731). Criticism of his work was taken as a negative reflection on the Committee, and after Laughlin's testimony in 1924, Johnson told him, "don't worry about criticism. You have developed a valuable research and demonstrated a most startling state of affairs. We shall pursue these biological studies further" (Laughlin, *Europe*, 1311). Indeed, they did. In a little more than ten weeks after Laughlin's appearance before the Committee, on 26 May 1924, the Johnson-Reed immigration quota bill became law.

The 1924 act was more restrictive than the 1921 act, which had set each nationality's quota at 3% of that group's percentage of the 1910 population; it reduced total immigration (per quota) as compared to the 1921 act from 358,000 to 164,000, a reduction of 54%. The 1924 act provided for the readjustment of the quota to the 1920 census, with each nationality's quota being its proportional percent of the population in the 1920 census multiplied by 150,000. This second phase of the act was scheduled to become effective in 1929, at which date the quota system was applied to Mexico and Canada as well. Chinese exclusions continued in this act and were not lifted until 1943.

Laughlin remained active in testifying before the Committee until 1931 (when his primary supporters on the Committee, Reps. Johnson and Box, lost reelection bids). He appeared before the Committee on 28 April 1926 and 21 February 1928 on eugenical deportation, observing that "in our immigration law and practice, deportation is the last line of defense against contamination of American family stocks by alien hereditary degeneracy. The first line of defense is the attempt to exclude certain types and classes of antisocial and otherwise undesirable persons, from admission into the United States" (*Eugenical Aspects* 3). Selective immigration should admit only those whose offspring would tend

> to raise the level of American intelligence, and to improve the standard of all other hereditary qualities which we prize in the American people, such as honesty, industry, initiative, courage, natural reverence for law and order, altruistic instincts, artistic talents, ability to collaborate, ability to solve new problems, generally called inventiveness, and the

like. These qualities, besides sound bodies, are the fundamental inborn possessions of a superior race. (*Eugenical Aspects* 45)

What this eugenic standard of selective immigration meant in practice was made clear when Laughlin testified before the Committee on 5 April 1928 on immigration from the Western Hemisphere. He recommended a return to the original (1790) standard of naturalization, which limited acquired citizenship to "free white persons." He suggested adding a provision to the naturalization statute "that only white persons shall be naturalized as citizens," thus excluding from immigration, because ineligible for naturalization, Mexicans "of mixed Spanish and Indian or black blood, and the mixed blacks of the West Indies" (Laughlin, *Eugenical Aspects*, 718). To insure racial purity and to begin the reclamation of America as a white man's country, Laughlin proposed a standard of racial purity in the statutory definition of "white": "for the purpose of this act, a white person shall be defined as one all of whose ancestors are of Caucasian stock" (*Eugenical Aspects* 718). Essentially, the position that Laughlin advocated was a reiteration of the official policy recommendations of the Committee on Selective Immigration of the American Eugenics Society.

Indeed, the Committee did establish race at the center of American immigration policy and the legitimation of that position owed much to Laughlin's aggressive advocacy and tireless statistical compilations supporting the connection between eugenical standards of race and Americanism. In retrospective overview of the success of the Eugenics Research Association in 1927, it was noted that the group's services had been "of the highest value to the nation," especially in the area of immigration policy. Laughlin, in his first appearance before the Committee on Immigration and Naturalization, had irrefutably placed eugenics at the center of the debate on restriction; he had "immediately [taken] the whole question out of politics and placed it on a scientific and biological basis" ("A Retrospective" 94).

Laughlin had further served the Committee by providing it with "arguments to meet the opposition of those legislators who would restrict immigration according to the political needs of their own districts" and "that would protect it from political and racial attacks" ("A Retrospective" 94). It seemed anti-climactic to note that Laughlin's research and reports had "greatly influenced Congress in the passage of the acts restricting immigration" ("A Retrospective" 95). Of Madison Grant's influence on the restrictionist campaign during the same years, there is no more eloquent testimonial than the publication by the House Committee as an extract from its hearings on 24 December 1928 of the *List of Authoritative Works on Immigration by Madison Grant* (1929).

Thus did the eugenics movement, walking in the dark corners of newly emerging academic disciplines—anthropology, psychology, genetics, and biometrics—provide a philosophical and intellectual foundation to legitimate racially exclusive immigration policies in the 1920s. And those eugenically-based immigration policies remained the law of the land for four decades. During the Depression, the restriction of immigration from the Western Hemisphere that Laughlin and the American Eugenics Society had advocated was implemented; exclusion lasted until 1943. Not until the Immigration Reform Act of 1965 was the "national origins" quota system brought to an end.

While apparently the worst abuses of the racialized quota system have been abandoned, recent immigration liberalization has provoked a contemporary alliance of nativist, anti-immigration groups and the violent racist right. And the post 9/11 anxieties and fears provide a political climate of xenophobia, hyper-emotional patriotism, and paranoia about the invisible alien within that recall the social and political circumstances that characterized the earlier restrictionist movement. In a recent report of the Southern Poverty Law Center, the leader of today's anti-immigration movement is identified. He is John H. Tanton, an ophthalmologist from Michigan, who heads the Federation for American Immigration Reform (FAIR) that he founded in 1979. He is the co-author, with Wayne Lutton, of *The Immigrant Invasion* (2001), and publishes an anti-immigration periodical, *The Social Contract*, and the *FAIR Immigration Report* ("Effort to Curb Immigration" 3). The SPLC has identified twelve anti-immigration organizations, all with connections to Tanton, that are "increasingly able to affect Congressional decision-making" (3). Their political contacts with and lobbying of politicians have intensified since September 11 at a critical period when Congressmen are becoming more intensely concerned about immigration issues.

More ominous, given the history of the associations among nativists, eugenicists, and racialists discussed above, is the observation that many anti-immigration groups have been growing harder since 1988, when they first began openly working together with white supremacists. Today, many of their leading officials have joined racist organizations—groups like the white supremacist Council of Conservative Citizens and the American Patrol. And the anti-immigration activists have found an ally in Congress, Rep. Tom Tancredo (R-CO), whose Congressional Immigration Reform Caucus is the center for outspoken criticism of current immigration policy. The caucus' web site has links to many of the anti-immigration groups as well as to the American Patrol (see "Effort to Curb Immigration" 4).

And just as in the period of World War I, the popularizers, responding to public fears, raise the specter of cultural collapse. Pat Buchanan, quondam presidential candidate of the Reform Party, in *The Death of the West: How Dying Populations and Immigrant Invasions Imperil Our Country and Civilization,* has identified a "new divide" in American society in the post-September 11 world, one of "ethnicity and loyalty." For him, as for the eugenicists in the first three decades of the twentieth century, the "melting-pot" ideal has failed. As Buchanan sees it, "the immigrant tsunami rolling over America is not coming from 'all the races of Europe.' The largest population transfer in history is coming from all the races of Asia, Africa, and Latin America, and they are not 'melting and reforming'" (2).

Buchanan also shares eugenicist fears about differential fertility, the declining birthrate of the U.S. and of Europe, and the prospect that the tidal wave of colored immigrants will breed out the white population. He recommends a cap on annual immigration at 250,000, and concludes that

> no nation in history has gone through a demographic change of this magnitude in so short a time, and remained the same nation. . . . Uncontrolled immigration threatens to deconstruct the nation we grew up in and convert America into a conglomeration of peoples with almost nothing in common—not history, heroes, language, culture, faith, or ancestors. Balkanization beckons. (2)

And so, as the twenty-first century opens, the issues surrounding immigration policy continue to be at the very heart of the struggle over the definition of Americanism, and the same issues that sustained racialist-nativist policies in the 1920s—fear of the "breeding out" or the swamping of white America (the darkening of a continent), the threat to established Anglo-Saxon cultural values and the English language, and the degeneration or deconstruction of the American character—continue to drive the contemporary anti-immigration movement (see Lutton and Tanton ). While today's restrictionists no longer employ the rhetoric and the tropes of a discredited eugenical social science, popular attitudes still reflect the racialism of the earlier restrictionist crusade. It is clear that the central questions of racial identity form the core of the ongoing debate over the nature of American character and culture, and that immigration policy remains a primary discursive site and practical policy ground for the battle over the reconstruction of "true" Americanism.

## Works Cited

"A Retrospective of the Eugenics Research Association." *Eugenical News* XII.8 (Aug. 1927): 93-99.

Bouvier, Leon F. *Peaceful Invasions: Immigration and Changing America.* Lanham, NY: UP of America, 1992.

Buchanan, Patrick J. *The Death of the West: How Dying Populations and Immigrant Invasions Imperil Our Country and Civilization.* New York: St. Martin's P, 2002.

"Breeders Association Will Change Its Name." *American Breeders Magazine* 4 (1913): 177.

Cox, Ernest Sevier. "Repatriation of the American Negro." *Eugenical News* 21 (Nov.-Dec. 1936): 133-39.

"Effort to Curb Immigration is Curbed With Bigotry." *Southern Poverty Law Center Report.* July 2003: 3.

"The Field of Eugenics." *American Breeders Magazine* 2 (1911): 139-40.

"First Report of the Committee on Immigration of the Eugenics Section." *American Breeders Magazine* 3 (1912): 249-55.

Goddard, Henry H. "Heredity of Feeblemindedness." *American Breeders Magazine* 1 (1910): 165-78.

Grant, Madison. *Conquest of a Continent; or, the Expansion of Races in America.* New York: Charles Scribner's Sons, 1933.

– – –. *List of Authoritative Works on Immigration* (Washington, DC: GPO, 1928).

– – –. *The Passing of the Great Race; or, the Racial Basis of European History,* 1916. Rpt., 4th ed. New York: Scribners & Sons, 1923.

Gulick, Sidney L. "An Immigration Policy." *Journal of Heredity* 7 (Dec. 1916): 546-52.

Haller, M. H. *Eugenics: Hereditarian Attitudes in American Thought.* New Brunswick, NJ: Rutgers UP, 1963.

Kevles, Daniel J. *In the Name of Eugenics: Genetics and the Uses of Human Heredity.* Cambridge, MA: Harvard UP, 1995.

Laughlin, Harry H. *"Analysis of America's Melting Pot." Hearings Before the Committee on Immigration and Naturalization, House of Representatives, $67^{th}$ Congress, $3^{rd}$ Session, November 21, 1922. Serial 7-C.* Washington: GPO, 1923.

– – – . *Eugenical Aspects of Deportation. Hearings Before the Committee on Immigration and Naturalization, House of Representatives, $70^{th}$ Congress, $1^{st}$ Session, Feb. 21, 1928.* Washington: GPO, 1928.

– – – . *Europe as an Emigrant-Exporting Continent and the United States as an Immigrant-Receiving Country. Hearings of the Immigration and Naturalization Committee, House of Representatives, $68^{th}$ Congress, $1^{st}$ Session, 8 March 1924.* Washington: GPO, 1924.

– – – . *The Second International Exhibit of Eugenics Held Sept. 22 to Oct. 22, 1921 in Connection with the Second International Congress of Eugenics in the American Museum of Natural History, New York. An Account of the Organization of the Exhibit, the Classification of the Exhibits, and a Catalog Description of the Exhibits.* Baltimore: Williams & Wilkins Co., 1923.

Lutton, Wayne, and John Tanton. *The Immigration Invasion.* Monterey, VA: American Immigration Control Foundation, 2001.

Popenoe, Paul B., and Roswell Hill Johnson. *Applied Eugenics.* New York: Macmillan Co., 1933.

"Review of Ernest Sevier Cox's *White America.*" *Eugenical News* 9 (Jan. 1924): 3.

"Second Report of the Committee on Immigration of the Eugenics Section of the American Genetic Association." *Journal of Heredity* 5 (July 1914): 297-300.

Selden, Steven. *Inheriting Shame: The Story of Eugenics and Racism in America.* New York: Teachers College, Columbia UP, 1999.

"Some Present Aspects of Immigration: Fourth Report of the Committee on Immigration of the American Genetic Association." *Journal of Heredity* 10 (Feb. 1917): 68-70.

Stoddard, Lothrop T. *The Revolt Against Civilization: The Menace of the Under Man.* New York: Charles Scribner's Sons, 1922.

– – – . *The Rising Tide of Color Against White World Supremacy.* 1920. New York: Charles Scribner's Sons, 1922.

Tucker, William H. *The Science and Politics of Racial Research.* Urbana: Illinois UP, 1994.

Ward, Robert De Courcey. "The Immigration Problem Today." *Journal of Heredity* 11 (Sept.-Oct. 1921): 323-28.

– – – . "Our Immigration Laws From the Viewpoint of Eugenics." *American Breeders Magazine* 1 (1912): 20.

# Three-Quarter Enemies: Anti-Americanism in Austria-Hungary during World War I

## Roman Puff

### I. Introduction

Through the larger parts of the 19th century, there was some antagonism between Austria-Hungary and the United States of America. It derived mainly from the fact that the one understood itself as representing an older, aristocratic tradition, whereas the other thought of itself as being part of a younger, enlightened movement. When war broke out in Europe in 1914, this situation aggravated considerably: for most Americans, Europe underwent a deplorable regression towards a second Middle Ages (Austria-Hungary was con-sidered as being particularly backward) [1]. For the longer period of the war, the United States was content not to be involved. Walter Hines Page, for example, U.S. Ambassador in London, reporting about a meeting with the brother of the Serbian King, described him as "a ferocious Slav who wishes to fight, who talks like a mediaeval man and so loves the blood of his enemies that, if he can first kill enough of them, he is willing to be whipped," finishing his letter to President Wilson stating that "again and ever [he] thank[ed] Heaven for the Atlantic ocean." [2]

But detestation was mutual: reflecting political conflicts on topics like the supply of ammunition to Britain and France by Americans, the expulsion of Vienna's Ambassador Constantin Dumba from Washington, the conflict over the sinking of the Italian liner *Ancona*, the American demand for national self-domination or the American entrance into the war against Austria-Hungary's ally Germany, anti-Americanism became common in the Habsburg Monarchy. [3]

This was true for more or less all sectors of the Austro-Hungarian society, from the press to the Minister for Foreign Affairs, who is said to have abominated the United States for the reason of her being a "crude republic." In this paper, I want to shed some light on the sentiments of Austria-Hungary towards the United States in the final struggle of the empire and show how diplomats on both sides of the Atlantic reacted to the phenomenon. Finally, the anti-American attitude that Austrian decision-makers expressed during World War I as well as patterns of anti-American prejudices will be briefly considered.

## II. From Bad to Worse – the Evolution of Anti-Americanism in Great-War Austria-Hungary

After the United States had declared their neutrality in the European war in early August, 1914, the first major conflict between Vienna and Washington soon arose: the American declaration of neutrality stated that Americans were allowed to produce and sell "articles ordinarily known as 'contraband of war'" to the parties in the conflict.[4] In fact, because of their superiority on the seas, England and France were the only beneficiaries of that settlement. Nevertheless, Wilson and his staff argued correctly that this regulation was not biased, since it was the only way not to impair the given balance of power.[5] But public opinion in the Central Powers turned ever more hostile towards the United States, whether of the populations' own accord or stirred up by their governments.

In February 1916, the American Ambassador in Vienna, Frederic C. Penfield, who became quite sympathetic with his hosts as time went on,[6] reported to the Department of State that, though representatives of a neutral power – in fact, the only great power that had remained neutral at that stage – he and his staff were regarded as "three-quarter enemies" by the Austrians, regardless of the social strata they belonged to.[7] He added that almost daily the "employees of the Embassy would come to me with statements that they were being regarded by the Viennese almost as spies."[8] Around the same time he reported to Colonel House, Wilson's major policy-adviser, that the feeling against America in wartime Vienna was "stronger as against Russia, France, England or even Italy."[9]

In the creation of popular sentiments against the United States, the press played an important role. On May 15, 1916, immediately after the end of the Sussex crisis, for example, the Vienna weekly newspaper *Der Morgen* printed a quite offensive cartoon of President Wilson. Normally Penfield tried to ignore adversities like this, "giving no intimation of our being aware of the fact that there is a wide difference between . . . Austria-Hungary in war time and in peace."[10] But also the American Ambassador was at the end of his tether at times, and the offensive cartoon roused his resistance.

*Der Morgen* was a progressive/liberal paper which was said to be something like the organ of Austrian freemansonry.[11] Under the title "Jonathan the Righteous,"[12] the cartoon showed Wilson as "Iustitia," holding a pair of scales with ammunition on one side, and foodstuff like cocoa, tea and coffee on the other. In his hand he holds a sword with the word "neutrality" on it, and his eyes are blindfolded with a ribbon on which the German word for "war profit" can be read. Wilson/Iustitia is sitting on a pedestal which is decorated in stars and stripes and is inscribed with the Latin epigraph "Fiat Justitia! Pereat Mundus." Behind his back Russians, Italians, Frenchmen and Englishmen are hiding from the German chancellor Theodor von Bethmann-Hollweg.[13] He is pointing at a large crowd of women and children confined in barbed wire while stepping up to Wilson's pedestal, stating "Goodness! Wilson! You must be aware how Germany's women and children are to be exposed to hunger" with Wilson/Iustitia answering "But why am I Justice if I shouldn't be blind."[14]

When Penfield saw the cartoon, he immediately applied for an appointment with the Austrian foreign minister, Baron Istvan Burián. Burián "dilated" first upon the alleged abusive tone of the American press towards Austria-Hungary. But Penfield persisted, and finally got the promise that the United States were rendered "full justice and entire satisfaction" in the shape of a formal apology that was issued the next day.[15]

Baron Burián yielded in this as in other, similar incidents. Such cases occurred frequently, whenever a new conflict between Vienna – or even more often, Berlin – and Washington turned up. Quite logically, anti-American sentiments reached a new climax when the United States declared war on imperial Germany in early April 1917. Although

Wilson had declared in Congress that he wished to postpone "a discussion of our relations with the authorities at Vienna" at least "for the present,"[16] which prolonged the period of American neutrality against the Habsburg Monarchy, the Austrian press reacted furiously: Even the *Neue Freie Presse*, the flagship among Vienna's respectable newspapers, described Wilson in harsh words as a two-faced statesman who had doctored himself to appear like a peace campaigner but now was showing his true, sinful, megalomaniac ambition.[17] This might have passed as a normal political antagonism, had they not taken the opportunity to bash the United States lock, stock and barrel: What was this country – a country where "millions of children are used by industry, millions of women do night shifts" and compulsory insurance was unknown![18] – to declare war on Germany? Arguments like that, which clearly had nothing to do with the political conflict at stake and were issued in a newspaper that up to then had not championed labor rights and social security, simply made use of (and amplified thereby) anti-American sentiments – to what success can easily be drawn from the fact that they still sound quite familiar nearly a hundred years later.

But there was one important fact that set the situation of that time apart from today: Penfield did not forget to mention in his report to Washington about the *Der Morgen*-affair that the Austrian press was subject to strict censorship. This led him to conclude that its remarks must be interpreted as the official position of the Austro-Hungarian Government. This view was supported by the fact that Burián did not show an attitude towards the United States that was as favorable as it should have been. When Wilson forced the Ballhausplatz to withdraw its ambassador, Constantin Dumba, in the autumn of 1915, after he had got caught in the organisation of strikes in American war material factories, Burián was seriously offended: a "crude republic" like the United States forced him, representative of "the proudest empire in Europe,"[19] to withdraw his ambassador! According to Penfield, from that moment on the heart of the Austro-Hungarian Minister for Foreign Affairs was "chilled against our nation."[20]

As in similar cases, Burián's opinion regarding the United States did not result from personal experience. But this fact did not hinder him from stubbornly sticking to his prejudices when they were challenged. For example, when Dumba returned to Vienna after his expulsion from

Washington in October 1915, he had a strange experience: being one of the very few Austrians who made it back over the Atlantic after the outbreak of the war, he wanted to report to Burián about the situation in the United States. But when he started, he was interrupted by the minister who "showed neither interest nor understanding." Dumba was forced to listen to a lengthy talk of Burián about the state of relations between Vienna and Washington. After a while he left the foreign minister with his prejudices and half-truths.[21]

Yet Dumba himself was not immune to anti-American sentiments. Apart from his very unsympathetic personal attitude towards President Wilson, whom he experienced as a clumsy, out-of-touch intellectual,[22] he described the Americans in his memoirs as dull people, following their sheep instinct whenever they got the opportunity.[23]

When Burián was replaced by Ottokar Czernin in December 1916, the situation improved at least in one point: although Czernin, like his predecessor and most present-day Austrians, thought that Wilson showed a "startling ignorance" regarding the conditions in Europe "and specially Austria-Hungary," he at least admitted that the Americans were possibly "honest and sincere."[24] It obviously never occurred to the Minister for Foreign Affairs or any other person responsible to make use of the Vienna University library. There they had – and still have – stored a book that appeared in its European edition in London in 1904. The book is titled *The State: Elements of Historical and Practical Politics: A Sketch of Institutional History and Administration* (originally published in 1889). It describes all European states of that time in terms of their history, their constitutional and de facto political system, society, etc.; pages 333 to 347 are dedicated to Austria-Hungary. The author of this book was a university professor named Woodrow Wilson. Of course, the views on *The State* can – and do – differ considerably.[25] But be that as it may: Czernin's and the other Austrians' attitudes towards Wilson and the United States remained mere prejudice.

The negative attitude of the decision makers in Vienna towards the United States tended to trickle down within the ministries and to the local authorities. On the eve of the diplomatic break between Vienna and Washington, the Ministry for Foreign Affairs contacted the Army's Supreme Command's (the "Armeeoberkommando," located in Baden, 15 miles south of Vienna) to hear its view on how to treat Americans after that foreseeable event. Baden answered that things ought to be left as they were: American citizens should be neither interned nor confined and should remain "completely un-annoyed." This message was later changed: somebody deleted the word "completely" and added "The attention of the police will be drawn to them."[26]

Consequently, the approximately 2,000 American citizens[27] that stayed in Austria-Hungary after the severance of diplomatic relations in April 1917 often suffered from distrust and unfair treatment by the authorities, although the United States still was not at war with Austria-Hungary. In June 1917, for example, Arthur and Mathilde Baker, an American couple who had lived in Trieste for several years already, were ordered by the local police to leave the town within fifteen days. No explanation was given, but on request the police informed the Bakers that this had been ordered by the war surveillance office ("Kriegsüberwachungsamt"). Baker complained at the Spanish Embassy in Vienna, which was charged with representing the interests of the United States and its citizens after the diplomatic relations had been cut.[28] Through the intervention of the embassy Baker and his wife were permitted to stay in Trieste, but only "as long as they were not guilty of some offence," and again the Ministry for Foreign Affairs added "that they will be observed by the police."[29] But even when Americans wanted to leave the country, which in principle was allowed and possible via Switzerland, they often had to deal with arbitrary decisions by the Austro-Hungarian administration, and the Spanish Embassy often had to intervene to secure their rights.[30]

### III. What and What for? – A Policy-Instrument and Its Patterns

It is widely held that policy-makers in pre-World-War-I Europe held a comparatively high standard, if not in terms of their factual knowledge, then at least in terms of education, diplomacy, and style. But from the points made above, one would draw the conclusion that the World-War-I Austrian politicians were highly irrational in their attitude towards the United States. How to deal with this contradiction?

In February 1917, after the Central Powers had resumed unrestricted submarine warfare, the Austro-American relations were strained to the utmost. To avoid that Washington broke off diplomatic relations with Vienna as it had done with Berlin on February 3, the Austrian diplomats had to undertake an unprecedented balancing act: on the one hand, they desperately tried to convince the Americans that their support of Germany's unrestricted submarine warfare meant nothing, while on the other hand they had to prove to Berlin, which insisted on Austrian political if not military support, that they were still faithful to their ally. Their balancing poles were extensive diplomatic notes that argued with sophistication that, in reality, nothing had changed.[31] Following that track, with nothing substantial to offer in the principal matter of submarine warfare, Czernin politely promised "drastic steps taken by Government for preventing newspaper articles hostile to America" at a conference with Penfield in mid-February.[32]

This offer did not only prove that Penfield had been right in assuming that press-utterances should be interpreted as official statements of the Austro-Hungarian government. Also, obviously, at least for high-ranking decision-makers, anti-Americanism was not an irrational sentiment, but a political instrument. A "Righteous Jonathan," who was driven by mere greed instead of regard for international law, was a very suitable means to fasten the strained inner lines of a country at war and strengthen the legitimacy of the monarchy's cause as well as hide its military and political failures.

To make anti-Americanism an operational policy instrument, anti-American resentments must have existed in all major sectors of society, and it is clear that these resentments must have had historical roots in times long before the war. They were just spurred on by the press, in many cases on behalf of the government, the representatives of which often had anti-American dispositions themselves and found anti-Americanism an easy way of gaining public support for their policies.

But that is not the whole story, since finally a quite disturbing observation must be made: although the background of the underlying conflicts that led to the various eruptions of anti-Americanism changed by and then during the war, the pattern of anti-Americanism remained the same over the whole period. The United States in general and President Wilson in particular were not only described as ignorant or, at best, as well-meaning fools – with almost no exception they were described as greedy hypocrites: "Jonathan the Righteous," while stating that his action was an outflow of lawfulness, was blindfolded by a ribbon on which the words "war profit" could be read. The American children that were from being "used by industry" with a simultaneous, total lack of social security were described as being in that deplorable situation because American society was run by "multi-millionaires with the sense of demi-gods" who were selling their ruthless rule as "democracy."

These are only two examples from an extensive press production in a war that lasted over four years, but many more can be easily found. Nearly each time the Austro-Hungarian press portrayed the United States and "the" Americans as Janus-faced: while publicly proclaiming moral values like liberty, democracy, national self-domination and the rule of law, in reality they were moneygrubbers, unscrupulous opportunists only caring for their own benefits.

## Notes

[1] Ottavio Barié, *L'opinione intervenzionistica negli Stati Uniti, 1914-1917*. Biblioteca storica universitaria, ser. II, vol. XI. Milan: Varese, 1960. 84-85.

[2] W. H. Page to W. Wilson, July 29, 1914, *The Papers of Woodrow Wilson*. Ed Arthur S. Link. 69 Vols. Princeton 1966-1994, vol. XXX, 314-16 (subsequently referred to as *PWW*).

[3] For a detailed survey of these political conflicts see Angelo Ara, *L'Austria-Ungheria nella politica americana durante la prima guerra mondiale*, Rome: Ed. Dell'Ateneo 1973, and Roman Puff, "Uncle Sam und der Doppeladler. Die Beziehungen zwischen den USA zwischen Sarajevo und Kriegserklärung," master thesis, U of Vienna, 2003.

[4] Proclamation of Neutrality, Aug. 4, 1914, Papers Relating to the Foreign Relations of the United States, Supplement The World War, Washington 1928ff., 547-51 (subsequently referred to as FRUS [Vol.], Suppl. WW).

[5] For example Lansing's Memorandum for Wilson, Dec. 9, 1914, *PWW* XXXI, 432-46.

[6] Walter F. Bell, "American Embassies in Belligerent Europe, 1914-1918," diss., U of Iowa, 1983, 261-62.

[7] Penfield to Wilson, Feb. 14, 1916, FRUS 1916, Suppl. WW., 816-18.

[8] Penfield to Wilson, May 20, 1916, FRUS 1916, Suppl. WW., 273-75.

⁹ House to Wilson, Feb. 3, 1916, *PWW* XXXVI 124. House had met Penfield in Geneva on the occasion of his trip to Europe that had led to the famous "House-Grey-Memorandum."
¹⁰ Penfield to Wilson, Feb. 14, 1916.
¹¹ Kurt Paupié, *Handbuch des österreichischen Pressewesens*, 2 vols., Vienna 1959, vol. 1, 211f.
¹² This refers to Jonathan the Maccabean, a 2nd-century-BC Jewish political leader in Palestine, who because of his successes was very much in demand of the great powers of those days (Romans and the Diadochian Empires) but finally was murdered because of his scheming policy towards them (see Siegfried Herrmann, *Geschichte Israels in alttestamentarischer Zeit*, Munich 1980, 444-48, 451, 463). The story is told in the Old Testament, and Penfield, a practicing Catholic, surely understood every detail of its implications.
¹³ Obviously, *Der Morgen* took the cartoon from a German newspaper: although the German chancellor might have been a quite popular figure in 1916 Austria-Hungary it does not seem logical that the cartoon provides no references to Austria-Hungary at all.
¹⁴ *Der Morgen*, May 15, 1916, 9.
¹⁵ Penfield to Wilson, May 20, 1916. Wilson was so impressed by the action of his ambassador that he recommended it to the American ambassadors in London–Paris when they faced a similar situation some months later.
¹⁶ Wilson's speech to the Congress, April 2, 1917, *PWW* XLI, 519-527.
¹⁷ *Neue Freie Presse*, Morgenblatt, No. 18902, April 6, 1917, 1.
¹⁸ ibidem.
¹⁹ Penfield to Wilson, May 20, 1916.
²⁰ Penfield to Lansing, April 26, 1916, FRUS 1916, Suppl. WW, 269-70.
²¹ Constantin Dumba, *Dreibund- und Entente-Politik in der Alten und Neuen Welt*, Zurich–Vienna 1931, 436.
²² ibidem, 340.
²³ ibidem, 314, 324.
²⁴ Ottokar Czernin, *Im Weltkriege*, Berlin and Vienna 1919, 257.
²⁵ For Tibor Glant, for example, Wilson "developed no proper understanding of the major problems of the Habsburg monarchy" (*Through the Prism of the Habsburg Monarchy. Hungary in American Diplomacy and Public Opinion During World War I*. Atlantic Studies on Society in Change 95. Princeton–New York: Columbia UP, 1998, 60). Arthur May, however, thinks that "[w]ith clarity and penetration Wilson outlined the complicated structure and the fragilities of the Dual Monarchy on the Danube, which disposes of the myth that he was quite unfamiliar with the character and the problems of Austria-Hungary" ("Woodrow Wilson and Austria-Hungary to the End of 1917,"

*Festschrift for Heinrich Benedikt; überreicht zum 70. Geburtstag.* Ed. Hugo Hantsch und Alexander Novotny [Vienna: Verlag Notring der wissenschaftlichen Verbände Österreichs 1957, 213-42, 214]). In my opinion, Wilson's description of the Habsburg Monarchy is brief but tenable, particularly in its assessment of the ethnic conflicts in the empire.
[26] Telegram by phone to Baron Gautsch (the Ministry for Foreign Affairs' deputy at the Army's Supreme Command), April 5, 1917 (HHSta, Ministerium des Äußeren, Administrative Registratur, 36.607, file number 31299/11/1917).
[27] In January 1918, about 1,350 American citizens lived in the Austrian parts of the empire (Memorandum January 26, 1918, HHSta, Ministerium des Äußeren, Administrative Registratur, 36.608, no file number), in June 1918 the Hungarian Ministry of the Interior counted 651 for the Hungarian parts (Note verbale for the Spanish Embassy, HHSta, Ministerium des Äußeren, Administrative Registratur, 36.607, file 45011/11/1918). Although some Americans tried to leave the monarchy after April 1917, their number was very limited; therefore one can assume that the overall number didn't change considerably between the severance of the diplomatic relations and the end of the war.
[28] Note verbale for the Spanish Embassy, June 22, 1917 (HHSta, Ministerium des Äußeren, Administrative Registratur, 36.608, file 64746/11/1917).
[29] Memorandum, August 6, 1917 (HHSta, Ministerium des Äußeren, Administrative Registratur, 36.608, file 74844/11/1917).
[30] HHSta, Ministerium des Äußeren, Administrative Registratur, 36.608, bundle 47/4.
[31] For the details of that balancing act see Puff, 132-37.
[32] Penfield to Lansing, Feb. 19, 1917, FRUS 1917, Suppl. WW 1, 137.

# Austrian Anti-Americanism after World War II

## Günter Bischof

*Dedicated to my University of Innsbruck mentors
Sonja Bahn, Brigitte Scheer, and Arno Heller*

**Introduction**

Americanization and anti-Americanism are like Siamese twins. Whenever and wherever the influence of American political and military power, economic penetration and consumerism, the spreading popular culture and the American dream are felt and consciously registered by indigenous populations, countervailing defenses for the preservation of national identity are thrown up and the growing clamor of critiques of America is vociferously voiced. The French communist critic Roger Garaudy posits the dyad Americanism vs. anti-Americanism in these drastic terms: "This disease [Americanism] has spread all over the world and 'Anti-Americanism' is the fight against that disease from which we have to cure the American people themselves who are the victims of the financial, political and military oligarchies."[1] European discourses about America have at all times produced the 'killer oppositions' of *Traum* vs. *Albtraum*, as the Munich Americanist Berndt Ostendorf has reminded us. He further notes that "the transatlantic exchange has played itself out in a compulsive *folie à deux* for over three centuries with a remarkably stable set of choreographies, but with a rather uneven, historically specific set of performances."[2]

The question under review here is, has there ever been an Austro-specific anti-Americanism? My basic answer is that it is difficult to sort out a specific Austrian anti-Americanism that is recognizably different from the Western European variants. What John Hollander calls "irrational" anti-Americanism is most likely to be found on the political margins on the Right and the Left. The Austrian Left tended to follow the international trends of rabid Communist, mild Socialist, as well as U.S.-inspired New Left and pacifist Green anti-Americanisms. Austria may also be seen as going somewhat of a *Sonderweg* in the postwar European reaction to America due to its Cold War neutrality and its curious geopolitical status between East and West. This neutrality more recently has descended increasingly towards neutralism and what Hollander in his magisterial study of anti-Americanism calls the "moral equivalence" argument of seeing both Cold War superpowers as gargantuan imperialist monoliths with the frightful potential of civilization-ending nuclear arsenals (the "better red than dead" paradigm).[3]

Austria's self-perceived role as "bridge" between East and West during the Cold War naturally fostered such neutralist moral equivalence thinking. The "equidistance" between the two superpowers produced a distancing from the East-West conflict and an "island-of-the-blessed" mentality in the 1970s and 1980s that is unique to Austria. Increasing trade, tourism and cultural contact with Austria's neighbors to the East made traditional Austrian anti-communism – the counterpoint to the Cold War killer opposition Americanism vs. anti-Americanism – pale.

A note on the historiography: it also needs to be clearly said here that the study of anti-Americanism in Austria has hardly begun. Whereas at least since the 1980s scholarship on anti-Americanism in Germany, France, the Netherlands, Italy and the United Kingdom has gathered momentum, in Austria it has stayed dormant. Reinhold Wagnleitner's persistent work on the Americanization of Austria and Europe, which naturally also has produced some offspring of its twin anti-Americanism, is largely a one-man show.[4] In fact, David Elwood in a recent and very thoughtful survey of West European anti-Americanism notes that Richard Kuisel's work on France and Wagnleitner's on Austria marks a turning point in the study of the deeper dimensions of Americanization- and anti-Americanism-studies in Europe.[5]

Given this state of scholarship on Austrian anti-Americanism, what I have to say here, then, needs to be seen very much as *prolegomena*.

My theses here are highly tentative hypotheses that need to be discussed and refined.

## I. Traditional Stereotypes and Hitler's Legacy

The prevalent images of America have traditionally originated with elite accounts. In the 19th century Austrian noblemen, including Archduke Francis Ferdinand, had traveled to the United States to gather impressions of the new world (one can hardly speak of serious study). Usually they see their stereotypes confirmed, of filthy cities, beautiful landscapes and corrupt politics.[6] In the late 19th and early 20th centuries it was increasingly engineers, businessmen and scientists who went to American world's fairs and inspected factories and the new engines and production techniques. They came back and wrote travel accounts featuring the traditional European stereotypes of America the land of opportunity vs. capitalist acquisitive greed (*"Das Land der unbegrenzten Möglichkeiten"* vs. *"Das Land des unbehinderten Erwerbs"*). American management and mass production methods – Taylorism and Fordism – began their global conquest and took Austria by storm, too, in the 1920s.[7] So did Jazz and Hollywood movies in the interwar period. Apart from movies, which found a popular following, most of these encounters before World War II were elite encounters.[8] The images of America that they produced were usually along the lines of the deeply held stereotypes that have been proliferating in Europe from the beginning of the American Republic – *"America as Paradise"* vs. *"America the Barbarous."* There is a rich literature on these 19th-century images, perceptions and stereotypes, and Reinhold Wagnleitner has summarized them well in his *Coca-Colonisation.*[9]

It is important to know that these projections usually were based more on ignorance than on well-informed factual knowledge.[10] Marcus Cunliffe has observed an important trend in these projections. While, on the one hand, in the 19th century the professional and upper classes were traditionally anti-American, they tended to be pro-American in the 20th century. For the laboring class and the Left, on the other hand, America during the 19th century represented an opportunity to leave oppression and the class struggle behind and begin a new life. After

World War II the Left came to see the United States increasingly through simplistic Marxist lenses as imperialist, monopolistic, oligarchic, and hegemonic, and since the 1990s as relentlessly globalist.[11] It needs to be added that conservative elites would still hold anti-American views when it came to American popular culture imports to their countries. As Richard Pells put it: "upper-class Europeans were more apt to be anti-American, on cultural grounds, than were those on the lower rungs of the social and economic ladder." After World War II America increasingly became the scapegoat "for everything that had gone wrong in modern Europe."[12]

The rise of Nazism and World War II contributed much to change this traditional reservoir of images dramatically. Adolf Hitler's highly modern propaganda machine (radio and film) reinforced traditional negative prejudices about the United States as a racial melting pot internally divided under the direction of incompetent leaders. Gerhard Weinberg has demonstrated how Hitler's originally positive image of the United States changed towards a highly critical one in the course of the 1930s. Hitler, arguably the most prominent Austrian of the 20th century, initially saw the U.S. as a vigorous nation based on its massive German immigration. The turbulent impact of the Great Depression changed all that. Now Hitler, according to Weinberg, "combined his negative view of the racial melting pot, in which the scum naturally floated to the top, with his antipathy for American cultural influences as these were reflected in the developments of Weimar Germany that he most detested." In spite of the changing fortunes of Nazi Germany during the war, Hitler's negative view of the U.S. remained constant until his suicide in the Berlin bunker. Weinberg concludes: "This was a perception of the United States which combined the potential strength and danger with the actuality of weakness and disarray."[13] These are the images that Nazi propaganda bombarded the Germans (including Austrians) with throughout the war.

## II. The Occupation (1945-1955)

For Austrians, the American occupation above all came with plenty of food and economic aid. The memory of private American charity and benevolence through CARE packages is still alive among the Austrian wartime generation. Austria received one of the highest ratios of per capita aid in all of postwar Western Europe. Half a billion dollars in food aid between 1945 and 1948, one billion dollars in Marshall Plan aid from 1948 to 1952, and tens of millions of Marshall Plan induced counterpart funds after 1952, as well as some 100 million dollars in military aid after 1955.[14]

The Marshall Plan was sold with considerable fanfare about American generosity and peacefulness to the local population. Marshall Plan propaganda dispersed through films and traveling exhibits had a sharp anti-communist edge to it, too. This was part of the Cold War propaganda wars unleashed after the East-West conflict erupted after 1947. Hans-Jürgen Schröder has studied these ad campaigns for and against the Marshall Plan in Germany (and only partially for Austria).[15] It also needs to be added that dependency on American aid also caused resentment in Europe, as the State Department Bureau of European Affairs noted: "There is much evidence that the Europeans find continued United States economic aid psychologically galling."[16] Delivery of military aid was less disturbing since it contributed to the common defense. Even though the details of American defense efforts in Austria against Communist subversion were kept secret, the general trend of Western rearmament produced a steady stream of Communist press attacks against it in Austria and elsewhere.[17]

One of the most important *lacunae* in the scholarship of image transfers and the transformation of Austrian mental elite perceptions of America is a missing study of the numerous visitors programs to the United States throughout the Cold War. During these years some 7,000 mostly young Austrians visited the U.S. for extended periods of stay through programs such as the State Department's young visitors program, expert study tours financed through the Marshall Plan, the Fulbright student and faculty exchanges, as well as high school exchanges such as the American Field Service. Most returned with positive views about American society.[18]

Oliver Schmidt has provided us with a model study of analyzing 12,000 German visitors to the U.S. in the years 1945-1961 and the impact of these visits on shaping "democratic elites" and fostering "Atlanticism." Schmidt has also provided us with a first scholarly analysis of the vast benefits of the Salzburg Seminar for the launching of the American Studies movement in postwar Europe.[19] Volker Berghahn even more recently provided us with a fascinating study of the important work of the large philanthropic foundations in financing the "Congress of Cultural Freedom" and fighting the cultural and intellectual Cold Wars in Europe.[20] It is certainly true that in my personal case half-baked and stereotypical Karl May novels, Hollywood films and television images of America, stemming from a 1960s Austrian Catholic *Gymnasium* socialization, were thoroughly corrected during a post-*Matura* AFS year in California in 1972/73.[21]

The reservoir of Austrian anti-American stereotypes comes to light most clearly in Ingrid Bauer's oral history testimonies from the American zone in Salzburg. Today this is hard to believe, but in 1952 the U.S. Army spent 28.7 million dollars in Salzburg, which amounted to more revenue than Salzburg made from tourism that year. The free-spending American GI's impressed the Salzburgers, and above all the youngsters and the *Fräuleins* looking for suitable partners. The traditional images of both American wealth and "uncultured" backwardness kicked in as both were very freely displayed by the GIs. The El Dorado of American Army PX stores spilled out into the streets, the black market, and the imagination of Salzburgers – Jeans, nylons, chewing gum, Coca-cola, and all kinds of canned food for a hungry population. Amerika Houses, bookmobiles, the *Kurier* and Red-White-Red radio provided all kinds of "food" for physically and mentally starved souls from classic novels, movies, magazines, jazz and, in the 1950s, rock 'n' roll. American wealth was also displayed in a highly mobile U.S. Army where every GI seemed to be able to afford a car. The Austrian highbrow stereotype of the lowbrow American "hillbillies" was pervasive. The GIs were not expected to know Goethe or even Shakespeare: "*Kulturell haben wir schon ein bisschen auf die Amerikaner heruntergeschaut, weil wir spürten, dass sie in dieser Hinsicht nicht so ganz auf unserem Niveau sind.*" When one GI whistled themes from Beethoven's Fifth Symphony, the Salzburgers were floored. Turning the *Festspielhaus* into the variety show theater "Roxy" is what was expected of these cultural barbarians. Still the young girls considered the healthy and cocky young GIs as heroes from a different planet, and the youth found the American presence as a welcome liberation from the stultifying authoritarianism and paternalism of their parents' generation.[22]

Generationally speaking, the highbrow cultural anti-Americanism of the wartime generation clashed against the receptivity towards American pop culture of the postwar baby boomers. Reinhold Wagnleitner's *Coca-Colonisation und Kalter Krieg* can also be read as a partly autobiographical treatise on his generational rebellion, which was as marked in postwar Austria as it was in Germany and elsewhere in Europe. Wagnleitner has rightly noted that American popular culture attracted the young because of its countercultural and subversive character: "The major attraction of and opposition to American popular culture for young people lies in the fact that it always contains an element of rebellion: a rebellion against the tastes of politicians, priests, the military, and teachers."[23]

One of the most fascinating yet strangest sources where Western Europe's postwar intellectual anti-Americanism surfaces is the investigation of the early Eisenhower administration about the loss of American prestige. This loss of respect for America as the Western leading power came as a result of growing U.S. political and military hegemony abroad and the anti-Communist hysteria of McCarthyism at home. The fulcrum of Washington's concern was the fact that a growing number of Europeans considered McCarthyism as an American form of fascism. The Left in Europe was beginning to equate the United States and the Soviet Union (here may lie the origins of the moral equivalence argument). Washington was very worried that the growing anti-Americanism among Socialists in Western Europe might endanger the stable coalition governments – a constant worry that they harbored for Austria too.

Eisenhower's National Security Council ordered the Psychological Strategy Board to launch a thorough study of the decline in American prestige abroad. American mission chiefs reported back to Washington that Europeans were worried about the lack of American leadership in the world, and about Washington's inflexibility vis-à-vis communism, which prolonged the Cold War; there was a pervasive fear in Europe of nuclear war and American mismanagement of nuclear strategy (later so drastically expressed in Stanley Kubrick's 1964 movie *Dr. Strangelove*). Paradoxically, Europeans also feared American disengagement from the continent; they were concerned about the Republicans returning to isolationism. The PSB report noted: "Paradoxically, many of the same people who fear a decrease in American interest in Europe also fear United States 'domination' of Europe." McCarthyism was perceived in Europe as "an acute attack of anti-Communist hysteria" and an indication of the United States and its people being "intolerant of nonconformity" and motivated by "fierce and irresponsible hatred of Communism." Europeans perceived the investigations of McCarthy's "junketeering gumshoes" Cohn and Shine into European USIS libraries as "ridiculous and childish" and reeking of congressional "star chamber" methods. The PSB conclusions were sobering: "'McCarthyism' has become synonymous with neo-fascism in European minds, and is regarded by some European leaders as Communism's greatest present asset in Europe." In a debate about the lengthy PSB report an enraged President Eisenhower strangely dismissed these evaluations about the decline of America's prestige by American mission chiefs in Europe as being generated largely by "fellow traveling" Democrats in the U.S. embassies. In other words, he blamed the messengers of bad tidings and had the PSB report locked up.[24]

These concerns of the Eisenhower administration never saw the light of day, yet they would not go away either, as reports kept coming in about the loss of American prestige. McCarthy's fall quieted the critiques of McCarthyism abroad, but not European concerns about Washington's foreign policy unilateralism and lack of consultation with NATO allies. The "projection of Nazism, dehistoricized as fascism, onto America," as Dan Diner has observed for the New Left in Germany in the 1960s, seems to have been a European response to McCarthyism by the Left already in the 1950s.[25]

Cohn's and Shine's two-day visit to Vienna was part of a whirlwind tour of investigating abuse of U.S. information programs in Europe. What they really hoped to find for Senator McCarthy was a lack of anti-Communist fervor among State Department officials in Europe. In ridiculously brief – at times only ten-minute interviews – the two experts checked into security clearances of staff in *Kurier* and radio Rot-Weiss-Rot operations. They rattled American personnel by wanting to get a "complete picture" of United States Information Service operations. They went to the Amerika House Library and checked the card catalog to see whether the books of Communist authors such as Howard Fast, Agnes Smedley, and noted African American historian W.E.B. Du Bois had been pulled from the stacks after they had been put on the State Department proscription list. They wondered why the patriotic *American Legion Monthly* and *The Freeman* were not available in Vienna. Cohn complained that "there just aren't any magazines fighting communism" in the Amerika House Library in Vienna. The local correspondent of *Time* magazine asked Cohn whether he did not regard *Time* as anti-Communist. They also went to the Soviet Library to check the card catalog and found novels by Theodore Dreiser, Jack London, Upton Sinclair and Mark Twain available for an unsuspecting Viennese readership. During a press conference a correspondent asked them whether now that Mark Twain was represented in the Soviet Library, he ought to be banned in American libraries.[26]

The Salzburg Socialist *Demokratisches Volksblatt* noted in a story entitled "'Purge' in the Amerika Haus" that all German-language authors, including Thomas Mann, Franz Werfel, Stefan Zweig, Erich-Maria Remarque and Friedrich Torberg, had been purged and were no longer available. William Hale, the Public Affairs Officer, responded that in the early years of the occupation German-language authors were made available to the Austrian readership because the Hitler regime had removed many of them from the Austrian public libraries. But now that the Austrian libraries had re-acquired most of these authors, they no longer needed to be carried in Amerika House Libraries. The American authorities were not prepared to admit that such "purges" were related to the visit of Cohn and Shine, as the Catholic weekly *Die Furche* had suspected.[27]

### III. World-War-II Historical Revisionism and Cultural Anti-Americanism by the Old Right

The hypotheses of my brief case study of elements of anti-Americanism on the mental map of the Austrian Right is empirically based on a close reading of their lead intellectual publication, *Die Aula*. It needs to be stressed, however, that their anti-communism was at all times during the Cold War more vocal than their anti-Americanism. Hitler's legacies were fully intact in their mindset. In fact, the Austrian officer Lothar

Rendulic, one of Hitler's top generals in the Balkans theater and commander of Hitler's troops in the "Ostmark" in the final days of the war, was the principal strategic expert writing in *Die Aula*. In the 1960s General Rendulic commented regularly on developments of Western strategy in general and American nuclear policy in specific. The principal anti-American sentiment that emerges in the political arena is a critique of American hegemony in the West, one much less vocal than French "Gaullism." In the economic sphere resentment of American technological savvy and business influence in Europe grew, partly inspired by the bestseller *Le Défi Américaine* by the French journalist Jean-Jacques Servan-Schreiber. Anti-Americanism was particularly poignant in the German nationalist Right in the cultural and intellectual arenas. They resented mindless and immoral "Americanism" – consumerist materialism – spread through jazz, Hollywood and television. They also fought a stubborn campaign of "historical revisionism" in the "*Kriegsschuldfrage*," trying to shift the burden of the causes of World War II away from Germany onto the shoulders of the Anglo-American powers.

Given that the Austrian Right was still strongly German nationalist, they welcomed the American defense presence in Western Europe against the "red threat." They observed American domestic politics quite closely, particularly as partisan swings might affect the "German question." Being on Europe's "frontlines," they worried about American disengagement or détente with the Soviet Union that might hurt Germany's and Western Europe's defense position.[28] They complained about the "cowardly Americans" ("*feige Amerikaner*") – a stereotype among Wehrmacht soldiers that was quite prevalent during World War II. German nationalists expected the Americans to resist militarily when the Berlin wall was built in August 1961. Berlin, for the nationalist Right, was "the symbol of the [Western] will to resist the Communist assault from the East" ("*den vom Osten her anbrandenden Kommunismus*" – a diction originating in Nazi anti-Communism).[29]

General Rendulic's critiques of American preponderance in the world were prevalent in the nationalist-conservative camp in Western Europe at the time. After the crucial NATO meeting in Athens in May 1962, Rendulic bemoaned American "hegemony" and Washington's central control over all atomic weaponry in NATO strategy. He stressed that Western Europe played a decisive role in the defense of the West and should therefore have some say in the use of tactical nuclear devices – a demand that goes back to the mid-1950s.[30] Two years later he assaulted the basic American nuclear strategy of reducing Western Europe to a mere glacis (*"Vorfeld"*) for Western defense. Since American strategy intended to defend Western Europe in the initial phase with conventional forces only, Rendulic wondered whether they were prepared to use nuclear weapons at all for the defense of Europe. A deep mistrust of American willingness "to sacrifice New York for Hamburg" is, of course, an old European reflex. Rendulic pondered the question whether the American realized that the loss of Western Europe to communism would be the "first step towards the destruction of America."[31] Rendulic's geostrategic thinking here resembles Nazi long-term visions – would Stalin follow a similar step-by-step plan for world conquest that Hitler had pursued?

Another commentator, in fact, called this fear of Europe's decline into becoming the mere glacis of America's defense, "Gaullism." No one was more concerned than General Charles De Gaulle, after all, that Europe was losing its maneuverability as a power vis-à-vis America's growing political, economic, technological and military preponderance. Servan-Schreiber's assault on "the American technological invasion," argued one observer, converted many Germans, Italians, and Dutch into the Gaullist camp[32] – surely Austrians, too.

These French chauvinist concerns increased anti-Americanism in Western Europe. Both De Gaulle's strategic departure of leaving NATO in 1966 and Servan-Schreiber's *Die amerikanische Herausforderung* contributed as much to popularize anti-Americanism on the Right as did the gradual U.S. descent into the Vietnam quagmire, sparking the charge of "American imperialism" on the Left. Servan-Schreiber's emotional description of the American technological and economic colossus invading Europe and degrading the continent to an American "franchise colony" (*"Lizenz-Kolonie"*), articulated the European inferiority complex vis-à-vis the global hegemony of the American way of life. The French Minister of Education Alain Peyrefitte poured oil into the fire by also stressing the scientific gap: "Europe is in danger of falling as far behind the United States [in the natural and engineering sciences] as the Third World is behind Europe." American universities were far ahead of

European institutions in research funds and consequently in the development of innovative technologies. Therefore young Europeans – who wanted to be on the cutting edge in the natural sciences – attended American universities and often stayed in the U.S. The specter of the "brain drain" was raising its ugly head and was debated vigorously in Austria, too.[33] Without naming Servan-Schreiber, the *Aula* was perplexed about the growing fads of anti-Americanism coming out of Paris, and worried that in the long run this could be advantageous to the Soviet Union.[34] A study is badly needed about the discourse and reception of Servan-Schreiber's book on both the Austrian Left and Right and particularly its possible impact on fanning the flames of anti-Americanism.

While on the Right the 1960s anti-Americanism got louder and louder moving from political to economic issues, in the cultural arena it was always shrill, often bordering on the hysterical. Nowhere was Hitler's legacy more pronounced than in the nationalist Right's dark fears about the influence of *"negroider Jazz"* on European civilization. Jazz amounted to little more than mere irritating noise (*"aufreizende rhythmische Geräusche"*). Its improvisation was dilettantish (*"erhebt Schlamperei zum Gesetz"*). The bodily movements it aroused were not graceful swinging but awkward shaking (*"kein Schwingen sondern ein Schütteln"*). Given that jazz was played by inherently grotesque colored musicians (*"von den von Natur aus der Grotekse zuneigenden farbigen Musikanten"*), it is small wonder that this music was melodically and harmonically *"verhackt"* and *"verzerrt."* Jazz was the revenge of the Negroes on the white men who had enslaved them – *"Rache durch Rhythmus."* Since jazz was played by the hybrid black race (*"negroide Mischrasse von Amerika"*), the ultimate danger was its undermining of the racial fiber of Europe's youth:

> Der volkstumszersetzende Einfluss, den Jazz aber auf die europäischen Völker in weitestgehendem Masse ausgeübt hat und noch ausübt, wird auch von volkskundlichen Gesichtspunkten aus betrachtet und beurteilt werden müssen, was natürlich in hohem Masse Aufgabe der zuständigen Fach- und Erziehungskreise ist bzw. sein müsste.[35]

The repertoire of German nationalist perception of jazz as "degenerate music" going back to the Nazi era was still well and alive in the 1960s.

In 1964 Dominik Schausberger from Vienna took account for *Aula*-readers of the influence of "Americanism" in Austria and Europe. He contested the assumption made by Foreign Minister Bruno Kreisky that America combined political with moral leadership in the global arena. While Schausberger took little issue with America replacing Europe's political preponderance in the world after World War II, he doubted whether a nation that had killed 200,000 civilians in Dresden in a "act of satanic malice" (*"Akt satanischer Bosheit"*), could claim even an inch of morality. Worse, the Americans were guilty of an across-the-board "moral poisoning of the soul" (*"moralische Vergiftung der Seele"*). The monstrous Hollywood films flooding Europe were full of sex and violence and appealing to the lowest instincts; they were polluting Europe's youth. People we dancing to *"Negermusik"* instead of listening to Mozart, Beethoven and German folk songs. America was undermining European morals by setting new standards of violence such as pervasive Mafia mob action and asocial youth-gang behavior. Next to this cultural assault on the European value system, America's quest for accumulating material wealth was ruining Western civilization. This American "dance around the golden calf" was now copied fanatically by Europeans in their pursuit of "economic miracles." Ultimately, this "dance" could only end in a demographic catastrophe in Europe. Young couples pursued comfort and leisure time and higher incomes instead of bearing children. Every year millions of unborn children were killed, according to Schausberger. Instead, foreigners were brought into the land to do the hard work. Following in the footsteps of the satanic American pursuit of "mammon", concluded this *Aula* diatribe, could only end in biological death and suicide for European civilization.[36]

These dark ruminations were in the tradition of the pre-war Spenglerian mood of the decline of the West (*"Untergang des Abendlandes"*) and the attacks on "catastrophic" American civilization by the likes of Martin Heidegger. This "revolutionary conservatism," or "reactionary modernism," also influenced the Nazis' view of the United States.[37] Digging for American war crimes (the bombing of Dresden) and the pursuit of comfort and wealth with its genocidal outcome for the West established a moral equivalency between the Third Reich and the United States. The projection of genocidal policies onto the United States – so prevalent in Germany in the Vietnam era – was a strategy to reduce the historical culpability of Germany,[38] and by extension also of the former Austrian Nazis. What we find in the sedimentation of German nationalist layers of thought on America is a continuum from rational critiques of strategy in the political arena to irrational anti-American ranting and raving in the cultural arena. Paul Hollander's distinction between just critiques of American policies vis-à-vis an irrational scapegoating for all the ills of modernization and the alienation from modern society being blamed on America is a helpful one to understand anti-Americanism and its deeper sources in Europe in general, and Austria in particular.[39]

In German nationalist thinking on the Right the deep origins of the *"Kriegsschuldfrage"* go back to Woodrow Wilson's "betrayal" of Germany in the late months of World War I and his "unjust Versailles dictate." The Germans naively trusted Wilson who pressured them into a premature armistice. Wilson's infamous Fourteen Points formed the blueprint for his peace settlement; they turned out to be deceptive. Wilson's plan was not self-determination *for* but *against* all Germans in Central Europe. His conduct during the "dictate" at Versailles was as revanchist as that of Clemenceau and Lloyd George. The Fourteen Points, then, were not a program for peace and justice but "psychological warfare" to deceive the Germans, in this German nationalist view. Sigmund Freud and William C. Bullitt were on the mark in their psychological portrait of Wilson – he was a "nutcase" for the mental hospital. The true reason for American intervention in World War I was that the American "dollar imperialism" needed to defeat the Germans in order to control the continent and inherit power over the Europeans.[40] The nationalist Right charged that Wilson's puritanical ambition to become the liberator of the small nations directly produced the "first" division of Germany and ultimately presented half of Europe to Stalin due to the betrayal of his own peace program based on the Fourteen Points.[41]

World War II originated for the same reasons – the British and the Americans refused to tolerate a European continent with German preponderance. When Germany after World War I wanted to opt out of a gold-based international currency system, the U.S. was forced to intervene once again to preserve the global leadership of its "dollar imperialism."[42]

Whenever books by Anglo-American authors contested the "*Alleinschuld*" of Germany and put the blame on the United Kingdom and the United States for unleashing the war, the *Aula* eagerly joined the debate. Like David Irwin more recently, in the mid-1960s the American historian David L. Hoggan was lionized by the nationalist Right for his "painstaking research." Hoggan blamed the British Tories for starting the war and pulling the French in too. According to this view, Churchill allegedly told the German ambassador in 1937: "If Germany will get to be too strong, it will be crushed again." However, the "*Greuelpropaganda*" of the British and German mainstream press and even secret service interventions, charged the *Aula*, unleashed "grotesque campaigns" ["*Hetze*"] against people like Hoggan. Self-inflicted "German guilt propaganda campaign" reached psychopathic proportions, lamented the *Aula*, and undermined the basis for a future German peace treaty.[43]

Allied war crimes committed in the air war against Germany were another prominent recurring theme in the historical revisionism of the nationalist Right. When Sir Charles Webster's and Noble Frankland's four-volume work on the strategic air offensive against Germany appeared in 1961, the *Aula* gleefully pounced on it. Here the British admitted that their terror bombing of the German civilian population had failed since it never broke the German will to fight on. The veil of lies ("*Lügenschleier*") of Britain's own "unmastered past" was torn down. Churchill was fully exposed as the "murderer of Dresden." Now the question needed to be asked when the Allies would be put on trial for "genocide and war crimes" in Katyn, Hiroshima, Nagasaki, Berlin and Dresden, and for the expulsion and liquidation of millions of Germans from Eastern Europe.[44]

The ultimate goal of Churchill's terror bombing and Roosevelt's Morgenthau Plan had been to fatally weaken Germany. Postwar denazification and the blizzard of lies about German war guilt continued this campaign of keeping Germany weak and not permitting any new self-confidence to emerge. Denazification pursued the sinister strategy of dividing the people into "good" and "bad" Germans, which was nothing less than the old Roman strategy first enunciated by Tacitus to let the Germans "disembowel" each other ("*selbstzerfleischen*"); the

Germans then and now continued this tradition of self-hate so its enemies could sleep peacefully.[45]

For the 60th anniversary of Hitler's invasion of Poland in 1999, the *Aula* once again revived the issues of Roosevelt's and Churchill's confrontational policies that had unleashed World War II. This time the old canards were complemented by new revisionist evidence from Soviet archives alleging that Hitler attacked the Soviet Union in order to preempt an attack planned by Stalin.[46] Jörg Haider's moral equivalency argument of denouncing both Stalin and Churchill as war criminals in the same breath has, we can see, very deep roots in the thinking of the German nationalist Right.

The historical revisionism of the nationalist Right in Germany and Austria, shifting the blame for World War II into the Allied camp, has a clear anti-American and anti-British edge to it. This anti-Americanism is peculiar to the German nationalist-conservative Right – and the German nationalists in Austria clearly share this mentality with their German brethren. Constantly "refighting" the outcome of World War II and placing the responsibility for the outbreak of the war and the crimes committed on the Western allies too, is a form of anti-Americanism that seems unique to those who lost the war in Central Europe.

## IV. The American/European Cross-Fertilization of Anti-Americanism in the New Left (1955-1968)

The worldwide rebellious youth movements of the 1960s have been researched rather well for most of Europe and the United States, but are remarkably "under"-searched in Austria.[47] This may partly be due to the fact that the "1968ers" rebellion was less radical and pervasive in Austria than elsewhere in Western Europe. The youthful rebels had many political and cultural causes. Above all they protested against the stultifying lifestyles of their authoritarian and paternalistic parents' generation – in Austria often represented by "Nazi" fathers, strict teachers, and the prevailing Catholic milieu of stern village priests.

Again we encounter the inherent paradox and deep-seated ambivalence towards all things American.[48] While the European youngsters rebelled against the imperialism and racism of the American government, they were at the same time culturally fully Americanized and attuned to counter-cultural lifestyles; in their subversive political manifestations they copied their American counterparts. This reminds us of the crucial point that Paul Hollander has made – most anti-Americanism in the world is inspired by the long critical tradition of American views about the United States.[49] There is a long tradition of cross-fertilization between American and European critiques of the American experiment. In the 1960s these interactions simply seem to have intensified due not least to the fact that the information age and the ease and cheapness of modern travel made such interactions more facile and much faster in the "global village." Neutralist Austrians, sitting on the fence in the East-West conflict, did not fully participate in these trends; often they adopted milder versions imported with a time lag from West Germany.[50] When Dan Diner postulates that the German "stance towards America is an indicator for the westernization of Germany,"[51] we might adapt this for Austria by noting that Austria's stance vis-à-vis America and West Germany is an indicator for its westernization. So many of Austria's imports from America came by way of West German mediation.

The political spectrum on the Left in Austria in the 1960s holds some surprises. The Communists were predictable in their knee-jerk anti-Americanism. Their charge of American "imperialism" and "monopoly capitalism" was the stock-in-trade of communist propaganda throughout the Cold War. The Socialist Old Left was remarkably free of anti-Americanism. The New Left acted rather tame in Austria during 1968 and its aftermath.

The far-left Communists did not have a voice of their own but followed the propaganda line of the Kremlin. Hence the lurid headlines and the contents of the Communist *Volksstimme* are not remarkable. This daily reported the details of the heroic "liberation struggle" of the North Vietnamese People's Republic against the "imperialist Americans" faithfully according to the party line. The Central Committee followed the successes and the heroism of the South Vietnamese liberation front during the Tet offensive with great admiration. "Naked American aggression" was bankrupt, yet the Americans lied to the world and escalated the war. The Communists demanded that neutral Austria join the rest of the world in calling for an end both to the bombing campaign and the war of extermination. The Communists joined public protests against the "barbarian imperialist war" and expressed their "solidarity" with the Vietnamese liberation struggle. Communist speakers brandished the Austrian bourgeois press for not reporting the full extent of brutal American crimes committed against the civilian population ("*Greuel*" is the code word so prominent in 20th-century political propaganda). The *Volksstimme*'s huge banner headlines trumpeted "US-Massacres among Civilians" and reported the destruction of entire cities by the U.S. armed forces. The Communist daily asserted the Americans planned to deploy tactical nuclear weapons in Vietnam and immediately launched a campaign against this "atomic lunacy." The *Volksstimme* gave a lot of attention to the American and European anti-war movement and featured an interview with Jean-Paul Sartre, the prominent French critic of the Vietnam war and American imperialism. "The International Tribunal against American War Crimes in Vietnam" was also prominently featured. Maybe the most bizarre assertion was that the old SS hero Otto Skorzeny was an adviser for the Americans in Vietnam.[52]

A case study of the Socialists' lead programmatic journal *Die Zukunft* for the late 1960s reveals a remarkably mild view of the United States in the mainstream SPÖ. American domestic and foreign policy were carefully reported by knowledgeable correspondents like Otto Leichter in New York and editor Karl Czernetz in Vienna. Leichter interpreted Johnson's victory against the "rightwing extremist" Nelson Rockefeller, who was willing to leave the decision about the use of nuclear weapons in the hands of the generals, as a victory against a recurrence of McCarthyism.[53] The cultural perceptions of the U.S. could not be more different than those of the Austrian Old Right and the Old Left. While the *Aula* lamented that the violence, sex and trash in Hollywood movies were leading to the demise of Western civilization, the *Zukunft* featured a long review of the "Wild West" movies and their archetypal celebration of the American frontier spirit and its romantic way of life.[54]

If critiques were voiced against America and U.S. foreign policy it usually came in the guise of American critics such as Senator William Fulbright, who was seen as an American "*Linker.*" In a lead article about the "crisis of world politics" in 1968, Karl Czernetz cited *New*

*York Times* columnist C. L. Sulzberger extensively, who lambasted the U.S. as the "weakest superpower in history." America was internally deeply divided by the "race question" and the growing resistance against its playing global policeman. America was "a broken giant," asserted Sulzberger, and was becoming a danger to the world.[55] The contradictions of the "negro question" were discussed and the growing internal divisions and radicalization of the black movement stressed.[56] American "monopoly capitalism" was analyzed through the prism of a long book review of the American Marxist economists Paul A. Baran and Paul Sweezy. The severe Cold War export controls imposed by the U.S. on shipments of strategic goods to Eastern Europe, which were so detrimental to European interests, were analyzed by a Swedish observer.[57] The "arrogance of American power" was touched upon by reviewing Senator Fulbright's book of the same title and "American neo-imperialism" in a long summary of Servan-Schreiber's *Le Défi Américaine*.[58] Karl Ausch concluded his review of Servan-Schreiber by noting how far removed Austria was from the dynamism of the world economy analyzed in the French bestseller. Rather than criticizing Servan-Schreiber he took the hidebound spirit in the Austrian economy to task. In Austria "economic problems were solved by postponing decisions." Austria was the corporatist land where economic problems were endlessly discussed but not solved (*"das Land der Zünftler und Phäaken, in dem wirtschaftliche Problem nicht gelöst, sondern zerredet werden"*).[59]

Was "1968" in Austria only a "tame revolution" that lasted for a mere "hot fifteen minutes"?[60] New Left ideas and lifestyles were an American phenomenon adopted by the Austrian baby-boomer generation. It was a rebellion against the stultifying authority of the wartime generation by adopting subversive American counter-cultural habits of the heart and a full immersion in American popular culture.[61] It has been noted above that the process of the Americanization of the Austrian youth started in the 1950s. In the 1960s the "movement cultures" of these societal upheavals associated with the lifestyle rebellions, civil rights revolution, the Vietnam peace movement (and the Western exploitation of the Third World), and university reforms turned more radical in the United States, Germany and France.[62] In Austria the notorious "orgy" in lecture hall I of the University of Vienna was indeed a short-lived affair; moreover, the authorities came down hard on such radical protests. A Committee on Indochina was formed by the younger left wing of the SPÖ, protesting the Vietnam War. There was a milder version of student unrest, heated debates about the antiauthoritarian Summerhill model of education pioneered in England, some infatuation with romantic revolutionary movements in the Third World, as well as considerable attraction to Latin American liberation theology as a form of protest against the hidebound Austrian Catholic church. The most intellectual of the baby-boomers in the 1960s were much more concerned with their fathers' unmastered Nazi past than coming to terms with the institution of slavery in the American civil rights movement. Anti-fascism arguably had a higher priority for the New Left in Austria than anti-Americanism, even though that may have started to change in the 1970s.[63]

If some events on American campuses and in West Germany and France had revolutionary character, in Austria it all seemed to amount to the youngsters' simmering resentment against all entrenched reactionary systems, particularly in the social and cultural arenas. The pot never boiled over like in Berkeley, Berlin or Paris. Alexandra Friedrich has shown that Austrian research on the 1960s and 1968, particularly in a comparative context, is still far behind Western Europe.[64] But that also may have to do with the fact that 1968 in Austria happened to be remarkable sedate when compared with other Western European countries. Not being part of the NATO alliance system probably meant less pressure from Washington on Vienna to tow the line in the Vietnam conflict.

The *"ausgebliebene Revolution"* – the revolt that did not happen – in Austria during the 1960s is a fact. Austria was different and maybe a *Sonderfall* again. The legacies of the Nazi era radiated deeply into the postwar Austrian mentality and not only in conservative circles. In the art scene, the 1950s still experienced a restoration of pre-war paradigms. Robert Fleck has shown how artists like Friedensreich Hundertwasser and Arnulf Rainer were socialized in the Nazi era and did not fully encounter the liberating exhilaration of modern art until the 1960s. We must not forget that the restorative climate in traditional high-brow culture was guided by hidebound ÖVP ministers of education with "Austro-Fascist" pasts such as Heinrich Drimmel.[65] Only with time lags did the rebellious movement cultures of the 1960s assert themselves during the later 1970s. The *"Arena-Bewegung"* and the environmental protests in Zwentendorf and Hainburg, however, were home grown and had little to do with American models.[66]

West German anti-nuclear protests were much stronger and more widespread than Austrian ones.[67] I doubt whether Dan Diner's assertion of a West German "anti-imperialist revisionism from the left-wing" holds true for Austria. Diner sees the 1970s representing "the peak of anti-imperialism," blaming the United States "for all conceivable atrocities." For one, Austria did not have pacifist anti-NATO/anti-American icons like writer Hans Magnus Enzensberger and "peace researchers" like Alfred Mechtersheimer.[68] After all, the "double-track" decision stationed new medium range nuclear missiles on West German and not on Austrian soil, where an entrenched neutralism left many oblivious to the nuclear danger of the Cold War world and its complex discourses. While the British, American and West German anti-nuclear weapons protest of the 1980s had a heated anti-American edge to it – in West Germany the need of stationing American troops was widely questioned for the first time – in Austria anti-nuclear protests concentrated on civilian nuclear power plants (Zwentendorf, and Wackersdorf in Bavaria); such protests were not inherently anti-American. The serious scholarly study of these cultural changes in the 1970s and 1980s has hardly begun.[69] Growing Austrian anti-Ameri-canism as a result of American interventionism in the 1990s (Balkans crises) and President George W. Bush's new strategy of preemption in the wake of the 9/11 attacks will also have to demand the future attention of historians.[70]

## V. Conclusion: The Upsurge of Anti-Americanism after the End of the Cold War

The larger analytical problem with all critiques of America, "Americanism", and "Americanization" – or the "globalization" paradigm today – is this: where exactly is the border line where a just and rational critique of America quietly slips over into the irrational arena of anti-Americanism.[71] Or as critics on the Left and Right put it in today's context – how can one criticize Bush's foreign policies without being hit with the bludgeon of anti-americanism. The Indian novelist and critic of American globalist capitalism Arundhati Roy has recently observed: "Anti-Americanism is in the process of being consecrated into an ideology." She complains that "[t]he term is usually used by the American establishment to discredit and, not falsely – but shall we say inaccurately – define its critics." Particularly after the terrorist attacks of 9/11, American "bruised national pride" brands everyone anti-American whose arguments they do not want to hear. Roy concludes: "This sly conflation of America's music, literature, the breathtaking physical beauty of the land, the ordinary pleasures of ordinary people with criticism of the U.S. government's foreign policy is a deliberate and extremely effective strategy."[72]

On the one hand, American capitalism drives the globalist world system today and can be analyzed and criticized as a model of a political economy that is enormously greedy and coldly unmindful of the social problems produced in its wake. On the other hand, the anti-globalization crusaders in Davos, Seattle, Salzburg, Genoa, or Washington, with their vocal protests against share-holder inspired "turbo capitalism" and American-dominated international institutions (World Bank, IMF, World Economic Forum), carry an inherently anti-American message.[73] Yale Law School professor Amy Chua has noted the strange irony that the very American idea of spreading free markets and democracy globally, is at the same time sparking global anti-Americanism today: "Throughout the world, global markets are bitterly perceived as reinforcing American wealth and dominance." Chua adds: "At the same time, global populist and democratic movements give strength, legitimacy, and voice to the impoverished, frustrated, excluded masses of the world—in other words, precisely the people most susceptible to anti-American demagoguery." This world-wide "anger of the damned" against the forces of globalization will haunt Europe and America for years to come.[74]

The universal resentment of American post-Cold War "hyper power" – American hegemonic predominance in the world – has generated enormous reservoirs of anti-Americanism in Austria and around the world. This time around, however, it is not only located on the margins of the political spectrum.[75] Coupled with Austria's unsettled geopolitical position after the end of the Cold War, the realignments of world politics after 1989 have produced inchoate fears among Austrians about the future of their dearly-held neutral status and neutralist identity. Whenever American – or United Nations-backed – interventions occurred in recent years (Gulf War 1991, Bosnia 1994ff., Kosovo 1999, and now Iraq), Austrian critiques of American militarism have been coupled with domestic partisan political infighting over Austria's neutral status. The pacifist Green Party and its knee-jerk anti-militarism is inherently anti-American.[76] Surprisingly, the adherence within the SPÖ to Austria's status of neutrality is partly populist (ca. 70 percent of Austrians have persistently been pro-neutrality and anti-NATO in the 1990s), and partly 1960s New Left anti-militarist/anti-American.

In the 1990s Anti-Americanism began to prosper in the Old and the New Left. Günter Nenning's *Profil* columns during the Gulf War are paragons of unalloyed anti-Americanism. Punishing Saddam Hussein's invasion of Kuwait, in the mind of old Leftist-turned-populist Nenning, was a mixture of "justice, egoism and hypocrisy" (*"Gerechtigkeit, Egoismus und Heuchelei"*). The American pretense that they were fighting against naked aggression and for Kuwait's independence, showed the "typical thin veneer of a moralistic cover of the crusaders" (*"Das moralische Mäntelchen ist so dünn wie bei Kreuzzüglern fast immer"*). Two weeks before the 1991 Gulf War started in mid-January, Nenning predicted a *"Supervietnam"* for George Bush: *"George Bush wird eingehen, und zwar als grösster Flop der jüngsten Weltgeschichte in diese."*[77] Nenning never ate his words. Neither did other Left journalistic accounts of Reagan's foreign policy in Latin America in the 1980s or of America in the 1990s, such as the journalist Harald Irnberger's, or the novelist-turned-America-observer Josef Haslinger's.[78] The critique of George W. Bush's post-9/11 foreign policy of "preemptive interventionism" in general and its implementation in the war against Iraq reached across the political spectrum in Austria and has further fanned the red-hot flames of anti-Americanism; it demands careful study.[79]

This Austrian geopolitical neutralism, particularly strong amongst the "greenish" younger generation, is paralleled by an even more inchoate cultural anti-Americanism. All forms of what could be termed the "franchise imperialism" of the global American "turbo capitalism" of the 1990s have met a growing wave of anti-globalization critiques.

The triumph of American-style fast food culture in a more mobile and stressed-out Austrian population – increasingly also dominated by two working-parents households – has produced predictable reactions against the uniformity of "McDonaldization" and more recently the "Starbucksization" of Austria. You can always count on the knee-jerk reactions of old leftists like Günter Nenning raising the bogey of modernization as Americanization: "This melting down and stamping into uniformity – this McDonaldization – all eating and drinking the same (oh, what a state of prosperity and welfare!) – this is not the 'multicultural society' but inhumanity itself, utterly desolate."[80] Americans do wonder "why they hate us."[81] But they hardly would agree with Immanuel Wallerstein that the "Pax Americana" is over.[82] The demise of American hegemony in the world is wishful thinking by old leftists rather than reflecting the status of real American power in the world today.

Austrian anti-Americanism today is hardly unique. Swedish journalist Herbert Soderstrom's assessment for Sweden rings true for Austria as well: "I have tried to find some critique of the United States that is uniquely Swedish, but I have not found a single opinion, a single nuance that has not already been expressed by American critics."[83] Maybe the "post-fascist" climate of Austria in the 1950s and 1960s and the specific critiques of America produced by the nationalist-conservative Right come closest to a specific Austrian version of anti-Americanism. It may be different from the rest of Europe but hardly from the dark views of America in the West German nationalist Right.

**Notes**

For their commentaries and critiques of this paper I would like to thank Reinhold Wagnleitner, Berndt Ostendorf, David Ellwood and Andy Markovits. Michael Draxlbauer's and Thomas Fröschl's editing of the paper has much improved it.

[1] Roger Garaudy, "What Is Anti-Americanism?," unpublished paper.
[2] Berndt Ostendorf, "Americanization and Anti-Americanism in the Age of Globalization," unpublished lecture.
[3] Paul Hollander, *Anti-Americanism: Irrational & Rational* (New Brunswick, NJ: Transaction, 1995) xlv ff., 387, and *passim*.

[4] For the complete and very rich list of his publications in the Americanization field over the past twenty years see Reinhold Wagnleitner, "'No Commodity Is Quite So Strange As This Thing Called Cultural Exchange': The Foreign Politics of American Pop Culture Hegemony," *Amerikastudien/American Studies* 46.3 (2001): 443-70 (bibliography 468-70).

[5] David Elwood, *Anti-Americanism in Western Europe: A Comparative Perspective* (Occasional Paper European Studies Seminar Series #3), The Johns Hopkins University Bologna Center, April 1999. The celebrated studies are, of course, Reinhold Wagnleitner, *Coca-Colonisation und Kalter Krieg: Die Kulturmission der USA in Österreich nach dem Zweiten Weltkrieg* (Wien: Verlag für Gesellschaftskritik 1991), published in English as *Coca-Colonization and Cold War: The Cultural Mission of the United States in Austria after the Second World War*, trans. Diana M. Wolf (Chapel Hill: U of North Carolina P, 1994), and Richard Kuisel, *Seducing the French: The Dilemma of Americanization* (Berkeley: U of California P, 1993).

[6] Justin Stagl, Ulrich Graf Arco-Zinneberg, Verena Winiwarter, and Georg Rigele, "Eine Reise um die Erde.... Adelige Weltanschauung und Naturbild um 1900. 'Das Tagebuch meiner Reise um die Erde 1892-1993' von Erzherzog Franz Ferdinand," unpublished research report, Vienna 1999.

[7] Helmut Lackner, "Travel Accounts from the U.S. and Their Influence on Taylorism, Fordism and Productivity in Austria," *The Americanization of Austria in the Twentieth Century* (Contemporary Austria Studies, vol. 12), ed. Günter Bischof and Anton Pelinka (New Brunswick, NJ: Transaction, 2004) [forthcoming]. For the German response, see Philipp Gassert, "Nationalsozialismus, Amerikanismus, Technologie: Zur Kritik der amerikanischen Moderne im Dritten Reich," *Technologie und Kultur: Europas Blick auf Amerika vom 18. bis zum 20. Jahrhundert*, ed. Michael Wala and Ursula Lehmkuhl (Cologne: Böhlau, 2000) 148-72.

[8] The classic study of the "Americanization" of Europe after World War I is Frank Costigliola's *Awkward Dominion: American Political, Economic and Cultural Relations with Europe, 1919-1933* (Ithaca, NY: Cornell UP, 1984).

[9] The best introduction to these older images is the magisterial study by C. Van Woodward, *The Old World's New World* (New York: Oxford UP, 1991); see also Jan W. Schulte Nordholt, "Anti-Americanism in European Culture: Its Early Manifestations," *Anti-Americanism in Europe*, ed. Rob Kroes and Maarten van Rossem (Amsterdam: Free UP, 1986) 7-19, Thomas Fröschl, "Antiamerikanismus in Europa und Lateinamerika. Sieben historische Dimensionen," *Atlantische Geschichte* (= Wiener Zeitschrift zur Geschichte der Neuzeit, 3.Jg., Heft 2), ed. Thomas Fröschl (Innsbruck: StudienVerlag 2003): 82-97, and Simon Schama, "The Unloved American. Two Centuries of

Alienating Europe," *The New Yorker*, March 10, 2003, 34-39; for German projections see *The German-American Encounter. Conflict and Cooperation between Two Cultures 1800-2000*, ed. Frank Trommler and Elliott Shore (New York: Berghahn, 2001); Dan Diner, *America in the Eyes of Germans: An Essay on Anti-Americanism*, trans. Allison Brown and with an introduction by Sander L. Gilman (Princeton: Marcus Wiener, 1996) 1-103; see also Wagnleitner's fine summary of this imagology, *Coca-Colonisation* 9-56; there are also useful essays on Austrian images of America in *Nordamerikastudien: Historische und literaturwissenschaftliche Forschungen aus österreichischen Universitäten zu den Vereinigten Staaten und Kanada* (Wiener Beitrage zur Geschichte der Neuzeit, vol. 24), ed. Thomas Fröschl, Margarete Grandner, and Brigitta Bader-Zaar (Vienna: Verlag für Geschichte und Politik, 2000).

[10] Austrian prejudice against the United States is one of Wagnleitner's recurring themes, see *Coca-Colonisation* 45, 49, 55.

[11] Marcus Cunliffe, "The Anatomy of Anti-Americanism," *Anti-Americanism*, ed. Kroes and Van Rossem 20-36.

[12] Richard Pells, *Not Like US: How Europeans Have Loved, Hated, and Transformed American Culture since World War II* (New York: Basic Books, 1997) 160, 162.

[13] Gerhard Weinberg's path-breaking essay "Hitler's Image of the United States" first appeared in the *American Historical Review* 69.4 (July 1964): 1006-21, and was reprinted in his *World War II in the Balance: Behind the Scenes of World War II* (Hanover: U of New England P, 1981) 53-74. The quotations in my text are from Weinberg's summary of this essay in the next chapter in this volume, "Germany's Declaration of War on the United States: A New Look," 75ff.

[14] For the exact numbers on American aid to Austria and Marshall Plan per-capita distributions, see the tables in Günter Bischof, *Austria in the First Cold War 1945-55: The Leverage of the Weak* (Basingstoke: Macmillan, 1999) 102; for details on macro- and microeconomic benefits to Austria, see *The Marshall Plan in Austria*, ed. Günter Bischof, Anton Pelinka, and Dieter Stiefel (*Contemporary Austrian Studies*, vol. 8) (New Brunswick, NJ: Transaction, 2000).

[15] Hans-Jürgen Schröder, "Marshall-Plan-Werbung in Österreich und West-Deutschland," *80 Dollar: 50 Jahre ERP-Fonds und Marshall-Plan in Österreich 1948-1998*, ed. Dieter Stiefel and Günter Bischof (Vienna: Ueberreuter, 1999) 315-42 (see particularly the reprint of posters between pp. 324 and 325).

[16] Merchant to Dulles, August 24, 1953, with attached Draft Memorandum Prepared in the Bureau of European Affairs, in: U.S. Department of State, ed., *Foreign Relations of the United States 1952-1954*, vol. I/Part II: *General:*

*Economic and Political Matters* (Washington, D.C.: Government Printing Office 1983) 1475 [*FRUS*].

[17] Günter Bischof, "'Austria looks to the West': Kommunistische Putschgefahr, geheime Wiederbewaffnung und Westorientierung am Anfang der fünfziger Jahre," *Österreich in den Fünfzigern*, ed. Thomas Albrich, Klaus Eisterer, Michael Gehler, and Rolf Steininger (Innsbruck: Studienverlag 1995) 183-210; Christian Stifter, *Die Wiederaufrüstung in Österreich: Die geheime Remilitarisierung der westlichen Besatzungszonen 1945-1955* (Innsbruck: Studienverlag, 1997).

[18] I have traced some of these visitors programs in greater detail in "Two Sides of the Medal. The Americanization of Austria and Austrian Anti-Americanism," paper delivered at the conference "American Culture in Europe. Americanisation & Anti-Americanism since 1945," The Rothermere American Institute, University of Oxford, September 2003.

[19] Oliver M. A. Schmidt, "A Civil Empire by Co-optation: German-American Exchange Programs as Cultural Diplomacy, 1945-1961," diss., Harvard U; idem, "No Innocents Abroad: The Salzburg Impetus and American Studies in Europe," *"Here, There and Everywhere": The Foreign Politics of American Popular Culture*, ed. Reinhold Wagnleitner and Elaine Tyler May (Hanover, NH: U of New England P, 2000) 64-79.

[20] Volker R. Berghahn, *American and the Intellectual Cold Wars in Europe* (Princeton: Princeton UP, 2001).

[21] For a brief description of my personal experience, see Günter Bischof, "AFS and the Making of an Austrian Americanist," *Intercultura* (May 1999) 30.

[22] Ingrid Bauer, et al., *Welcome Ami Go Home: Die amerikanische Besatzung in Salzburg 1945-1955. Erinnerungslandschaften aus einem Oral-History Projekt* (Salzburg: Anton Pustet Verlag, 1998) 207-81 (citations 214ff., 272ff.); see also Reinhold Wagnleitner's brief sketch outlining many of these themes, "Der kulturelle Einfluss der US-Besatzung," *Befreit und Besetzt: Stadt Salzburg 1945-1955*, ed. Erich Marx (Salzburg: Verlag Anton Pustet, 1996) 137-51.

[23] Wagnleitner, "No Commodity Is Quite So Strange," 447.

[24] The full documentation of the debate about the decline of American prestige abroad is in *FRUS 1952-1954*, I/2, 1458-1556 (the State Department draft memorandum and the PSB report of September 11, 1953, are 1469-1527, the paradox in the Europeans' position is noted on p. 1475). I have summarized this debate in "The Politics of Anti-Communism in the Executive Branch During the Early Cold War: Truman, Eisenhower and McCarthy(ism)," *Anti-Communism and McCarthyism in the United States (1946-1954): Essays on the*

*Politics and Culture of the Cold War*, ed. André Kaenel (Paris: Editions Messene, 1995) 55-77, 162-66 (appendices 2 and 3).
[25] Diner 130.
[26] See the long report on the Cohn and Shine visit by the Public Affairs Officer William Harlan Hale from the U.S. Embassy of April 20, 1953, *FRUS 1952-1954*, I/2, 1447-53. See also the Memorandum of Conversation by Ben Thibodeaux about his contentious 10-minute talk with Cohn and Shine about the USIA program in Austria and Austrian East-West trade and whether the Austrians broke trade controls concerning strategic and semi-strategic goods, Thibodeaux to Collins, April 24, 1953, Austrian Desk Files 195-54, Lot 56 D 294, Box 4, Record Group [RG] 59, National Archives and Records Administration [NARA], Suitland, MD.
[27] See James Espy to Dowling, June 18, 1953, with a translation of the article, and the attached Memorandum Hopman to Hale, explaining the American response to the "purge" article, Austrian Desk Files, 1050-54, Lot 56 D 294, Box 5, RG 59, NARA.
[28] Silesius, "Was bringt uns Kennedy," *Die Aula* 11 (March 1961): 1-3.
[29] Silesius, "Weihnachts- und Neujahrsgedanken," *Die Aula* 12 (Nov. 1961): 2-3.
[30] Lothar Rendulic, "Vormacht Amerika," *Die Aula* 12 (June 1962): 1-2. These fascinating debates over the control of the NATO nuclear arsenal caused a lot of strain in the alliance and have been given major attention in recent scholarship, see Marc Trachtenberg, *A Constructed Peace; The Making of the European Settlement 1945-1963* (Princeton: Princeton UP, 1999) 283-35, and Lawrence Freedman, *Kennedy's Wars: Berlin, Cuba, Laos, and Vietnam* (New York: Oxford UP, 2000) 45-120.
[31] Lothar Rendulic, "Europa als Vorfeld Amerikas," *Die Aula* 14 (Feb. 1964): 1.
[32] Peter Menke-Glückert, "Europas technische Zukunft," *Die Aula*, Sonderfolge (Nov. 1969): 25. Menke-Glückert was the chief of the science division of the OECD in Paris and gave this talk at the "12. Tag der Freiheitlichen Akademier." It had already been previously published with the more telling title "Der Amerikanismus und Europa" in Jan. 1969: 4-10.
[33] Ibid.
[34] "Europäische Gehirnwäsche," *Die Aula* 17 (May 1967): 12.
[35] Max Merz, "Unsere Zeit und der Jazz," *Die Aula* 14 (Oct. 1963): 6-8.
[36] Dominik Schausberger, "Bilanz des Amerikanismus," *Die Aula* 14 (April 1964): 2-5. Interestingly, the editors changed the title from "Bilanz Amerikas" to "Bilanz des Amerikanismus" since it was dealing with the spirit (*"Geist"*) the Americans were spreading globally. The Kennedy assassination and the world

championship bout between and a criminal and a draft resister [Liston vs. Clay?] only confirmed the author's analysis.

[37] James W. Caesar, *Reconstructing America. The Symbol of America in Modern Thought* (New Haven: Yale UP, 1997) 162-213.

[38] This is Dan Diner's argument, see *America in the Eyes of the Germans* 117ff.

[39] Hollander xii-xiv.

[40] "Historische Kritik," *Die Aula* 18 (Jan. 1968): 14.

[41] W. W. von Wolmar, "Erste Teilung Deutschlands," *Die Aula* 11 (May 1961): 3-4.

[42] Karl Hanss, "Der wahre Grund für die entscheidende Rolle Washingtons bei der Einkreisung und Vernichtung Deutschlands," *Die Aula* 13 (Sept. 1962): 17.

[43] Edmund Marheska, "Forschung und Propaganda zur Kriegschuldfrage," *Die Aula* 16 (Dec. 1966): 12-13. The propaganda campaign against Hoggan as a "liar, forger and charlatan" reached its zenith when he toured Germany and Austria. In Heidelberg he lectured to 800 people and in Munich to 1,000 about Allied war guilt. Both the Leopold-von-Ranke Prize and the Ulrich-von-Hutten Prize were bestowed on the young American scholar for his "fine scholarship." Only in Austria were Hoggan's lectures, scheduled by the "*freiheitliche Akademikerverbände*," prohibited by the Interior Ministry. "Communist protesters" gathered in front of the lecture hall where Hoggan was supposed to speak. See R. Sonde, "Ehrenrettung wieder Willen," *Die Aula* 14 (June 1964): 11-12.

[44] Karl Hanss, "Die Wahrheit ist auf dem Wege," *Die Aula* 12 (Nov. 1961): 9-11.

[45] Silesius, "Die Sünden wider den Geist," *Die Aula* 12 (Oct. 1961): 3-5.

[46] "Krieg und Kriegsschuldfrage," *Die Aula* 9 (Sept. 1999): 23-30. The authors of stories on September 1, 1939, Stalin's "*Überfall*," and the British role were Emil Schlee, Wolfgang Strauss, and Lothar Höbelt, respectively.

[47] Alexandra Friedrich makes this point in her fine review essay "1968 in Austria," *Austria in the European Union* (*Contemporary Austrian Studies*, vol. 10), ed. Günter Bischof, Anton Pelinka, and Michael Gehler (New Brunswick, NJ: Transaction, 2003) 324-33.

[48] See also the essays in *Transactions, Transgressions, Transformations. American Culture in Western Europe and Japan*, ed. Heide Fehrenbach and Uta G. Poiger (New York: Berghahn, 2000).

[49] Hollander 385, 400, 402, and passim.

[50] The cultural and time lags may have been a crucial element in the relative moderateness of the Austrian movement; see Rolf Schwendter, "Das Jahr 1968: War es eine kulturelle Zäsur?," *Österreich 1945-1995: Gesellschaft, Politik, Kultur*, ed. Reinhard Sieder, Heinz Steinert, and Emmerich Tálos, 2nd ed. (Vienna: Verlag für Gesellschaftskritik, 1996) 166-75.

[51] Diner 108.
[52] This evidence is gathered from a reading of the February 1968 *Volksstimme*. See, for example, the headlines "Gegen die Brutalität des US-Imperialismus," 8 Feb.; "Sie wollen A-Bomben einsetzen!, US-Massaker unter Zivilisten," 10 Feb. and 13 Feb.; the Sartre interview, "Amerika kann nicht siegen," 10 Feb.; "Man muss kein Nazi sein, um Kriegsverbrechen zu begehen," 17 Feb.; and "US-Berater Skorzeny?," 5 March.
[53] Otto Leichter, "Was veränderten die amerikanischen Wahlen?," *Die Zukunft* 11 (Jan. 1965): 6-9.
[54] Walter Hollstein, "Die Furchtlosen: Bemerkungen zum Wildwestfilm," *Die Zukunft* 13/14 (July 1965): 54-58.
[55] Karl Czernetz, "Krise der Weltpolitik," *Die Zukunft* 19 (Oct. 1967): 1-5 (Sulzberger citations 3).
[56] Herbert Dominik, "Weiße Dreieinigkeit: US-Negerpolitik zwischen Versprechen und Erfüllung," *Die Zukunft* 19 (Oct. 1967): 8-11.
[57] Peter Anders [pseudonym], "Der amerikanische Kapitalismus," *Die Zukunft* 23/24 (Dec. 1967): 12-15; Gunnar Adler-Karlson, "Des Westens heimliche Waffen," ibid., 18-21.
[58] "Amerika – kritisch betrachtet," *Die Zukunft* 10 (May 1968): 29-30; Karl Ausch, "Europa und der amerikanische Neo-Imperialismus," *Die Zukunft* 18 (Sept. 1968): 7-9.
[59] Ibid., 9.
[60] In the first serious study of 1968 in Austria, Fritz Keller entitled the book somewhat hyperbolically *Wien, Mai 1968 – Eine heiße Viertelstunde* (Vienna: Junius, 1983). See also the more recent study by Paulus Ebner and Karl Vocelka, *Die zahme Revolution: '68 und was davon blieb* (Vienna: Ueberreuter, 1998). See also the review essay by Friedrich, "1968 in Austria".
[61] Karl Stocker shows how these phenomena conquered the Austrian provinces as well, "'Wir wollen alles ganz anders machen': Die 68er Bewegung in der österreichischen Provinz. Ein Fallbeispiel," *Österreich 1945-1995*, ed. Sieder et al., 176-85.
[62] For a comparative approach, see the fine monograph by Arthur Marwick, *The Sixties. Cultural Revolution in Britain, France, Italy, and the United States, c.1958-1974* (Oxford: Oxford UP, 1998), and the collection *1968: The World Transformed*, ed. Carole Fink, Philipp Gassert, and Detlef Junker (Washington, DC: German Historical Institute and Cambridge UP, 1998).
[63] Schwendter, "Das Jahr 1968," 166-75; Friedrich, "1968 in Austria," 324-33.
[64] Friedrich, "1968 in Austria," 324-25.
[65] See Robert Fleck's insightful essay "Kunst in einer Zeit der Restauration: Die Rekonstruktion einer Szene moderner Kunst in der österreichischen Nach-

kriegszeit," *Inventur 45/55: Österreich im ersten Jahrzehnt der Zweiten Republik,* ed. Wolfgang Kos and Georg Rigele (Vienna: Sonderzahl, 1996) 441-71. For the role of reactionary Education Ministry officials in the establishment of an Austrian identity, see Peter Thaler, *The Ambivalence of Identity: The Austrian Experience of Nation-Building in a Modern Society* (West Lafayette, IN: Purdue UP, 2001) 51-109.

[66] Schwendter stresses that the caesura in Austria does not come in 1968 but in the 1970s, see "Das Jahr 1968," 167ff.

[67] Diner 136ff; Hollander 378ff.

[68] Diner 136.

[69] A fascinating introduction into the mental and ideological world of Austrians' intimate relationship with their environment is Wolfgang Kos, "Imagereservoir Landschaft: Landschaftsmoden und ideologische Gemütslagen seit 1945," *Österreich 1945-1995*, ed. Sieder et al., 599-624.

[70] For a more general analysis of American foreign policy pre- and post-9/11, see Andrew J. Bacevich, *American Empire. The Realities & Consequences of U.S. Diplomacy* (Cambridge, MA: Harvard UP, 2002); Harald Müller, *Amerika schlägt zurück. Die Weltordnung nach dem 11. September* (Frankfurt a. M.: Fischer, 2003).

[71] This is one of the principal challenges that Hollander poses for his study, giving it the new subtitle "Irrational & Rational" in the second edition, see his new introduction to *Anti-Americanism* xii.

[72] Arundhati Roy, Lannan Speech (print excerpt), 29 Sept. 2002. The old Austrian German nationalist FPÖ politician Otto Scrinzi argues similarly that after September 11 all just critiques of American hegemonic policies are dismissed as "inhumane anti-Americanism." See "Das amerikanische Jahrhundert nach dem 11. September," *Die Aula* (Sept. 2002).

[73] *New York Times* 4 Feb. 2002.

[74] Amy Chua, "A World on the Edge," *Wilson Quarterly* 26 (Autumn 2002): 62-77 (citation 67).

[75] Andrei S. Markovits, "Der Ton Macht die Musik: The Anti-American Baseline of European Public Discourse," unpublished paper delivered at the Organization of American Historians annual meeting in Memphis, TN, April 5, 2003.

[76] The Green party politician Peter Pilz has provided a classical statement of contemporary Austrian anti-Americanism. In his view, George W. Bush ("Bin Bush") is trying to take over the world with his global crusade against terrorism. See Peter Pilz, *Mit Gott gegen Alle. Amerikas Kampf um Die Weltherrschaft* (Stuttgart: DVA, 2003) 15, 37, 56, 169. For critiques of Bush's foreign policy in a similarly anti-American vein see Emmanuel Todd,

*Weltmacht USA. Ein Nachruf*, transl. Ursel Schäfer and Enrico Heinemann (Munich: Piper, 2002); Till Bastian, *55 Gründe mit den USA nicht solidarisch zu sein und schon gar nicht bedingungslos* (Munich: Pendo, 2002); Hans-Jürgen Heinrichs, *Die gekränkte Supermacht. Amerika auf der Couch* (Düsseldorf: Artemis & Winkler, 2003).

[77] Günter Nenning, "Morgen, 15. Jänner, geschieht gar nix", *Profil* 14 Jan. 1991: 57; "Warum ich mich geirrt habe," *Profil* 21 Jan. 1991: 45; "George Laokoon," *Profil* 4 Feb. 1991: 55.

[78] Harald Irnberger and Ingrit Seibert, *Zentralamerika: Opfer, Akteure, Profiteure* (Göttingen: Lamuv Verlag, 1998); Josef Haslinger, *Das Elend Amerikas: Elf Versuche über ein gelobtes Land* (Frankfurt: Fischer, 1992). To his credit, Haslinger has refined his perspective, noting that he suffers from the new (nebulous) anti-Americanism, whereas years ago he used to be part of it. In an open letter to Bush he presents himself as a "notorious friend of America" and thoughtfully analyzes the new wave of European anti-Americanism situated no longer on the margins but moving into the bourgeois center; see his ". . . könnte es sein, dass Sie so denken, sehr geehrter Mr. President?," *Der Standard*, 10 Sept. 2002.

[79] For a beginning, see Günter Bischof, "American Empire and Its Discontents. The United States and Europe Today," *Towards a European Constitution? Historical, Political and Comparative Aspects. Europe – U.S.*, ed. Michael Gehler, Günter Bischof, Rolf Steininger and Ludger Kühnhardt (Vienna: Böhlau, 2004) [forthcoming].

[80] Nenning, quoted in Ellwood, *Anti-Americanism in Western Europe* 21-22. Oddly, Nenning is presented in Ellwood as an "ex-socialist now 'left-nationalist'" German writer.

[81] Bruce Stokes, "Why do they hate us? The roots of terrorism," *Great Decisions* (2002 ed.) 9-18; see also Mark Hertsgaard, *The Shadow of the Eagle. Why America Fascinates and Infuriates the World* (New York: Farrar, Straus and Giroux, 2002); Ziauddin Sardar and Merryl Wyn Davies, *Why Do People Hate America?* (new ed. Cambridge: Icon Books, 2003).

[82] Immanuel Wallerstein, "The Eagle Has Crash Landed," *Foreign Policy* July/Aug. 2002: 60-68.

[83] Soderstrom, cited in Hollander 407.

**Part II: (Anti-)Americanisms in Some 20th-Century Literary Texts**

# Surrounding Johann Breitwieser: A Comparative Literary Study in Representation

## Vincent Kling

### 1. Phrasemaker Hilmar Kabas

The late Kurt Albert Mayer modestly introduces his two "*Miniaturen aus der Gründerzeit*" entitled *Die Wienbilder der amerikanischen Delegierten John Hay und Charles Francis Adams jr.* with a disclaimer about his ability as a historian, only to have the excellence of the ensuing work belie the disclaimer. He upholds a traditional boundary between disciplines by noting that in his own research, "Die Betrachtungsweise bleibt die des Literaturwissenschaftlers," and then removes that boundary in the very next clause, "für den alle geschriebenen Geschichten Thema der Forschung sind, egal ob nun im Englischen *story* oder *history* genannt" (7). The essay presented now, expanding on an address at a conference organized largely by Mayer, follows his lead (but falls short of his skill) in adopting both meanings of *Geschichte*, history as well as literature.

Is there ever a "what" separate from its "how"? Representation is essential to both history and literature, a bridge of discourse across their common border. No history can be independent of some historiographical approach, and any literary narrative coheres only from the viewpoint of its telling. Especially in urban settings, because they are so public, representation of events is the frame inside which those events can be understood in the first place. The city as "Erfahrungsraum" (Mattl-Wurm 175), as a concentrated locus for perceiving and processing stimuli via the media and other networks of communication, gives events or phenomena meanings that would otherwise not be articulated. Writing about fashions in clothing, for example, Sylvia Mattl-Wurm states a principle of representation that holds true for any study of cultural phenomena against the backdrop of a large city: "Urbanität lebt bekanntlich vom kreativen Umgang mit der eigenen Erscheinung" (137), as she puts it. New social accommodations to increased leisure in the early nineteenth century created effective settings for the "eigene Erscheinung"; the ballrooms, amusement parks, coffeehouses, taverns and other large gathering places for popular entertainment that began springing up in the Biedermeier age functioned not just as places of individual diversion but also as "neue großstädtische Kommunikationszentren" (Öhlinger 46). When the result of the "eigene Erscheinung," the self-presentation, causes a strong reaction—positive or negative—in these "Kommunikationszentren," then that reaction, the representation of the *Erscheinung* at large, becomes an index of the urban culture's value systems.

The present essay focuses on Vienna, but Vienna in turn, like so many other cities of Europe, has long shaped its identity in part from comparisons and contrasts with real or fancied urban conditions in the United States. The campaign phrase from a Viennese municipal election in the 1990s, "Wien darf nicht Chicago werden," attributed to Freedom Party functionary Hilmar Kabas, earned ridicule for its primitive, xenophobic scare tactics based on supposed criminal behavior among "foreign elements," but it had documentable success in swaying voters and went on to establish itself as a byword through the German-speaking world, to the chagrin of image-making tourist bureaus and city officials (Johler). (As this essay is being written, the film version of the musical *Chicago* is having a successful run in Vienna.) With all the due irony usually accompanying its use, that slogan captures one mode of apprehending attitudes to crime and race accurately enough to make it a valid starting point for exploring some Austrian self-images that arise out of projections onto the United States, while its proposal of a direct comparison makes the exploration a logical activity for a comparatist whose "Betrachtungsweise bleibt die des Literaturwissenschaftlers."

## 2. Achieving by Transgressing

The violent gangsters of the Chicago Mafia became folk heroes in an age of bland, fatuous public leaders, so much so that watchdog groups formed by the movie industry and some religious denominations to devise production codes and censor film content were impelled far more strongly by the danger of glorifying crime and criminals than by the eternal allure of sex (Skinner). Walter E. Richartz notes of the Jazz Age, "Die gewählten Präsidenten . . . waren farblos und passiv; bewundert wurden Al Capone und seine Mordgenossen" (90). Vienna also suffered from a vacuum of legitimate available role models; Kaiser Franz Joseph embodied the empire in his person alone, but he was the quintessential "Mann ohne Eigenschaften," especially as described in Egon Friedell's classic, devastating assessment of him as a total nonentity (313). The emperor's featurelessness is emblematic of a whole society without leaders to emulate. The vacuum was filled in part by the dynamic mayor Karl Lueger, one of the first geniuses of self-representation against an urban backdrop (Öhlinger 137-43), but in even greater part by the "criminal mastermind" Johann "Schani" Breitwieser, beloved to the point of canonization, and all the more because he exercised technical ingenuity in his crimes, not brutality. His legend grew to such mythic status among the working class, especially in Meidling and Ottakring, that his funeral on April 1, 1919 attracted upwards of forty thousand mourners, and "alljährlich am Allerheiligentag war es den hinterbliebenen Angehörigen nicht möglich, an das Grab, das von einer dichten Menschenmauer umgeben war und um das herum Hunderte von Kerzen brannten, auch nur heranzukommen" (Maderthaner 157). Breitwieser's heroic, even saintly, status is rooted in both a general capitalistic myth of success played out most fully in America and a more specific Austrian social dynamic. Both helped extend his appeal beyond his own class into struggling, potentially rebellious segments of the lower middle class as well.

    By 1900, the trope of "log cabin to White House" was firmly established in the American social myth of upward mobility, and the popular "rags-to-riches" novels by Horatio Alger about newspaper boys becoming captains of industry and finance were read with fascination as examples of the unlimited opportunities open to those—at least those boys—willing to live clean and work hard. This American dream came true very rarely, but it did sometimes happen, as witness examples, with appropriate iconography, like Benjamin Franklin arriving in Philadelphia with only two loaves of bread, Abraham Lincoln growing up poor in a log cabin, and Andrew Carnegie journeying to America in steerage.[1]

The older British rags-to-riches legend of Dick Whittington, the poor boy who becomes Lord Mayor of London with help from his cat, was relegated to fairy tale in England, while the home-grown American variation was embraced as a feasible social model. Even politically leftist authors who scourged the mendacity of the capitalistic success myth showed their fascination with it by their constant resort to heightened language, prophetic and Biblical in tone, when they addressed it. The thundering rhetoric of the "muckrakers" active in the Theodore Roosevelt era, deriving as much from Jeremiah as from Zola, betrays the awe in which those writers held the daunting power of the corporations and institutions they indicted. The iconography of John Dos Passos's *U.S.A.* trilogy pays capitalist rags-to-riches achievers the tribute of negative apotheosis, elevating them to demonic status; its pages bristle with sarcastic but captivated accounts of self-made capitalist moguls, "devils" like Henry Ford, Thomas Alva Edison, Andrew Carnegie, J. Pierpont Morgan, and Frederick W. Taylor, icons no less absorbing to Dos Passos than his progressivist heroes, "angels" like John Reed, Big Bill Haywood, Thorstein Veblen, Randolph Bourne, and Frank Lloyd Wright. Similarly, in his fierce poetic outcry "Howl," structured like a psalm, Allen Ginsberg personifies the cannibalistic materialism and inhuman achievement-oriented consumerism of the 1950s as the hideous Old-Testament pagan god Moloch.

In Austria, by contrast, significant movement upward from the working class, because it was a flat impossibility (Öhlinger 164-65), was not a strong dynamic of literature or of life. The successful careerist or *Aufsteiger* was not an unknown quantity in Vienna, especially in the rapid expansion of mercantile arrangements and urban structures in the eighteenth century. Following what could be called the Faninal pattern, after the *nouveau riche* in Hugo von Hofmannsthal's *Der Rosenkavalier* who makes a huge fortune as a military outfitter in Maria Theresa's wars, men who had begun humbly—financiers and suppliers like Johann Fries (1719-1785) or scholars and scientists like the celebrated physician Leopold Auenbrugger (1722-1809)—came to play influential public roles, were welcomed at court, and even attained aristocratic rank (Mattl-Wurm 101-02; 83-84). Such men seem never to have been viewed by the Viennese as general models, however; they remained exceptional cases, and Austrian literature reveals little mythologizing of their kind. On the contrary: stories like Franz Werfel's "Der Tod des Kleinbürgers" or Josef Haslinger's "Tod des Kleinhäuslers Ignaz Hayek" are more typical of social dynamics in Austrian literature than tales of rising from the lower classes.[2]

During his reign, Emperor Franz Joseph contributed further to upward mobility by creating whole cadres of nobles wryly dubbed in court circles the *"Sehadel"*—*"Wen er sah, den adelte er"* (a clumsy but serviceable translation would be "He made a peer out of everyone within sight"). This distinction was conferred on men from the worlds of technology, finance, and industry, but by the routine, anonymous nature of their occupations, members of the working class could never be granted such honors. Affluence, position, status already had to be in evidence; with perhaps one exception, the head of the Social Democratic Party Franz Schuhmeier (1864-1913), the lower social strata were shut out to an extent that had virtually never been the case in America. Lueger took advantage of his popularity to rig his reform program such that the lower middle class was favored and the propertyless, poverty-stricken working class kept disenfranchised. Throughout his term of office, municipal administration, voting rights, and public services were "orientiert an den Interessen des kleingewerblichen Mittelstands" and correspondingly "für den Großteil der Bevölkerung immer noch unbefriedigend" (Öhlinger 191). It should be added in this context that Schuhmeier's renown as a "Volkstribun" (Maderthaner 156) depended on his continued strict adherence to his working-class identity. In a memorial tribute, Leon Trotsky, who had observed Schuhmeier closely for some years, called him a "class mirror." Mobility upward from his roots through emulation of the capitalist success myth would have destroyed his credibility. (The working class represented by Schuhmeier could not have taken it as a sign of growing acceptance or progress, either, that he was shot and killed in 1913 by Paul Kunschak, the brother of Leopold Kunschak, founder of the association which would later became the Christian Socialist Party [Öhlinger 193]).

Entrapment in poverty with no prospects of improvement made transgressive patterns of expression, legal or otherwise, almost the only means of articulating hopes and fears. The poverty did not even have to be so great, for that matter. Alongside the lofty moral messages contained in the earnest Viennese *Volksstücke* of Ludwig Anzengruber and others, plays that uphold middle-class morality at its most conventional and restrictive, were the irreverent clowns of improvisational popular comedy, types like Kasperl and Hanswurst, transgressive to the point of open subversion in using their bawdry and quick wit to overthrow entrenched pieties about bourgeois order and political conformism (Bauer 152-53). These comedies grew ever more popular among both the working class and the middle class in Vienna (Mattl-Wurm 147-48) just when they were being banished from the stage in Germany. It is telling, for example, to note the degree to which Weinberl and Christopherl, the employees of Zangler's "*vermischte Warenhandlung*" in Johann Nepomuk Nestroy's *Einen Jux will er sich machen*, feel trapped for life in wage slavery, even though they are treated comparatively well on the whole. They have no chance for advancement within the system, so they run off to enjoy an escapade before the doors close on them forever (Nestroy 164-73). The theatrical mode of defying repressive authority culminated in Nestroy, in fact; his *couplets* were improvised glosses on political and social topics that flouted censorship and earned him more than one night in jail (Bauer 151-52). The line along which this culture of transgression in theatrical form reaches across historical eras and social classes extends to the present, through legendary, daring cabaret presentations that tweaked National Socialist leaders in attendance, through the provocativeness of Helmut Qualtinger or the challenges to bodily taboos by the Vienna Group and the Actionists, to the current weekly perpetrations of Hermes Phettberg at the Cabaret Stadnikow.

Among the very poor, who could not afford a theater ticket, a directly transgressive stylization of self was a more immediate means of representation in the theater, the "Erfahrungsraum," of the city.[3] As Wolfgang Maderthaner and Lutz Musner say about one popular but feared type, the "Wiener Strizzi . . . wird . . . als Inbegriff des Plattenbruders zu einer öffentlichen Figur, die weniger etwas über ihn selbst aussagt als über die Sehnsucht der Deklassierten, sich gegen die herrschende Ordnung und gegen unmenschliche Lebensbedingungen aufzulehnen" (156). What these poverty-stricken "Deklassierte" saw in the life of Johann Breitwieser is the ultimate expression of this yearning; as Maderthaner and Musner continue,

> In keinem anderen Fall . . . konzentrieren sich Hoffnungen und Sehnsüchte, latente Rebellion und Renitenz, Sozialromantik und Projektionen eines anderen, besseren und gerechteren Lebens der vorstädtischen Elendsbevölkerung in der Person des Schränkers, "Eisenschlitzers" und Einbrechers Johann "Schani" Breitwieser, "König von Meidling" und "Robin Hood von Wien".

In spite of—or more likely because of—prison sentences and desertion from the army in World War I, Breitwieser was revered, even canonized, for robbing the rich and giving to the poor, providing for the needy out of his takings, and maintaining such faithful contact with his beloved "little people" that the police reputedly looked the other way when they recognized him on the street in Ottakring (Maderthaner 165). His mode of charity oddly but distinctly echoes the private philanthropies of American plutocrats like Andrew Carnegie or John D. Rockefeller, who dispensed largesse through individual generosity without reference to larger social or political institutions and were thus able to reinforce their personal images as contributors to society.

Breitwieser was of course also admired for being able to pursue the lifestyle of the rich and famous; like the mansions of the American multi-millionaires, though hardly on the same scale, his opulently furnished villa in St. Andrä-Wördern, a setting beyond the wildest dreams of Meidling or Ottakring, was the main proof that he had gone from rags to riches in the American sense, or that, to cite the Viennese phrase, "*er hat es zu etwas gebracht.*" Modest as that goal was compared to palatial mansions on Fifth Avenue and in Newport, it was one that a man of Breitwieser's background had to resort to crime to fulfill, since he could never have attained it through legal means (Öhlinger 164-65). Egon Erwin Kisch touched on a very widespread popular feeling in his assessment of Breitwieser as "Ein Mann der Tat, des Mutes, des Ernstes und der Intelligenz" (27). These glowing terms capture an attitude that reveals how strongly Breitwieser exemplified the achiever pattern within the transgressor pattern, or vice versa. American romantic images of the Lone Ranger and the Wild West outlaw or of the Mafia kingpin suggest that heroic status of the individualistic, fantasy-fulfilling variety was largely unavailable within the stable system of middle-class "getting ahead" in the United States, while much of Breitwieser's fascination arises precisely from his representing himself in an environment that replicated the surroundings and the qualities of the hard-working, law-abiding *Aufsteiger*.

### 3. Pastoral Archetype, Technical Wizard

In their summary of Breitwieser—a distillation of what his contemporaries wrote about him—as "dem Wiener Vorstadtkriminellen mit populärem Robin Hood-Charme und amerikanischem Know-how" (165), Maderthaner and Musner touch on two additional opposing elements of the urban dynamic. Expanding that brief juxtaposition here will show its elements also helping to contribute to understanding Breitwieser's legendary representative status. He functioned at once as the embodiment of a fantasy involving a vanished agrarian, pastoral world and of a power dream based on mastery of the latest technology and equipment.

Numbers documenting the explosive growth of the Viennese population (close to a tenfold increase from 1800 to 1910, all administrative districts included [Öhlinger 6; 56-57]), bear out that many of those jammed into hovels around 1900 must have been first- or second-generation country people with direct or freshly inherited memories of rural life. Walter Öhlinger notes that the Industrial Revolution "ging auch in Österreich mit der Auflösung der bestehenden Gesellschaftsstrukturen in den ländlichen Gebieten einher.... Als Folge der sich auflösenden Feudalgesellschaft begannen unzählige Menschen, ihr Glück in der Stadt zu suchen" (56). Under the pressure of this displacement, the popular imagination no less than the literary began stylizing agrarian memories into an idealized vision of *Heimat*, a variant of pastoral and a point at which folklore and oral tradition intersect with consciously literary production. W. G. Sebald, tracing "die gesellschaftliche Bedingtheit der literarischen Weltsicht" (9), writes:

> Der Heimatbegriff ist verhältnismäßig neuen Datums. Er prägte sich in eben dem Grad aus, in dem in der Heimat kein Verweilen mehr war, in dem einzelne und ganze gesellschaftliche Gruppen sich gezwungen

sahen, ihr den Rücken zu kehren und auszuwandern. . . . Je mehr von
der Heimat die Rede ist, desto weniger gibt es sie. (11-12)

The huge upsurge of interest among the literate throughout the industrialized world in pre-industrial myths, legends, and stories; the romanticizing of handicrafts and village life; the emergence of the specifically historical novel (*Middlemarch, Henry Esmond, Witiko, Huckleberry Finn*) set in a simpler, purer time bear witness, as do many other manifestations, to the paradox of a culture's longing for exactly what its expansionism had forcibly done away with: "Der Begriff steht . . . in reziprokem Verhältnis zu dem, worauf er sich bezieht" (Sebald 12). That opposition is captured by Dos Passos's portrait of the aged Henry Ford as a "passionate antiquarian" who "rebuilt his father's farmhouse and put it back exactly in the state he remembered it in as a boy" and who "scoured the country for fiddlers to play old-fashioned squaredances" (III 57).

> When he bought the Wayside Inn near Sudbury, Massachusetts, he
> had the new highway where newmodel cars roared and slithered and
> hissed oilily past (*the new noise of the automobile*)
> moved away from the door,
> put back the old bad road,
> so that everything might be
> the way it used to be,
> in the days of horses and buggies.

Millionaires could have entire vistas changed back to pre-industrial Arcadias; poets could invoke the Ancient Mariner or "die Götter Griechenlands" or "le génie du Christianisme"; artisans of means like William Morris could hark back to Caxton and produce handmade books; scholars like the Brothers Grimm could investigate the pre-medieval roots of their language and literature, as a byproduct of which they often revived and recorded long-standing tales transmitted orally as folklore for centuries, in that way bridging a gap between pre-literate and literate cultures.

Seen in light of a widespread wish fantasy that encompassed all classes, from destitute former country dwellers with homespun lore and rural memories now stranded ten to a room in Meidling, through the middle-class passion for historicizing evident in the costumed pageants of Hans Makart and the architecture of the Ringstraße, to King Ludwig II of Bavaria with his medieval-Teutonic Wagner cult and his fairy-tale castles, the frequency of contemporary references to Breitwieser as a Robin Hood figure suggests resonance with pastoral, prelapsarian legends of life before agrarian displacement. Robin Hood is a figure from the last frontier, fighting for simple justice by taking the law into his own hands and away from heartless functionaries, court and town officials, sheriffs as tax collectors, and property-owning oppressors. Robbing the rich to give to the poor—but what rich and what poor? All the institutions he fights because of their power to harm the defenseless and exploit the poor are post-agrarian, related to the whole array of mercantile, urban, courtly, and money-economy arrangements to which he stands in such contrast. The poor whom he helps are from obsolescent social strata, evicted small farmers, displaced humble clerics, unprotected women and children. They are often outcasts, victims of new social and economic structures to which they cannot accommodate. Robin Hood's loyalty to them arises partly from the old chivalric oaths to protect women and children—a wellspring of courtesy and considerateness now cynically forgotten by the new merchants, courtiers, and toadying law enforcers—partly from identification through his own status as a banished outcast (for reasons never clarified), and partly from fealty, contemptuous of all pragmatic accommodation, to the king he serves, Richard the Lionheart, himself in turn an outcast from England and the symbol of a purer, more chivalric world free of greed and scheming (Fortunaso; Lupack). The more closely Robin Hood is observed in his social aspect, the more closely he and Breitwieser reveal most of the above factors in common. In parallel to Robin Hood's activities, Breitwieser had by about 1916 or 1917 confined himself to robbing only from banks, insurance companies, and other strongly hated capitalistic institutions, so the legend grew that he was not even in it for himself. He came increasingly to be judged as one motivated by sheer compassion, as a great, noble soul "der nur stehle, um andere zu bereichern" (Maderthaner 164).

    Beyond the social configuration, Robin Hood also bears the marks of an ancient mythic archetype, the woodland god or spirit, an embodiment and apotheosis of nature itself, the primal Green Man or

Green Knight of folklore and Arthurian romance. Who does not know that his only weapons are the old-fashioned bow and arrow, which he uses so skillfully; that he dwells deep within Sherwood Forest, from which he emerges when and where he is needed; that he wears only green, with a feathered hat like an animal's crest; that his retinue scorns worldly social distinctions of gender and class; that he asserts his elemental need, spurning deeds and contracts, by boldly hunting game in the royal preserves; that he despises court frippery and lives with his Merry Men off the land? His very name identifies him with the forest elf or daemon known in folklore as Robin Goodfellow and as Puck in Shakespeare's *A Midsummer Night's Dream*, a spirit himself and the servant of spirits, the incarnation of nature's cycle and an elemental force of nature dangerously subversive of civilized ways. Not that the population of Meidling or Ottakring knew Shakespeare or participated in consciously artsy revivals of legend, but the elemental power of nature gods and spirits to confer meaning on life is what made a Robin Hood or a Robin Goodfellow into a universal archetype in the first place, a figure of yearning and wish fulfillment that goes beyond literacy or even consciousness (Fortunaso; Lupack). More than functioning as an avenger in human social arrangements, Robin Hood embodies the stabilizing power of nature itself, a foremost element in myths of *Heimat*.[4]

After Breitwieser's death in a shoot-out with police, what especially intrigued those who already admired him and gained him even wider respect, as attested in newpaper accounts, was the high-tech elegance of his criminal career. Photographs of his villa show the standard tasteful, affluent furnishings in the most conventional decorator-magazine style, but the house beautiful contained a whole concealed world as well: "im fensterlosen Kellergeschoß stieß man auf ein vollkommen ausgestattetes Laboratorium moderner Technologie . . . und eine durchaus auf der Höhe ihrer Zeit stehende technische Bibliothek" (Maderthaner 157). Kisch describes police officers frozen in shock when they discovered relatively simple "Wachstabletten, Schlüsselbunde, Dietriche, Feilen" but then also "Maschinen, Drehbänke, Schraubstöcke, eine Feldschmiede. . . . Ein autogener Schweißapparat für Hitzeentwicklung von dreitausendsechshundert Grad war vollständig aufmontiert, gebrauchsbereit" (26). With professional skill, Breitwieser applied all that

technology—metallurgy, welding, explosives, electricity, and the like—
to his already legendary crimes. Basement rooms, hidden laboratories,
unsuspected gadgetry—by the turn of the twentieth century, such
components of a fantasy involving technological prowess had grown
pervasive, transcending good and evil to encompass Drs. Frankenstein,
Moriarty, Caligari, Mabuse, No, and Strangelove; Captains Nemo and
Midnight; Batman; Flash Gordon; 007; criminal masterminds; mad and
noble scientists; and high-tech spies of every stripe.[5] And here it was,
played out by a local boy in the quiet environs of St. Andrä-Wördern, a
location so staid that the police dispatched to capture Breitwieser were
at first convinced they had been sent to the wrong place (Kisch 22).

The attainment of such wealth and power through expensive up-to-
date technology by one of their own must have been a thrilling wish
fulfillment to people unable ever to afford a meat meal (Öhlinger 58-
60), the more so in again invoking the American plutocratic model, but
without threat. Breitwieser's ability to master and profit from complex
technologies creates another strange but suggestive parallel between him
and many of the acclaimed multi-millionaires, especially types like
Edison, Ford, and Taylor, all depicted in the standard iconography as
staying up at night to teach themselves hydraulics, telegraphy, internal
combustion, methods of steel production, or whatever other technological developments would help them pull themselves up by their boot-
straps and build that better mousetrap (Dos Passos I 297-301 [Edison],
III 19-25 [Ford], and III 47-57 [Taylor]). Unlike the conspicuous and
super-human American "giants of industry," however, Breitwieser was
able to represent himself as both a primal spirit of nature, an outlaw too
elemental to observe shallow social conventions, and an advanced
wizard of technology, in that way reconciling a polarity in which both
apparently opposite figures symbolize social fantasies of total control
over one's destiny and fortune. As Maderthaner and Musner express it,
Breitwieser projected the image "eines konsequenten Modernisierers
und Technik-Fanatikers, der sein Gewerbe revolutionierte und zugleich
im durchaus prämodernen Stil eines 'Sozialrebellen' zu agieren
verstand" (157).

Combining those modes allowed Breitwieser to inspire admiration
without fear. Modern literature everywhere mirrors the anxieties of an
increasingly technological world; even a mere listing of the utopian and

especially dystopian treatments from about 1870 would require a bibliography pages long. Historians as well attest to this fear from the beginning of the industrial age; Öhlinger argues that the withdrawal of Biedermeier life into a domestic idyll resulted not from love of quietism for its own sake but from "die enormen Spannungsfelder, in denen sich die Menschen damals bewegten"; not the least menacing was "eine Welt voller rasanter technischer Veränderungen" (29-30). Wolfgang Schivelbusch documents the terror produced by the very sight of an early railway's "maschinelles Ensemble" (21-34; 106-12), for instance, and Richartz reviews in this context documented anecdotes of the kind in which a rural English curate collapsed in shock at the speed of one of George Stephenson's first locomotives and had to be temporarily confined to a mental institution (172-73).[6]

Over time, though, the terrifying turned at least partly into the exhilirating, as technology became a means of pursuing leisure and—literally—a vehicle for preserving agrarian dreams, further creating power over nature through power over machinery. As time and space became industrialized (Schivelbusch's subtitle), technology gained acceptance as a boon. The railroad could transport those outside the city to all the cultural and shopping opportunities unavailable at home (Schivelbusch 158-74), but it was the movement the other way that satisfied deeper urban fantasies. In his section titled "Technik als Vergnügen," Öhlinger mentions that the expansion of the railway system, from the modest "Standseilbahn auf dem Leopoldsberg" and the "Kahlenbergerbahn" to the more extensive southern railway system made a "Fahrt durch die Idylle" a matter of ease, and he reminds us that lines now used for commuting and other business purposes were almost exclusively drawn on for leisure activities like country outings when they were first put into service (50). It is notable, too, that the Viennese immediately and affectionately began referring to the city trolley system as "die Elektrische" when it was converted from horse-drawn power (Öhlinger 147); far from resistance or doubt, this designation shows that the updated technology was hailed.

A reliable index to the acceptance of technology was its prominence as a feature of happy popular music. With his characteristic sovereign irony, Robert Musil—who hated music, by the way—notes in a related context in *Der Mann ohne Eigenschaften*: "In Goethes Welt ist das Klappern der Webstühle noch eine Störung gewesen, in der Zeit Ulrichs begann man das Lied der Maschinensäle, Niethämmer und Fabriksirenen schon zu entdecken" (36). Johann Strauss the Elder's "Tivoli-Rutsch-Walzer," written in honor of a new "mechanical" attraction, was only the first of dozens of compositions he and his son would compose either as direct commissions or in tandem with new technologies—the openings of railroad lines ("Vergnügungszug-Polka"), the availability of newspapers ("Morgenblätter"), faster access to the Vienna Woods ("Geschichten aus dem Wiener Wald"), improved conditions on the regulated Danube ("An der schönen blauen Donau"), and other technological sources of leisure and entertainment (Öhlinger 46-47; 106-07). Similar value was ascribed to technology in American popular music as well, suggesting a general phenomenon as well as a profit-minded respect in the United States for the younger Johann Strauss's commercial success. Package rail excursions to beaches and mountains were celebrated through musical tributes to familiar resorts ("On the Boardwalk in Atlantic City"), while other songs extolled cross-country rail networks that could transport people to new horizons for new opportunities ("On the Acheson, Topeka, and Santa Fe"). Europeans in general romanticized their past, and the Viennese integrated technology into Arcadian clichés about their present surroundings, but Americans were still celebrating a bright future on a frontier that had in fact closed. From the plea to "send me a kiss by wire" (1899) through the "clang, clang, clang" of the trolley (1944) on which boy meets girl, technology was also favored as an innocent means of promoting innocent love.[7]

## 4. Destroyed Self, Superhuman Identity

Technology could not have contributed so integrally to the mythologizing of a criminal, however, if it had corresponded to only this breezy side of social fantasizing, if it had facilitated only diversion in the spirit of "We bring good things to life," to quote another ubiquitous advertising slogan by General Electric. It is from a psychological, individual standpoint, rather than a social, communal one, that we can ascertain the power of technology to shape icons of demonic or angelic function. On that more elemental level, mechanization can cause human annihilation, the destruction of the identity and of the very soul, with representation no longer possible because there is no self left to represent; or it can turn a "*Mann ohne Eigenschaften*" into a visionary superman of power and courage projecting a self-image released from the dull constraints of everyday reality.

The negative and positive psychological aspects were both common cultural property. Expressing anxieties that cross national borders, for instance, Jules Paul Barbier adapted a play by Jules Barbier and Michel Carré—it in turn conflated stories of E. T. A. Hoffmann and Adalbert von Chamisso—to create a libretto, *Les contes d'Hoffmann*, in which Hoffmann fights a losing battle against a series of evil physicians and mad scientists who convince him that an automaton is a real woman, kill his artist-lover, and steal his reflection in the mirror, cackling all the while in triumph and malice at first having co-opted the poet to physical science and then having destroyed him. On the positive side, it was also a French writer, latter-day rationalist Jules Verne, who touched a universal chord with his novels of wondrous technical mastery, elevating the champions of gadgetry to superhuman ability while allowing them to keep their admirable human traits—like Johann Breitwieser!

How inextricably individual identity and representation had become interwoven with technology, for better or worse, comes clear in our context by observing two very different Austrian novelists who again articulated the dynamics of their specific culture through comparison with American models and forces. In that perenially recurrent strategy of representation, Rudolf Brunngraber draws on the irony of contained indignation, while Robert Musil exercises the detachment of comic irony to show the effects of specifically American technological influence.

The opening sentence of Brunngraber's novel *Karl und das zwanzigste Jahrhundert* directly juxtaposes the main character Karl Lakner and the American efficiency expert Frederick W. Taylor and his methods at the Midvale Steel Company in Philadelphia.[8] Needless to say, Lakner, not even born as of when Taylor "1880 als Erster konsequent den Gedanken der Rationalisierung faßte" (Brunngraber 5), is defeated, thousands of miles away, by processes of production efficiency that make individual human workers into expendable cogs and levers on an assembly line. Disadvantaged from the start as a child of the working class, Karl "scheint durch seine Herkunft für das Unglück programmiert" (Schmidt-Dengler 86). Progressively more disillusioned, he comes to believe that "Die Wirtschaft ist das Schicksal," and his "Schicksal" drives him to suicide (Schmidt-Dengler 88). If this novel were filled only with the standard rhetoric of anti-capitalistic demonization ("Rockefeller, der Oktopus, der Polyp" gobbling up the world's oil supply [7]), it would be just another feverish period rant. Its integrity derives instead from its highly unusual narrative method and structure, which counterbalance the ever-present moral indignation. Brunngraber invokes vehement reader reactions to a whole array of heartless tycoons, robber barons, capitalist exploiters, corrupt Republican political operators and then keeps those reactions in emotional check by applying strictly statistical methods of sociological analysis that he had learned from Otto Neurath, the one member of the "Vienna Circle" who identified himself as a social scientist (Schmidt-Dengler 84-85).

Brunngraber uses his skill at individual characterization to show Karl deprived of individuality. From the very beginning, Karl is placed within the statistical context of impersonal forces that have direct bearing on every aspect of his life. The narrator says, for instance, "im Jahr 1893 kam Karl Lakner zur Welt," but at once revises that statement: "einer von den 40 Millionen schreienden Würmern, die damals geboren wurden, war der Anfang eines Menschen, der sich später seiner als Karl Lakner bewußt wurde" (19). At no point is Karl ever able to have an experience or make a decision aside from a level of statistically depicted "scientific" inexorability going far past Zola's Naturalist method in showing the determinism of heredity and environment in a completely mechanized world.[9] For that matter, Karl never even gets to say anything. The irony of Brunngraber's objectifying narrative method arises in its increasing, rather than mitigating, the poignancy and moral indignation over the triumph of Taylorism and American production methods at the expense of human beings. The larger and more impersonal the statistical forces we see operating on Karl—population figures, food distribution tables, unemployment trends, health reports—the more inescapable and thus the more pitiable his fate grows. Charts and graphs are more pitiless than the Greek gods; individuals become meaningless to the point of losing all personal identity. Karl's total impotence dramatizes how implacable is the increasingly dehumanizing "march of progress" through ever-increased efficiency. The final chapter, in which a spare newspaper article laconically records his suicide under the wheels of a train, is titled, with ironic appropriateness, "Die Welt geht weiter." A prostitute was witness to the suicide, hinting at Karl as a debased Anna Karenina who never had the love. In an example of Brunngraber's ability to use apparently neutral montage effects for a contained emotional effect, the same chapter reprints another newspaper article in which an expert scientist estimates the amounts of different chemicals in a human body and the uses to which they can be put. As Schmidt-Dengler notes, Brunngraber applies statistical analysis according to the most accepted social-science methods to show how inadequate statistical analysis is in apprehending human nature and human fate (86). A rational force for progress when viewed from the social perspective, technology—expressed in its language of charts and graphs—becomes an evil in the psychological view, Taylorism a juggernaut unable to take account of individuals and totally impersonal in its inevitable effect of making them redundant.[10]

Literacy and formal education gave the middle classes more leverage over their outward fate than Karl Lakner had, but Robert Musil's ironic refraction in *Der Mann ohne Eigenschaften* of the usual elements tracing a hero's emergence to adulthood in the *Bildungsroman* suggests that Ulrich's eagerness to crush technology to his bosom by becoming an engineer may be a form of annihilation not much preferable to being crushed under the wheels of a train. Ulrich's self-image gains in inverse proportion to his forfeiture of authentic self-realization. Mastery by leading the strenuous life is the apparent gain, but Musil's marmoreal irony guides readers through the layers of Ulrich's insecurity and uncertainty, of his capitulation to an attractive image of the self while in search of a genuine self such that he remains "*ohne Eigenschaften*." At best, nothing has been gained, and much may have been lost, by his desire to bestride the narrow world like a colossus.[11]

"Ulrich war, als er die Lehrsäle der Mechanik betrat, vom ersten Augenblick an fieberhaft befangen" (Musil 37). Only when strictly procedural methods or processes like engineering come to take the place of an ethos or a religion do they have the power to enthrall by touching the core of identity in this way. Identity depends on being able to make ethical value judgments, to accept one mode of representation and reject another, so technology and its mechanical processes must, as in Ulrich's case, have projected onto them value systems in order to furnish a sense of self. As for a whole society, this quasi-religious reassignment or displacement of ethical systems from older arrangements is what makes virtual worship of Breitwieser possible, in part on the basis of his technological prowess. Just as society at large did not see the basic logical and ethical fallacies of social Darwinism, eugenics, and other projections of an ethos onto a method, so Ulrich does not see that his new identity is defective, because it rests on the fallacy of confusing the means with the end, or rather makes them the same, elevating the use of the tool to the reason for using the tool. In the second of his three attempts to become "ein bedeutender Mann" (Musil 35), recorded in a chapter subtitled "Ansätze zu einer Moral des Mannes ohne Eigenschaften," Ulrich meditates as follows:

> Wozu braucht man noch den Apollon von Belvedere, wenn man die neuen Formen eines Turbodynamo oder das Gliederspiel einer Dampfmaschinensteuerung vor Augen hat! . . . wenn man einen Rechenschieber besitzt, und jemand kommt mit großen Behauptungen oder großen Gefühlen, so sagt man: Bitte einen Augenblick, wir wollen vorerst die Fehlergrenzen und den wahrscheinlichsten Wert von alledem berechnen! (37)

(Hubris is revisited here as technological cocksureness. The passage echoes Jocasta's mockery in *Oedipus Rex* of those benighted and old-fashioned enough to believe in the gods and heed their oracles.) What Ulrich does not notice, too, is the merely cosmetic aspect, the shallowness, of his up-to-date viewpoint. "Superseded" abstractions which cannot be determined by numbers are being preserved in different form. They are the same abstractions with a numerical basis, so the deeper paradigm has not changed, as Musil's narrator makes even more clear. No matter how thoroughly scientific their professional outlook, technocrats,

wenn sie etwas Besonderes von sich hermachen wollen, setzen sie sich
nicht auf den Wolkenkratzer, sondern aufs hohe Roß, sind geschwind
wie der Wind und scharfsichtig, nicht wie ein Riesenrefraktor, sondern
wie ein Adler. . . . Es bedeutet also kein gar kleines Glück, wenn man
darauf kommt, . . . daß der Mensch in allem, was ihm für das Höhere
gilt, sich weit altmodischer benimmt, als es seine Maschinen sind. (37)

The shallow may be deep enough, though, if it furnishes the promise of
an *Eigenschaft* or two by lending the simulacrum of an identity. Ulrich's
passion for engineering is animated by the romance of

> eine kraftvolle Vorstellung vom Ingenieurwesen. Sie bildete den
> Rahmen eines reizvollen zukünftigen Selbstbildnisses, das einen Mann
> mit entschlossen Zügen zeigte, der eine Shagpfeife zwischen den
> Zähnen hält, eine Sportmütze auf hat und in herrlichen Reitstiefeln
> zwischen Kapstadt und Kanada unterwegs ist, um gewaltige Entwürfe
> für sein Geschäftshaus zu verwirklichen (37-38).

This fantasy of swashbuckling machismo is an amalgam of Napoleon
(see Emerson 727-45), Teddy Roosevelt, Cecil Rhodes, Nietzsche's
*Übermensch* on the cheap, and other nineteenth-century power icons,
crusading, self-righteous carriers of big sticks anticipated by
Schopenhauer in his parodistic essay "Die Kunst, Recht zu behalten,"
about how to bully the opponent into silence by any means fair or foul.
The cheesy posturing traits of, say, Mirko Jelusich's strong-man
heroes—Cromwell, Julius Caesar, Hannibal—are all captured by Musil
with a few masterstrokes of sovereign irony as he sketches the lines
along which fascism gained in attractiveness; males use the power
technology lends them to bolster, not alter, the compensatory martial
images on which they build their self-representation. In the end, these
technowizards are just as deprived of individual identity as Karl Lakner,
harnessed through the need for a male image by a power they thought
they had harnessed.

The specifically American aspect of Musil's analysis is its
indebtedness to Emerson, himself lovingly parodied here; the most
skeptical and ironic of writers draws on the most idealistic and hortatory
in his moral explorations. Geoffrey C. Howes points out Emerson's
influence on Musil (233-37), but he does not mention this key chapter,

in which Ulrich justifies his adolescent swaggering by citing a motto of Emerson's, one he thinks ought to be over the door of every workshop: "Die Menschen wandeln auf Erden als Weissagungen der Zukunft, und alle ihre Taten sind Versuche und Proben, denn jede Tat kann durch die nächste übertroffen werden!" (38). No wonder Howes omits this passage, for Emerson never said any such thing. As the narrator reveals, "Genau genommen war dieser Satz sogar von Ulrich und aus mehreren Sätzen von Emerson zusammengestellt" (38). Instead of borrowing from images of American technological superiority, Musil reverses the usual terms and further points his irony by assigning a cutthroat progressivist spirit to the European. After all, Emerson's idealism is connected to a thoroughgoing optimism that came to ring hollow in its naivete while yet attracting Musil and other Austrian writers. As Howes puts it, "In those days Emerson seemed to be on the side of confidence, newness, reform, antidecadence, and the spiritual transcendence of materialism" (236). For Europeans of Musil's generation, those qualities had been filtered through Schopenhauer, Nietzsche, and Freud into something more problematic, and so it is Musil's strategy when concentrating on Ulrich to invoke the memory of Emerson's idealism, but with purposeful misquotation, distortion, and splicing of the best-known Emersonian principles and sayings.[12] Only by mutilating Emerson's call to a transcendent identity can the self-serving technocrat justify his forfeiture of identity in favor of image.

## 5. The Unleashed Id

Representation depends on organizing separate data into a coherent governing narrative, whether assembled primarily from actuality or imagination. The category of narrative covers both senses of *Geschichte*, as Mayer pointed out (7), making secondary for our purpose the question of the source in actual life or fiction and validating a comparison between two modalities normally separate. Musil was one of a few Austrian novelists—another was Heimito von Doderer in *Die Dämonen*—whose fictional criminals, psychopaths operating within the hypersophisticated and civilized world of affluent middle-class Vienna, are at the opposite extreme of social estimation from Johann

Breitwieser. Both Musil's Moosbrugger and Doderer's Meisgeier[13] are so totally unconstrained by social controls in their criminal deeds as to be primal forces threatening mayhem, as clear in representing deepseated social dread and anxiety as Brietwieser was to his class a primal force of hope and reassurance. Breitwieser integrated and articulated the dreams of his admirers, while Moosbrugger and Meisgeier are filled with loathing for humanity in general and for pleasure and happiness in particular. Far from helping others in Robin-Hood style, both are fixated on their own impulses and desires to a homicidal degree and to the total exclusion of everything else. Moosbrugger is a fear-drenched but hypnotic projection of violence by a jaded, polished, oversecure, achievement-oriented middle class, acting out the dark dreams beneath conformism and respectability, while Meisgeier stands as a chaotic force lodged in the subconscious and reaching out to destroy the settled values and traditional structures of a more modest social order.

The horror they evoke is at least as attractive as it is repulsive. Ulrich is mesmerized when he sees Moosbrugger in person, as is all of "good" society: "es ereignete sich . . . daß die krankhaften Ausschreitungen Moosbruggers, als sie noch kaum bekannt geworden waren, schon von tausenden Menschen, welche die Sensationsgier der Zeitungen tadeln, als 'endlich einmal etwas Interessantes' empfunden wurden" (69). Through newspaper stories that with hollow piety express horror while piling on the details, these solid citizens gobble up every grisly particular of Moosbrugger's ghastly mutilations of prostitutes (68). What readers find most intriguing is Moosbrugger's vehement refusal to accept professional evaluations of the ceaseless raging voices in his head as signs of mental or emotional illness (71-72); he takes pride in the remarkable intelligence ascertained by testing, but he hates all psychiatrists, tries to confound them in court, and is insulted at talk of confining him to an insane asylum instead of the prison to which he feels he has earned full rights of residence (72). If we keep in mind the range and depth of Musil's irony, it will not be hard to see in Mossbrugger a brilliant evocation of all that is potentially chaotic in a middle class eager to regulate sexual impulses and orderly conduct but unable to turn its eyes away from his self-rationalized violence. More an embodiment of than a contrast to dynamics many would rather not recognize, Mossbrugger is a representation on the individual level of the

"*Masse*" (Elias Canetti understood its energies as reaching across classes) unleashed before the burning of the Palace of Justice and the subsequent riot on July 15, 1927, the crystallizing point in Canetti's understanding of mass action (Canetti 560-67).

Doderer's Meisgeier is a manifestation of the same subrational forces, but indebted more to Freud than to Canetti. Meisgeier is the pure aggressive id without constraints. Unlike Moosbrugger, he is never known to society at large; he works underground, reaching up out of sewers to create mayhem and to murder indiscriminately from sheer concentrated malice. He is too unpresentable ever to be even the fashionable psychopath of the headlines. Killed in the same riots of July, 1927, Meisgeier dies almost totally unknown (Doderer 1265-70; 1328-31), but that is perhaps what is most frightening about him, for Doderer depicts him as a universal demon, a force for chaos, more animal than human, anonymously inhabiting the dreams of even the healthiest people psychologically.

As opposed to Moosbrugger, who mirrors a whole society's potential for extreme disorder, Meisgeier reflects the most savage components of the individual soul. Vulture-like in his ugliness, he is nonetheless irresistible to women, even when they know he will harm them; Anna "Didi" Diwald has no choice but to accompany him on his campaign of destruction, going down into the sewers and to her death with her will to resist paralyzed (1265-70). Besides exercising erotic power through personal contact, he dwells in the minds of persons who have no conscious idea who he is as the ultimate representation of everything fearful that rises up from dark depths. His terrifying murders correspond to some horror inside the minds of persons who are anything but psychopathic. No character in *Die Dämonen* is more balanced, open, self-aware, and marked by integrity than the humble, humanly great Anna Kapsreiter; no figure in Doderer fulfills more completely Freud's famous dictum that the surest sign of mental health is the ability to love and work successfully. Even so, her "Nachtbuch" (Doderer 393-98; 530-34), with its dreams of monstrous clawed cephalopods creeping up out of sewers and underground passages, seemingly no more than an individual record of indefinite presentiments in highly symbolic form, later turns out to be a nearly literal description of Meisgeier's emergence from the depths. "Kaps" lives quietly in Lichtenthal, a model of domestic peace, but she could not have such fantasies of primal dread, such intuitions of impending violence, if they were not already within her. Her "Nachtbuch" clearly has tapped into archetypes of chaos, where she encounters on the deepest level of collective unconscious the universal horror of annihilation that Meisgeier represents. It is too disturbing to realize that Meisgeier lives in us all, so we try to hide him in the depths. Yet no one is exempt from the struggles the determined id raises to achieve its gratification at any price of rampage or destruction.

## 6. In Black and White

Meisgeier, then, is the hidden demon at the opposite pole from the public angel of mercy, the sainted Robin Hood of Meidling. He could not be consciously hated, because he was never consciously known. Outside the work in which he appears, genre plays its part as well; like Moosbrugger, Meisgeier is a character in a novel, a genre absorbed in private, not usually performed for audiences. Another famous literary criminal, however, the title character of Ernst Krenek's opera *Jonny spielt auf*, had an immediate and widespread impact, causing a furore as either a brash but welcome new (black) face or a feared, hated transgressor after his debut on the stage of the Vienna State Opera on December 31, 1927. As Krenek himself wryly noted, Jonny was a far cry from the usual New Year's Eve fare of *Die Fledermaus*; the tacit contrast to soothing Viennese tradition could not have been more complete (*Im Atem der Zeit* 650). An African-American jazz musician— played by a white singer in blackface, of course[14]—Jonny makes off with a stolen Amati violin and turns the head of more than one woman, including the diva Anita. Contemporary audiences loved it; hidebound upholders of "German" culture hated it; political mobs goaded by the "NS-Agitationsmaschinerie" rioted over it as a "'freche jüdisch-negerische Besudelung' . . ., ein Paradebeispiel 'entarteter Kunst'" (Dobretsberger). With the hindsight of seventy-plus years, it looks as if each group was responding to a different facet of criminal representation.

Krenek's stated intentions delighted "advanced" 1920s audiences thrilled by the novelty of telephones and automobiles in a grand opera: "Diesen Johnny habe ich den Vertretern der hoffnunglos verfahrenen europäischen Kunst und Geistigkeit als Naturprinzip und Urkraft entgegengesetzt" (*Im Zweifelsfalle* 20). The composer Max is honorable in his integrity, but he and his frozen European culture are symbolized by a glacier. The virtuoso violinist Daniello has all the showy tricks, the artsy pseudo-loftiness, the crowd-pleasing mannerisms of the fraud, and he is the performer, the person who presents and represents "high" culture, a debased "Kunst und Geistigkeit," before audiences. Not only is there something shabby about his art, but he is morally dubious, too, calling Jonny a "Bestie" and ordering him to leave with a hatefully racist "Ote toi [sic], négrillon!" (*Jonny* 68). Being a virtuoso has nothing to do with being a decent human being, and thoughtful audiences would have seen that the cultivated Europeans who demonize Jonny into the other are guilty of projection. Daniello is as driven by undisciplined lust as Jonny, and Anita—stylized as the great lady, the artist, the bringer of beauty and representative of higher things—is consumed by libido; her watchword as she goes with Daniello to his room is "Wieder das Blut" (*Jonny* 70).

The crime culturally informed reactionaries bewailed was the destruction of genuine culture by lewd American cacophony. When Krenek wrote in retrospect, "Andere haben wiederum entdeckt, daß ich das barbarische Wesen eines kulturlosen Amerikanismus unter der Form der triumphierenden Jazzmusik glorifizieren wolle" (*Im Zweifelsfalle* 15), he was not exaggerating actual reactions. Hans Pfitzner's true-blue German attitude is typical; those who favor American popular music "befördern auch den Untergang aller europäischen Kultur, deren oberster Quell und Zuflucht Deutschland immer noch war, und helfen, die internationale Seelenlosigkeit, den pseudo- oder anationalen Amerikanismus auf unser Festland zu pflanzen" (Pfitzner qtd. in Kurth 33-34). Besides the usual nationalistic jargon, Pfitzner and kindred spirits are coding reactions against a lasciviousness they reject in Jonny and do not even notice in Daniello and Anita, against the "primitivism" supposedly inherent in persons of color, against the greed for money and fame that drives Jonny but from which cultivated Europeans are protected by their loftier vision. For these reactionary critics, Jonny is a figure onto which all fears of change in the era after World War I could be projected. While appreciative audiences cheered, they displayed a defensive Teutonic indignation.

In its twisted way, the rioting of the National Socialists was the most perceptive reaction and the one that best illuminates our context. Jonny is black, of course (more of that in a moment), and that would have automatically raised hackles, but there is nothing Jewish about him or his creator, so the code words "jüdisch-negerische Besudelung" are more generic than actually descriptive. The Nazis responded to what they were able to name, even if it wasn't there, but the real horror of Jonny is that he is the Dionysian counterpart to the more Apollonian image of a "Schani" Breitwieser. He is riotous and lustful, driven by greed and instant gratification, a force for disorder and overthrow of stable social arrangements. And like Dionysos himself, he has the power to entrance and enthrall those around him, to gain their consent from within. He does not ravish women, for instance, but awakens their primal sexual feelings without overmuch persuasion. In his music and in his person, he is indeed the "Naturprinzip" and "Urkraft" Krenek called him (*Im Zweifelsfalle* 20), and the fascination he exercises is dangerous. He is shown at the end of the opera atop a globe, having conquered the world with his music while the Europeans look on transfixed. Jonny is the eruptive American Dionysos to whom civilized Europeans actually want to succumb, and that is what the Nazis might have instinctively recognized and hated. As Krenek says, he "wird die Urlaute seiner Heimat, die motorischen Rhythmen seiner amerikanischen Tänze einer Gesellschaft in die Ohren geigen, *die nichts begehrt, als von ihm genommen zu werden*" (*Im Zweifelsfalle* 20; emphasis added). Breitwieser could create order beyond the law; Jonny creates lawless upheaval. Breitwieser could selflessly balance injustices; Jonny cares about nothing but himself. Breitwieser outsmarted a technological society; Jonny thinks only with his phallus and its musical extension, his violin. Breitwieser made everything all right and had a tacit, respectful understanding with the police; Jonny leaves a trail of mayhem and has an understanding with no one at all. Breitwieser is, in short, a fantasy fulfillment in which the id is relegated to its functional, productive place; Jonny is pure id, a frightening brother under the skin of Meisgeier and Mossbrugger.

As for skin, even the psychopaths were at least white, to say nothing of Breitwieser, totally and literally a "homeboy," a smart, white, ethnically German boy from Meidling. Identity with him is close enough for Kisch to write in almost a personal tone when lamenting the fate that led Breitwieser—as if incidentally—to follow a criminal path (27). How eager would Musil's Ulrich have been to approach Moosbrugger from a spirit of identity if the criminal had been black? Racism, or at least a sense of the black as the other, has been a feature of life in Vienna for centuries; even honored citizens could at times be considered freaks, as in the well-attested case of the black African Angelo Soliman (1721-1796), a civil servant of high rank whose body was nonetheless subjected to an autopsy after his death merely because he was "different". It would be a lie or a delusion to claim that Vienna, and Austria at large, have worked free of racial and ethnic prejudices as of 2003, but racism is not what it was. One sign is that the xenophobic Freedom Party has repeatedly been losing ground in a series of recent provincial and municipal elections.

In literature, always a social barometer, the black has paradoxically become an Austrian homeboy or homegirl, the person both inside and outside Viennese culture at the same time and therefore both familiar and distanced enough to register the society with unusual perceptiveness. This otherness is now exactly what can make the black a more, not less, valid representation of the Viennese, the person who by both fitting in and not fitting in is more keenly observant than those more self-evidently integrated. The title character of Peter Henisch's novel *Schwarzer Peter* starts right off pointing up the discrepancy: "Sie werden lachen, aber ich komme aus Wien. Auch wenn ich möglicherweise nicht ganz so aussehe. Vienna. Austria. Europe. Ob Sie es glauben oder nicht" (7). Visiting Vienna after twenty years in the United States, Peter commands views, critical insights, and wisdom that white residents of the city could never know, and in such a way as to be even more an embodiment of the city in which he spent his childhood than many other Viennese. In his way, this mixed-race musician is as "urwienerisch" as Breitwieser was often said to be (Maderthaner 163). What could be more Viennese than bewitching listeners through music from the soul? The exact feature that made Jonny a dangerous, exotic novelty to the other characters in the play and to audiences outside it in

1927 is what builds a bridge between Peter and the Viennese, beguiled by his New Orleans jazz and blues, in 2000. Through music he articulates his own soul—and theirs.[15]

Magnolia Brown, the central character of Lilian Faschinger's novel *Wiener Passion*, is also a mixed-race child, but she was raised in the United States from birth by a mother who spoke German with her. In Vienna for the first time as an adult, and living with an old relative, she discovers a manuscript revealing painful family history purposely unexplored by those who have stayed. While the Viennese great-aunt tends to suppress the few items of the past she is aware of, Magnolia scrutinizes her heritage, making it cohere by delving deep into it and finding through it what the present means. Confronting taboos and secrets wrapped in strategic forgetting is not just some abstract exercise in *Vergangenheitsbewältigung* for Magnolia; her uncompromising pursuit of the truth creates needed upheaval in her life by showing her for the first time what love and fulfillment of self really consist in. While the indigenous Viennese prefer numbness to painful truth, Magnolia gives momentum to a world in which she induces renewal and growth. Her singing teacher, a mama's-boy invalid, becomes her lover and recovers, released from crippling hypochondria to convey with unhampered fervor the heritage of Schubert and Mahler. The *Winterreise* and the *Kindertotenlieder* no longer articulate a decadent cult of death but point in their emotional integrity and formal perfection to enhanced life. Both characters achieve coherence through music, Peter by bringing the new music of America to Vienna, Magnolia by revitalizing the old music of Vienna as an American.

## 7. Colorful City

We can close the book and walk around the city now. Though white, the writer of this essay resembles Peter and Magnolia in being strongly connected to Vienna but not physically present all the time. The advantage gained from spending several months a year and then going away is that gradual changes are quickly apparent on returning. Mixed-race couples, almost never to be seen five years ago, are now not uncommon. Groups of school children on their class trips are at least one-third African, Asian, Turkish, or Latin American. Black Africans are very much more frequent than in, say, 1998, and they are clearly registered as less alien than they were. Blacks and Asians are hip features of print advertising, and European MTV would not think of not featuring at least one mixed-race DJ. The clerk who helps me in the local post office is Korean; many city employees, especially those dealing with residency permits, have Turkish, Iranian, or Arabic names but Austrian citizenship, like Herr Park from the post office. When Turkey advanced in the summer of 2002 to the final rounds of a soccer championship, many Viennese of German-white heritage and ethnicity stood on the sidewalks waving and applauding as happy drivers went by, flying Turkish flags and honking their horns. Xenophobia, stereotyping, and racism are still painfully evident, but a video of casual street scenes in Vienna from 1993 would be far less colorful than one from 2003, and on the whole, the city appears to be adjusting, blessedly free of the skinhead attacks that have taken place in other large European cities. The change can be seen in the young; the Vienna choirboys, the quintessence of traditional culture, are as a group not nearly as blond and blue-eyed as they were a decade ago, and schoolkids on the streetcar are worried about who has the coolest cell phone or the latest sneakers, not whether their friends are yellow, copper, or brown. Hearing Herr Park speak pure Viennese colloquial dialect seems to strike me odder than it does his other customers.

At the transportation terminal at Kagran some weeks ago, I stopped to watch passengers coming down the escalator. For almost a full minute, I saw almost no all-white Viennese. Among other languages I could at least recognize, I heard Tagalog, Arabic, Turkish, Brazilian Portuguese, and Senegalese French. It was almost as if the scene were a staged parade of multiculturalism, and I kept wondering why it looked so familiar until it came to me—I could have been back in Chicago.

## Notes

[1] One American and one Austrian novel—their authors coincidentally had the same last name—read as almost deliberate rebuttals of the "rags-to-riches" American dream; Henry Roth's *Call It Sleep* (1934) depicts through the

autobiographical character David Schearl the poverty and misery of Jewish immigrants on Manhattan's Lower East Side around 1905-1910, while Joseph Roth's *Hiob: Roman eines einfachen Mannes*, published in 1930 by a writer who never visited America, shows just as graphically the grueling conditions in this same slum district at the same time through the fate of Mendel Singer. The respective spiritual redemptions of David and Mendel are unrelated to any improvement in their outward status; the characters remain as materially poor at the end as they were at the beginning, though they are reborn inwardly.

[2] Ernst Lothar's novel *Der Engel mit der Posaune* depicts a family of piano manufacturers rising gradually to wealth in all the accepted capitalistic ways, but it is indicative of the difference between American and Austrian patterns that Hans Alt, the heir to the family business and fortune, grows into one of those radiantly pure souls like Valentin in Ferdinand Raimund's play *Der Verschwender*, uncorrupted, rooted in primal virtues, casting off material ostentation, and scornful of power and social position even before his business is Aryanized and he becomes an ascetic and social outcast notable for his profound spiritual fulfillment as a defiantly proud Austrian in the National Socialist years.

[3] The earnest and sometimes violent street theater of massive demonstrations belongs in this category as well. Öhlinger (136-68) and Maderthaner and Musner, throughout their book, describe the marches—for work, for affordable grocery prices, for voting rights—that took place periodically from the late 1860s on. The burning of the Justizpalast on July 15, 1927 was the culmination of this movement and has been judged by writers of "Geschichte" in both senses as a turning point in Austrian history. Karl Kraus, Heimito von Doderer, Elias Canetti, and Erich Fried are only a few of the authors who drew on this event as the basis for comprehensive analyses of Austrian political and social problems. (With a small but sad number of exceptions, almost all demonstrations after 1945 have been relatively peaceful and often unexpectedly successful.)

[4] These may also be some of the reasons why Hollywood's version of Robin Hood, as personified by Errol Flynn (1938), enjoyed such huge success in the years of the Great Depression and the growing menace of totalitarianism. (Another Austrian connection, if not an essential one—the music for the film was by Erich Wolfgang Korngold.)

[5] The reaction against romanticizing technology in spy stories and "tales of international intrigue" began relatively early, with the novels of Joseph Conrad (*Nostromo* and *The Secret Agent*) and continued with the "entertainments" of Graham Greene in a later generation (*The Ministry of Fear*). It increased during the Cold War; counterbalancing the extreme gadgetry and derring-do of Ian

Fleming's James Bond novels, John le Carré's *The Spy Who Came In from the Cold* signaled an age of somber, even squalid tales in which technology is at best absurdly irrelevant and at worst actively harmful. In Austrian literature, what romance there might have been about technology in spy stories was debunked in the gritty novels of Milo Dor and Reinhard Federmann from the 1950s—*Internationale Zone* and *Und wenn sie nicht gestorben sind* . . ., for example. It seems symptomatic of American persistence in the romantic view that the examples in English mentioned here are all from Great Britain. Foolishly naïve Holly Martins of *The Third Man* remains the American symbol of misplaced trust. Except for a few dark novels of intense disillusionment, often directly or indirectly involving the assassination of John F. Kennedy (Don DeLillo's *Libra*, for instance, or Thomas Pynchon's *The Crying of Lot 49*, with its vision of universal conspiracy), technological prowess, and its attendant basic belief in "the government," has not essentially been called into question; the American high-tech thriller continues to thrill, as shown by the sales figures of Tom Clancy and John Grisham. By contrast, American awareness of the dangers arising from technology has usually come from non-fiction; John Hersey's *Hiroshima* or Rachel Carson's *Silent Spring* are two absolute classics, more nuanced and sophisticated than the earlier, crudely effective "problem" novels of Upton Sinclair and other "muckrakers," likewise written with polemical intent.

[6] The contours of this fear are explored in two fascinating but relatively lesser-known examples. Alfred Döblin's novel *Berge, Meere und Giganten* (1924) depicts a once totally urbanized world of the twenty-seventh century in which a few remaining "Siedler"—worshipers of fire in a post-technological age—have returned to nature and lead a fulfilling life after the collapse of technology through extreme overproduction and global wars. Though neither American nor Austrian, Döblin calls for mention here because his novel appears almost purposely answered by Doderer's "Divertimento No. IV" (1926-1927), in which any return to a pre-industrial Arcadian paradise proves impossible, because it is essential part of human activity to devise ever more sophisticated implements and weapons, a process that the leader of the agrarian colony is powerless to prevent by decree. Technology is inherent to human invention and will inevitably assert itself.

[7] The "Trolley Song" from the 1944 film *Meet Me in St. Louis* is one of the last "innocent" tributes to technology in American popular culture, and it is worth noting that the film is set in the Arcadian past of 1904, not in contemporary wartime. After 1945, technology increasingly became an instrument of conspicuous consumerism and a means of representing affluence through domestic gadgetry like hi-fi equipment, cars—traded in every year, of course—

and kitchen appliances, and through ostentatious planned vacations, now defined as scheduled breaks from the primary activity of the job, not just weekend jaunts. (This aspect of creeping American-style consumerism in Austria is mirrored perfectly as a motif in Doderer's story "Tod einer Dame im Sommer.") Technology also became a hallmark of military or "defense" superiority, from "atoms for peace" and new agricultural methods of greater crop yield—the rhetoric was that hunger was about to be wiped out forever worldwide—to nuclear weaponry, enabling threats of "massive retaliation," and rocket science. Loewen points out (254-70) how an advertising slogan once used by General Electric, "Progress Is Our Most Important Product," illustrates that technology had taken on a more serious, "onward-and-upward" aspect after World War II, a tone anticipated by the "Century of Progress" World's Fair in Chicago in 1933. Only twenty years separate Judy Garland's bucolic scene with the "Trolley Song" from Dr. Strangelove's retreat into an underground bunker to outlast the nuclear winter he has brought on.

[8] Taylor also figures as one of Dos Passos's ruthless demons (III 19-25), and his production methods haunt the brilliant conveyor-belt and automation scenes of Charlie Chaplin's *Modern Times*.

[9] Writing in 1982, Schmidt-Dengler referred to *Karl und das zwanzigste Jahrhundert* as "so etwas wie ein Unikum in der Literaturgeschichte" (84). When the novel was new, Theodor Kramer acknowledged its uniqueness by titling his review "Eine neue literarische Form?."

[10] When *Karl und das zwanzigste Jahrhundert* was first published in 1932, it enjoyed huge popularity in the German-speaking world. It was translated into English "under the aegis of Dorothy Thompson," as Waldinger mentions (342), and was likewise well received, if by a smaller readership. "In the year 1943 the *New Republic* conducted a symposium on the theme *Books Read Too Little*; Sinclair Lewis placed *Karl and the Twentieth Century* at the head of his list" (Waldinger 342).

[11] Luft provides a pertinent summary insight: "Musil offers the most balanced perspective, advocating a sophisticated scientific view of the world against a variety of metaphysical perspectives, while also attempting to come to terms with the realities of the world of feelings" (3).

[12] Space limits preclude a parallel listing of passages, but the three consecutive chapters about Ulrich's coming of age (I: 9, "Erster von drei Versuchen, ein bedeutender Mann zu werden"; 10, "Der zweite Versuch. Ansätze zu einer Moral des Mannes ohne Eigenschaften"; 11, "Der wichtigste Versuch"—Musil 35-41) can be seen through their turns of phrase to parody Emerson's essays "Self-Reliance," "Nature," and "The American Scholar." Ulrich turns to theo-

retical mathematics in Chapter 11, a more scholarly pursuit called into question in its turn by Hermann Broch in his novel *Die unbekannte Größe* (1933).

[13] Their intense mutual antipathy would have made a comparison between them unwelcome to either Musil or Doderer, but the resemblance of the criminals' names would provide a point of departure for exploring Musil's influence on Doderer (who at this point would be turning in his grave).

[14] The latest revival at the Vienna State Opera, with performances in December 2002 and May 2003, capitalizes on the extreme discrepancy between "black" Jonny and his popular portrayer, the winsome and almost stereotypically Nordic, blond, blue-eyed Bo Skovhus.

[15] The first question this writer would ask Henisch is if he knows James Baldwin's great story "Sonny's Blues," in which music likewise reveals and articulates the emotional depth of the main character.

## Works Cited

Bauer, Roger. "Wandlungen des Geschmacks und der dramatischen Konventionen im biedermeierlichen Wien." *Laßt sie koaxen, Die kritischen Frösch' in Preußen und Sachsen!: Zwei Jahrhunderte Literatur in Österreich*. Vienna: Europa, 1977. 150-66. Rpt. of Horst Rüdiger, Dieter Gutzen, et al. *Teilnahme und Spiegelung: Festschrift für Rüdiger Horst*. Berlin: de Gruyter, 1975. 385-96.

Brunngraber, Rudolf. *Karl und das zwanzigste Jahrhundert*. 1932. Nördlingen: Greno, 1988.

Canetti, Elias. *Die Fackel im Ohr. Lebensgeschichte 1921-1931*. 1980. Frankfurt/Main: Zweitausendeins, 2001.

Dobretsberger, Christine. "Der kühle Silberlaut des Mondes." *Wiener Zeitung*, 18 Dec. 2002: 9.

Doderer, Heimito von. *Die Dämonen: Nach der Chronik des Sektionsrates Geyrenhoff*. 1956. Munich: Beck, 1995.

Dos Passos, John. *U. S. A.* (I. *The 42nd Parallel*, II. *1919*, III. *The Big Money*.) New York: Modern Library, 1939.

Emerson, Ralph Waldo. *Essays and Lectures*. Ed. Joel Porte. Library of America 15. New York: Library Classics of the United States, 1983.

Faschinger, Lilian. *Wiener Passion*. Cologne: Kiepenheuer & Witsch, 1999.

Fortunaso, Robert. *Robin Hood: The Facts and the Fiction.* 25 Mar. 2003. <http://www.geocities.com/longo44au/index 2>.

Friedell, Egon. *Kulturgeschichte der Neuzeit.* Vol. 1: *Die Krisis der europäischen Seele von der schwarzen Pest bis zum Ersten Weltkrieg.* 1927. Munich: dtv, 1976. Rpt. 2001. 2 vols.

Henisch, Peter. *Schwarzer Peter.* Salzburg and Vienna: Residenz, 2000.

Howes, Geoffrey. "Emerson's Image in Turn-of-the-Century Austria: The Cases of Kassner, Friedell, and Musil." *Modern Austrian Literature* 22 (1989): 227-40.

Johler, Reinhard. "'Wien bleibt Wien' – 'Wien ist anders' – 'Wien darf nicht Chicago werden': Zur Rhetorik gegenwärtiger Urbanitätdiskurse in Wien." *Berliner Blätter: Ethnographische und Ethnologische Beiträge* 17 (2000): 51-60.

Kisch, Egon Erwin. "Wie der Einbrecher Breitwieser erschossen wurde." *Der rasende Reporter.* Berlin: Aufbau, 1995. 21-27.

Kramer, Theodor. "Eine neue literarische Form?" *Tage-Buch*, 27 Aug. 1932. 4 Apr. 2003. <http://www.uni-mainz.de/~hilst005Brunngraber>.

Krenek, Ernst. *Im Atem der Zeit: Erinnerungen an die Moderne.* Tr. Friedrich Saathen. Rev. Tr. Sabine Schulte. Hamburg: Hoffmann und Campe, 1998.

– – –. *Jonny spielt auf.* Krenek. *Prosa. Dramen. Verse.* Munich and Vienna: Langen-Müller, 1965. 59-99.

– – –. "Johnny spielt auf." *Im Zweifelsfalle: Aufsätze zur Musik.* Munich: Europa, 1985. 13-32.

Kurth, Ulrich. "'Ich pfeif auf Tugend und Moral': Zum Foxtrott in den zwanziger Jahren." *Ich will aber gerade vom Leben singen. . . : Über populäre Musik vom ausgehenden 19. Jahrhundert bis zum Ende der Weimarer Republik.* Ed. Sabine Schutte. Reinbek: Rowohlt, 1987. 365-84. Rpt. (abridged) in Ernst Krenek. *Der Sprung über den Schatten.* Bielefeld Opera. Cond. David de Villiers. CPO 999 0820-2, 1989. 30-34.

Loewen, James. W. *Lies My Teacher Told Me: Everything Your American History Textbook Got Wrong.* 1995. New York: Touchstone, 1996.

Lothar, Ernst. *Der Engel mit der Posaune.* Salzburg: Silberboot, 1949.

Luft, David S. *Eros and Inwardness in Vienna: Weininger, Musil, Doderer.* Chicago: U of Chicago P, 2003.

Lupack, Alan. *The Robin Hood Project at the University of Rochester.* 25 Mar. 2003. <http://www.lib.rochester.edu/camelot/rh/rhhome.stm>.

Maderthaner, Wolfgang; and Lutz Musner. *Die Anarchie der Vorstadt: Das andere Wien um 1900.* 2nd. ed. Frankfurt am Main: Campus, 2000.

Mattl-Wurm, Sylvia. *Wien vom Barock bis zur Aufklärung.* Vol. 4. *Geschichte Wiens.* Vienna: Pichler, 1999. 6 vols.

Mayer, Kurt Albert. *Die Wienbilder der amerikanischen Delegierten John Hay und Charles Francis Adams jr.* Vienna: n.p., 1995.

Musil, Robert. *Der Mann ohne Eigenschaften.* 1930-1932. Vol. 1. Ed. Adolf Frisé. 1978. Reinbek: Rowohlt, 2000. 2 vols.

Nestroy, Johann Nepomuk. *Einen Jux will er sich machen. Ausgewählte Werke.* Ed. Joseph Gregor. Vienna: Globus, 1959. 151-243.

Öhlinger, Walter. *Wien im Aufbruch zur Moderne.* Vol. 5. *Geschichte Wiens.* Vienna: Pichler, 1999. 6 vols.

Richartz, Walter E. "Fünfzig Jahre Skandal im Weißen Haus oder Das Würstchen als Präsident." In Richartz. *Vorwärts ins Paradies: Aufsätze zu Literatur und Wissenschaft.* 1979. Zurich: Diogenes, 1988. 76-99.

– – –. "Das Neueste aus Laputa oder Scheppern für die Wissenschaft?" *Vorwärts ins Paradies.* 128-93.

Roth, Joseph. *Hiob: Roman eines einfachen Mannes.* 1930. Cologne: Kiepenheuer & Witsch, 2002.

Schivelbusch, Wolfgang. *Geschichte der Eisenbahnreise: Zur Industrialisierung von Raum umd Zeit im 19. Jahrhundert.* 1977. Frankfurt/Main: Fischer, 2000.

Schmidt-Dengler, Wendelin. "Statistik und Roman: Über Otto Neurath und Rudolf Brunngraber." *Arbeiterbildung in der Zwischenkriegszeit: Otto Neurath – Gerd Arntz.* Ed. Friedrich Stadler. Vienna: Löcker, 1982. 119-24. Rpt. in Schmidt-Dengler. *Ohne Nostalgie: Zur österreichischen Literatur der Zwischenkriegszeit.* Literaturgeschichte in Studien und Quellen 7. Ed. Klaus Amann, Hubert Lengauer, and Karl Wagner. Vienna: Böhlau, 2002. 82-91.

Schopenhauer, Arthur. "Die Kunst, Recht zu behalten." 10 Apr. 2003. <http://www.institut-halbach.de/g_streit/recht>.

Sebald, W. G. *Unheimliche Heimat: Essays zur österreichischen Literatur.* 1991. Frankfurt/Main: Fischer, 1995.

Skinner, James M. *The Cross and the Cinema: The Legion of Decency and the National Catholic Office for Motion Pictures, 1933-1970.* New York: Praeger, 1993.

Trotsky, Leon. "At the Coffin of Franz Schuhmeier." Memorial Tribute. 8 Feb. 1913. *Marxist Writers.* 24 Mar. 2003. <http://www.marxists.org/achive/trotsky/works/1940/profiles/franzschumeier [sic]>.

Waldinger, Ernst. "Rudolf Brunngraber: Novelistic Innovator." *Books Abroad* 26 (1952): 340-44.

# Anti-Americanisms in Contemporary Canadian Fiction

## Verena Klein

### Backdrop Addresses Cowboy

Star-spangled cowboy
sauntering out of the almost-
silly West, on your face
a porcelain grin,
tugging a papier-mâché cactus
on wheels behind you with a string,

you are innocent as a bathtub
full of bullets.

Your righteous eyes, your laconic
trigger-fingers
people in the streets with villains:
as you move, the air in front of you
blossoms with targets

and you leave behind you a heroic
trail of desolation:
beer bottles
slaughtered by the side
of the road, bird-
skulls bleaching in the sunset.

I ought to be watching
from behind a cliff or a cardboard

storefront
when the shooting starts, hands
clasped
in admiration,
but I am elsewhere.

Then what about me

what about the I
confronting you on that border
you are always trying to cross?

I am the horizon
you ride towards, the thing you can
never lasso

I am also what surrounds you:
my brain
scattered with your
tin cans, bones, empty shells,
the litter of your invasions.

I am the space you desecrate
as you pass through.

This poem by Margaret Atwood emphasizes the ambivalent feelings many Canadians have towards the United States. Since the foundation of the dominion in 1867, but especially since the 1950s, Canada has been concerned with the formation of a distinct national identity. The search for a Canadian identity as well as the struggles for dissociation from the United States feature in many Canadian texts. In the following, I will discuss Anti-American attitudes in *The Englishman's Boy* and *Green Grass, Running Water*, two frequently discussed Canadian novels from the 1990s.

*The Englishman's Boy* by the Saskatchewan author Guy Vanderhaeghe was published in 1996 and won the Governor General's Award the same year. Like *Green Grass, Running Water* (1993) by Thomas King, who is of Cherokee, Greek and German descent, it excited the interest of a large community of readers and literary critics. In both novels, three Anti-American attitudes are particularly prominent. Both question the rules of traditional historiography and attempt to deconstruct official versions of American history by giving voice to alternative historical accounts. They also disparage stereotypes of Indianness prevalent in North American society and show their negative impact on Hollywood's film industry, of which they paint a rather unfavorable picture. Moreover, both novels critique the position of the United States as a superpower, which is illustrated by the U.S. citizens' condescending treatment of non-Americans in the novels.

## 1. No Truths, Only Stories

In *Green Grass, Running Water*, the narrator informs the trickster Coyote that "there are no truths. . . . Only stories" (432). This statement summarizes an essential idea that both novels give voice to. Both speak in favor of alternative versions of history and question the possibility of a faithful representation of the past, thus reflecting the trends of modern historiography. Before the advent of postmodernism historical novels were believed to 'hold up a mirror' to the past and to represent the past 'as it really was.' It was commonly assumed that although the past as such does not exist anymore, an able historian or writer of historical fiction could make it still visible through "proper methodological procedures and critical awareness" (Wylie 10).

In the second half of the twentieth century the concepts underlying history and historical writing underwent substantial change, and the "traditional view of history as a picture of the past" (Wylie 4) was given up. Since the advent of postmodernism historiography has been much more fragmented, self-conscious and self-reflexive. In other words, contemporary historians and writers of historical fiction strongly question the possibility of an objective representation of the past and are much more preoccupied with the creation of a more heterogeneous picture—or pictures—of history. As history is no longer regarded as a unified story, the revelation of alternative accounts of historical events and the focus on marginal groups in society are considered the main task of contemporary historiography.

The subversion of traditional historical discourse and its move towards self-reflexivity has also brought history and literature closer together. Since the writing of history always implies an act of interpretation, the work of historians, it has been argued, is not much different from the task of literary writers. Hayden White, who contends that history and literature share many characteristics, points out that historical facts

> are *made* into a story by the suppression or subordination of certain of them and the highlighting of others, by characterization, motific repetition, variation of tone and point of view, alternative descriptive strategies, and the like—in short, all of the techniques that we would normally expect to find in the emplotment of a novel or play. (84)

Contemporary Canadian fiction, such as *The Englishman's Boy* or *Green Grass, Running Water,* clearly reflects these new trends in historiography. Vanderhaeghe's novel focuses on the Cypress Hills Massacre of 1873, an episode frequently overlooked in North American history. From the point of view of a young man, simply referred to as the "Englishman's boy," Vanderhaeghe relates the events leading to the massacre. After his master's death, the Englishman's boy joins a group of wolfers from Montana who are on their way to Canada, where they hope to catch a group of horse thieves. Unable to find these, the brutal wolfers kill a group of innocent Assiniboine Indians in what are today the Canadian prairie provinces. A second, fictitious story which Vanderhaeghe skillfully intertwines with the account of the massacre is centered on the U.S.-American millionaire Damon Ira Chance, who attempts to make the Cypress Hills Massacre into a Hollywood Western in the 1920s.

Chance's main motivation to shoot the Western is not only to bring a frequently overlooked fact of history closer to the U.S.-American audience but also to contribute to the shaping of an U.S.-American historical truth. In order to gather more information on the massacre, Chance hires Harry Vincent, a young script writer, who ironically comes from Canada, to interview Shorty McAdoo, a legendary cowboy, who is said to have participated in the Cypress Hills Massacre. Only gradually is it brought home to the reader that Shorty is the "Englishman's boy" whose story is told in the second half of the novel. When Harry shows the draft for his movie script to Chance, the latter does not accept Harry's version because it is based on McAdoo's account and forces him to change the script. Contrary to what really happened, Chance makes Harry state that the Assiniboine—and not the U.S.-American wolfers—started the fire. Chance's suppression of McAdoo's account of the massacre illustrates the techniques of traditional historiography, typically based on the account of the victors. Herb Wylie points out: "In this light, historical discourse appears as an act of power, the assertion of a particular reading of certain historical material and certain points of view, and the projection of a particular ideology, which traditionally, unsurprisingly, has been that of the victor" (12). In the case of *The Englishman's Boy* the victors clearly are the cruel wolfers, whom Chance regards as brave frontiersmen. Thus he justifies the modification of Harry Vincent's movie script in the following way: "The picture of the rawhide frontiersman is entitled to hang in the mind of every American. To hang illuminated by lightning—the cold eyes, the steady hand, the long rifle revealed in brightness. . . . Rewrite it" (242-43). Through the depiction of Chance's behavior Guy Vanderhaeghe paints a highly critical picture of the United States, maintaining that it does not acknowledge alternative versions of history. All accounts of the Cypress Hills Massacre seen from a point of view other than the U.S.-American need to be suppressed if they challenge national myths such as the integrity of the frontiersmen. However, by including Shorty McAdoo's version of the massacre—and thus a description of the brutal behavior of the wolfers—into the novel, Vanderhaeghe manages to create a more heterogeneous picture of the event. Thus, his novel invites readers to look critically at the North American past and encourages them to form their own opinion.

Despite the fact that Thomas King's *Green Grass, Running Water* cannot be classified as a typical historical novel because it is too "carnivalesque" (Wylie xvii), it nonetheless subverts dominant versions of North American history in a way comparable to *The Englishman's Boy*. Like Vanderhaeghe's novel, *Green Grass, Running Water* is constructed along two alternating story lines, one of which depicts in a highly entertaining way the lives of a group of Blackfoot on a reserve in Alberta. The other half of the novel consists of four Native North American creation stories, told and simultaneously lived through by the tricksters First Woman, Thought Woman, Changing Woman and Old Woman, who are accompanied by Coyote. In Native North American mythology they are so-called First People, or to use William Bright's words, "members of a race of mythic prototypes who lived before humans existed" (xi). It is in these retellings of the creation story that Thomas King's critique of dominant versions of history is best visible.

Although *Green Grass, Running Water* is set in Canada and repeatedly lampoons the United States, King does not confine his critique to the North American continent but addresses it to Western society in general, basing it on a parody of the "master-narrative" of Western society, the Bible. In order to understand all of King's allusions, a profound knowledge of Native North American as well as Western cultural and religious traditions is required, as biblical stories—traditionally said to relate "absolute truth" (Wilke 83)—are juxtaposed as well as intertwined with traditional Native North American myths. This skillful juxtaposition of aboriginal and Western values leads readers to a thorough re-examination of North American society. Gundula Wilke explains: "The appropriation and re-telling of an existing text becomes the parodic inversion of the original text, questioning its values and its influence and therefore establishing a counter-discourse with alternative spiritual visions" (83).

The creation myths contained in *Green Grass, Running Water* follow a repetitive pattern. In each story a mythic female falls out of the Sky World into the Water World. Such a beginning, argues Sharon Bailey, is characteristic of Blackfoot creation myths (44). Then, each of the women meets a famous male figure from the Bible. Whereas First

Woman and Changing Woman meet God and Noah from the Old Testament, Thought Woman and Old Woman encounter A[rch] A[ngel] Gabriel and Jesus from the New Testament. Each of these biblical figures attempts to subjugate the mythic trickster women but does not succeed in doing so. At the end of each creation myth each of the women takes on the identity of a famous literary male character: Lone Ranger, Ishmael, Robinson Crusoe and Hawkeye, respectively. In the disguise of their adopted male identities the four Indians participate in the second half of the novel where they work hard in order to "fix" the lives of a Blackfoot reserve in Alberta. Thus, the four mythical Indian characters function as a linking element between the two halves of the novel.

The juxtaposition of biblical and Native North American stories clearly highlights the underlying ideological framework of both cultures. Whereas the guiding principles in Native North American mythology as represented in *Green Grass, Running Water* are respect and equality, King presents Christianity, seen in the novel as the dominating force in North American society, as organized by strict hierarchy. The Christian God's desire to be omnipotent is a continuous source of critique throughout the novel—and his power is already undermined on the very first page:

> So.
> In the beginning, there was nothing. Just the water.
>
> Coyote was there, but Coyote was asleep. That Coyote was asleep and that Coyote was dreaming. When that Coyote dreams, anything can happen.
> I can tell you that. (1)

King depicts the Western God as one of Coyote's dreams that "gets loose" (1). However, in contrast to Coyote, who is a playful figure concerned with the interrelatedness of all aspects of life, the Christian God soon attempts to dominate the trickster and rule the world: "I don't want to be a little god, says that god. I want to be a big god!" (3). In plainer terms, King's Western God seeks to solidify his power over the universe. Although the disputes between God and Coyote at first sight seem to be only entertaining, they help readers understand that "the monotheist version of *creatio ex nihilo*—creation of the earth from nothing—achieves its singular and univocal status only by suppressing all other voices in this highly contested terrain" (Donaldson 32). Not only does King subvert Christian religious beliefs by making God a creation of Coyote's, but he also shows that the Western thought system owes its omnipresence on the North American continent to the suppression of aboriginal views.

All the creation stories related in *Green Grass, Running Water* promote a strong sense of community. In the first story, for instance, First Woman meets God in the Garden of Eden, and "everything is perfect. And everything is beautiful. And everything is boring" (40). As soon as God finds out that First Woman has been offered and has accepted food, he scolds her: "Anybody who eats my stuff is going to be very sorry . . . There are rules, you know. . . . Christian rules" (73). This confrontation between God and First Woman foregrounds their differing value systems. Whereas First Woman knows that her existence is connected to all other forms of life on earth—a concern which is expressed in King's novel through the admonition to "mind [one's] relations" (39)—and thus spends her time in the Garden of Eden helping others and "looking for things that are bent and need fixing" (40-41), the Western God is completely ignorant of this interrelatedness. Thus, when First Woman proposes to share the food she has been offered, God does not accept her invitation. First Woman, realizing what a "stingy person" (73) God is and understanding that he does not share her values, decides to leave the Garden of Eden together with "Adhamn" before God even has the time to expel her. Thus she shows that the seemingly omnipotent biblical God has no power over tricksters. (King's humorous rewriting of Adam's name further underlines First Woman's disinterest in Christian rules, about which she simply does not give "a damn".)

In addition to "minding their relations" and sharing their resources, the tricksters in King's creation stories are all equal whereas in the biblical stories included in the novel women are subjugated to men. King denounces women's inferiority in Western society in a number of exhilarating scenes in which First Woman, Thought Woman, Changing Woman and Old Woman each meet a male biblical character who is so used to the Christian gender rules that he automatically regards the native women as inferior and assumes that they will do what he desires.

However, the trickster women do not accept this inferior role; they show no signs of submission and treat the biblical men as they would treat everybody else, as the following passage, describing the first encounter between Changing Woman and Noah, exemplifies:

> Who are you? says the little man.
> I'm Changing Woman, says Changing Woman.
> Any relation to Eve? says the little man. She sinned, you know. That's why I'm in a canoe full of animals. That's why I'm in a canoe full of poop.
> Are you all right? Changing Woman asks Old Coyote.
> Psssst, says Old Coyote.
> Why are you talking to animals? says the little man. This is a Christian ship. Animals don't talk. We got rules.
> I fell out of the sky, says Changing Woman. I'm very sorry that I landed on Old Coyote.
> The sky! shouts the little man. Hallelujah! A gift from heaven. My name's Noah, and you must be my new wife.
> I doubt that, says Changing Woman.
> Lemme see your breasts, says Noah. I like women with big breasts. I hope God remembered that.
> Don't do it, says one of the Turtles. He'll just get excited and rock the canoe.
> I have no intention of showing him my breasts, says Changing Woman.
> Talking to the animals again, shouts Noah. That's almost bestiality, and it's against the rules.
> What rules?
> Christian rules. (159-60)

The rules of the Bible have no power over the trickster women in *Green Grass, Running Water* so that neither does God manage to expel First Woman from the Garden of Eden nor does Noah succeed in his attempts to "court" Changing Woman.

## 2. "Real" Indians

In addition to subverting dominant versions of North American history, both novels criticize stereotypes of the continent's aboriginal peoples. Both *The Englishman's Boy* and *Green Grass, Running Water* not only disparage clichés of Indianness but also highlight their mostly negative effects on the Indians themselves. As Vine Deloria ironically remarks:

> The American public feels most comfortable with the mythical Indians of stereotype-land who were always THERE. These Indians are fierce, they wear feathers and grunt. Most of us don't fit this idealized figure since we grunt only when overeating, which is seldom. . . . To be an Indian in modern American society is in a very real sense to be unreal and ahistorical. (45)

In 1922 Walter Lippmann defined a stereotype as a "picture inside [one's] head" (qtd. in Dovido et al. 279). Although present-day scientists have somewhat modified Lippmann's definition they still regard a stereotype as "a cognitive structure containing the perceiver's knowledge, beliefs, and expectancies about some human social group" (Mackie et al. 42). The creation of such belief patterns presupposes the categorization of individuals in different social groups (Mackie et al. 44). It is argued that human beings tend to categorize others in order to be able to deal more easily with the substantial amount of information they receive every day about their fellow human beings. Diane Mackie and her colleagues point out that "once an individual is categorized as a group member, the observer can assume that that person possesses many features characteristic of group members, even in the absence of empirical evidence about that individual" (45). Besides facilitating the handling of information about others, categorization "emphasizes the self-evaluative benefits of differentiating one's own group from other groups" (45). Since an individual's social identity is mainly based on group membership(s), the categorization of people contributes to a better understanding of the individual's own social group(s) and increases people's awareness of their own character traits and of the characteristics of the groups they belong to. The considerable impact of stereotypes on society, psychologists explain, is derived from the mostly negative emotions that are associated with them. In other words, when a person or object is repeatedly associated with a particular emotion, the person or object comes to elicit that emotion after a certain time. The creation of such negative stereotypes can be particularly harmful to ethnic groups since they can easily turn into self-fulfilling prophecies, thus making the negative belief patterns come true.

In *Green Grass, Running Water* Thomas King attempts to do away with stereotypes of North American Indianness through his humorous depiction of the so-called "Dead Dog Café," owned by the Canadian Blackfoot Latisha. The main reason for the popularity of the café lies in the marketing strategy Latisha applies. Although she uses mostly chicken or beef for the food she prepares, her customers, who are frequently tourists from the United States, are led to believe that she is actually selling them dog meat. Although the tourists intuitively realize that the meat they are served is not dog meat at all, the dog-meat myth of the café caters to their stereotypes about Indians. Besides, the "Dead Dog Café" refers to the impoverished Indians of the past who were forced to eat their dogs, as Jane Flick points out (149). Furthermore, the name of the café can be regarded as a playful joke based on Nietzsche's assertion of God's death, and thus as a harsh critique of Christianity (see Flick 149).

North American stereotypes of Indianness in both novels are depicted even more strongly in connection with Hollywood's film industry. *Green Grass, Running Water,* for instance, features Portland Looking Bear, a Canadian Blackfoot actor, who ekes out an existence by miming Indian characters in Hollywood Westerns. After a while, however, the movie moguls force Portland to change his name because they do not consider it "Indian" enough. Only when Portland changes his name to something as unrealistic as "Iron Eyes Screeching Eagle" is he allowed to continue acting. However, his luck is short-lived because soon the movie producers force him to wear a rubber nose, as his nose does not look native enough to them. Making Portland adapt his nose to the North American stereotype of Indianness exemplifies the importance of the face for the formation of stereotypes. Many stereotypes, Leslie Zebrowitz argues, are based on the face because it is still believed that people's character traits can be deduced from their appearance, in particular from their face (84). Portland, however, cannot bring himself to wear the rubber nose and is thus soon out of work. Instead, the movie producers hire white actors and transform them into the stereotypical "Indians" they want (*Green Grass, Running Water* 166).

Both novels also criticize that in Hollywood Westerns of the past the white cowboys are always the winners and the Indians always the losers. As already mentioned, the film producer Damon Ira Chance in

*The Englishman's Boy* does not accept Harry Vincent's film script on account of the assertion that the wolfers and not the Assiniboine started the massacre. Despite the fact that Harry quits the job as soon as he realizes that Chance is not interested in the historical truth, Chance shoots the Western, but is later killed by a friend of McAdoo's. A similar point is made in *Green Grass, Running Water*, where in all the Westerns in which Portland Looking Bear participates the cowboys win and the Indians lose. When Portland's son Charlie asks his mother whether his father also played heroes, such as "a lawyer or a policeman or a cowboy," she laughingly replies: "He could have. . . . But that was back before they had any Indian heroes" (166). Thus, in order to change the stereotypical pattern of the traditional Western at least in fiction Thomas King makes the trickster Coyote change a John Wayne Western so that for once the Indians win and the cowboys lose.

## 3. American Power

In 1968 Susan Sontag wrote about the United States: "Everything that one feels about this country is, or ought to be, conditioned by the awareness of American *power:* of America as the arch-imperium of the planet, holding man's biological as well as his historical future in its King Kong paws" (32). More than thirty years later not much has changed: the United States still are the most powerful nation of the world, the leading economic and military power. Already a decade ago, Noam Chomsky stressed that even though since the 1970s "the state capitalist world [has] moved towards a tripolar structure with economic power centered in the United States, Japan, and the German-based European Community" (1), military power has remained focused on the United States, which "remains the only power with the will and the capacity to exercise force on a global scale—even more freely than before, with the fading of the Soviet deterrent" (2). It is thus only logical that the U.S.-American dominance of economic and military world structures has also led to repercussions on a cultural level and to the Americanization of many parts of the globe.

In their respective novels Vanderhaeghe and King criticize that its powerful position in the world has led the United States to look down on others, not only abroad, but also at home. Harry Vincent in *The Englishman's Boy,* for instance, disapprovingly notices Hollywood's movie moguls' cruel treatment of cowboys, observing that the cowboys are simply held like cattle in a big "hiring tank" where they have to wait until they are needed:

> At dawn, I drive out to Universal City where more white hats ride the range than on any other spread in southern California. The program feature is king at Universal and the king of program features is the Western, cheap to make and profitable. . . . This Western factory also has its own herds of cattle, horses, and mules, grazing a huge pasture, ready to serve at a moment's notice. But it also requires a reliable reserve of two-legged stock to work as doubles, stunt men, and extras. Uncle Carl's solution to the problem of ready supply is to construct a big hiring tank fenced with wire to hold cowboys corralled inside the studio gates and out of mischief until they are needed. Anybody looking for employment is penned there until Universal directors give him the nod and cut him out of the remuda for a day's shooting. (66)

Moreover, Hollywood's movie moguls also force the cowboys to perform life-threatening stunts that are often fatal, as in the case of young Miles, a friend of Shorty McAdoo's, who dies while doing a "Running W":

> A Running W is how horses were thrown in movie action scenes before the SPCA put a stop to it. A Running W worked like this. A post called a deadman was driven solidly into the ground, out of camera view. Two lines of piano wire were run from the horse's fetlocks up its front legs and back underneath the girth of the saddle; the remaining several hundred feet of piano wire were coiled beside the deadman and the ends of the coils snubbed tight to the post buried in the ground. The stunt man's job was to ride a horse at a hard gallop until it ran out of line and the wire yanked its legs out from under it, hurt and crippled a lot of men. It was not popular with cowhands. (70)

Not only cowboys but also Indians are treated badly by U.S.-American characters in both novels. In *Green Grass, Running Water* this is shown through the cruel treatment of a Blackfoot family who wants to cross the border from Canada to the United States in order to take part in the annual Sun Dance. A young U.S. border guard confiscates the family's dancing outfits and lays them on the asphalt. When the father politely tells the guard that the dancing outfits are sacred and thus should not be laid on the asphalt the border guard righteously replies: "Guess we're the ones to say what's right and what's not right. . . . Isn't that right?" (284). The border guard does not even try to listen to the Blackfoot family and shows no respect for their sacred dancing outfits. In his eyes, they are just eagle feathers. When the family explains that they need their outfits he threatens them: "I can always put you in jail, if that's what you'd like" (284). It is little surprising that in the face of this alternative, the family decides to head back home.

The lack of respect and the condescension towards Indian traditions are not only evident in the border guard's behavior but also in the restitution of the outfits to the family. Instead of sincerely apologizing, a judge, this time a Canadian, "the Honorable Robert Loblaw" (311), turns the restitution of the outfits into his professional victory. In other words, the judge is more interested in making himself a name than in the incident itself. The judge's attitude towards the affair can be clearly seen in his complete disinterest in the family's tribal identity: he keeps referring to them as Cree.

The most entertaining as well as profound critique of American omnipotence is evident in Thomas King's character George Morningstar, the husband of Latisha, owner of the Dead Dog Café. When the Canadian Blackfoot Latisha first meets the U.S.-American George Morningstar she is enticed by his behavior as well as by his native-sounding name. After their marriage, however, their happiness is rather short-lived. Morningstar, despite his promising name, is unable to hold a job for more than three months so that Latisha has to look after her children alone. Moreover, he beats her and finally leaves her when she is pregnant with their third child. In a nutshell, Morningstar unites the most negative character traits. Yet although he has completely failed as husband and father, he is still full of self-confidence. His pride is entirely founded on his U.S. citizenship and he regards himself as superior to everyone else, especially to Canadians. Morningstar's self-righteousness can be clearly seen in the following passage.

> Early on in their marriage, George began to point out what he said he perceived to be the essential differences between Canadians and Americans.

"Americans are independent," George told her one day. "Canadians are dependent." Latisha told him she didn't think that he could make such a sweeping statement, that those kinds of generalizations were almost always false.
"It's all observation, Country," George continued. "Empirical evidence. In sociological terms, the United States is an independent sovereign nation and Canada is a domestic dependent nation. Put fifty Canadians in a room with one American, and the American will be in charge in no time."
George didn't say it with any pride, particularly. It was, for him, a statement of fact, an unassailable truth, a matter akin to genetics or instinct.
"Americans are adventurous," George declared. "Canadians are conservative. Look at western expansion and the frontier experience. Lewis and Clark were Americans."
What about Samuel de Champlain and Jacques Cartier? Latisha had asked.
"Europeans." George laughed, and then he gave her a hug. "Don't take it personally, Country." (172)

George's nationalistic attitude, however, makes Latisha only all the more convinced of raising her children as Canadians:

> In the end, simple avoidance proved to be the easiest course, and whenever George started to warm up, Latisha would take Christian into the bedroom and nurse him. There, in the warm darkness, she would stroke her son's head and whisper ferociously over and over again until it became a chant, a mantra, "You are a Canadian. You are a Canadian. You are a Canadian." (175-76)

George Morningstar clearly has not managed to Americanize his Canadian wife.

**Conclusion**

Anti-American critique in contemporary Canadian fiction is multi-layered and wide-ranged, as can be seen in *Green Grass, Running Water* and *The Englishman's Boy*. King's and Vanderhaeghe's novels share three facets of Anti-Americanism: they speak in favor of alternative versions of history, attempt to deconstruct stereotypes of Indianness and lampoon U.S.-American haughtiness towards others. Whereas Thomas King bases his critical examination of the United States on a parody of the Bible, Guy Vanderhaeghe uses a widely unknown event of 19th-century North American history, the Cypress Hills Massacre, as a starting point for his critical portrait of the United States and in particular of Hollywood's film industry.

However, even if this article has tried to show that both novels view the United States from a highly critical angle it should always be borne in mind that the action of both novels takes place on both sides of the border, in the United States as well as in Canada. Thomas King states: "I guess I'm supposed to say that I believe in the line that exists between the U.S. and Canada, but for me it's an imaginary line. It's a line from somebody else's imagination; it's not my imagination" (King in Linton 217). In other words, Canada is not flawless either—but this needs to be examined elsewhere.

**Works Cited**

Atwood, Margaret. "Backdrop Addresses Cowboy." *The New Romans: Candid Canadian Opinions of the U.S.* Ed. A. W. Purdy. New York: St. Martin's P, 1968. 10.

Bailey, Sharon M. "The Arbitrary Nature of the Story: Poking Fun at Oral and Written Authority in Thomas King's *Green Grass, Running Water.*" *World Literature Today* 73.1 (Winter 1999): 43-52.

Bright, William, ed. *A Coyote Reader.* Berkeley: U of California P, 1993.

Chomsky, Noam. *Deterring Democracy.* London: Verso, 1991.

Deloria, Vine. "Indians Today, the Real and the Unreal." *American Cultural Studies: A Reader.* Ed. John Hartley and Roberta E. Pearson. Oxford: Oxford UP, 2000. 44-52.

Donaldson, Laura E. "Noah Meets Old Coyote, or Singing in the Rain: Intertextuality in Thomas King's *Green Grass, Running Water.*" *Studies in American Indian Literature* 7.2 (Summer 1995): 27-43.

Dovido, John F., John C. Brigham, Blair T. Johnson, and Samuel L. Gaertner. "Stereotyping, Prejudice, and Discrimination: Another Look." *Stereo-*

*types and Stereotyping.* Ed. C. Neil Macrae et al. New York: The Guilford P, 1996. 276-319.

Flick, Jane. "Reading Notes for Thomas King's *Green Grass, Running Water.*" *Canadian Literature* 161 (1999): 140-72.

King, Thomas. *Green Grass, Running Water.* 1993. New York: Bantam Books, 1994.

Linton, Patricia. "'And Here's How It Happened': Trickster Discourse in Thomas King's *Green Grass, Running Water.*" *Modern Fiction Studies* 45.1 (Spring 1999): 212-34.

Mackie, Diane M., David L. Hamilton, Joshua Susskind, and Francine Rosselli. "Social Psychological Foundations of Stereotype Foundation." *Stereotypes and Stereotyping.* Ed. Neil C. Macrae et al. New York: Guilford P, 1996. 41-78.

Sontag, Susan. "What's Happening to America?" *American Cultural Studies: A Reader.* Ed. John Hartley and Roberta E. Pearson. Oxford: Oxford UP, 2000. 32-38.

Vanderhaeghe, Guy. *The Englishman's Boy.* 1996. London: Anchor, 1998.

White, Hayden. *Tropics of Discourse: Essays in Cultural Criticism.* Baltimore: The Johns Hopkins UP, 1978.

Wilke, Gundula. "Re-Writing the Bible: Thomas King's *Green Grass, Running Water.*" *Across the Lines: Intertextuality and Transcultural Communication in the New Literatures in English.* Ed. Wolfgang Klooss. Amsterdam: Rodopi, 1998. 83-90.

Wylie, Herb. *Speculative Fictions: Contemporary Canadian Novelists and the Writing of History.* Montreal: McGill-Queen's UP, 2002.

Zebrowitz, Leslie. "Physical Appearance as a Basis of Stereotyping." *Stereotypes and Stereotyping.* Ed. Neil C. Macrae et al. New York: Guilford P, 1996. 79-120.

# Americanisms under the Critical Eye of African-American Poet, Writer, Singer and Musician Gil Scott-Heron: the "Movie" Poems

## Sylvia Schiefer

Gil Scott-Heron published his first two novels, *The Vulture* and *The Nigger Factory*, as well as his first book of poetry, *Small Talk at 125th and Lenox*, in the early 1970s. Between 1970 and 1994 he produced 20 records. Most of them were created in collaboration with composer Brian Jackson and a group of musicians called the Amnesia Express. A selection of the poetry featured on these albums was published in two collections, *So Far, So Good* in 1990, and *Now and Then* in 2000.

In this paper I will focus on the "movie" poems, which were created in 1981 and 1984 as the artist's reaction to the election and re-election of Ronald Reagan as president of the United States. These poems offer a critical view on a wide variety of American clichés: the glitter and glamour of Hollywood, the cowboy myth, the heroism of warfare, the demonstration of strength and unity, and the great American dream of equal opportunities for everyone. Demonstrating the illusions which cover up the imperfections of American society, the "movie" poems highlight the gap between American values and American actualities.

With the election of George W. Bush as president of the United States in the year 2000 these poems have gained new relevance. In the following I will demonstrate that these poems do not only criticize American actualities of 1981 and 1984, but that they also show that many of the issues addressed have not changed much over the last 20 years. A critical analysis reveals striking parallels between now and then.

The first poem, "'B' Movie", was written in 1981. This poem can be split up into three parts: an introduction, the actual poem, and a one-line tune, which is repeated again and again at the end of the recorded version on Scott-Heron's album *Reflections*. This tune is not included in the written version of the poem. But in this paper the artist's performance on record will be considered as well, because it offers additional information and new aspects for a closer interpretation.

With the introduction Gil Scott-Heron sets the stage for the actual poem, as he explains the preconditions upon which we enter the world of the 'B' movies.

First, he criticizes the American election system when he says that "we've been convinced that 26% of the registered voters, not even 26% of the American people, but 26% of the registered voters form a mandate, or a landslide" ("'B' Movie" 8). With these words the artist does not only question the system itself but also the legitimacy of the thus elected president.

Second, Scott-Heron criticizes the show elements that have come to dominate politics, especially election campaigns. This does not only apply to Ronald Reagan, who indeed had been a professional actor before he started his political career, but to all politicians. In fact, politicians at all times have to be actors in certain ways, as it is often their performance and not their substance that is foregrounded in the media. It is their performance that attracts people and not their actions. And, as Scott-Heron says, as soon as we let ourselves be deceived by the image that is created around a candidate, we all become part of the show.

Third, the artist addresses the effects of economic change. He argues that people find it hard to accommodate to new circumstances. In the 1980s these were changes brought about by an increase of imports and a decrease of exports. This is what Scott-Heron means when he argues that "America has changed from a producer to a consumer" (8). At present, such changes are caused by globalization and the new economy, and Scott-Heron's argument still holds true: people have problems to adapt. What he says about natural resources still holds true as well: "Natural resources and minerals will control your world" (8). In the case of the United States the most important natural resource that comes to mind is oil. Many battles have been and probably will be fought in order to secure a permanent supply of oil. One of the reasons why George Bush senior battled Iraq in the early 1990s was to secure

America's access to the oil reserves in Kuwait. At present George W. Bush is also fighting Iraq, and it would be ignorant to believe that oil has not played an important role in his decision to go to war.

Fourth, Scott-Heron addresses people's tendency towards nostalgia. Every time things get difficult people tend to look back to the so-called "good old times," which were probably as tough as they are now, just different. But still, there is this inclination to look backwards: "They want to go back as far as they can, even if it turns out to be only last week. Not to face now or the future, but to face backwards" (9). And this past is strongly glorified: "yesterday was the time of our cinema heroes riding to the rescue at the last minute; the day of the man on the white horse or the man in the white hat, coming to save America at the last moment. Someone always came to save America at the last moment" (9). So, when people are facing backwards they are actually looking for a hero, a leader they can trust to solve their problems, an almighty father figure who can handle everything.

But this desire is extremely dangerous, as Scott-Heron demonstrates with the next lines: "unfortunately John Wayne was no longer available, so they settled for Ronald the Raygun" (9). By turning Ronald Reagan's name into Ronald the Raygun the poet alludes to the president's role in the cold war. And at this point we should also keep in mind that the current president's plans to build a new satellite defense system are quite similar to Reagan's "Star Wars" concept of nuclear deterrence. By contrasting Hollywood star John Wayne to 'B' movie actor Ronald Reagan Scott-Heron illustrates that, first, people normally do not get the star they actually want but a second-choice hero that is available, and second, that the concept of cinema heroes does not work in reality at all. Even John Wayne could not act in real life like the John Wayne in the movies.

At this point we cross the line between reality and fiction: "it has turned into something that we can only look at like a 'B' movie" (9). If we want to have cinema heroes, we have to change our perspective. We have to deceive ourselves in order to create the illusion of a reality as it is presented in a movie. We have to enter another world and go "back to those inglorious days before heroes were zeros . . . to the days of the wondrous 'B' movie," as is stated in the first lines of the poem (10).

At the beginning of the poem the most important positions in the film crew are filled. The producer "underwritten by all the millionaires necessary, will be 'Casper' the defensive Weinburger. No more animated a choice is available" (10). Caspar "Cap" Weinberger was Reagan's Secretary of Defense. As the head of the president's "Star Wars" program he played a powerful role in the cabinet. Punning on the politician's name the poet links him to the cartoon figure "Casper the friendly ghost" as well as to fast food.

The director "will be 'Attila' the Haig, running around declaring himself 'In charge and in control!' The ultimate realization of inmates taking over at the asylum" (10). Alexander Haig, Reagan's Secretary of State, here linked to Attila the belligerent King of the Huns, is further ridiculed through his own words. After Watergate Haig declared himself "in charge and in control," although he actually had totally lost control of the situation.

The poet's irony becomes even more subtle, when he further argues that the "screenplay will be adapted from the book called *Voodoo Economics* by George 'Papa Doc' Bush" (10). "Voodoo Economics" was the term used by George Bush senior in order to criticize Reagan's economic concepts, when they competed for the position of the presidential candidate for the Republican party. By naming him "Papa Doc" Scott-Heron actually links Reagan's successor and father of the current president of the United States to "Papa Doc" Duvalier, the former dictator of Haiti. From a present point of view, this word play could be extended even further by referring to George Bush junior as "Baby Doc."

When he finally suggests that the "theme song will be done by The Village People. That most military tune 'Macho Man.' A theme song for saber rattling and selling wars door-to-door" (10), Scott-Heron's irony reaches its peak. Wars are not sold door-to-door. This expression, taken from business language, is used to reveal the government's attitude towards war. War is business, too. And everybody who is only a little familiar with the song "Macho Man" knows that this is not a military tune at all. And surely the Reagan administration, very conservative, very straight, did not want to be connected in any way to The Village People, this group of gay singers in fancy costumes.

In a next step Scott-Heron explains the way in which the movie has to be made. First of all there have to be many clichés, like "Tall in the saddle," or "Riding on or off into the sunset," or "Qadafi, get off my planet by sunset" (10). As the words "country" or "land" are replaced by "planet" in this last quote, the poet thus also accuses his fellow Americans of being arrogant enough to perceive of the whole world as their own. From a present point of view, we could go one step further and replace the name Qadafi by Saddam Hussein and put the quote right into the current president's mouth.

The second element the movie needs is toughness. Scott-Heron starts this argument with examples that are not necessarily negative, when he states that the hero has to be "Marine tough . . . Bogart-tough, Cagney-tough . . . Hollywood-tough" and "John Wayne-tough," but then the artist suddenly drifts into a rather ordinary context when he says that the hero also has to be "cheap steak-tough," and he ends this line with "and Bonzo-substantial" (10). Bonzo was the name of a chimpanzee who co-starred in a movie with Ronald Reagan. So, what is actually being said here, is that as long as the hero is tough enough he does not have to have more substance than an ape. (This argument becomes even more hilarious from a present point of view, as the current president of the United States is compared to a chimp on the internet. On the web site www.bushorchimp.com one finds pictures that relate different facial expressions of George W. Bush junior to those of a chimp.)

Clichés and toughness, these are the most important elements of the 'B' movie which is presented in this poem. And as soon as they are sufficiently present, the audience does not care so much about who is actually starring anymore, as Gil Scott-Heron expresses in the next lines: "Put your order in, America, and quick as Kodak we duplicate, with the accent on the dupe" (10). It is not the man himself that is important, but the image he incorporates and the clichés he transports. And as we accept these duplicates of heroes, we are duped ourselves. But, as the artist further argues, people are all too ready to trick or deceive themselves: "It's a clear case of selective amnesia: remembering what we want to remember and forgetting what we choose to forget" (11). We are willing to forget anything that does not fit our illusion of reality. And if we choose our leaders according to this concept, we are prone to follow "the new Captain Bligh on the new Ship of Fools" (11). We get a hero who leads us in the wrong direction. But as we are not on the *Bounty* but on the Ship of Fools we do not even notice that, and we let him proceed.

Being fools we can probably also agree to the following argument: "Civil Rights. Gay Rights. Women's Rights. They're all wrong! Call in the cavalry to disrupt this perception of freedom gone wild. First one of them wants freedom and then the whole damn world wants freedom" (11). With these words Scott-Heron touches the very heart of the American nation. The United States is proud to uphold freedom and equal rights, which are perceived as the quintessential American values. But, taking a closer look at history, we have to ask ourselves: For whom? For everybody, or just the white majority? For everybody, or just the heterosexual majority? For everybody, or just the dominant male portion of the population? And if we expand our view, the issue gets even more complicated and further questions are raised. Does America want freedom and equal rights for every nation or just for the United States, or maybe just for every nation that is based on structures that are similar to those of the United States? These questions also immediately come to one's mind if one recalls the current president's recent statements, in which he has made clear that anybody who is not with America, is consequently against it.

With such arguments, complicated issues are reduced to very simple, old-fashioned concepts. But, as Gil Scott-Heron has stated in his introduction and repeats here, this seems to be exactly what people are longing for when things get too difficult: "Nostalgia. That's what America wants. The good old days. When we 'gave them hell!' . . . To a time when movies were in black and white and so was everything else" (11). When times get harder, people are longing for clear and familiar patterns that allow them to easily distinguish right from wrong, so that they can draw a clean line between friend and enemy. At present George W. Bush is trying to meet this need of the American people by frequently using the words "good" and "evil."

Reality, however, is different, as the poet remarks in the language of the stock exchange: "Racism is up. Human Rights are down. Peace is shaky. War items are hot. . . . Jobs are down, money is scarce and Common Sense is at an all-time low with heavy trading" (12). But we do not even realize the actual situation anymore because of the illusion we have created to live in, as Scott-Heron concludes the written version of his poem: "Movies were looking better than ever and now no one is looking because we're all starring in a 'B' movie" (12).

On the recording, however, the artist offers something like an exit strategy. There is this tune which consists of only one line: "This ain't really your life, ain't really your life, ain't really, ain't really nothing but a movie" (*Reflections*). This line is repeated again and again and again until the words become barely identifiable. And we end up with this wave of sound which seems to be irresistible. This tune functions like a meditation chant which drags you in and forces you to think about present realities, and therefore it also works like a wake-up call inviting you to open your mind and take a fresh look at the world around you.

The second poem, "Re-Ron," was written in 1984 as the artist's reaction to Ronald Reagan's re-election. With the title of this poem Gil Scott-Heron ironically addresses the aspect of boredom that comes with repetition. The movie which is characterized in this poem is not only a 'B' movie, but even worse, it is the re-run of a 'B' movie. Therefore, it does not only lack quality but also originality, as is stated in the chorus of this song: "We don't need no Re-Ron . . . We've seen all the Re-Rons before" ("Re-Ron" 13). And in a variation of this line the poet adds: "A Re-Ron, the late late show. A black and white flick from ages ago" (15), thus demonstrating that it also is not apt to fulfill the requirements of the present.

What is so striking about this second poem is that Scott-Heron has become more explicit. He does not work so much with subtle irony anymore, but formulates his position in clearer, more concrete statements as the quotes above also demonstrate. This new, more aggressive element is also expressed in the music, which works with harder and faster beats as opposed to the smooth and jazzy melody backing the first poem. Taking a look at the whole corpus of Scott-Heron's musical work, we can see that such beats are really not typical of him.

The artist has become harder because the situation has tightened and he feels that the government is "[b]anging on the war drums and we're listening to the rhythms" (13). As this observation characterizes present developments as well, this line functions as another strong demonstration of the striking parallels between the past and the present. Furthermore, the artist also addresses the common political stance of Ronald Reagan and Maggie Thatcher, thus criticizing the co-operation between the United States and the United Kingdom in global issues, especially concerning warfare (cf. "Re-Ron" 15). At present George W. Bush and Tony Blair demonstrate a similar uniformity of attitudes. The present situation, thus, not only shows that history really repeats itself but also reminds of Scott-Heron's words: in certain situations it simply seems as if there were "20 years gone at the point of a gun" (16).

The demonstration of strength and militancy also adds a new aspect to the concept of toughness that has been discussed before. Our hero does not only have to be our savior but also our warrior. He does not only have to defend his position but fight for it. But still, this is just a variation of an old concept: "The same old lines and the same clichés. Perfectly rehearsed. Obscuring wrong and right. He says he's defending some bullshit while he's picking a fight" (16). Scott-Heron strongly suggests that we should rather find new answers to old problems than rely on old patterns to master new challenges, otherwise we will end up in "a time machine stuck in reverse and filming new scenes" (16).

**Works cited**

Scott-Heron, Gil. "'B' Movie." 1981. *Now and Then: The Poems of Gil Scott-Heron*. Edinburgh: Payback Press, 2000. 8-12.

– – –. "Re-Ron." 1984. *Now and Then: The Poems of Gil Scott-Heron*. Edinburgh: Payback Press, 2000. 13-16.

– – –. *Reflections*. Arista, AL 9566, 1981.

**Part III: (Anti-)Americanisms in Popular Culture, Sport and the Media**

# Inarticulate, Violent White American Men

## Greta Olson

### Introduction

Because the topic of this volume is anti-Americanism, I wish to focus on a single image of what we Europeans (I am an expatriate American who is well assimilated in German culture and thus have the status of a *Grenzgänger*, or border crosser) love to hate about Americans. When considering what makes many European individuals maintain anti-American sentiments, one finds a number of despised and contested cultural icons to choose from, including McDonald's, the American arms industry (particularly in connection with the current crisis with Iraq), excessive energy expenditures, silicone-enhanced Barbie doll blondes, violent Hollywood movies, etc. The list goes on.

By focusing on the figure of the inarticulate, violent white American man, I recognize that I am dealing with a generalization. However, since this clichéd figure receives so much media coverage and generates heated criticism, it appears worthwhile to delineate his features closely and note how he appears in the Austrian and German as well as in the American context. After defining the dangerous white American man, I will explore the origins of this figure or trope and its textual manifestation in post-war American drama. Some causes for the emergence of the figure of the 'pissed-off' white American man will then be mentioned. Finally, I will conclude with a discussion of exclusion as an identity-building process.

### Defining the Cliché

A recent article by the webzine *ZYN!* describes Americans in bitterly derogatory—if farcical—tones:

Die Siedler in der neuen Welt entschieden sich für eine demokratische Verfassung, da es unter ihnen niemanden gab, der das Format zum König gehabt hätte. Ihr Hobby war es, Indianer abzuschlachten. Als die Ureinwohner wegen dieser Freizeitbeschäftigung auszusterben drohten, importierten die Yankees Afrikaner: Jetzt konnten sie sich mit den Schwarzen die Zeit vertreiben. Um die Afroamerikaner für das erlittene Unrecht zu entschädigen, versorgt die US-Regierung die Schwarzen jetzt billig mit Drogen ("Der häßliche Amerikaner").[1]

If in ridiculously exaggerated terms, the figure I wish to investigate emerges out of the above description. Racist, violent and white, his gender is implicit; it is visible in his power over and his violence towards Native and African Americans. This farcical description from *ZYN!*, notable for its utter lack of political correctness, bespeaks the most extreme vision of the ugly, violent white American man in the Austro-German context.

What about the American context?

Recently, the American media voiced enormous surprise that the Washington, DC area sniper—otherwise known as "the Beltway Killer"—was identified as two African Americans. This surprise speaks for the salience of the image of the violent white American man in the United States. Prosecutors had been certain that the gunman who shot 13 people in 21 days in October 2002, plus two in Alabama in late September, and who seemed to disappear from dragnets into the blue, must fit into the expected profile of a serial killer as a twisted genius, white middle-class man between twenty and forty years of age. In the manhunt for the perpetrator, two gun-toting white men from the DC area, who fit the expected profile, were in fact questioned by the police. By contrast, prosecutors literally passed over the 41-year-old African American John Mohammed and his sidekick John Lee Malvo—who were subsequently charged with ten murders—when Mohammed was found sleeping in his car near the sight of one of the shooting murders on October 8. Various leads identifying a black man in a dark-colored car were ignored, because prosecutors were sure they were looking for a lone Caucasian in a white van. Expecting the sniper to be an "intelligent, well-organized white male" (Wingert 18), police had been searching for someone who resembled other highly publicized serial killers such as

David Berkowitz, aka "Son of Sam," who stalked and killed mostly women in the late 70s. Needless to say, the white killer they were looking for is a man with a bone to chew, whose hidden fury at the world or his perceived enemies leads him to choose and kill his victims randomly. Where does this image come from?

Perhaps the most salient figure of the frighteningly violent and dangerously inexpressive white man is Michael Douglas in his portrayal of William Foster, or Bill "De-fens," as he comes to be known from the vanity plate on his car that refers to his former job in the defense industry. I am referring to the 1992 movie *Falling Down*. Bill epitomizes a stereotypical image of the clean-cut, white-collar Caucasian American. He has a brush cut, is dressed in a nerdy fashion in a white button-down shirt and a stripped black tie. Four engineer pencils adorn his breast pocket. Decidedly unfashionable, his glasses have a thick black horn rim frame that bespeaks middle-class tax-paying solidarity. He appears to typify a nerdy kind of upright and responsible, mainstream American male.

The movie begins in a Los Angeles traffic jam. We are made to sense Bill's frustration at sitting in an endless traffic jam and feel the heat of the Los Angeles day via long close-ups of his sweating face, broken air conditioner, and the flies that land on his neck. We witness his slow mounting disgust at the individuals in the cars around him: children who fight inside a bus, women who apply make-up endlessly— their mouths turned into grotesque caricatures of gaping holes with fat fleshy red rims—, two white men who yell into a cell phone. Bill—but significantly we do not yet know his name—gets out of his car in the middle of a traffic jam and begins to walk away, much to the consternation of the car drivers around him. When Bill gets out of his car and announces that he is "going home," he is an everyman, or, to borrow Joseph Conrad's phrase, he is "one of us."[2] That he is one of us, or part of a larger collective group, is signified by the men who challenge Bill when he gets out of his car and then move his car off the roadway after he has abandoned it. Like Bill, they are also white, middle-aged, white-collar workers: one is a cop and the other a salesman. The suggestion is that Bill could be any of the white men trapped in their cars during any morning's traffic jam, a man who is caught in a life amongst grotesque caricatures of women, screaming children, and loud, shouting men. Any one of them could break out, go AWOL and desert his respective cage on the highway.

Our first indication of just how AWOL Bill has gone occurs after he has run out of change for the phone. He enters a small grocery store and asks for change. In heavily-accented English the owner insists that Bill has to buy something if he wants to have change, and Bill grows incensed when he is asked for eighty-five cents for a coke. Not only the price but the grocery store owner's pronunciation infuriates him: "You come to my country, you take my money, you don't even have the grace to learn my language," he retorts. When the owner reacts fearfully to Bill's threatened violence and starts to defend himself by grabbing a baseball bat hidden underneath the counter, Bill wrestles it away from him and starts to destroy the store by batting down the merchandise and the displays. He grows even angrier when the owner shields himself from Bill's swings with the bat and tells him to take the money in the register. "Do you think I am a thief?!" the infuriated Bill wants to know. He demands to know what each item in the store costs. After a last bash at a beer display he finally pays the 50 cents he thinks the Coke should cost and leaves the store.

Baseball bat—an icon of American manhood in itself—in tow, Bill begins to walk in the direction of his ex-wife's house and sits down on a block of graffiti-covered concrete to rest. Soon he is challenged by two expensively-dressed young Hispanic men who inform him that he is trespassing on their property and wonder aloud at his having failed to have read the sign on the concrete blocks where he sits. Again Bill reacts with self-righteous rage. The sign is graffiti, he protests, and it is not written in English. Demanding Bill's briefcase as a fine, the two young men are surprised at Bill's hidden bat and the fury with which he swings it at them. Temporarily, they are frightened away.

Without repeating the whole of the plot, let it suffice to say that Bill's 'voyage home' turns into a rampage in which his weapons grow bigger and deadlier and the victims of his violence go from being non-white Americans to food chains which use false advertising, corrupt municipal agencies that close roads for non-existent construction work so as to maintain inflated budgets, rich plastic surgeons who live in heavily-guarded mansions, and wealthy old white men whose sense of entitlement enables them to order trespassers off 'their' golf course. The movie is careful to render Bill's grievances general ones. Disturbingly, the objects of Bill's hate may well be ones that many moviegoers will agree on. De-fens is directly responsible 'only' for the deaths of the Latino youths, who turn out to be gang leaders, the Army Navy store owner, who is a homophobic fascist, and the rich white man who orders him off the golf course.

Treading carefully around America's sore spot concerning racism, the movie never portrays De-fens being hostile towards African Americans. Instead, moments of closeness and identification between Bill and black males are shown. Bill observes a black man who is dressed in the shirt and tie white-collar uniform almost identical to his own, who demonstrates outside of a bank that has refused to give him a loan with a sign proclaiming "I am not economically viable." This stranger loudly proclaims the story of how his life has been destroyed by the bank until police officers cart him off. From the window of the police car where he is now held captive the man looks at Bill directly and says in parting: "Don't forget me." De-fens answers "I won't." Economic downsizing—a common enemy—has cost Bill his job, we later learn, and this man his loan. An articulate African American boy teaches Bill how to fire the heat-seeking missile launcher that he has picked up at the army navy store. The two males, adult and boy, cuddle together after the launcher has been fired off, observing how it destroys a highway construction site.

So far the objects of Bill's violence have been a Korean store owner who in Bill's eyes overcharges, two Latino gang leaders, a food chain, and big money as represented by a rich plastic surgeon and two aging golfers. These groups may all be sources of anger to white men, who are not faring well economically, feel undervalued, and whose conformity to traditional masculine behavioral traits no longer guarantees them success. Finally, however, Bill's target is his ex-wife, who has remained with their daughter in the house where Bill also once lived and who has a restraining order against him. The ex-wife, large-breasted, with long hair—the visual iconography of movies is simplistic and telling—is stereotypically feminine. Unable to convince the police men and women of her growing terror of her former husband's potential violence, she is characterized by them as 'hysterical.' That she is shown baking a cake for her daughter's birthday using fresh strawberries signifies, I believe, her moral purity and figurative freshness. With no new man visible around her, she represents the image of the 'good girl' matron-in-distress.

Obviously, love and desire do at least in part motivate De-fens's wish to return to his former home, reclaim his turf, give his daughter a birthday present, and hold his ex-wife. The audience is made to identify with and empathize with his sense of loss when he views the home videos depicting his former wife and daughter. At first, a happy nuclear family is portrayed; later the videos show Bill's wife and child's growing fear of his violence and his need to control them.

Cornered at the end of the movie by the wise older white man, Detective Prendergast, who was behind him in the traffic jam, De-fens asks "When did I become the bad guy?" Unable to comprehend his moral collapse, his literally having fallen down, Bill De-fens cannot justify his actions. Perhaps the movie's odd logic might explain or mitigate his violence towards the thugs, the grocer with poor English skills, the Nazi surplus store owner, and the rich golf player. Yet now another middle-class white man calls Bill on his intention to shoot his ex-wife and child and then himself. Ultimately, the object of Bill's violence is the female other, whom he regards as having betrayed him.

Bill De-fens is an everyman, made to represent every white, middle-class, disaffected American man who despises inflationary prices and false advertising, immigrants who cannot pronounce American 'properly,' Hispanic gangs, and the injustice represented by the excessive wealth and conspicuous display of the Super Rich. The once-responsible white American man has run amok. De-fens's inability to voice his discontent becomes so great that violence appears to be his only recourse. What are the causes of the inarticulate fury of men like De-fens, of de-fensive white American males? Where did these men come from? In other words, when did the Bill De-fenses of America become the bad guys?

**Textual Predecessors of De-fens and Other Violent White Men**

Before discussing the causes for the emergence of the angry-white-man figure, I want to name some earlier characters who have contributed to his development. Some of Bill De-fens's textual predecessors can be found in post-war American drama.[3] I want to name two dramatis personae that have become cultural icons as well as some later interpretations of the violent white man figure:

1) Stanley Kowalski in Tennessee Williams's *A Streetcar Named Desire* (1947) serves as one father to De-fens's frustrated and violent masculinity. Full of blue-collar brawn, cunning, and anti-intellectual as well as anti-class sentiments, Stanley is of the red-blooded man tradition in American literature that began with turn-of-the-century authors like Frank Norris and Jack London. Stanley despises women when they are not quiet and sexually and verbally subordinate, as is his wife Stella and as he forces his sister-in-law Blanche to become.

Stanley displays a distrust of Blanche Dubois's embellishments, complex language and pretensions of ladylike behavior. He tells her that he despises women who need to be told that they are good-looking (136-37). Although Stanley is obviously aware of Blanche's sexual appeal, he refuses to behave in any way that might suggest his having a need for or a dependency on women. Stanley beats Stella when she demands that the men break up their poker party. There is evidence that he has done so in the past when the neighbor Eunice yells at Stanley: "You whelp of a Polack, you! I hope they do haul you in and turn the fire hose on you, same as the last time!" (154). Displaying his need to control and subjugate his wife, Stanley accuses her of ripping the shirt that he has just pulled of his body (198). Stanley justifies his having told his friend Mitch about Blanche's sexually deviant past on the basis of the male bond between them. As he explains to Stella: "We were in the same outfit together – Two-forty-first Engineers. We work in the same plant and now on the same bowling team. You think I could face him if—" (190). War, the work place, and the bowling rink constitute sites of closeness and identification for men like Stanley; these sites are radically separate from the feminized world of Blanche with her fine words, music, perfume, and dimmed lights.

Stanley reacts with fury to his wife and her sister's likening of him to an animal and their references to his having a Polish background. Throwing his dishes on the floor and eating with his fingers, he tells Stella to remember that a man is the king of his castle, and that he is an American: "I am not a Polack. People from Poland are Poles, not

Polacks. But what I am is a one hundred percent American, born and raised in the greatest country on earth and proud as hell of it, so don't ever call me a Polack" (197). Stanley's rape of Blanche represents an act of violent dominion analogous to an army's invasion of an enemy country. Blanche's resultant pain and humiliation re-enforce Stanley's dominance and show that Stanley has regained the right to completely control his wife Stella, the discourse of their home, and his mastery over a world that threatens to make him feel that he is a foreigner and an animal rather than a 'man.' Stella reacts to Blanche's report of the rape with disbelief—"I couldn't believe her story and go on living with Stanley" (217). While Mitch calls Stanley a braggart and a bull, he refrains from interfering with his having Blanche be committed to an asylum. These reactions make it clear that Stanley's violent reclamation of his powerful dominion over his household has been acknowledged, perhaps even condoned, by his friend and wife. Stanley to my eyes represents one model of violent American manhood: He embodies the threat of sanctioned violence which is mostly held under control. Furthermore, Stanley's character initiates a tendency to glorify and sexualize American male violence which continues in blockbuster action movies today such as Sylvester Stallone's *Rambo* trilogy.[4]

2) A second textual predecessor to Bill De-fens is Willy Loman from Arthur Miller's *Death of a Salesman* (1949). Willy, of course, offers a very different picture of violent tendencies in white American men. A familiar and culturally resonant figure, Willy is unable to fulfill the standards of manhood he has ascribed to and eventually destroys himself.

Like De-fens, Willy Loman is a white-collar worker, who has played by the rules of the American-dream game: to work and cheat hard, to impress through convincing self-presentation. Speaking to the imagined presence of his dead, long-departed and much more conventionally successful brother Ben, Willy explains that because he had so little contact with their father he hardly knows himself: "Can't you stay a few days? You're just what I need, Ben, because I—I have a fine position here, but I—well, Dad left when I was such a baby and I never had a chance to talk to him and I still feel—kind of temporary about myself" (40). This lack of self-knowledge is also commented on by Biff after Willy's suicide with the words: "He never knew who he was." In his history of American manhood Michael Kimmel uses Willy's stated sense of temporariness to describe the state of American men after 1945. Citing their fear of over-conformity to a cookie-cutter mode of boring suburban domestication and simultaneous need to repress their urge to break out with undomesticated masculine behavior, Kimmel classifies 50s men as deeply unhappy. According to him, their unhappiness paved the way for the crisis of masculinity that still besieges American men today.

As in so many post-war American dramas, the second act of *Death of a Salesman* finds its climax in the violent confrontation between male family members. Willy screams at his son Biff, who tries to attack his father physically. The men nearly come to blows twice, before Willy kills himself to enable his family collect on a twenty-thousand dollar insurance premium. Needed conversations occur neither between Willy and his beleaguered wife Linda nor between Willy and his malcontent sons, but only between Willy and the imaginary figure of Ben. Willy represents a second icon of violent American manhood, that of the disoriented and disempowered man who resorts to violence as a way to end or free himself from circumstances that have grown intolerable. He is a predecessor of the so-called victimized American man.

Moving from the original models of violent white men to other realizations of this figure, other post-war dramatic figures also resemble De-fens in their fury at the world. De-fens's anger can also be found in the lower middle-class character of Teach from David Mamet's *American Buffalo* (1975). This intense, intimate play between three characters depicts men's frustrations and troubled interrelationships. Don, Bob, and Teach meet in the older man Don's junkshop, where Bob, a former junkie, acts as a sort of apprentice gofer to Don in exchange for guidance from the older man. Teach is the loose gun in the group: He has lost too much in a card game the night before and is desperate for money. Teach's distrust of the lesbian couple Ruthie and Grace—"Only . . . from the mouth of a Southern bulldyke asshole ingrate of a vicious nowhere cunt can this trash come" (157)—and his disdain for the youthful, uncertain, and, hence, in his eyes, effeminate Bob, demonstrate his insistence on conforming to what he sees as traditional mores of masculinity. Teach expresses his inarticulate energy and faltering sense of his own maleness in his desire to do a robbery and propensity towards violence. When his desire to go on the job is frustrated by the other men in various ways, Teach becomes enraged and hits Bob. His fury and frustration growing, he—anticipating Defens—picks up a metal stick and proceeds to trash Don's junkshop. His words become a credo for the disaffected American man:

> My Whole Cocksucking life.
> The Whole Entire World.
> There Is No Law.
> There Is No Right And Wrong.
> The World Is Lies.
> There Is No Friendship.
> Every Fucking Thing.
> Every God-forsaken Thing. (253-254)

Here a rage at an unhinged world is expressed. According to Teach, nothing works as it should. Traditional ordering principles such as law, friendship, and right and wrong have vanished. Lost to Teach is what Lacan calls "the name of the father," the ordering principle based on and identified with an abstracted principle of paternal authority that enables individuals to make sense of the world (67).

Very often in post-war drama and other genres wrath at the upside-down world is directed at what is identified as other: women, less masculine men and minorities. Note the words with which one real estate salesman assails another co-worker for having blown a job in another Mamet play, *Glengarry Glen Ross* (1984). The play is named after a junk property in Florida, a tract of undeveloped land that four competing real estate brokers try to sell to unwitting customers. The men have been put in a brutal contest to close sales: the winner will take home a six thousand dollar bonus and a new Cadillac; the losers, by contrast, will be fired. In the scene I am quoting from the most successful of the four contenders, the testosterone-filled Roma, has just been contradicted by his boss in front of a customer who is trying to cancel the deal he made the night before to buy junk property in Florida. Having witnessed his trustworthiness be completely undermined, Roma screams at the man whom he expected to lie for him:

You stupid fucking cunt. You, Williamson . . . I'm talking to you, shithead. You just cost me *six thousand dollars*. (Pause). Six thousand dollars. And one Cadillac. That's right: What are you going to do about it. What are you going to do about it asshole. You fucking *shit*. Where did you learn your *trade*. You stupid fucking *cunt*. You *idiot* Whoever told you you could work with *men*? [And later] You fucking *child* . . . (58-59)

Here weakness, stupidity, the inability to do work, and personal betrayal are all associated with women, who are reduced and emblemized by the word "cunt." This figure of the despised other is gendered as feminine and as non-adult, as we see in the words "[y]ou fucking *child*." Significantly, the bad salesman is put down for not being 'man' enough. This speech demonstrates how the feminized other is identified both as a threat to the male character and the image of everything he defines as non-masculine.[5]

In another play concerning male rage, misogynist and age-prejudiced violence takes on a racial slur. Al, the ex-con boyfriend of the go-go girl protagonist Chrissy, from David Rabe's *In the Boom Boom Room* (1972/1986), grows violent when he imagines that his girlfriend has been looking lustfully at a black woman. What really throws him over the edge, however, is when she defends herself by saying that she has also seen him occasionally look at African American men. Imagining this to be a slur about his having a sexual interest in black men, Al engages in an orgy of misogynistic racialist hate:

> I'll burn you your fuckin' snatch clean you, do you hear me? I'll put a hot poker up you, make you clean, you hear me? I spit at 'em on the street. Niggers ain't shit, man; they ain't nothin'. Two and three of 'em used to beat me up when I was a kid. They used to jump me, take me to knuckle city, but I'd get one of 'em alone it was different. I used to grind 'em up, spit 'em out. Niggers ain't shit, man! One on one they'd be tough for a little, but little by little—kick 'em in the shins—they'd come apart. No endurance. Couldn't last, see: and I think it was because a their nutrition; they wasn't getting' food like I was. I mean, they was all poorer than me, even, and two or three of 'em would do a job on me. Then I'd get one of 'em, and I'd clock'm—I'd put out his lights. But now they're getting better food or somethin', they're getting good nutrition—I mean, you seen the size of some a them spooks. It

never used to be that way. It never used to be that way. I mean, they ain't shit; niggers ain't shit. (*It has all rushed out of him like vomit and hysteria, leaving him shaken, nearly exhausted.*) (120)

After this horrifying speech and Al's subsequent brutal beating of his girlfriend to her cries of "Don't hit my face, don't hit my stomach" (124), the play ends. In a closing image the audience sees a masked Chrissy dancing topless at another go-go joint. Obviously, her descent into the grind of sexual exploitation has been furthered by the beating from Al that has left her face disfigured. Al's sense of his own victimization, his reported memories of having been beaten up by darker-skinned youths, fuels his desire to destroy the other: woman and "nigger" become identified in his mind as his hated opponent. They are reduced to "a snatch" and "shit" respectively.

Sam Shepard's plays have also been remarked for their frequent portrayal of masculine violence: Doors are smashed, furniture broken, and walls broken down, for instance, in *Buried Child* (1979), *True West* (1980), and *Fool for Love* (1983). In *A Lie of the Mind* (1986) Shepard dramatizes the story of a man, who has nearly beaten his wife to death, and his brother, who visits her family home to see if she has survived this latest of serial beatings. This brother is subsequently accidentally shot by the wife's father and repeatedly threatened by her own violent brother. A man's violence towards the woman he supposedly loves is answered by other men's violence. That Shepard has been so admired for the physicality of his productions, for his having brought vitality and freshness to the theater in the form of "destruction" and a "masculine approach to the stage" (Wade 119), bespeaks the attraction of violence enacted by men on the stage as well as on the screen.

In his survey of American drama Robert Vorlicky points out that post-war theater overwhelmingly features casts that are white, violent, and male. The white man's placement at the heart of American drama speaks for both his privileged position in American society and for anxieties about the stability of his dominant position. In plays like the ones I have quoted from above, men display a fear of a loss of control. This identity-forming moment proves an incentive for them to commit violent acts. Typically, their violence is directed towards whatever character is identified as other—the boyish former addict, the man who refuses to lie, the girlfriend who is identified with "niggers." In a system that conceives of masculine and feminine and self and other as radical opposites, whatever is not male enough is feminine, lacking, and other. The object of violence is the other, because s/he is childlike, gay, of a different color, or simply not masculine enough. Ultimately then the other is constituted as feminine. Only by excluding and destroying the other and any suggestion that there could be so-called feminine character traits in himself can the angry white man shore up his identity and prove that he is a 'man.' Violence in these plays manifests a violent defense of an unstable sense of self.[6]

**Causes**

Having described manifestations of the violent white American man in movies and plays, I wish to speculate about why this figure has emerged so prominently. Researchers in cultural, men's and literary studies all document reasons for the white man's fury and inability to articulate himself. The figure of the troubled and troubling violent Caucasian man has now become the subject of intense media debate and interest. Even the conservative rag *The Economist* worries about the confused state of Anglo-American men. According to a recent article there, the main cause for male anxiety (and violence) is the undermining of the traditional masculine role as economic provider: Women now regularly outperform men in school as well as in post-secondary education; increasingly, men have to take on service-oriented jobs that require flexibility and offer no guarantees of power or advancement—formally dubious prerogatives of women's work; job insecurity that arose in the American recession has never really disappeared, as was evidenced by the recent net.com bust. Second, men feel that women have the right to choose family or career or some changing balance between the two as opposed to themselves, who are belittled for wanting to stay home or are involuntarily separated from their children by family courts' seemingly arbitrary allotment of child custody to women and financial responsibility to fathers. Third, middle-class white men are beset with anxiety about the sexual prowess and the objectification of their bodies by women and concurrent injunctions to be fit, toned, and, perhaps, lifted ("Downsized Male").

In her effectively named book *Stiffed: The Betrayal of the American Man* (1999), Susan Faludi argues that men currently suffer from a sense of having been deeply deluded by the values they were raised with. For the baby-boomer generation, values such as the worth of taming the frontier, being leaders at home and serving loyally in the work place as well as, if necessary, in war have been dislocated. Furthermore, men's sense of dislocation has been caused by their lack of having had present fathers, by war and service having been made shameful after Vietnam, and by their wives no longer wishing to take on the traditional, feminine care-taker role. Interestingly, Faludi cites that seeming embodiment of American masculinity Sylvester Stallone to illustrate another current frustration among men. Stallone's effort to transcend his image as the muscular, if monosyllabic, Rocky has been frustrated by the public's refusal to allow him to do so (580-93). Using Stallone's story, Faludi describes men's sense of having been victimized by a culture that has turned them into fetishized purchasable ornaments just as it has traditionally done to women. Questioning men in a domestic-violence group, she teases out the answer that bouts of violence are accompanied by a sense of release and of being in control of a world that is otherwise difficult to manage (8-9). In other words, a sense of being powerless and hence not 'masculine' enough precipitates acts of violence against women. Masculine identity then is created by or experienced in violence.

Most convincingly, David Savran explains the malaise of American white men by reviewing their economic losses during the 70s and 80s. Financial loss was combined with the aftermath of the Vietnam War and the burgeoning economic growth of middle-class African Americans and women. Economic changes were caused by the transition from an industrial-manufacturing society to a service-oriented one and the so-called 'trickle-down' economics of the Reagan era—that is, give to the rich and eventually something will get to the poor bastards. These changes led to the consolidation of wealth among America's richest individuals (think of the older men on the golf course in *Falling Down*) and a real 18% loss of income to average workers (Savran 192). Such changes could be blamed on women and minorities, who were in fact gaining some economic and political ground, even if these groups were not at all at fault for white men's woes. The media's sensationalistic reporting of the Bakke case contributed to the scapegoating of America's minorities. Allan Bakke, an ex-marine and Vietnam Vet, took the University of California Medical School to court for having allegedly violated his constitutional rights by using a quota system in their admissions policy. In 1978 the Supreme Court ruled in the Bakke decision that using quotas in affirmative action programs was not constitutional. Reports on this decision turned the white man into a victim of so-called racism and racial minorities into the authors of white men's problems (Savran 193, 346). Not the economy was at fault for the loss of white men's privileges, according to this view, but women and blacks were stealing jobs from 'real Americans,' in other words, white, male ones. And so the image of the white man as victim that has to resort to violence to defend himself was born.[7] This angry white man acts out his fury and sense of betrayal in film and drama. He embodies a "politics of resentment and retaliation" (Kimmen 326) that can be found not only in drama and film but also in the homophobia and racism of singers like Axl Rose of Guns N' Roses and, to a lesser degree, Eminem.[8]

Two points need to be made: 1) The disaffection felt by many white, middle-class American men is real, if misplaced; the violence this disaffection results in is directed often to those who 'need' and 'deserve' it least: women, minorities, and children. 2) The image of the white American man as a victim is simultaneously a sensationalistic media construct. As witnessed by the coverage of the Bakke decision, the portrayal of this construct sells news.

**Concluding Thoughts**

The review of angry white men from Bill De-fens to Stanley Kowalski and Teach shows that American dramas and films are a field where questions of masculine identity are being worked out. That these texts enact masculinity as gay bashing, covertly or overtly misogynist, consistently violent, and lily white reflects patriarchal hegemony and racism on the one hand. On the other hand the image of the angry white man also speaks to anxiety about just how strong the white man really is. In drama and film men are overly represented and processes of excluding 'the other' through acts of violence constantly occur. The excluded here is anyone who differs, whether because this person is not masculine, due to their 'effeminate' relations to women or overt emotionality, or is in some sense considered deviant. By deviant I mean anything that is not a straight, white and male.

The philosophers Emmanuel Lévinas and Bernhard Waldenfels as well as social psychologists have taught how the creation of identity goes hand in hand with the exclusion of an identified other.[9] While the victimized and victimizing violent white American man excludes a racialized and genderized other and resorts to violence to shore up the faulty dam of his own identity, we as critical students of culture and literature must be aware of our desire to exclude and vilify this man in order to assure ourselves of our own multicultural and humanist values.

**Notes**

[1] "The settlers of the new world decided to have a democratic constitution, because no one among them had the necessary stature to be king. Their hobby was slaughtering Indians. When the Native Americans grew in danger of becoming extinct due to this leisure time activity, the Yankees started to import Africans: Now they could pass the time with Blacks. To recompense African Americans for the injustice they had suffered from, the U.S. government supplied them with cheap drugs." (Trans. G.O.)

[2] In *Lord Jim* (1900), Marlowe, an experienced seaman, takes a deep interest in the fate of the young English officer Jim, who abandoned his ship and its 200 passengers when it appeared to be sinking. Marlowe's sense of disbelief that Jim, the son of a pastor, could have committed such a cowardly act is reflected in his repeated use of the term "one of us." This phrase expresses both a sense of group membership—Marlowe is speaking to other officers—and a class-oriented sense that cowardliness is unthinkable for a gentleman. As in *Lord Jim*, the audience of *Falling Down* is encouraged to sympathize with the protagonist and the group of men with which he is identified. That the viewer's sympathies can be controlled in this manner works on the assumption that he or she will automatically identify with this group. Needless to say, this may be more problematic for the woman viewer.

[3] Students of literature may object to the freedom with which this essay jumps between figures such as Son of Sam, Bill De-fens, and characters from post-war dramas. They may rightly say that I fail to address questions of genre. This

is a problem in talking about the cliché-ridden figure of the angry, white man, who is in part historical reality, media construct, and theatrical enactment. Briefly, let me agree with Clive Bloom that there are qualities that make the theatrical space a particularly powerful one for working out issues of conflict and identity. This may be one reason that we find the angry white man figure so often in post-war dramas: "The visceral, three-dimensionality of the theatrical space, at once *muscular* presence and fragile voice, is the sinful nature of raw knowledge. Unlike film and television, even and especially unlike commercial radio, the theatre offers an *authenticity* which is shocking and peculiarly distressing" (2-3). (I might, however, object to Bloom's genderization of action and voice). Presenting another view, the anthropologist Victor Turner allows that both represent "collaborative, social performative systems" (31-32) where rituals of identity can be played out.

[4] In a discussion of Williams's plays as an expression of their author's inability to express his non-conformist sexuality, Mark Lilly writes of Stanley in the context of the traditional admiration for "the brutish male" (72): "The tradition is best represented by Stanley Kowalski. Violent, drunken, unpredictable and insensitive, it is almost as if these characteristics are an appropriately pleasing complement to his hard musculature" (73).

[5] For an extended reading of the play as an explication of American notions of white, capitalist masculinity, see Vorlicky 25-56.

[6] For a more explicit explanation of how the other is defined as feminine, see Vorlicky: "And in this gender-based circuit of cultural codings, women and homosexuals share the position of the coded Other. Thus, realist male-cast drama is essentially a misogynistic, homophobic canon. A male character's conflict between social talk and personal talk, between violent action and non-violent behavior, between a social role and individualization, is rooted in his attitude toward the Other, in his attitude toward women. The point is that traditional male-cast plays exist for the sole purpose of furnishing a very specific designation of maleness: in this kind of play, Men are defined as not-Women" (256).

[7] Rather than in violence, men's sense of victimization has also given rise to the growth of the men's movement as typified by Robert Bly and Sam Keen's work. Bly's *Iron John* and the workshops that grew out of the book contend that exclusively male initiation or re-initiation rituals are needed for men to find their lost fathers and the Wild Man within themselves, their unconscious and masculine core. *Iron John* suggests that men can only overcome their "suffering" and fulfil "their longing for father and mentor connections" (27) by finding their lost fathers. Without doubt, it is better for men to react to their

sense of displacement by going off and getting in touch with their hidden Wild Men in rituals than in acting out aggressively.

[8] Kimmel quotes the following lyrics from Rose's song "One in a Million": "Immigrants and faggots / They make no sense to me / They come to our country / And think they'll do as they please . . ." (326).

[9] See, for instance, Lévinas's *Entre Nous: On Thinking-of-the-Other* and Waldenfels's *Topographie des Fremden: Studien zur Phänomenologie des Fremden 1.*

**Works Cited**

Bly, Robert. *Iron John: A Book about Men.* Reading, MA: Addison-Wesley, 1990.

Bloom, Clive, ed. "Introduction." *American Drama.* Houndmills: Macmillan, 1995. 1-5.

Conrad, Joseph. *Lord Jim.* 1900. Ed. Cedric Watts and Robert Hampson. Harmondsworth: Penguin, 1986.

"Der häßliche Amerikaner." *Stern Online.* 25 Nov. 2002 <http://www.zyn.de/stern_online>.

"Downsized Male: Sometimes It's Hard to Be a Man." Special Christmas issue of *The Economist.* 22 Dec.-4 Jan. 2002: 60-62.

*Falling Down.* Dir. Joel Shumacher. Perf. Michael Douglas, Robert Duvall, Barbara Hershey and Rachel Ticotin. Warner Brothers, 1992.

Faludi, Susan. *Stiffed: The Betrayal of the American Man.* New York: William Morrow, 1999.

Lacan, Jacques. *Ècrits: A Selection.* Trans. Alan Sheridan. New York: Norton, 1977.

Lévinas, Emmanuel. *Entre Nous: On Thinking-of-the-Other.* New York: Columbia UP, 1998.

Lilly, Mark. "Tennessee Williams." *American Drama.* Ed. Clive Bloom. Houndmills: Macmillan, 1995. 70-81.

Kimmel, Michael. "'Temporary About Myself': White-Collar Conformists and Suburban Playboys, 1945-1960." *Manhood in America: A Cultural History*. New York: The Free P, 1996. 223-258.

Mamet, David. *American Buffalo. Plays: 1*. London: Methuen, 1994. 147-258.

– – –. *Glengarry Glen Ross. Plays: 3*. London: Methuen, 1996. 1-66.

Miller, Arthur. *Death of a Salesman: Certain Private Conversations in Two Acts and a Requiem*. 1949. London: Penguin Classics, 2000.

Rabe, David. *In the Boom Boom Room*. 1972/1975. Revised version. New York: Grove P, 1986.

Savran, David. *Taking It Like a Man: White Masculinity, Masochism, and Contemporary American Culture*. Princeton, NJ: Princeton UP, 1998.

Shepard, Sam. *A Lie of the Mind. A Lie of the Mind and The War in Heaven*. New York: New American Library. 1-130.

Turner, Victor. *An Anthropology of Performance*. New York: PAJ Publications, 1986.

Vorlicky, Robert. *Act Like a Man: Challenging Masculinities in American Drama*. Ann Arbor: Michigan UP, 1995.

Wade, Leslie A. *Sam Shepard and the American Theatre*. Westport, CT: Praeger Publishers, 1997.

Waldenfels, Bernhard. *Topographie des Fremden: Studien zur Phänomenologie des Fremden 1*. Frankfurt: Suhrkamp, 1997.

Williams, Tennessee. *A Streetcar Named Desire*. 1947. *A Streetcar Named Desire and Other Plays*. Ed. E. Martin Browne. London: Penguin. 113-226.

Wingert, Pat, et al. "Descent Into Evil." *Newsweek* 4 Nov. 2002: 16-27.

# Barbie's (American) Success Story

## Carmen Birkle

### 1. Introduction

Popular culture has long been an ignored field in academia and particularly in literary studies. However, with the rise of new academic methods and an increasing concern for an understanding of production in its cultural, social, and historical contexts, the discipline of Cultural Studies was inaugurated in the 1950s in Birmingham, England, and has developed in various ways and directions into the twenty-first century. Including popular culture in a reading of society no longer needs much justification in most English Departments. What the analysis of popular culture has added to our understanding of societies are ideas such as the need for a deconstruction of power structures in cultural production, for a recanonization in literature, and the recognition that popular and mass culture make available interesting and significant insights into mainstream culture. In that sense, the history of the Barbie doll in America is a tool with which to read American history over the last five decades.

In 1999, Barbie doll's 40th birthday was one of the highlights of an American success story that originally had begun in Germany in 1958 when Ruth and Elliot Handler, founders of Mattel Toys, brought the German "Lilli Puppe" to the United States, Americanized it, and presented it at the New York Toy Fair in February 1959 as "Barbie doll." Ever since, Barbie has written a success story with far-reaching impacts on young girls. She has become a cultural icon that has shaped cultures around the world. At the same time, the doll is a product of a highly sophisticated toy industry that both satisfies and provokes mostly young girls' desires for beauty and success. Barbie as a commodity (with the Mattel company as its producer) has instilled beauty ideals and values in more than one generation of teenage girls. The history of the development of the doll shows that the Barbie phenomenon cannot be discussed without looking at social and cultural developments over the last forty years. On the one hand, Barbie has remained independent, unmarried, without children, has not grown old, and is most frequently shown in the private sphere of her house, and among friends. On the other hand, she has gone ethnic and national without losing the emphasis on white American beauty ideals which, in more recent years, have also been connected to a professional success story. In my paper, I will look at some of the various roles and identities Barbie has embodied over the years, and I will argue that her story is the story of cultural perceptions of, on the one hand, ethnic and national stereotypes and, on the other, the female body and femininity, expressed in concepts of sexuality, fashion, and professions.

## 2. The Origins of Barbie

Sometime in 1958, Ruth and Elliot Handler discovered a new toy that would revolutionize the world. On their trip to Germany and Switzerland in search of a new doll for their daughter Barbara, they found the German Lilli doll in a shop, bought the rights to the doll in the same year, took it to America, and introduced it to their customers at the New York Toy Fair in February 1959. This date marks the birth of Barbie doll. What the Handlers did not tell their customers was that the Lilli doll in Germany was an almost pornographic representation of a woman which was sold mostly to men in tobacco stores and bars as a sex object. The idea for such a doll went back to a 1952 cartoon created by Richard Beuthin for the infamous German newspaper *Bildzeitung* which shows Lilli as "a sexy young lady who plays with her admirers" (Deutsch 8). This cartoon was so successful that, in 1955, Max Weißbrodt modeled an actual doll based on this cartoon. However, the Lilli doll did not suit the Handlers' idea of an ideal doll for their daughter, but it did at least have the three-dimensionality that all her paper dolls lacked. The producers of Mattel were convinced that there was a market for such a doll. The company began to remodel the original figure of the Lilli doll, but essentially left the features and size intact. While Ruth Handler at first only wanted to replace her daughter's paper dolls with "a three-dimensional fashion doll" (Urla and Swedlund 399), one of the major reasons why she had acquired the Lilli doll for her daughter was that the latter preferred to play with dolls that had adult instead of a child's features. As an adult doll, Barbie catered to the desires of young girls to be grown-ups, to dress like adult women, and to be independent. Barbie doll embodied all of this from the moment of its inception and thus allowed for teenage dreams and visions. The new role young girls then learned to play was no longer that of mother to a baby doll, but that of woman in a male world.

At first, however, as Stefanie Deutsch argues,

> buyers weren't particularly excited about this new doll that was so different from the popular baby dolls. But the first series of 500,000 Barbie dolls and a million outfits (all produced in Japan) sold out quickly. Mattel marketed Barbie very intelligently. They introduced Barbie on TV during the popular *Mickey Mouse Club*. The doll was promoted also on Viewmaster disks. Shop displays were set up at counters with dressed dolls to show how the outfits would look on a doll. (23)

With the beginning of television advertising in the 1960s, "the advertisers would soon be able to announce: 'We do not promote products, we create behaviour'" (Virilio 28). Subsequently, Barbie went through various hair colors and hair lengths, slightly differing brown or blue eyeliners, but essentially the doll remained the same. Throughout the years, Mattel created various companions for Barbie, the first one being her boyfriend Ken, who was introduced in 1961 and named after the Handlers' son (Deutsch 27). Gradually, there was Midge, Barbie's girlfriend, and Midge's boyfriend Allan, as well as Barbie's little sister Skipper, and many others. In 1992, Mattel estimated "that in the United States over 95 percent of girls between the ages of 3 and 11 own at least one Barbie, and that the average number of dolls per owner is seven . . ." (Urla and Swedlund 398).

Eventually, Mattel created a world according to Barbie, and Barbie became more than just a doll. Barbie offered the possibility of identification for girls and teenagers and represented a concept of femininity that eventually became its trademark. This concept, represented in the female body and beauty ideals and in fashions and professions, has changed over the years – but only slightly so because Mattel has, of course, been unwilling to change such a successful product. Because of Barbie's relative stability, generations of women have grown up with the same ideas (of femininity), and therefore Barbie's, and by definition Mattel's, representations of ethnic and gender roles have become norms for young women not only in the United States of America but worldwide.

## 3. Barbie's Gender Identity

*Sexuality*

In the 1950s, post-war America saw a gradual decline in women's participation in the public workforce. While women had contributed considerably to America's industrial and business life during WW II, the return of their fathers, husbands, brothers, and sons from war slowly reestablished traditional gender role distributions. Women once more saw their activities restricted to the private sphere; they realized with a certain unease that it was once more their responsibility to keep the house, raise the children, and cook dinner. In 1963, in her seminal study *The Feminine Mystique*, Betty Friedan elaborated on what she called "the problem that has no name." She argued that women's dissatisfaction with their lives was caused by the limited role choices available to them. Friedan pointed at society's attempt at reinstituting clear-cut binary oppositions with women in their roles as wives, housewives, and mothers. Parallel to this traditional image of women, the 1950s witnessed the public appearance of the "child-seducer" in the figure of Lolita, the protagonist of Vladimir Nabokov's novel *Lolita* (1955) (Debouzy 139). Taking into consideration Barbie's origins in a German sex symbol, the Lilli doll, it is possible to conclude that the 1950s' images of women were constructed through the binary labels of women as "angel in the house" and "whore." The Barbie doll embodies precisely those contradictory images. On the one hand, it represents traditional femininity and is an "angel"; on the other hand, it offers the potential of sexual fantasies for both young girls and adults. In her article "Older Heads on Younger Bodies," Erica Rand claims: "As has often been noted, Barbie's body signals sexuality to adults. It is a commonplace that Barbie might induce precocious sexual thinking, and adult narratives indicate that Barbie often signaled sexuality to children" (387-88).

In 1997, the Danish group Aqua successfully marketed their quite catchy song "Barbie Girl," cashing in on Barbie's representation of sexuality. The song plays with the idea of a sexual relationship or at least a quite openly flirtatious game between Barbie and Ken. Barbie's voice is almost childlike; she emphasizes her girlish features and the fun she has when partying. Barbie's offer to Ken, "You can touch; you can play; You can say I'm always yours" and "imagination, life is your creation," and Ken's response, "You're my doll," suggest Ken's ownership of and control over Barbie. She plays the little girl seducing and being seduced by Ken: "I'm a blonde, single girl in the fantasy world. . . . I can act like a star; I can beg on my knees." Ken's voice is that of an adult, deep and resonant, singing "Kiss me here, touch me there, hanky-panky" and "Come on Barbie, let's go party." When Barbie admits that she is having so much fun, he responds with quite openly sexual undertones: "Well, Barbie, we are just getting started!" And Barbie's response is: "Oh, I love you, Ken!" (Interestingly, recent news [February 2004] tell us that Barbie and Ken have separated.) This song is full of images of the woman as a child, as a sex object, voluntarily submitting herself to the powerful man. Because of the song's sexual implications, Mattel sued the group and MCA Records. According to Lucky Bensonhurst,

> the case turned out to be one in a virtual blitz of legal activity as one lawsuit after another began to fill the courts of America aimed at anyone depicting Barbie in extremely or even slightly naughty ways, or in fact any way not personally endorsed or authorized by Mattel. To wit: "I think of Barbie as a universally accepted vehicle that kids project their imaginations into – we have an obligation to keep it pure," says Mattel's chief operating officer, Bruce Stein.

As Bensonhurst claims, MCA Records so far has been the only one to triumph over Mattel.

Barbie's submissive sexuality has also led to strong feminist protests in the 1960s and 70s (Debouzy 143) and to a ban in Montpelier,

VT, where Barbie is "reviled as the ultimate symbol of two evils – commercialism and sexism. Plus she's plastic" (Strohmeyer). Since the 1950s were also the time of reconstruction after World War II with a significant rise in consumerism and commercialization, Mattel seized the opportunity to outwardly market Barbie as a children's toy without erasing the underlying sexual implications. After Lilli's Americanization as Barbie, the producers did not significantly alter the doll's body. Its features such as a large bust, very long legs, and thin hips remained unchanged and prominent and began to suggest a beauty ideal which had derived from male fantasies, considering the birth of Barbie as Lilli. According to Jacqueline Urla and Alan C. Swedlund, Barbie's disproportional body features are "what worries many feminists. As our measurements show, Barbie's body differs wildly from anything approximating 'average' female body weight and proportions" (419).

Through Mattel's clever marketing, these male fantasies gradually turned into a seemingly "universal" value; girls and young women were constantly confronted with these ideals that became norms, and increasingly internalized them. In 1991, Naomi Wolf called this phenomenon *The Beauty Myth* and subtitled her book: *How Images of Beauty Are Used against Women*. Her references to backlash tendencies in the 1980s and early 90s supported by this beauty myth can also be applied to the 1950s since then, too, the beauty myth with Barbie as its most prominent physical representation was used to control women (Wolf 10-11). The cultural critic Camille Paglia asserts:

> I definitely believe that toy sales are a key to the *Zeitgeist*. Barbie not only became a major sexual persona influencing celebrity style from Farrah Fawcett to Ivana Trump, but she ominously prefigured the destabilization of sexual identity that would lead, among other things, to an epidemic of anorexia and bulimia among white middle-class girls.

While bulimia and anorexia as forms of self-denial render young women "gradually more androgynous in appearance," Barbie "is able to remain powerfully sexualized" (Urla and Swedlund 420) and suggests that she has control over her body. In addition to sexuality, "her excessive slenderness also signifies a rebellious manifestation of willpower, a visual denial of the maternal ideal symbolized by pendulous breasts;

rounded stomach and hips. Hers is a body of hard edges, distinct borders, self-control. It is literally impenetrable" (Urla and Swedlund 420). The ambiguity lying in self-control on the one hand and adherence to an almost self-destructive and utopian beauty ideal on the other is to a large extent responsible for the perpetuation of Barbie's success story.

## The World of Fashion

This simultaneous fascination with and rejection of Barbie's physical features is further emphasized in the doll's marketing as a fashion statement. Over the years, Mattel has worked very hard to convey traditional femininity through Barbie's clothes. Fashion is an expression of identity and moods (Becker and Schütte 9), either self-chosen or imposed. And fashion makes it possible to play with identities. Barbie can easily be a good housewife and a woman at home in the glittering party world. Her clothes are created by fashion designers, and her collection is tremendous and steadily increasing. For each life situation and profession she has the right clothes. While designers offer these images of perfection, girls and teenagers imitate and accept them but also play with them according to their own fantasies and thus turn Barbie into "the prototype of the 'transformer dolls'" (Urla and Swedlund 406):

> It is sensible to assume that the children who play with Barbie are themselves creative users, who respond variously to the messages about femininity encoded in her fashions and appearance. Not only do many children make their own clothes for their Barbie dolls, but anecdotes abound of the imaginative uses of Barbie. (Urla and Swedlund 421)

After all, clothes can be taken off and put back on so that Erica Rand concludes: "Barbie is what she wears. She performs her gender" ("We Girls" 204).

One of the most successful and rather traditional Barbie costumes is her wedding dress, although according to her biography Barbie is not married [Ill. 1]. Being married would imply an ageing as well as a maternal woman and would thus destroy the image of being forever young. In 2002, Mattel attempted to introduce the first pregnant Barbie. Midge, mother of three-year-old Ryan and wife to Alan, is pregnant, with "a detachable stomach with a curled-up baby inside" ("Wal-Mart"). Although Mattel argued that the doll "can help parents discuss pregnancy without having to resort to graphic descriptions of the reproductive process" (qtd. in "Wal-Mart"), according to Wal-Mart, customers were "'unhappy with the offering,'" justifying the pulling off of the doll from the shelves. While the wedding-dress offers "one of Barbie's most true-to-life social-context accessories: compulsory heterosexuality," a final marriage would, according to Mattel, "cut off the fantasy" (qtd. in Rand, "We Girls" 197) of little girls. The first wedding dress was created in 1989. There was a Wedding Fantasy Barbie in 1991 and a Dream Wedding Barbie in 1992, but "the text on the box explains that Barbie is merely fantasizing about what her wedding will be like" (Rand, "We Girls" 197).

## *Drag Barbie*

Because fashion allows for a play with identities, i.e., what you wear indicates who you are, people have experimented with Barbie identities other than femininity. The desire to undermine and subvert norms of identity has led to the creation of Barbie as drag queen and the establishment of "a whole genre of Barbie satire, known as 'Barbie Noire' . . ." (Urla and Swedlund 421). The combination of "male" and "dress" disrupts the mainstream notion of heterosexuality and the clearly defined gender positions of femininity and masculinity. While drag queen Barbie literally embodies unlimited identity constructions, Mattel successfully sued Paul Hansen, who had sold "Exorcist Barbie" and "Drag Queen Barbie," and thus revealed the restrictions commercially imposed on these constructions.

## *Profession*

Directly connected to the fashion world is the professional world. Barbie started out as a doll in a striped bathing suit, no visible profession attached to it. She subsequently became a nurse, a beach girl, a babysitter, Miss America, a ballerina, an aerobics dancer, a tennis player, and a rock star. These professions were available to her in the 1960s. From the 1970s onward, she became a pilot, "Astronaut Barbie" (1986), "Dr. Barbie" (1988), a businesswoman with laptop and cell phone, and even ran for president in the year 2000. By now, she has had roughly 75 careers. On November 13, 2002, Hollywood affirmed Barbie's stardom. Assisted by Barbara Handler, Barbie left her imprints in a swimming-pool full of concrete: "In einem Swimmingpool voll Zement durfte die Kultpuppe Barbie ihre zierlichen Fußabdrücke in Hollywood hinterlassen. Barbara Handler, die Tochter des Barbie-Schöpfers, griff ihr bei der Ehrung helfend unter die Plastikärmchen" ("Starwelt").

On the one hand, because of her professions, she is a symbol of women's independence, not depending on a husband or any man's support. On the other hand, her independence remains controlled by Mattel. The image she conveys to her admirers is that if you are beautiful you are successful, or in other words, beauty and success go hand in hand. The detrimental effects of this image to girls is quite obvious in bulimia, anorexia, and other self-effacing and self-destructive body images as well as in a loss of self-confidence because of the, in most cases, unsuccessful striving for these beauty ideals. As Mattel with its lawsuits has made painfully clear, Barbie's independence is fake. The "slogan 'We girls can do anything, right Barbie?' [by Mattel] is a question as pseudorhetorical as Barbie's body is pseudoproportional" (Rand, "We Girls" 198). According to Rand, "Barbie can't do everything, and neither can we girls . . ." ("We Girls" 198). As soon as the imagination goes beyond Mattel's understanding of Barbie, this imagination is censored.

The ambiguous feelings evoked by the representation of Barbie's professional and fashion life are lucidly expressed in Janet Evanovich's detective novel *High Five*, in which her protagonist, the bounty hunter Stephanie Plum, uses the image of Barbie without underpants in order to describe her ambivalence about her own profession:

> When I was a little girl I used to dress Barbie up without underpants. On the outside, she'd look like the perfect lady. Tasteful plastic heels, tailored suits. But underneath, she was naked. I'm a bail enforcement agent now – also known as a fugitive apprehension agent, also known

as a bounty hunter. . . . being a bail enforcement agent is sort of like being bare-bottom Barbie. It's about having a secret. And it's about wearing a lot of bravado on the outside when you're really operating without underpants. Okay, maybe it's not like that for all enforcement agents, but I frequently feel like my privates are alfresco. Figuratively speaking, of course. (1)

In this quotation, femininity, fashion, and profession come across as performances. The outward appearance of the doll suggests success and socially sanctioned femininity while the emphasis on the absence of underwear implies women's (sexual) vulnerability but also constitutes an act of resistance to gender role dictates imposed by society.

**4. Barbie's Ethnic and National Identities**

Barbie's potential for transformation also lends itself to the acquisition of ethnic and national identities. Barbie starts her career as the all-American or American Golden Girl most attractive to girls from white middle-class families. While the 1960s' feminist movement set off a debate about the concept of femininity suggested by Barbie, the Civil Rights Movement with its demand for racial equality and an end to discrimination provoked changes in the toy industry as well. In 1967, Mattel introduced a black version of Francie, but because of her white counterpart the doll was not successful. In 1968, Mattel replaced Francie with black Christie, a friend of Barbie's, and gave her a black boyfriend, Brad, in 1970. Christie was not too successful either. In 1980, Mattel introduced Black Barbie, "the first doll with Afro-style hair," but she also "appears to have suffered from a low advertising profile and low sales . . ." (Urla and Swedlund 404). A Hispanic Barbie was introduced around 1980. In 1991, Mattel added the African-American doll Shani and her friends Asha and Nichelle together with Shani's boyfriend Jamal. According to Urla and Swedlund, the "packaging also announced that these dolls' bodies and facial features were meant to be more like those of real African American women, although they too can interchange clothes with Barbie" (405). But the more than twenty years of Barbie's white middle-class life could not easily be erased. While white girls did not see any need to identify with black dolls, black girls had so much internalized whiteness as a beauty ideal that they did not accept black versions in any significant way, not even in dream versions. "Until 1990, the only doll advertised on television was white" (Debouzy 141). The only ethnic version that has been successful is the Native American young woman Pocahontas from the Disney movie *Pocahontas* (1995) turned into a Barbie doll.

Until the 1980s, the doll had been largely a national, American phenomenon, except for its production in Japan and later in Korea and the Philippines since the 1950s. Because of the doll's success, Mattel extended its markets worldwide and began to create, for example, Asian dolls, which however were "usually westernized ethnic dolls" (Debouzy 141). By now, the company has spread worldwide. While Barbie's features have mostly remained the same, her clothes represent national identities. Gradually, there are Mexican, Russian, Korean, Canadian, Peruvian, Filipina, and German Barbies dressed in national costumes. There are examples of Japanese, Italian and Parisian, Irish and Swiss, Swedish and Spanish Barbie dolls, and a Greek Barbie doll with "a candle for girls to hold through religious processions" (Deutsch 158). In 1990, Mattel created a very interesting version of a German Barbie doll. It is called "Friendship I (Berlin Wall) Barbie" and "was sold only in East Germany after the fall of the Berlin Wall to celebrate this event" (Deutsch 158) [Ill. 2]. It is a regular blond Barbie in a prom-like dress. On the surrounding box there are children of various ethnic backgrounds, among them white children, an Asian, and a black child, mostly girls with one boy barely visible on the right margin. The British, Spanish, and European flags are clearly visible to suggest community.

Apart from the fact that this internationalization of Barbie is a highly successful marketing strategy, it also represents Americanization – or even Germanization, if you think of Barbie's origins. Barbie has become a global commodity like many other products and companies such as McDonald's or Disney. However, the American Barbie is not simply imposed on other countries; instead, she is nationalized in outward appearance so that non-American girls have something to recognize and identify with. Non-American Barbies can thus be considered transculturated or hybridized. At the same time, all Barbies share the same hardly changing images of women, femininity, and beauty.

## 5. Barbie's Success Story: A Conclusion

Barbie's 40th birthday in 1999 and Mattel's continuous successful marketing of this doll have revealed that images of femininity have been changing, but barely so. Barbie's body has lost nothing of its sex appeal; its black, Hispanic, Asian, and other ethnic and national versions cannot hide its homogeneity within diversity. It is still the white Barbie that sells best. And while Barbie has developed from a housewife into a businesswoman and politician, the beauty myth is more prevalent than ever. Naomi Wolf correlates recognizable backlash tendencies in the 1980s and 90s – also analyzed by Susan Faludi in her book *Backlash* in 1991 – with this renewed vigor in the promotion of beauty ideals:

> The contemporary backlash is so violent because the ideology of beauty is the last one remaining of the old feminine ideologies that still has the power to control those women whom second wave feminism would have otherwise made relatively uncontrollable: It has grown stronger to take over the work of social coercion that myths about motherhood, domesticity, chastity, and passivity, no longer can manage. It is seeking right now to undo psychologically and covertly all the good things that feminism did for women materially and overtly. (10-11)

Today, the all-feminine Barbie has strong competitors in the Japanese cartoon figures of *Pokémon* and *Digimon* or in the computer-animated doll Lara Croft. But Barbie's story is an American success story, and she is a strong player in the global world of toys. With her many professions and changeable colors, hairstyles, clothes, ethnic and national backgrounds, she seems to suggest that cultural identity is flexible. But the images of sexuality and gender and gender role distributions that Barbie embodies have remained surprisingly (?) stable – not to say conservative – and seem to be universally accepted in their binary constructions of femininity and masculinity. After all, the toy industry is a consumer-oriented mass-production enterprise, and therefore this stability may not be all that surprising.

## Works Cited

Aqua. "Barbie Girl." *Aquarium*. CD. Universal Music (Denmark), 1997.

Becker, Susanne, and Stefanie Schütte. "Der Stoff, aus dem der Zeitgeist ist." *Magisch angezogen: Mode, Medien, Markenwelten*. Ed. Susanne Becker and Stefanie Schütte. München: Beck, 1999. 9-12.

Bensonhurst, Lucky. "Bright Lights, Big Titties: It's a Corporate Barbie World, Part I." 1998. 6 November 2002 <htto://www.goteamfrog.org/gotohell/national/barbie1summer98.html>.

Boy, Billy. *Barbie: Her Life and Times*. New York: Crown, 1987.

Debouzy, Marianne. "The Barbie Doll." *European Readings of American Popular Culture*. Ed. John Dean and Jean-Paul Gabilliet. Westport, CT: Greenwood P, 1996. 139-46.

Deutsch, Stefanie. *Barbie: The First 30 Years, 1959 through 1989. An Identification and Value Guide*. Paducah, KY: Collector Books, 1996.

Evanovich, Janet. *High Five*. New York: St. Martin's, 1999.

Faludi, Susan. *Backlash: The Undeclared War against American Women*. New York: Doubleday, 1991.

Friedan, Betty. *The Feminine Mystique*. 1963. New York: Norton, 1983.

Lord, M. G. *Forever Barbie: The Unauthorized Biography of a Real Doll*. New York: Morrow, 1994.

Motz, Marilyn Ferris. "'I Want to Be a Barbie Doll When I Grow Up': The Cultural Significance of the Barbie Doll." *Popular Culture Reader*. Ed. D. Geist und J. Nachbar. Bowling Green, OH: Popular, 1983.

Paglia, Camille. "Pornographically_Android_Barbie." 2000. 6 November 2002 <http://www.salon.com/mwt/feature/1997/11/26moments.html>.

Rand, Erica. *Barbie's Queer Accessories*. Durham: Duke UP, 1995.

– – –. "Older Heads on Younger Bodies." *The Children's Culture Reader*. Ed. Henry Jenkins. New York: New York UP, 1998. 382-93.

– – –. "We Girls Can Do Anything, Right Barbie? Lesbian Consumption in Postmodern Circulation." *The Lesbian Postmodern*. Ed. Laura Doan. New York: Columbia UP, 1994. 189-209.

Rogers, Mary. *Barbie Culture*. London: Sage, 1999.

Schmale, Holger. "Barbie und Co. machen Karriere." *Allgemeine Zeitung Mainz* 8 April 2000.

"Starwelt." *Kurier* 16 November 2002: 14.

Strohmeyer, Sarah. "Barbie Banned in Vermont." 2000. 6 November 2002 <http://www.salon.com/mwt/feature/1997/11/26banned.html>.

Urla, Jacqueline, and Alan C. Swedlund. "The Anthropometry of Barbie: Unsettling Ideals of the Feminine Body in Popular Culture." *Feminism and the Body*. Ed. Londa Schiebinger. Oxford: OUP, 2000. 397-428.

Virilio, Paul. *Ground Zero*. Trans. Chris Turner. London: Verso, 2002.

"Wal-Mart Pulls Pregnant Barbie Pal from Shelves." 14 Feb. 2003 <http://biz.yahoo.com/rc/021226/retail_walmart_1.html>.

Wolf, Naomi. *The Beauty Myth: How Images of Beauty Are Used against Women*. New York: Morrow, 1991.

Ill. 1: "Wedding Day Porcelain Barbie." Deutsch 140. © Mattel, Inc.

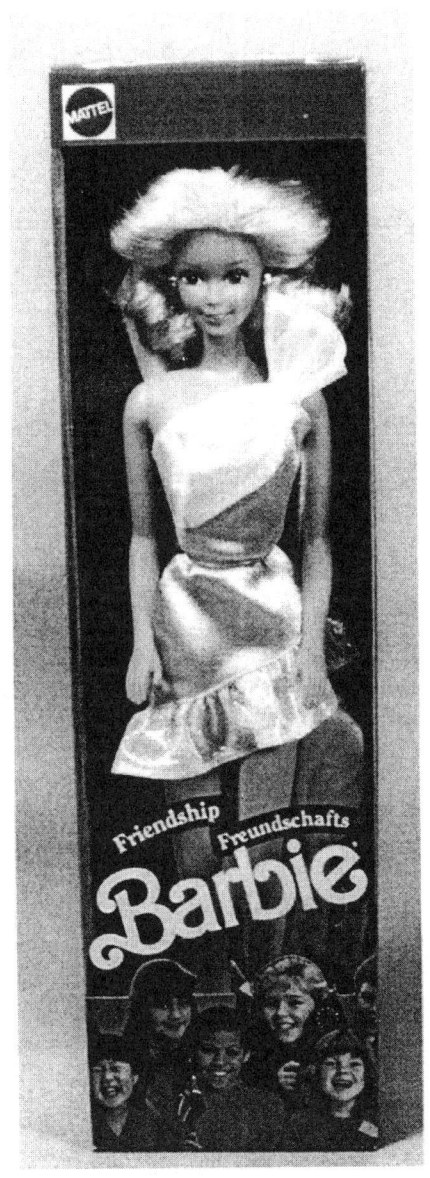

Ill. 2: "Friendship I (Berlin Wall) Barbie." Deutsch 158. © Mattel, Inc.

# The Black Athlete's Battle Royal of the 1960s: Anti-American Protests in American Sports

## Duco van Oostrum

One of the only times sports stars are listened to outside the sporting arena is when they protest. When Jackie Robinson broke the color line in 1947, he was told never to retaliate, never to speak back—the best mode of action was to beat his racist hecklers in "America's game." Referred to as the "noble experiment," Robinson's entry into baseball was as much about fitting into a uniform as about the ability to "play ball":

> Next he had to find the ideal player for his project, which came to be called "Rickey's noble experiment." This player had to be one who could take abuse, name-calling, rejection by fans and sportswriters and fellow players not only on opposing teams but on his own. He had to be able to stand up in the face of merciless persecution and not retaliate. On the other hand, he had to be a contradiction in human terms; he still had to have spirit. He could not be an "Uncle Tom." His ability to turn the other cheek had to be predicated on his determination to gain acceptance. Once having proven his ability as player, teammate, and man, he had to be able to cast off humbleness and stand up as a full-fledged participant whose triumph did not carry the poison of bitterness. (Robinson/Duckett 28)

Remarkably, the model precedes the actual human baseball player, and Jackie Robinson has to step into the uniform of this "noble experiment." In his autobiography, *I Never Had It Made*, ghost-written by his friend Alfred Duckett and written after his playing days were over, Robinson recounts the trials and experiences that made him the embodiment of an experiment. One of the pivotal moments occurs when he is taunted by opposing players from the Philadelphia Phillies in a 1947 game:

For one wild and rage-crazed minute I thought, "To hell with Mr. Rickey's 'noble experiment. It's clear it won't succeed. I have made every effort to work hard, to get myself into shape. My best is not enough for them." I thought what a glorious, cleansing thing it would be to let go. To hell with the image of the patient black freak I was supposed to create. I could throw down my bat, stride over to that Phillies dugout, grab one of those white sons of bitches and smash his teeth in with my despised black fist. Then I could walk away from it all. I'd never become a sports star. But my son could tell his son someday what his daddy could have been if he hadn't been too much of a man. (60)

I have quoted at length here from Robinson's autobiography to indicate that from the first moment of racial integration in major American team sports (very different from individual sports such as athletics and boxing), the African American athlete battles with racial images. Individuality contrasts with "playing the game"—i.e. conforming to type.

When black athletes starting speaking back in the 1960s, however, the response was loud and clear: they should just play ball. Even within the context of Civil Rights, athletes were in a different ballpark, observed by the leaders as examples of African Americans succeeding in slowly integrating America. Robinson himself was deeply engrained in Civil Rights and politics (making some unfortunate choices) and after the initial years of 'turning the other cheek,' he had become one of the most vocal players on the field, to the dismay of many sportswriters. Arnold Rampersad in his biography of Robinson cites Martin Luther King's 1962 tribute (Robinson had been elected into the Hall of Fame) to Robinson:

> Spelling out the meaning of Jackie Robinson's example, King defended Robinson's right, challenged by some observers who saw him as a faded athlete perilously beyond his depth, to speak out on matters such as politics, segregation, and civil rights. "He had the right," King insisted stoutly, "because back in the days when integration wasn't fashionable, he underwent the trauma and the humiliation and the loneliness which comes with being a pilgrim walking the lonesome byways toward the high road of Freedom. He

was a sit-inner before sit-ins, a freedom rider before freedom rides." (7)

In the 1960s, sports became an arena at the center of 'American freedom' and Civil Rights. Muhammad Ali's shocking decision not to fight in Vietnam brought home the disjunction between 'black athlete' and human.[1] He divided America:

> But who is this white man, no older than me, appointed by another white man, all the way down from the white man in the White House? Who is he to tell me to go to Asia, Africa or anywhere else in the world to fight people who never threw a rock at me or America? Who is this descendant of the slave masters to order a descendant of slaves to fight other people in their own country? (Ali/Durham 168)

The image of the contented black athlete, happy to be a model for integrating America, was shattered. It culminated at the 1968 Olympics, with Tommie Lee Smith's and John Carlos's Black Panther salute during the playing of the national anthem – this was the most visible political demonstration yet of the Black American athlete in the sports arena.

Amy Bass, in her recent book focusing on the 1968 Olympics, *Not the Triumph but the Struggle*, is right. Something changed in the "representations of the black athlete" and in the "many ways the black athlete [was] constructed in American cultural life" (xvi) during the 1960s. The voicelessness of the previous generations and their individual struggles now found a collective focus in action. Harry Edwards's Olympic Project for Human Rights, which tried to organize African American athletes into a boycott of the 1968 Olympics, sought to address international race inequalities through sports, advocating boycotts of South Africa and Rhodesia. His political action, and his personal choice to accept a fellowship at Cornell rather than embark on an athletic career, created a new visual phenomenon, Bass argues, the "black athlete." From a mixed terminology of "Negro athlete" to "athlete of color," spurred by Malcolm X's insistence on black pride, came this single, all-inclusive label, the black athlete. As dubious as that singular designation may appear, it offered African American athletes a forum from which to speak outside the arena.

The link to the sports arena, however, is a highly dubious structure for African American dissent. Bass's groundbreaking work in media politics also finds resonance in African American cultural expression, such as literature and autobiography. A focus on textual construction of the representation of the black athlete through literature, autobiography (ghost-written and all) and film produces striking moments of opposition to this label of the "black athlete." The overlaps between other African American male models such as that of "the noble experiment" or even Frederick Douglass's "heroic slave" are compelling. Here I would like to put this juxtaposition between model athlete and individual in the context of one of the ur-texts of African American literature, Ralph Ellison's novel *Invisible Man* (1947).

By reading the "Battle Royal" scene in *Invisible Man* as a structural analysis of race and sports, I would like to examine the potential for protest in the sports arena for African American athletes. Within regulated spaces and bound by specific rules, the sports arena allows for limited freedom within the Game. Even outside the sports field boundaries, athletes are punished if they transgress their identities as sports stars. Writing or speaking on issues away from the arena, the athletes are re-positioned into the safe structure of sports boundaries.

In the "Prologue," the Invisible Man, while smoking a reefer, listens to Louis Armstrong playing and singing, "What did I do to be so black and blue?" Music fills his mind as he traverses the meanings and contradictions of black invisibilities. As a young boy, he gave a Booker T. Washington-like graduation oration at his town's (Greenwood) high school. For his achievement, he was then invited to give his speech at a "gathering of the town's leading white folk" (17). This gathering turns out to be centered around a Battle Royal, ten black young men boxing blindfolded until two remain. The boxing ring is the centerpiece in the ballroom, with all attention drawn to the black athletes in the middle. Around this sporting event, other entertainment is in place, all involving spectacles of race, but no music. The evening starts with the boys in shorts, on stage, gazing at a white female stripper with an American flag tattooed on her belly. On this stage, black sports and white women perform together in a staging of black and female bodies. The arena is sexualized, as the men ("boys") try to conceal their erections in the face of the naked white American woman. After this erotic event, the "boxing" can commence. For the athletes, the evening presents a good night's work with excellent wages (five dollars). In fact, the boxers resent the Invisible Man's presence since he replaces one of the regulars. He actually feels himself intellectually superior to "these tough guys" and is afraid that "fighting a battle royal might detract from the dignity of my speech" (17). For the audience, however, the black intellectual shares the boxing ring with the black athlete. The structure of the Battle Royal, furthermore, tries to minimize athletic skill and makes winning and losing a matter of chance rather than prowess. The blindfolds ensure a scene of absolute mayhem. Amidst the onslaught, it turns out that the regular athletes have teamed up to conspire against the intruder. The Invisible Man is left to face Tatlock, the biggest and most skilled boxer, for the grand prize of the evening. Then, in a remarkable moment, he offers Tatlock a bribe, first five, and then seven dollars. Finally, he tries to win: "I fought back with hopeless desperation. I wanted to deliver my speech more than anything else in the world, because I felt that only these men could judge truly my ability, and now this stupid clown was ruining my chances" (25). But as he hears someone in the audience yell, "I got my money on the big boy," confusion sets in again. "Should I try to win against the voice out there? Would not this go against my speech, and was not this a moment for humility, for non-resistance?" At that moment, Tatlock settles the dilemma for him and knocks him out. In the daze that follows, all the men are led to an electrified rug, and sprinkled with supposedly gold pieces. Everyone battles for the fake coins on the rug, continuing in spite of the shocks. Finally, the men are told to get dressed and get their money. As the men leave, the Invisible Man is led back into the ballroom. Introduced as the "smartest boy in Greenwood," he then delivers his speech, fairly straightforwardly plagiarized from Booker T. Washington's Atlanta address. Barely able to speak because of the blood oozing from his mouth, he stumbles onto the words "social equality" (31). The outrage in the audience is only ameliorated after he corrects himself as he says: "social responsibility." In his right 'place' again, he finishes. As a reward, he receives a calfskin briefcase and a scholarship to the state college for Negroes (32). As he says, without irony, "I was overjoyed" (32).

Ellison's paradigm of invisibility of 1947 finds one of its most visible moments in the sports arena of the 1920s. Significantly, the structural arrangements leave little space for resistance. Inside the spectacle, racial battles rage, phrased in bloody games win or lose. While they slug it out in a man against man fight, winning is the only thing that counts, not resistance against the audience. The rules within the ring determine identity there. Yet outside the ring, the men are framed in a structure of spectatorship. Seduced by the spoils of cash and sex, the black athletes are willing participants in a scene of ultimate typology. The invisible man himself labels Tatlock a "stupid clown." In this case, sports for black athletes works very much within the parameters of John Hoberman's controversial *Darwin's Athletes*:

> The first section of the book describes the origins of the African American preoccupation with athletic achievement and shows how this cultural syndrome has subverted more productive developmental strategies founded on academic and professional achievement. It argues that Western racism inflicted on African Americans a physicalized (and eventually athleticized) identity from which they have yet to escape. The cult of black athleticism continues a racist tradition that has long emphasized the motor skills and manual training of African Americans. While the idea of black athletic superiority serves the fantasy needs of blacks as well as whites, providing symbolic victories and a renewal of survivalist thinking about black toughness, the sports fixation is also emblematic of an entire complex of black problems, which includes the adolescent violence and academic failure that have come to symbolize the black male for most Americans. (xxxiv)

What is so challenging about the Battle Royal scene of *Invisible Man* is the link between education and sport—both are terrains for white entertainment. On the boxing platform, the Invisible Man delivers his speech about race progress. The contemporary phrase "social responsibility" is lifted straight from the language of African American participation in sport—play by the rules and be a role model, an example for your race. The black man is an athlete first and if he speaks, he should follow the rules—know your place on the pitch and in the classroom. The field is exclusively male. The Battle Royal, I will argue, interrogates this masculine racial field of sport in lucid and terrifying detail: the stage and audience 'make' the black athlete; the shift from a team sport to an individual one challenges ideas of collective action, especially with comparatively vast monetary rewards waiting for the winner; the conformity of all athletes to perform these roles and their enjoyment; the link of black male athleticism and sexuality to the white female body; the link of the black intellectual and black athleticism; the pleasure in athletic skill for its own sake. Furthermore, the small-town setting creates local celebrity, providing a glimpse of visibility to the young men in a section of town from which they would normally be barred. (Where they go to after the main event is unreadable in this remarkable novel.)

Ellison's novel of 1947 is not a description of sports in the 1960s. In the 1960s a small group of extraordinary black athletes came to dominate some important sports. The athletes' blindfolds were removed and they could demonstrate talent, skill, innovation, and freedom inside the sports field. Winning and playing the game could now be attributed to agency. While athletics and boxing had always been a terrain of visibility for the black athlete (just think of Jesse Owen and Joe Louis – with massive problems in terms of representation there as well, of course), the major American team sports, baseball, football, and basketball, were far more resistant to integrated participation. In boxing, Cassius Clay/Muhammad Ali transformed the sport into aesthetics; Norman Mailer placed the 1975 fight with George Foreman on an equal footing with art: "Back in America everybody was already yelling that the fight was fixed. Yes. So was *The Night Watch* and *Portrait of the Artist as a Young Man*."[2] "I am the professor of boxing," Ali exclaims in Mailer's text (212). In baseball, Hank Aaron, Willie Mays, and Bob Gibson formed part of an African American elite. In football, Jim Brown ran the show, and in basketball, Bill Russell and Wilt Chamberlain established one of the all-time sporting rivalries. For all the athletes, removing the blindfold meant finding an aesthetic realm in play. On the sports field, the game lived up to individual and communal expression.

One of the best examples of this aesthetic wholeness occurs in Russell's autobiography (written by Civil Rights historian Taylor Branch):

At that special level all sorts of odd things happened. The game would be in a white heat of competition, and yet somehow I wouldn't feel competitive—which is a miracle in itself. I'd be putting out the maximum effort, straining, coughing up parts of my lungs as we ran, and yet I never felt the pain. The game would move so quickly that every fake, cut and pass would be surprising, and yet nothing could surprise me. It was almost as if we were playing in slow motion. During those spells I could almost sense how the next play would develop and where the next shot would be taken. Even before the other team brought the ball in bounds, I could feel it so keenly that I'd want to shout to my team-mates, "It's come there!"—except that I knew everything would change if I did. MY premonitions would be consistently correct, and I always felt then that I not only knew all the Celtics by heart but also the opposing players, and that they all knew me. There have been many times in my career when I felt moved or joyful, but there were the moments when I had chills pulsing up and down. (Russell/Branch 156-57)

*The Sporting News* chose Bill Russell as athlete of the 1960s. Perhaps more than Martin Luther King, Jr. and Malcolm X, the African American athletes came to be representative of what Houston Baker calls a "Black Public Sphere," which counters the "fantasies" of "mass media propaganda" (15). As Cornel West phrases it in the new foreword to Jackie Robinson's ghost-written autobiography, *I Never Had It Made*: "More even than either Abraham Lincoln and the Civil War, or Martin Luther King, Jr. and the Civil Rights movement, Jackie Robinson graphically symbolized and personified the challenge to the vicious legacy and ideology of white supremacy in American history" (x). Racial integration on the sports field changed the arena. Bill Russell recalls the tremendous impact the locker room scene made on his grandfather:

> After a few minutes we saw him standing not far away. Panic shot through both of us: the Old Man was crying. . . . What's the matter, Papa?" Mister Charlie asked anxiously. The Old Man looked up at us and made a slow pronouncement. "I never thought I'd live to see the day when the water would run off a white man onto a black man," he said, "and the water would run off a black man onto a white man." He kept shaking his head. "I've been to church all of my days, but I never

thought I'd see anything like this. You know, I can tell those two men *like* each other." (47)

Many of the black athletes' autobiographies detail conversion narratives of their white teammates. Jackie Robinson's incident with Kentuckian teammate, shortstop Pee Wee Reese, is perhaps the most familiar:

> In Boston during a period when the heckling pressure seemed unbearable, some of the Boston players began to heckle Reese. They were riding him about being a Southerner and playing ball with a black man. Pee Wee didn't answer them. Without a glance in their direction, he left his position and walked over to me. His words weren't important. I don't even remember what he said. It was the gesture of comradeship and support that counted. (65)

Bill Bradley in his autobiography also details how being in the presence of black athletes completely changed his ideas of himself:

> Living together eighteen hours a day for six months a year forces one to see a person, not a race. Sure there is black language, and black attitudes, and a black suspicion, but each man is different. Generalities about race become unacceptable against the diversity of human traits. And yet I have changed in some ways because of my black friends. It is hard to say exactly how but after witnessing their joys, fears, perceptions, and spontaneous reactions for seven years I am different. I regard authority a little more skeptically than I once did. I am more interested in experiencing life that in analyzing it. . . . But, above all, I see how much I don't know and can never know about black people. (139-40)

Many texts, such as those of Hank Aaron and Chet Walker, for example, point to the work of the black athlete in desegregating individual towns. By making the sporting structure interracial, change occurs inside. Their narratives from the sporting scene revise the Invisible Man's speech. Their 'work,' as Hank Aaron, for example, makes clear in the preface to *I Had a Hammer*, is also to "hammer out a little justice":

> The way I see it, it's a great thing to be the man who hit the most home runs, but it's a greater thing to be the man who did the most with the

home runs he hit. So as long as there's a chance that maybe I can hammer out a little justice now and then, or a little opportunity here and there, I intend to do as I always have—keep swinging. I'm taking my cuts as you read this. I'm telling my story, and when everything's said and done, maybe it'll mean more than a bunch of home runs. I can only hope and keep hammering. (4)

These individual stories of elite black athletes stress their actions on the sport field as actions with ramifications off it. While these are mainly stories of celebrities, of those 'who have it made,' their individual stories seek to emphasize, or 'hammer home,' the truth about the African Americans who remain in their hometowns. Stories of individual upward mobility through sport for African Americans (the seductive dream narrative) contrast with stories of 'home.' Robinson's autobiography is particularly telling as it insists that he "never had it made." The main action of the book, in fact, to the disappointment of many sports fans (see reviews on amazon.com and elsewhere) takes place in the 1960s, as Robinson goes from one unfortunate political choice to another—backing Richard Nixon against John F. Kennedy; supporting Nelson Rockefeller; his various business enterprises; testifying against Paul Robeson in 1949. He closes his book with: "However there is one irrefutable fact of my life which has determined much of what happened to me: I was a black man in a white world. *I never had it made*" (275). He cannot leave the structure of the sport arena; his book reminds one of the Invisible Man's speech after his battle.

The success of the black athlete visualizes him as a representative of a group. As Hoberman argues, the visibility of the black athlete remains essentially a typology. The individual black athletes and their individual stories uncomfortably form a genre of a collective experience. While Amy Bass focuses on the 1968 Olympics as a "collective making" of the black athlete, I think the stories and experiences of individuals point to other significant moments, created very much on local, regional territories rather than globally televised sporting events. The 1960s saw for the first time a group of elite black athletes, wealthy, independent and of vast importance to particular American team sports. The difference between individual and team sport cannot be overstated, and in particular the difference between

'American' sports and global sports. The track and field athletes have never attained the same symbolic status within the United States as baseball, football, and basketball players have.

Before the 1968 Olympics, irrespective of Harry Edwards, high profile black athletes (those who 'had it made') were keen to see themselves as part of a new class. Similar to the current African American sports 'club' of Charles Barkley, Michael Jordan, Tiger Woods, Roy Green, Ahmad Rashaad, and Quinn Buckner, the black elite athletes bonded as a separate group in both sports culture and American society.[3] As a group, they were acutely aware of their images as "black athletes" and their importance as role models for the African American community.

In 1966, there was a remarkable meeting of black athletes in a hotel in Cleveland. Jim Brown, running back for the Cleveland Browns, set up a Boxing Company together with some of Ali's closest advisors (Brown would receive 10% of revenue). But before the first fight could be organized Ali announced he refused to be inducted in the U.S. army. As Jim Brown (or Steve Delsohn) writes in his autobiography, *Out of Bounds*, "Ali's announcement shocked and angered" (291). He decided to call a meeting:

> I called my team-mate, John Wooten, our Executive Director of the Black Economic Union, told him to call a group of black athletes, ask them to come to Cleveland. Rumors were flying about why Ali "really" wouldn't fight in Vietnam. I wanted Ali to sit down with these athletes, explain his declaration. I knew Ali would need support, broader than what he had. By having a community of famous black athletes behind him, it would show the press, the public, Ali was backed by more than just the Muslims. (291)

Brown gathered a remarkable group of athletes: Bill Russell, Kareem Abdul Jabbar (then Lew Alcindor, UCLA), Sid Williams and Walter Beach (Cleveland Browns), Curtis McClinton (Kansas City Chiefs), Bobby Mitchell and Jim Shorter (Washington Redskins), Willie Davis (Green Bay Packers), Gale Sayers (Chicago Bears), John Wooten. Ali grasps the importance of the occasion:

> One morning I receive a telegram from Jim Brown, the football hero of the Cleveland Browns, asking me to meet with a group of prominent black athletes who want to question me on my draft stand. Of all the pressure on me to conform, none has yet come from black people, who mostly have been opposed to my going to Viet Nam. The press reports that the black athletes have been called to persuade me to 'support the government'. I fly into Cleveland wondering why a group of black athletes, who have never assembled for anything other than sports, want to see me. (*The Greatest* 173)

The political gathering of black athletes to question another black athlete about his decision whether or not to join the army seems far removed from the sports arena. Yet somehow these athletes are supposed to test Ali's commitment to American ideology. Interestingly enough, most of the athletes are quite confused about their own position. Jim Brown's motives cannot be separated from his financial stakes, and he admits that he was authorized to broker a deal on behalf of the government. Both Jim Brown and Bill Russell are well known for raising issues of race outside the sports field. Yet from them comes the call for Ali to please explain himself. In Thomas Hauser's biography of Ali, the athletes all recall they are there to support Ali. Kareem, for example, remembers:

> Jim Brown took the lead in the discussion, but he kept it as an open forum. He told us that our status as heroes in the black community could help gather support for Ali. But Ali didn't need our help, because as far as the black community was concerned, he already had everybody's heart. (Hauser 178)

Within the professional team sport game, the stakes are high. All athletes have lived the American sports dream and are indebted to an American myth. This myth, though, structurally resembles the sporting scene of the Battle Royal. Their professional contracts are closely intertwined with a mostly white American spectatorship. While their skill protects them against some repercussions, an anti-governmental stance will seriously damage individual careers and their accustomed life styles. The rewards in the short term for being a good team player are attractive—Jim Brown, Wilt Chamberlain, Magic Johnson, for example, write with glee about their life styles of luxury and sex.

Following an entire section on race in his autobiography, Brown then writes a chapter on white women; Johnson is keen to blame his HIV status on having had sex with 5,000 women. Wilt Chamberlain, in *A View from Above*, proudly proclaims his sexual prowess to the world:

> I'm one of the lucky ones. So don't be shocked to hear that if I had to count my sexual encounters, I would be closing in on twenty thousand women. Yes, that's correct, *twenty thousand different ladies*. At my age, that equals out to having sex with 1.2 women a day, every day since I was fifteen years old. (251)

The entertainment in the Battle Royal clearly puts the stripper with the American flag on the same stage as the black athlete. The label "black athlete" is extraordinarily gender-specific. Wilma Rudolph and other female black athletes do not enter into this discussion. Harry Edwards himself now acknowledges that one of the failures of the Olympic Project for Human Rights was the absence of women:

> We also didn't do the job we should have done in terms of women. Even with all of those black women athletes in the Olympics, we never really approached them. In today's language that means we were sexist, an indictment that could be extended to the whole civil rights movement. ("What Happened to the Revolt Black Athlete?")

Contradicting his earlier declaration of why he wanted a meeting, Brown makes it clear that the athletes are there to persuade Ali to rescind his decision:

> They were there to hear him out, determine if he was sincere, whether they would support him. Unaware of Ali's intransigence, they were also there to raise questions and potential alternatives. Ali started preaching! He delivered a sermon on the Mother Ship, Elijah, the Nation of Islam. Despite the tension outside, it was funny as hell. Ali was in there with some of the top black athletes in America, whose intent was moderation and balance. But Ali was such a dazzling speaker, he damn near converted a few into the Nation of Islam. (292)

Yet Ali leaves the group speechless and rather shamefaced. As he writes in his autobiography: "I talk and they listen. And when it's over, most of them seem confused as to why they're there in the first place. Brown announces to the press that they finally found me 'sincere in my beliefs'" (173).

This meeting and Ali's decision changed the sport scene. Ali's exile deprived him of income and his art, as he sees his boxing. To many, though, he has since become the representative voice for political action in sport. Russell even admits that he envied Ali for his decision: "He has an absolute and sincere fate" (see Hauser 179). Lew Alcindor later converted to Islam after reading Malcolm X's autobiography. What about the other athletes and their political action, though? It appears to be all or nothing. Tommie Smith and John Carlos were permanently suspended after their protest and now sell autographed posters on their websites.[4] From within the sport, the competitive desire for winning is still equated with gaining respect outside the arena; the Invisible Man is seduced by the power associated with winning and will cheat the sport for it. Bill Russell resists that seduction in the spiritual moments of the sport; yet the impossibility of transposing those moments outside the boundaries of the court frustrates. The visibility on the sports court makes the athlete into a model, or, as Bill Bradley phrases it, "more a playmate than an adult" (111). This two-dimensional cartoon-like character (think also of Michael Jordan in the 1996 film *Space Jam*) in African American sports becomes a 'race man.' Resistance or compliance with this model of race in sport is itself already a racist implication. The well-known conflict between individual and collective action in African American culture finds a public stage in sports. The Olympic Project for Human Rights collapsed when athletes asserted their individual desires to play the game. When Charles Barkley declared, "I am not a role model," he, in Todd Boyd's words, "openly challenged the relationship between individual and group as it pertains to African Americans" (139). The Invisible Man is invisible because he fits the typology set up for him on the stage as boxer and speaker; his own allegiance collapses as he tries to bribe Tatlock and then tries to beat the "clown."

When Harry Edwards set up the Olympic Project for Human Rights, he envisioned that the black athletes would lead a revolt:

> In essence then, the black revolution in America has not been carried into the locker room, as one sports writer has stated. What has

happened is that the black athlete has left the façade of locker room equality and justice to take his long vacant place as a primary participant in the black revolution. (xxviii)

But, as became evident, playing the game and protesting its American values transgressed boundaries. The men in the Battle Royal box after a belly-dancing display of the American flag. An allegiance to the Game means an allegiance to the Flag.

Two contrasting images from previous Olympic Games could not illustrate the difference in attitude towards the United States of America by medal-winning black American men better: the black panther salute of Tommie Smith and John Carlos at the 1968 games in Mexico City and the American flag draped around Michael Jordan's body at the 1992 games in Barcelona. While a shoeless Smith and Carlos lowered their heads for the Stars and Stripes and raised their gloved fists "for the power and unity in black America" (Carlos/Smith), Michael Jordan, Magic Johnson, and Charles Barkley enveloped themselves in the flags and flaunted their branded shoes. The flags did not symbolize a new united America, but covered the Reebok logo on the award uniform. Their contracts to other corporations (Nike) led to the American Flag being used as a literal cover of conflicting interests. The Harry Edwards-inspired protests had immense personal consequences for Smith and Carlos. They sacrificed individual glory for political communal action. Jordan maintained and increased his individual interests, his iconic status in the African American community, and his symbolic representation of a nation.

Athletes as far apart as Jim Brown and Charles Barkley proclaim Ali their idol. But this is too easy. Ali lost four years of his career; yet when he returned he bizarrely played the race card against Joe Frazier and George Foreman; Foreman himself had stirred plenty of controversy himself by waving a tiny American flag after winning his gold medal at the 1968 Olympics. Barkley proclaims his famous "I am not a role model" in a Nike commercial. Jim Brown's Hollywood career lands him performances such as assistant coach in *Any Given Sunday*. Even Ali becomes an emblem of a nostalgic America as he lights the torch in the 1996 Atlanta Olympics. Sports can absorb all political action; the games must go on.

## Notes

I would like to acknowledge the support of the British Academy and the AHRB in conducting this research. I am also grateful for the helpful suggestions made by Dominic Shellard and the editors.

[1] Cf. Isserman and Kazin's *America Divided: The Civil War of the 1960s*. As in many textbooks about cultural history, scant attention is being paid here to a paradigm of sports within culture.
[2] Mailer, *The Fight* 210.
[3] See Jack McCallum's extraordinary interview with Charles Barkley in the March 11, 2002 edition of *Sports Illustrated*.
[4] See <http://www.tommiesmith.com> and <http://www.johncarlos.com>.

## Works Cited

Ali, Muhammad, with Richard Durham. *The Greatest: My Own Story*. London: Hart-Davis, MacGibbon, 1976.

Aaron, Hank, with Lonnie Wheeler. *I Had A Hammer: The Hank Aaron Story*. New York: HarperCollins, 1991.

Baker, Houston, Jr. "Critical Memory and the Black Public Sphere." *Public Culture* 7.1 (Fall 1994): 7-37.

Bass, Amy. *Not the Triumph But the Struggle: The 1968 Olympics and the Making of the Black Athlete*. Minneapolis/London: U of Minnesota P, 2002.

Boyd, Todd. "The Day the Niggaz Took Over: Basketball, Commodity Culture, and Black Masculinity," *Out of Bounds: Sports, Media, and the Politics of Identity*, ed. Aaron Baker and Todd Boyd. Bloomington: Indiana UP, 1997. 123-42.

Bradley, Bill. *Life On the Run*. New York: Vintage, 1995.

Brown, Jim, with Steve Dehlson. *Out of Bounds*. New York: Zebra Books, 1989.

Chamberlain, Wilt. *A View from Above*. New York: Villard Books, 1991.

Edwards, Harry. *The Revolt of the Black Athlete*. New York: Free P, 1969.

Ellison, Ralph. *Invisible Man*. 1947. New York: Vintage, 1972.

Hauser, Thomas. *Muhammad Ali: His Life and Times.* New York: Pan Books, 1992.

Hoberman, John. *Darwin's Athletes: How Sport has Damaged Black America and Preserved the Myth of Race.* Boston: Houghton Mifflin, 1997.

Isserman, Maurice, and Michael Kazin. *America Divided: The Civil War of the 1960s.* Oxford: Oxford UP, 2000.

Mailer, Norman. *The Fight.* London: Penguin, 1975.

McCallum, Jack. "Citizen Barkley." *Sports Illustrated* 96.11 (March 2002): 32-38.

Rampersad, Arnold. *Jackie Robinson: A Biography.* New York: Alfred Knopf, 1997.

Robinson, Jackie, with Alfred Duckett, *I Never Had it Made.* 1972. New Jersey: Ecco Press, 1995.

Russell, Bill, and Taylor Branch. *Second Wind.* New York: Random House, 1979.

Walker, Chet, with Chris Messenger. *Long Time Coming: A Black Athlete's Coming-of-Age in America.* New York: Grove P, 1995.

"What Happened to the Revolt Black Athlete? *A Look Back Thirty Years Later*," Interview with Harry Edwards by David Leonard, *Colorlines* 5.1 (summer 1998). 13 Jan. 2004 <http://www.arc.org/C_Lines/CLArchive/story1_1_01.html>.

# "On Behalf of a Proud, Determined, and Grateful Nation": Americanism in Sports

## Monika Messner

Throughout the history of American sports, the relation between sports and the construction of a national identity has always been of special importance. Nationalism and patriotism as well as national loyalty and military strength are displayed and reinforced through sports.[1] Seldom has a country more vividly demonstrated the linkage between sports and national interests than the USA in their long history of using sports as a vehicle for Americanism. I will therefore briefly summarize how sports in general, and sport participation among immigrants in particular, has been promoted in order to undermine traditional ethnic values and to replace them with an Americanized way of looking at the world. Then, I will focus on baseball as the national pastime and on how this game both mirrors and defines what it means to be American. Finally, I will deal with sports as a metaphor for the ideals that helped the United States to recover from the attacks of September 11, 2001. In sports spectacles such as the Super Bowl, the World Series, or the 2002 Olympic Games in Salt Lake City – all of them receiving extensive media coverage – sports truly served as an "opiate" for the people, diverting the masses from more substantial post-9/11-questions like the Bush administration's assault on civil liberties, skyrocketing military expenditure, and U.S. isolationism, with a fabricated dream world of glamor and excitement.

The origin of sports in America (and America will here be taken as synonymous with the United States) goes back to the colonial period. During that time, orthodox Puritan norms, particularly in New England, restricted the desire to engage in certain activities. The southern states had a more liberal attitude towards sports participation. According to Benjamin Rader, the emergence of a lively sports culture in the South was especially due to the "growth of the powerful landed gentry" (10). But because the upper classes considered their interest in sports primarily as a tribute to their British roots, it was not until independence that a distinctive American identity, emphasizing the difference from British/European models, began to materialize.

During the nineteenth century, the emergence of a distinct "Americanness" went hand in hand with a massive transformation of American society as a whole as well as with substantial changes in American sports culture. While sports participation and spectatorship were strongly linked with both elitist attitudes and social class at the beginning of the century, the development of modern sports as a mass phenomenon accelerated between the Civil War and World War I. The influence of industrialization, urbanization, transport, and mass communication was instrumental in the growth of American sports (cf. Betts 256). But at least as significant as the impact of the technological revolution on the rise of the modern sporting culture was the reconstruction of American society as a whole after the Civil War. The re-unified state was in search of new patterns and symbols that could help create a unified national culture and identity. Inevitably, this shaping of a national consciousness was closely related to the emergence of American sports that were "national in scope and 'Americanizing' in effect" (Mrozek xvi).

By the beginning of the twentieth century, the pervasion of sports with national and patriotic symbols was paralleled by a general tendency toward nationalism, which showed itself in the nation's emerging role as a global power, together with the movement toward immigration restriction and overseas imperialism. Sports was largely seen as an integral part in the production of a national cultural identity, and consequently many Americans believed that "organized sports provided the social glue for a nation of diverse classes, regions, ethnic and racial groups, and competing loyalties" (Pope, "Folk Highway" 327). This process of 'Americanizing' the nation's sporting culture is particularly reflected in the history of nineteenth-century ethnic sports clubs. As many immigrants tried to maintain their sporting traditions with such 'non-American' sports as soccer or cricket, the practice of using the prevailing sports culture to assimilate ethnic groups into the American way of life was much disputed. But as the twentieth century approached, many immigrants had already adopted the national sports: by playing American games they had finally "embraced and affirmed their place in the American community" (Pope, "Folk Highway" 331). Pope's statement poignantly illustrates the interdependency between sports and the American way of life – both were not only imposed on but also embraced by the immigrants. By the end of World War I, the use of sports to surpass ethnic and linguistic differences as well as to support American ideals had become an indispensable feature in the construction and reproduction of a national identity.

Although sports play a significant part in creating a sense of what it means to be American, they are also a terrain in which dominant groups seek to maintain their authority while their subordinates practice forms of cultural resistance. The European immigrants' efforts to maintain their ethnic sports culture was a first – though not too successful – attempt to resist Americanization. A much more dramatic form of resistance was displayed at the 1968 Olympic Games in Mexico City, when U.S. sprinters John Carlos and Tommy Smith gave the Black Power salute on the winner's podium to protest against the injustices black Americans were facing. Both athletes were subsequently suspended from the Games by the American Olympic Committee – a fact that proves the political facet of sports, which is often downplayed or even denied. But despite the fact that sports was labeled as a form of social glue, such forms of resistance show that much remains to be achieved before one can claim that the American people are truly united by sports. At this stage, however, it is still fitting to speak of American sports – especially in the professional leagues – as being an appropriate expression of the nation's identity as a whole. The control of sports as well as of the nation is in the hands of capital in general, and of rich white men specifically.[2]

In the process, there emerged a distinct American sporting culture in which considerable emphasis was placed on the team sports of baseball, football, basketball, and ice hockey. This emphasis on team sports seems to be a peculiar characteristic of American sports, considering the fact that the theme of individualism is so central to American society. But 'joining the team' has become the essence of the dominant American sports culture that represents a "combination of individualism and cooperation, a form of collective endeavor which nonetheless encourages the development of individuality" (Guttmann 138). Arguably, the most significant of these American games, in terms of representing what it means to be American, is baseball.

"A revealing metaphor for American society and values," "promoting democracy and good government," or "a true expression of the American spirit" are constantly repeated phrases in most literature on baseball.[3] But what is it about baseball that makes it the quintessential American game? The ground for baseball's mystic character was already laid in 1839, when, according to the legend, Abner Doubleday – a student at West Point later to become a Union general in the Civil War – first set out the rules of modern baseball in Cooperstown, NY. Although it is now clear that Doubleday had no recorded connection to baseball, the game's creation myth stands for the psychological need to provide the national pastime with an indigenous origin. The true beginning of baseball as a development of "a wide variety of English stick-and-ball games did not suit the mythology of a phenomenon that had become so quintessentially American" (Pope, *Patriotic Games* 71). Apart from granting baseball purely American origins, the Doubleday myth links the game with rural roots, thus establishing a relation between baseball and core values of an older way of American life. But like the creation myth itself, the rural associations were more legend than fact (Guttmann 100). Considering the game's mystique, it is no surprise that baseball had become a mass cultural movement by the 1880s. At this stage, however, the level of public interest shown in professional baseball was unprecedented. Further aspects, among them specific working-class occupations, Irish ethnicity, the development of a railroad-based entertainment industry, and increased sponsorship, contributed to the rise of baseball as the national pastime.

By the 1920s, "claims about baseball's nationally unifying characteristics were ubiquitous in American social commentary" (Pope, *Patriotic Games* 77). Between the two world wars, baseball established itself as America's undisputed national game. It did so by reflecting and helping to strengthen allegedly prototypical American values such as democracy, opportunity, fair play, individualism, team spirit, and competitiveness. In *America's National Game*, Albert G. Spalding had claimed that Base Ball owes its prestige as our National Game to the fact that as no other form of sport it is the exponent of American Courage, Confidence, Combativeness; American Dash, Discipline, Determination; American Energy, Eagerness, Enthusiasm; American Pluck, Persistency, Performance; American Spirit, Sagacity, Success; American Vim, Vigor, Virility" (3).[4]

Whether these values actually operated either in baseball or in American society as a whole and how far they can all even coexist is debatable. What matters, however, is that large numbers of Americans believed in these values, in their inherent Americanness and in their link to baseball. Especially the 'common man' could identify with baseball, even though it had become a profit-making enterprise run by far from common men.

Despite the fact that team owners more and more exploited the game for business purposes, baseball was still seen as a field of dreams, as a metaphor embodying "some of the central preoccupations of that cultural fantasy we like to think of as the American Dream" (Crella 550). This strong association of baseball with the basic concerns of the American Dream, such as opportunity and democracy, has inevitably linked the game with American nationalism. Baseball has been seen as a means of expressing patriotism and nationalism, and of promoting American prestige. For all these reasons, it has even been referred to as a "badge of Americanism" (Seymour ). This badge of patriotic pride is annually displayed, for example, at the opening of the baseball season or by the linkage of baseball with Fourth of July celebrations. The singing of the national anthem before games, which has become a regular feature since World War II, is intended to further unite the game and the nation. Besides all these demonstrations of loyalty to the state, one should not ignore the fact that many American presidents have associated themselves with sports in general and baseball in particular, thereby establishing, in the minds of the American people, a link between baseball and the nation-state.

Baseball's other immediate function, although more debatable, is no less significant. The game traditionally has also provided a sense of belonging otherwise absent from the new life experiences of immigrants. Baseball was considered as a crucial means to 'Americanize' these immigrants. They were advised to learn the national game in order to assimilate and to become Americans. Certainly, a major factor in the popularity of baseball among immigrants was that the game strengthened their group identity while at the same time promoting Americanism and answering questions about what it meant to be an American. According to the baseball historian Harold Seymour,

> The argot of baseball supplied a common means of communication and strengthened the bond which the game helped to establish among those sorely in need of it – the mass of urban dwellers and immigrants living in the anonymity and impersonal vortex of large industrial cities. . . . With the loss of the traditional ties known in rural society, baseball gave to many the feeling of belonging (1).

Though baseball definitely was of great help in acculturating immigrants, the game's long association with the American Dream was only true for certain sections of the population. Despite the fact that there are many success stories of players of African American, Asian American and Hispanic/Latino origin, these groups were long excluded from professional baseball. Richard Crepeau poignantly describes the downside of the national pastime: "Baseball was portrayed as a force for democracy, opportunity, and Americanization; it was a microcosm of the great American melting pot. [But] if American baseball was a melting pot, the Jew had difficulty melting and the black American never got into the pot" (163, 165). Indeed, it was not until after World War II that Jackie Robinsons's arrival with the Brooklyn Dodgers in 1947 broke baseball's color bar. Of course, politics was a major reason for Jackie Robinson's draft.

The use of sports as a showcase for political propaganda is nowhere more present than in the Olympic Games. Among the lowlights exemplifying nationalism at the Olympic Games were the 1936 Nazi Olympics in Berlin and the killings of eleven Israeli athletes and coaches at the 1972 Olympics in Munich. The concept of sports as a mirror reflecting political tensions was particularly evident during the Cold War, when sports clearly had a part to play in the promotion of American values. International events – and again particularly the Olympic Games – were ideologically exploited.[5] But after the terrorist attacks of September 11, 2001, the role of sports as a means to spread and promote American ideals and values, and also to reassure oneself of one's greatness in a difficult time, seems to be more prevalent than ever before. Although largely unnoticed, President Bush's departure from the original opening lines of the 2002 Olympic Games in Salt Lake City illustrated how the U.S. use sports events as propaganda for the U.S. war effort and the fight against the "axis of evil." By putting the phrase "On behalf of a proud, determined, and grateful nation" in before the official lines, George W. Bush explicitly linked patriotic and Olympic virtues. For Bush, the Olympics clearly served as a metaphor for the ideals that helped America recover from the attacks and as a stage to promote a global war against terrorism. Perhaps more than ever, these games were about more than sports. And with his largest TV audience ever, Bush decided to send an unambiguous message of endurance and strength to both the American people and the international community, when in reality many Americans were still anxious, insecure, and self-questioning.

Super Bowl XXXVI was similarly charged with patriotic messages. The pre-game show featured former presidents Carter, Ford, Bush, Clinton, plus Nancy Reagan, reading segments from Abraham Lincoln speeches, NFL players reading passages from the Declaration of Independence, and a broadcast from the troops in Afghanistan waiting for the Super Bowl coverage. All these iconic images and messages associated football with American history and mythology and the events of September 11. Some of the key images and words were the collapse of the WTC towers, firefighters hoisting the American flag, an image of Lincoln followed by President Bush Sr.'s words "piled high with difficulty," the Iwo Jima Memorial, the Lincoln Memorial statue, a football player appearing against the background of the image of JFK saying "Ask not what your country can do for you," the Pearl Harbor Memorial, and the Statue of Liberty.

All these scenes, blended with extremely emotive music and the presidential voices, formed a highly manipulative experience: they created an atmosphere of "either you are with us or against us," leaving no space for dissident voices stressing the complexity of the whole matter; they created the feeling that blind loyalty to the United States is a patriotic duty.

Obviously, this rather brief analysis of sports and its use in the construction and reproduction of an American national identity cannot account for the intricacies of the topic. However, summarizing the history of sports in America, together with examining baseball as the quintessential American game and showing how sports promotes American values and ideals after September 11, helps to trace just how deeply sports as a vehicle of creating national identity is rooted in the American national consciousness.

## Notes

[1] In this context, the reinforcement of Americanism works on two levels. First, national pride is strengthened by singing the national anthem before every game, often combined with honoring the veterans of the wars Americans have been involved in (microlevel). Second, sports is a great part of the inner circle of characteristics that make up an American, i.e. to *be* American means to go to the games, to know the statistics of your team, and to identify with the game (macrolevel).

[2] At this point, it is important to mention that sports has been institutionalized as white and it still is a white industry, which is illustrated by the fact that all NFL and MLB team owners are white. In this context, sports sociologists often refer to sports as a microcosm of society. According to Stanley Eitzen, American sports and society share "the basic elements and expressions of bureaucratization, commercialization, racism, sexism, homophobia, greed, exploitation of the powerless, alienation, and the ethnocentrism" (4).

[3] Cf. Robert Elias, "A Fit for a Fractured Society: Baseball and the American Promise," in Elias, 3-33, and Allen Guttmann, "Why Baseball Was Our National Game?," in Guttman, 91-116.

[4] Spalding's quote is a further addition to the construction of all the myths related to baseball. In this context, it is interesting that all the categories Spalding mentions are active, whereas baseball as a sport is often perceived to be rather static and strategic.

[5] The perfect example of how national ideology and sports go together took place in the 2002 Olympic Games in Salt Lake City. The U.S. ice hockey team that defeated the Soviet team in the Lake Placid Olympics in 1980 – a time when the USSR was (according to Ronald Reagan) still "the evil empire" – ignited the Olympic flame in Salt Lake City. Certainly, the intention behind this rather provocative action was to demonstrate national pride by calling up this special moment of national joy and to reassure oneself of one's greatness, strength, and dominant status.

## Works Cited

Betts, John Rickards. "The Technological Revolution and the Rise of Sport, 1850-1900." *Mississippi Valley Historical Review* 40 (1953): 231-56.

Crella, George. "Baseball and the American Dream." *Massachusetts Review* 16 (1975): 550-67.

Crepeau, Richard C. *Baseball: America's Diamond Mind, 1919-1941*. Orlando: U Presses of Florida, 1980.

Eitzen, D. Stanley. "American Sport at Century's End." *Sport in Contemporary Society*. Ed. D. Stanley Eitzen. 6th ed. New York: Worth, 2000. 4-9.

Elias, Robert. *Baseball and the American Dream. Race, Class, Gender and the National Pastime*. Armonk, NY and London: M. E. Sharpe, 2001.

Guttmann, Allen. *From Ritual to Record. The Nature of Modern Sports*. New York: Columbia UP, 1978.

Mrozek, Donald J. *Sport and American Mentality, 1880-1910*. Knoxville: U of Tennessee P, 1983.

Pope, Steven W. "Negotiating the 'Folk Highway' of the Nation: Sport, Public Culture and American Identity, 1870-1940." *Journal of Social History* 27.2 (1993): 327-40.

– – –. *Patriotic Games. Sporting Traditions in the American Imagination, 1876-1926*. New York: Oxford UP, 1997.

Rader, Benjamin. *American Sports: From the Age of Folk Games to the Age of Spectators*. 3rd ed. Englewood Cliffs: Prentice Hall, 1996.

Seymour, Harold. "Baseball: Badge of Americanism." *Cooperstown Symposium on Baseball and the American Culture: 1989.* Ed. Alvin L. Hall. Westport, CT: Meckler, 1991. 1-22.

Spalding, Albert G. *America's National Game.* 1911. Lincoln: U of Nebraska P, 1992.

# Advertising and the 'Americanization' of Western Europe

## Andreas Weissenbäck

### I.

Advertising is an archetypal discourse of modern capitalism. It is routinely at issue in the many debates on the Americanization of European culture. This is not surprising since many critics have come to treat American culture and capitalist culture as almost synonymous. In the terms of Reinhold Wagnleitner, for instance, the opaque slogan 'Americanization' is described as "the development of a consumption-oriented social order within capitalist societies" (7). In the wake of such a definition, there follows characteristically the dystopian vision of a uniform capitalist monoculture, a Westernization of the world. In this vision the United States assumes a hegemonic position whose expansionist culture threatens to marginalize other, more vulnerable ones. Americanization has then become a convenient buzzword for a rather bewildering array of ideas about domination: America over Europe, the 'West' over the 'rest' of the planet, the center over the periphery, the modern world over the traditional one, and free market ideology over almost anything else.

Modern capitalism is certainly not innocent in the shaping of a global culture. In fact, there can be little doubt that a large number of cultural practices in modern life have become commodified – converted into things that you can buy and sell. A shopping component has been added to many social domains and institutions whose concern is not producing commodities in the narrower economic sense. It is equally evident that the United States has played a vital role in the implementation of a consumption-oriented social order in Western Europe since World War II. In the terms of Wagnleitner (who was exposed in his formative years to this cultural transformation in Austria during the Allied occupation):

> In a Europe that had been devastated, the USA became synonymous with modernity . . . America signified the defeat of the old, the traditional, the small, the narrow – and the poor. . . . In short: the American Dream – of the pursuit of happiness as the pursuit of consumption – became, more than ever before, a European Dream" (Wagnleitner, "Diplomacy" 2)

I am not sure if Wagnleitner's definition of Americanization is valid today. Is it a legitimate claim at the beginning of the 21st century to maintain that the rise of global corporate capitalism is due to American agency? For sure, the elision of capitalist culture and American culture comes ready to hand for critics of both: it gives a name to the complex and ambiguous lived experience of global modernity, which is notoriously difficult to define. Has the United States then assumed the role of a scapegoat, a position where it takes all the blame for the drawbacks of an over-arching process of modernization?

In order to pursue this question, I have chosen advertising as a medium of analysis. Advertising is paid and non-personal communication from an identified sponsor, used to persuade or influence an audience via the media. Moreover, it is cultural discourse in the sense that it is considered a suitable instrument to measure the "ideological temperature" in a society (Vestergaard 153). In other words, advertising makes processes of social and cultural change surface acutely. Studying a society's adverts allows us a glimpse at its very soul. If this thesis is correct, Europeans must be heavily 'Americanized,' for Americanisms in European advertising are beyond count. Indeed, it is convenient and popular to say that our lives are relentlessly being Americanized.

Hoping to gain some insight into the myth of the Americanization of Europe, I want to address two central questions: why are Americanisms so popular in European advertising? Is the proliferation of Americanisms in advertising indicative of an Americanization of its viewers? To come to terms with the vast scope of the topic, this paper will be confined to a discussion of pictorial elements. Americanisms will then come to mean American iconography. With respect to structure, I will first outline the salient trend in modern advertising towards increased visualization. Second, I want to explore some of the functions of American iconography in Austrian advertising, thus accounting for their persistent popularity in this country. The concluding section analyzes a demonstration text to illustrate my observations.

## II.

In recent years modern advertising has seen a dramatic increase in the use of evocative pictures. The visual mode has clearly become more important in most adverts, while at the same time language as the main instrument of persuasion tends to decline. Part of the reason for this development stems from spectacular advances made in telecommunications technology. In the age of digitalization, the two modes of language and pictures have technically become equal at the level of representation. Today, a multi-skilled person can ask at every point: "Should I express this idea in words or pictures?"

However, technology only gave form to a need which was already there. The need for effective visuals derives from the most characteristic feature of all advertising: its strategic or goal-oriented discourse. Most advertising attempts to persuade people to consume: explicitly, in pursuit of their own happiness, to make them happier, prettier, faster – implicitly, for the company to make a profit. Accordingly, this dual strategy impels modern advertising to shift the balance in the display of goal on one hand, and content on the other. In the category of hard-sell advertising, which dominated the market until the late sixties, the orientation towards goals is – at least partially – laid out for the consumer. You, the consumer, are explicitly told to buy the commodity because of its purported beneficial qualities. Conversely, in the more modern soft-sell advertising the goals are kept out of the consumer's awareness.[1] There is no invitation to buy the product; sometimes the product is not even mentioned. Just do it.

Over the last three decades or so, modern market economies have seen a tremendous surge in soft-sell advertising. Its success hinges crucially on the company's ability to establish an image for the product it advertises. Image here designates a mental picture of something, a conception, an idea, an impression. The product's properties as a physical object are enhanced in the process of image-building. The product comes to have cultural properties in addition to physical ones. One way of building an image is to employ celebrities who will endorse a specific product. The success that a famous person embodies will rub off on the product. Subsequently, the consumer will be aestheticized through the act of purchase. Hence, a company such as Nike – as much as selling sports apparel – sells celebrities like the Brazilian soccer player Ronaldo or U.S. golf champion Tiger Woods. The image has clearly overtaken the product as the key to earned income.

Image-advertising has become necessary in part because current market conditions require that different companies market very similar products. Can you really tell apart *Pepsi* from *Coca-Cola*? These similar products are in competition for a market that is both limited and saturated. If the products are identical in their physical properties, a difference has to be created in the advertising. To establish a product as different, its identity has to be constructed. At the same time, categories of potential buyers for products are often (no longer) specifiable in terms of independently existing types of social membership (gender, class, regional and ethnic group, etc.): they also have to be constructed in the advertising. Also, the image of the producers and distributors of a product has to be harmonized with the images of the product and its potential consumers. The advert becomes a microcosm which potential consumer, producer, and product can jointly inhabit.

What advertisers gain from visual images is their "evocative capacity in the simulation of a lifestyle, which is generally more powerful and immediate than that of language" (Fairclough, *Discourse* 211). Visuals as a mode of communication are much more ambiguous than language as their deficits in precision and clarity are outweighed by their richness of information: being less explicit also means being able to communicate more things at once. Pictures, like music, call for interpretation. This way the addressee is forced to participate actively (though often subconsciously) in the process of perception. The addressee thus follows an image constructed for him or her.

In general, the salience of the image has been taken to be "one of the main characteristics of contemporary post-modern culture" (Fairclough, *Discourse* 208). Advertising is certainly not the only discourse type to be mentioned here, although it is certainly at the forefront of the development towards increased visualization. In advertising visuals are often used to circumvent standards of truthfulness. This is particularly evident in adverts for health-damaging products like cigarettes or alcohol, which are frequently promoted with images of youth, attractiveness, seductiveness, and wealth. The consumer tends to believe visual images more easily because of the strength expressed in the (obsolete but still widely believed) saying that "the camera doesn't lie."

## III.

As stated in the introduction, U.S.-American atmosphere is ubiquitous in the advertising of many European countries. The spectrum ranges from 'Cowboys and Indians' in the 'Wild West,' the 'Self-made Man' and Hollywood glamor to what still can be aptly described as the 'American Way of Life.' There is also a characteristic emphasis on American superior technology. Knowing that American iconography would not be used if it did not produce the desired results, we can ask: what is the appeal of these concepts?

Let us start by distinguishing three types of categories of 'Americanisms' in European advertisements. First, there are U.S.-based global brands like *Coca-Cola*, *McDonald's*, *Calvin Klein*, *Levi's*, *Nike*, *Marlboro* and others, some of which have even become synonyms for American cultural dominance itself.[2] In their efforts to incorporate all societies into their ambits, these companies normally rely on American imagery in their marketing strategies – selling American products means selling American popular culture. Their 'Americanness' is an intrinsic part of their product's identity.

The second category is European firms whose product invites association with the United States. For instance, the Italian jeans manufacturer *Diesel* promotes its commodity in Germany and Austria using an authentic frontier scene: a sepia-colored photo, which depicts a horse-drawn wagon with a family of eight on it. The historical link between America and blue jeans as a pioneer's item of clothing is an obvious one. Chewing gum is another example in this category.

The third category is certainly the most peculiar one: Americanisms used by European companies who operate in a strictly European market and whose products do not relate to the United States in any way. The Austrian brewery *Stiegl* uses the well-known dilapidated gas station in the deserted West of American road movies for its television spot. Of course, the commercial includes the quasi-erotic encounter between attractive men and women, with a bearded old-timer ogling the scene suspiciously. A few years ago, the paper tissue company *Feh* advertised its product in Austrian cinemas by a 'lone cowboy' type of commercial, which was itself a parody of the well-known *Marlboro* advertisements. The German automobile company *Audi* produced a commercial for the European market using the openness of the American West as the battlefield for what seems to be a variation of the old cat-and-mouse game. (This advert will be analyzed in the last section of this paper.)

'America' here echoes its general appeal as a signifier of freedom, individualism and modernity. It functions as a realm of opportunity, as open space, as a place where man [sic] can live untarnished and unencumbered some distance from rigid social control. Even in the early days of European advertising in the late 19th century, pictures of the American West were highly popular.[3] Today, probably the most conspicuous example of this appeal is the Marlboro Man, who has been roaming the country with overwhelming single-mindedness for over half a century. The longevity of his existence is truly impressive. Considering the prominent position which escapism holds in modern consumers' hierarchy of needs, America's position as a symbol of freedom is likely to intensify in the future. After all, advertisers can easily make use of this tailor-made and universally understood concept of freedom embodied in the pictures of the American West.

Still, I am reluctant to conclude that the trend makes these adverts American or their audiences Americanized. The adverts simply reflect what their audiences have grown up on in the last fifty years or so. Their iconography recalls our own European bedtime stories drawing on American ingredients: stories which often revolve around facets of the American frontier mythology and images which were constructed by Karl May in the 19th and Hollywood in the 20th century.

> The Hollywood film – with its emphasis on individualism, competition, the cleansing forces of the market, the freedom of choice, and especially the melting pot – became the most influential iconographic

inventory of the capitalist ethos and US democracy in the twentieth century. (Wagnleitner, *Coca-Colonization* 225)

Arguing along similar lines, Benjamin Barber has coined the term "Hollyworld" to describe the ubiquity of Hollywood as a text of power. He refers to the past century as the "Movie Century," an era in which "film and video and the images they mediate have replaced print and books and the words they once brokered as the chief instrumentalities of human communication, persuasion, and entertainment" (88).

Precisely because the America portrayed in Hollywood is now universally acknowledged, its images have attained the status of an Esperanto for the eye. In the words of Rob Kroes: "America's national symbols and myths have been translated into an international iconographic language, a visual lingua franca. They have been turned into free-floating signifiers, internationally understood, free for everyone to use" ("Advertising" 276).

As mentioned above, its images also represent Europeans' collective subconscious of growing up in a post-World-War-II Europe in which American icons were proliferating. Europeans have come to indigenize American iconography. They have used American cultural language and have absorbed American codes and made them their own. They have woven American icons into the fabric of their own cultural discourse. Why else would baseball caps with the acronym 'NYPD' on them be bestsellers at Austrian country fairs? It is vital to note, however, that the cultural language may have been creolized, but it has not become American. It is still recognizably German, French or Polish.

In my view, it is a common weakness of the Americanization argument to deduce deep ideological effects from the simple presence of cultural artifacts. It would take a leap of inference to conclude from the presence of American iconography an Americanization of its viewers. Yet this trend is characteristically found in totalizing critiques of modern capitalism. The argument tends to ignore the fact that transfer of culture always entails interpretation, adaptation, and indigenization, as "the receiving culture brings its own cultural resources to bear, in dialectical fashion, upon 'cultural imports'" (Tomlinson 84). Each side controls the other as they jointly evolve. Put more bluntly, culture is not a one-way-street.

A second argument which is sometimes forwarded is the idea that the hybrid nature of modern advertising – the tendency to string together elements from different contexts – is in itself distinctly American.[4] The assumption here is that initial shortages in resources and capital in the United States required cultural production to be modular in nature, creating something new by continually fragmenting, disassembling, and reassembling itself. Within the lines of this argument, it is a specifically American tendency to 'deconstruct' what appears to be a coherent whole only to put it back together differently. The hypothesis then is that European audiences have become Americanized because they have come to view the deconstructing logic of modern advertising as altogether natural. I think that the argument tends to lose its shape when viewed against the backdrop of today's cultural production in general. Which contemporary culture is not 'modular'? Similar to the use of American iconography, this approach may have a historic link to the United States, but clearly has gone international by now. We can think of many forms of cultural production today that can be seen as a building block, using individual bricks as empty signifiers and combining them into ever-changing, meaningful structures.

As an example I would like to discuss briefly the phenomenon of German-language rap. In simple terms, rap is by definition African American; its voice speaks from the ghetto, about the ghetto, to the ghetto. In sharp contrast to this, German rap bands like "Fettes Brot" come from white middle-class families and their lyrics address white middle-class audiences. There are no traces of African American culture whatsoever. An even more obvious example is rap singer Xavier Naidoo. Born in Germany into a family of Indian descent, he addresses topics like friendship, loneliness, and death. Both "Fettes Brot" and Xavier Naidoo carefully avoid the often homophobic lines typical of many American rappers. So both groups represent clear examples of a modular approach: a cultural phenomenon which may have had its onset in the United States has been deconstructed, adapted and turned into an avenue of artistic expression for German teenagers and others.

Advertising is then just one of many examples of cultural discourse that resort to a modular approach in their production. As a matter of fact, advertising is a textbook example of discourse that is extremely parasitic, feasting itself on its surroundings and other genres. The keyword here is intertextuality. This term describes the way one text, film, advert, artifact is echoed or reflected in another. It can be an important component of an advert's meaning in that the original text being referred to establishes a message which the second text can then use and elaborate on. In this way, the second text does not have to work so hard – it can take for granted that the original text has left a trace which it can use to its advantage. In Daniel Chandler's terms:

> Modern visual advertisements make extensive use of intertextuality in this way.... Instant identification of the appropriate interpretative code serves to identify the interpreter of the advertisement as a member of an exclusive club, with each act of interpretation serving to renew one's membership. (200)

The advert described below alludes directly to a film. It credits its audience with the necessary experience to make sense of such allusions and offers them the pleasure of recognition. We feel clever if we 'get' the connection.

## IV.

The commercial analyzed here is a spot for *Audi allroad Quattro*. It was shown on Austrian TV in the first half of 2002. The spot clearly toys with the audience's literacy in interpreting what I would like to call 'Hollywoodized' discourse. The commercial opens with the close-up of a lizard snapping at a fly. From a huge cloud of dust emerges an *Audi allroad Quattro*, apparently chased by an enormous black truck. The two vehicles are just inches apart. In the end we learn that the monster truck is being towed by the Audi. The message is that no task is too massive, unusual or quixotic to achieve for the new Audi: truly a car to meet any challenge.[5]

The commercial abounds with ingredients 'made in Hollywood': the lizard – an animal of the desert – and the humming of the fly set the scene. When the truck enters the stage, we can identify the setting as the American West. Immediately, we are watching a Hollywood road movie of some sort. The lizard abruptly snaps at the fly, and the viewer is invited to anticipate a cat-and-mouse game on a larger scale. Sure enough, there is a protagonist (the Audi), and an antagonist (the black truck) and they seem to be caught up in some sort of struggle. Even in the 21st century, this is still the classical format of storytelling in Hollywood. The majority of the viewers are likely to read what they see as a chase. This reading is supported by worried glances, which the driver in the Audi takes in the rear mirror. Dramatic music and sound effects heighten the tension. Naturally, there are numerous clues for the viewer to decide whom to side with: the Audi is silver and shiny, the driver looks trustworthy – and worried. The truck, on the other hand, is black, dusty and oil begrimed; the driver remains faceless yet seems aggressive. However, in a final ironic twist we learn that we have completely mistaken the situation. Car and truck are in alliance: the former is aiding the latter. (Here Hollywood's preference for happy endings is clearly evident.)

The advert is a direct quotation of the Hollywood movie *Duel* (1971), Steven Spielberg's debut as director. The film is about an innocuous salesman, David Mann, who – on the way to a business meeting – passes a truck on the road. For no given reason, this escalates into a deadly cat-and-mouse game with the truck driver relentlessly harassing, playing hide-and-seek with and trying to kill Mann. The key argument here is that the advert employs American iconography on two levels: it alludes directly to a Hollywood road movie, offering the viewers the opportunity to position themselves as members of an exclusive club. But even if viewers are not familiar with *Duel*, they are still presented with a massive portion of American imagery.

This brief demonstration may indicate how modern advertising – in its characteristic effort to establish an image for the product it promotes – reassembles icons, many of which may be American in origin. Their global dissemination over an extended period of time, however, has transformed these icons into part of an international imaginary repertoire. Global audiences have appropriated these symbols and myths, which they grew up on; they have largely made them their own. So even though many of the ingredients may derive from the United States, the resulting cultural artifact is not. In our sample advert it is a German brand of car, promoting a German automobile to a European audience.

In sum, we can contend that the discourse of advertising reflects a widespread fallacy in much of the critique of Americanization: the sheer presence of cultural phenomena is rashly taken to have fundamental ideological effects. If we take the very existence of American iconography in advertising as indicative of an Americanization of its viewers, we are using a rather restricted concept of culture – one that degrades culture to its material goods. Instead, a discussion of Americanization should address the notion of how our interaction with American cultural artifacts penetrates into the way we make sense of our lives. Let me conclude by saying that I am not denying the enormous power that some American companies wield over the development of global capitalism. But although the United States has been and still is a key player in the shaping of modern capitalism, it is now entangled in historic transformations much like other countries are. Many trends and developments for which America is blamed would have occurred anyway, even in the absence of the United States. It is owing to America's power that its voice is heard more often than others'. The United States' global influence is then one of quantity, not quality.

If anything, Western Europe was Americanized half a century ago. But then it was a process of self-colonization with the population eagerly awaiting and appropriating anything American. Now we are all joint inhabitants of the Global Village, some taller, some shorter.

## Notes

[1] See Beaugrande for a detailed analysis of the ideology of modern consumerism.
[2] Popular neologisms such as "McDonaldization," "Coca-Colonization" or "McWorld" illustrate the expansionist ambitions of many multinational corporations.
[3] Sandra Moriarty has shown in her history of advertising how European shipping lines and other emigration services have constructed America as the very site of freedom and escape.
[4] This thesis has been forwarded by Rob Kroes.
[5] Various media reconstructed the scene to find out whether the Audi can really tow a truck. Apparently, it can.

## Works Cited

Barber, Benjamin. *Jihad vs. McWorld: How Globalism and Tribalism are Reshaping the World.* New York: Ballantine Books, 1996.

Beaugrande, Robert. *New Foundations for a Science of Text and Discourse: Cognition, Communication, and the Freedom of Access to Knowledge and Society.* Norwood, NJ: Ablex, 1997.

Chandler, Daniel. *Semiotics: The Basics.* London: Routledge, 2002.

Fairclough, Norman. *Discourse and Social Change.* Cambridge: Polity P, 1992.

– – –. *Language and Power.* London: Longman, 1989.

Kroes, Rob. *If You've Seen One, You've Seen the Mall: Europeans and American Mass Culture.* Urbana: U of Illinois P, 1996.

– – –. "Advertising and American Icons of Freedom." *Here, There and Everywhere: The Foreign Politics of American Popular Culture.* Ed. Reinhold Wagnleitner and Elaine Tyler May. Hanover, NH: UP of New England, 2000. 273-287.

Moriarty, Sandra. *Creative Advertising.* Englewood Cliffs, NJ: Prentice Hall, 1991.

Ritzer, George. *The McDonaldization of Society.* Thousand Oaks, CA: Pine Forge P, 1993.

Tomlinson, John. *Globalization and Culture.* Cambridge: Polity P, 1999.

Vestergaard, Thorben, and Schrøder, Kim. *The Language of Advertising.* Oxford: Basil Blackwell, 1985.

Wagnleitner, Reinhold. *Coca-Colonization and the Cold War: The Cultural Mission of the United States in Austria after the Second World War.* Chapel Hill: U of North Carolina P, 1994.

– – –. "American Cultural Diplomacy, the Cinema, and the Cold War in Central Europe." April 1992. 3 March 2002. <http://www.cas.umn.edu/wp924.htm>.

# Spin-ning Wheel America: Americanism and Anti-Americanism Constructed by the Media

Claudia Schwarz

*Spider Woman, Spinning Wheel & Spin-off*

The Native American mythological figure Spider Woman holds the power to "spin" stories, which become reality as she tells them.[1] Likewise, most terms associated with "spinning" are strongly connected to the idea of creation. This idea is the thread I will "spin to" the contemporary media in connection with the creation of Americanism and Anti-Americanism.

Spinning, in its most common sense, means, "to draw out and twist fiber into yarn or thread" (Merriam-Webster). In sports "to put a spin on a ball" has the additional meaning of rotating a ball to make sure that it gets where it is directed to but also that it bounces up in an unexpected direction. These definitions share two elements: they both require someone to execute the action, a "spinner" in the first and a "player" in the second case, and they are both applicable to the media in the form of manufacturing "news" from raw material and pointing it in a certain direction. The results, i.e. what is "spun" by the media, can have a variety of effects. Whether these are planned actions or merely "spin-offs" remains to be discussed.

In this essay I will briefly outline the media's role in society, exemplify the editor's power to create myths that make up reality, and try to uncover the American-ness in the global media. This will lead to the discussion of the interaction between constructed Americanism and Anti-Americanism, focusing on the news coverage in the media (and leaving aside other genres like feature films or television shows). Even though the issue as such allows, even demands, a variety of perspectives, my approach will be philosophical with a clear literary viewpoint in reading the media as cultural (con)text.

## Invading the Public Forum

If it is still true, as English Renaissance philosopher Francis Bacon postulated, that knowledge is power, then it is (for us citizens living in a democratic system) in our own and society's interest "to possess knowledge of the external environment necessary to arrive at appropriate judgment of both personal and societal interests" (Garnham 364). To gain this kind of knowledge we need information, but also space for public debate, exchange, and discussion. However, a forum in its original sense of a marketplace where people meet in public and discuss current affairs no longer exists as a real place. Therefore, citizens have to find and create new ways to exchange their opinions. The German philosopher Jürgen Habermas argues that parts of the function of the forum have been taken over by the mass media. They extract communicational processes from the provinciality of time and space-restricted contexts. By providing an abstract simultaneity in a virtual net of remote communicational contexts, they create a public sphere and keep messages present for various contexts (cf. Habermas qtd. in Wiegerling 123). In other words, in a realm detached from physical restrictions, the media provide the space to openly debate issues of public interest. In the societal model of the three spheres both the private sphere (the free market) and the political sphere (the government) try to influence the debates taking place in the public sphere (the forum). Their aim is to invade the forum in order to direct public discussion and, thus, influence people's opinions. The free market uses advertising to achieve this aim; the government employs public-relations officers, or so-called "spin doctors."[2]

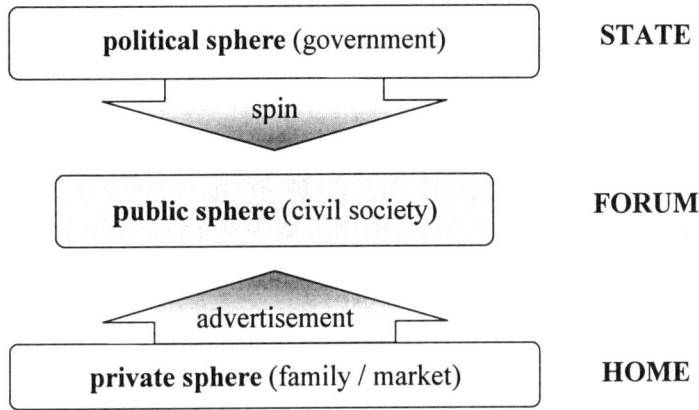

The ongoing struggle for a public sphere beyond the influence of systems has lately been transferred from the traditional to the new, computer-generated media. This newly-won virtual space was highly promising in the beginning because it developed independently from existing structures and restrictions. Moreover, the non-hierarchical concept of inter-connected computers in itself is highly democratic because its structure can be influenced and shaped by every participant. Therefore it is hardly surprising that the place where people meet in this virtual reality received its name from the ancient model, the forum. Today, millions of chat and news forums exist on the net and users eagerly discuss a huge variety of issues and exchange ideas. Of course, both the private and the political sphere have started to 'fish' in this World Wide Web.

**Editors at Work**

With the philosophical debate about the impossibility of objectivity in mind, it would be naïve to think of the media as a 'window' to the world, passively showing and reflecting what happens 'in reality.' Thus, the genesis of news reports should be regarded as a creative process with active editors at work forming and creating the content of reports.[3]

News is formed by journalists who filter items according to their importance and relevance, organize them within the whole set of what will be printed or aired, and shape them by adding or leaving out material. Arthur MacEwen, the first editor of the San Francisco *Examiner*, said that "news is whatever a good editor chooses to print" (qtd. in Boorstin 20). Hence, what becomes news depends on what editors consider newsworthy; it does not necessarily have to have much in common with reality. From the perspective of those who try to be present in the media, the central concern is to provide an issue or event that is of interest to journalists. Therefore, they start to edit their stories (or even create them) in order to make them newsworthy. Something about the media must have gone wrong when the question "Is it real?" became less important than "Is it newsworthy?" (cf. Boorstin 23).[4] Already in 1963, Daniel Boorstin warned against a "flood of pseudo-events" which he defined as happenings explicitly created for the media (19ff.). President Franklin D. Roosevelt, for example, was a master of "making 'facts'" (Boorstin 31), for which purpose he employed newspapermen, poets, playwrights, and speech writers. Roosevelt knew enough about the journalists' job to help them manufacture stories. Similarly, Senator Joseph R. McCarthy was known as a "natural genius at creating reportable happenings" (Boorstin 32). McCarthy even went so far as to hold a morning press conference "for the purpose of announcing an afternoon press conference" (Rovere in Boorstin 32-33). The news industry works according to its own rules, and those who know them are invited to join in the game. Obviously there are editors at work who are busy spinning the thread for the stories we live by.

The postmodern French philosopher Jean Baudrillard deals with the idea of Boorstin's pseudo-events and takes the argument one step further. He is concerned with the replacement of reality by signs when he states that "[s]imulation . . . is the generation by models of a real without origin or reality: a hyperreal" (169). In this hyperreality, both the consumer society's needs and demands are generated and therefore things lose their reality and are replaced by signs. Baudrillard leaves little space for hope because the system of simulation preserves itself. Since we are part of hyperreality as citizens, audience, and consumers alike, it seems impossible to step outside the system. As creators and distributors of the hyperreal, the media have an essential role in the preservation of the system. In his "The Gulf War Did Not Take Place" (1995), Baudrillard argues that the 1991 Gulf War was a war fought by and for the media, rather than in reality. He calls it a "Utopia of real time," and "the spectacle of the degradation of the event and its spectral evocation (the 'spiritualism of information': event, are you there? Gulf War, are you there?)" (246). In connection with the invasion of the public sphere and the way the media can be seen as the designers of a pseudo- or hyperreality, the media are the tool for influencing and creating public opinion. This is especially important for the authorities in times of crisis. Reporting about war has become part of the war, and for governments the media are just another front where they have to fight, to influence, to win.

A fictional and therefore more accessible example of how this could work is the film *Wag the Dog* (1997). Directed by Barry Levinson, this biting satire on America's media and the process of forming public opinion explains the "official way" of dealing with a White House crisis. Two weeks before election day the U.S. president is accused of having had an affair, and thus his re-election is in danger.[5] Robert De Niro plays "Mr. Fix Him," the president's secretive government operative with a vaguely defined job description, in other words, a spin doctor. His idea is to create an event that is of much greater importance than the president's *faux pas* so that the public would be distracted and, despite everything, vote for him. In short, what is needed is a war. Therefore, the spin doctor asks a famous Hollywood film producer, acted by Dustin Hoffman, to produce a war scenario in a film studio. The clip is to be aired on the news and taken for real by the public.[6] The task becomes a challenge for the producer. The eccentric team literally makes up a story about bombs, threats, and terrorism. A video clip is produced in a studio with a girl fleeing the terrorist regime in her bombed village. As the place of action they choose Albania, which – to the producers in the film – is "a country no-one knows anything about" (transcribed from the film). The plan works perfectly; the clip is broadcast, and within hours the United States seems to be at war. However, the CIA intervenes and ends this pseudo-event. The Hollywood producer does not want to accept that someone has ended the war he had created in the first place and gives in only when the spin doctor insists that "the war *has* ended; I saw it on TV" (from the film). So, the presidential team has to make up "Act Two," a story about a soldier who is trapped behind the enemy lines. Thus, an American hero is invented and musically supported by a newly composed apparent oldie, "Good Old Shoe." In spite of various difficulties, the president's re-election is eventually secure. When the film producer realizes that his inimitable contribution to the history of the United States will never become public, he threatens to make the background story public. To thwart this, he is secretly removed by the authorities. A short news report explains that the famous Hollywood producer died of a heart attack.

In a very amusing but also highly critical way, the satire examines the blurred lines between politics, media, and show business. The film reveals what forces are at work in times of crisis and times of war and underlines Baudrillard's argument that mediated reality is more enduring than the local physical reality. What counts in the end are the "facts" aired by the news channels. It is implied that citizens (the audience) cannot distinguish between real and fake. In the film, a whole nation is fooled by a small group's unscrupulous abuse of the media. This way of manipulating the audience is depicted as an American practice because of the obvious hints at the Hollywood industry and its drive for creating a perfect illusion. However, the phenomenon as such is not new because the media have always been used for propaganda in totalitarian states. The important difference here is that the film plays in the USA under the inscription of a "free press" and both the news broadcasting industry and the citizens have themselves been more or less "willingly fooled." As Baudrillard describes, we are running the risk of ending up in one of La Fontaine's fables: "the day there is a real war you will not even be able to tell the difference. The real victory of the simulators of war is to have drawn everyone into this rotten simulation" (253).

From the point of view of perceiving the media as cultural text, it is insignificant whether the story in *Wag the Dog* is probable or Baudrillard's observations about the unreality of the Gulf War are true. (Just as it is irrelevant whether Spider Woman exists or not.) It is more important to look at what those examples reveal about the culture from which they emerge. They point to a fear of the growing influence of the media on everyday life and a general concern about the production of news reports, which are completely detached from reality. It lies within the media's power to evaluate, transport, and explain facts about things that happen(ed). They analyze, they legitimize, they mobilize. They have an active and creative role in the construction of the myths – in the understanding of Roland Barthes – we live by.[7] Therefore, the media have an important function in society by setting the standards for what is culturally accepted. If one bears the current political world situation in mind, the underlying message of *Wag the Dog* and Baudrillard's argument are frighteningly topical.

**The Global Media are American**

One characteristic feature of the second half of the twentieth century was the growing significance of global chains of influence. Globalization is both a buzzword and a force shaping the world. The media are just one aspect of globalization in its manifold facets. Considering the worldwide exchange and distribution of the media we can think of ourselves as citizens in the "global village" in McLuhan's terms: "Earth in the next century will have its collective consciousness lifted off the planet's surface into a dense electronic symphony where all nations – if they still exist as separate entities – may live in a clutch of spontaneous synesthesia, painfully aware of the triumphs and wounds of one another" (*Global Village* 95). Technical developments in the field of communication have made the whole globe more or less accessible to any audience in real time. As McLuhan observes, "electronic technologies have begun to shake the distinction between inner and outer space, by blurring the difference between being here or there. The first hint of this condition came with the telephone. By increasing the speed of the private voice, it retrieved telepathy and gave everyone the feeling of being everywhere at once" (*Global Village* 148). Along with satellite TV broadcasting, the Internet as a new form of communication has finally broken down all national boundaries within which the invasion of the *forum* had taken place before. It is unnecessary to add that most technical inventions and innovations that helped to make the globe a village are American. One could say that globalization itself is an American invention.

Based on this aspect of globalization, two things are explicitly American about the world media today: one is the way the media are managed; the other is that they have become big business.

Media management is basically an American phenomenon. The inscription of the freedom of the press in the first article of the United States' Bill of Rights ("Congress shall make no law . . . abridging the freedom of speech or of the press") made it necessary for the people in power to influence the media on different levels. One of the leading media control critics, Noam Chomsky, wrote that the "U.S. pioneered the public relations industry. Its commitment was to 'control the public mind,' as its leaders put it." One example is the installation of the Presidential Press Conference in 1933, which professionalized dealing with the media in the United States. A more recent incident shows how this American way of managing the media – especially in times of crisis – has been adopted by other nations. According to a *Guardian* article of 26 October 2001, "The Pentagon has hired a PR company to help it win the propaganda war involving its military action in Afghanistan." In the same article it says that "[j]ust days after the September 11 attacks on the US, the Saudi government hired one of the world's biggest PR agencies, Burson Marsteller, to provide 'issues counseling and crisis management'" (Day). The attitude has prevailed that the media as the Fourth Estate are a key element in international political affairs. The media's direct impact on actions and on diplomacy is also referred to as the "CNN-effect" (Bell 20). The very fact that this phenomenon received its name from an American network is telling in terms of the United States' influence on global news broadcasting. Even though foreign policy is not created by the media, in this age of information it cannot be made without them. Therefore, the American example of managing the media has become a model for the world.

The media industry today is big business. The information sector is in a constant flux, and big global networks have become major shareholders because of the profits involved. News-producing institutions are in the hands of a few media giants like Rupert Murdoch's News Corporation Ltd., Time Warner Inc. (since 1996 including the Turner Broadcasting System), and United Press International (going back to E. W. Scripps). The directive in these mega-concerns is definitely not the idealized image of ethical journalism, but money and thus power (and vice versa). The two American big business slogans, "time is money" and "money makes the world go round," are directly applicable to the media, the first one in the form of live broadcasts, the second one in the structure of global networks.

In the classic study of the way American media have swept the world, Jeremy Turnstall concludes that the media are American in his book of the same title (1977). This historical account of the development of the world media and its Anglo-American predominance explains how other nations import contents, structure, and form from the United States because they cannot produce them all on their own: "In most of the world's countries the media are only there at all, on the present scale, as the result of imports in which the American media (with some British support) predominate. One major influence of American imported media lies in the styles and patterns that most other countries in the world have adopted and copied. This influence includes the very definition of what a *newspaper*, or a *feature film*, or a *television set* is" (Turnstall 17). The cultural implication is that the structures in connection with the production and genesis of national news reports are also American. Therefore, a culture's tastes in regard to what its citizens, as an audience, expect to see or read in the media, are Americanized. Thus, media imperialism results in cultural imperialism, which goes largely unnoticed because it looks too familiar to be disturbing. News broadcasts look more or less similar, that is, American, all over the world. In short, the global media follow the concept of a corporate identity made in the USA.

**Live Catastrophes**

In many respects, the terror attacks of September 11, 2001 have changed everything, and yet they have not. Millions of people watched the incredible horror scenario live on TV when the second airplane crashed into the World Trade Center. The fact that citizens all over the world became viewers of this live catastrophe made it seem unreal. The constant re-playing of the video clip created a global trauma.

We have seen the same pattern for televised catastrophe coverage before: in November 1963, when the Zapruder footage of John F.

Kennedy's assassination was endlessly rerun on TV and, in January 1986, when the space shuttle Challenger with a full crew on board exploded before running cameras. We will continue to encounter the same pattern, as the recent explosion of the space shuttle Columbia showed. Nevertheless, 9/11 was different, not only due to the dimension of the event but also due to the consequences brought to bear both on culture and politics.

After 9/11 it looked as if the drive for sensationalism, which is constantly pushed by the media industry, was satisfied for a while. This was also reflected in general viewing habits: after the immediate news boom triggered off by the attacks, there was a general decline in TV audiences. The only genre flourishing were the "lifestyle" shows, which can be interpreted as the people's longing for domestic ordinariness in a chaotic world. However, one year after the attacks, audience rates were more or less back to 'normal.' As *USA Today* put it in 2002, "9/11 didn't change 'everything' – but no one is quite the same" (Hampson 1).

## Interaction of Americanism and Anti-Americanism

Cultural standards are passed on to the audience by the media in the form of edited stories and biased utterances of opinion. Those "myths" (Barthes, again) are necessary to set the values in a community and help the citizens to structure their lives accordingly. This pattern has been used for centuries, especially in oral tradition. Whereas until recently those stories only affected a local community, the new media make them available to a global audience.[8] In effect, the influence on a local community of what is passed on by the media globally is hard to estimate. However, it is obvious that the same news material may be interpreted differently in different cultures. Paul Hollander concludes that this is one of the reasons for anti-Americanism abroad. In the form of nationalism, anti-capitalism, and protest against modernity, anti-Americanism is a defensive response to Americanization, which Hollander defines as "the spread of American values and ways of life threatening traditional values and ways of life" (444). Therefore, Americanism and anti-Americanism are closely connected because one can result in the other, depending on the cultural context. Of course, the knowledge of this interaction can be used intentionally to create both.

There is another notion that makes the use of this interaction especially attractive for the media. Generally speaking, the input an audience gets from the media, especially in news broadcasts, is oversimplified due to time and space restrictions. These reduced news-bits operate with binary categories in the form of good versus bad, acceptable versus unacceptable, etc. because they are quick and easy to understand. However, this "othering," "us versus them" pattern constructs false dichotomies. Nevertheless, it is used by the authorities and deliberately broadcast in news programs, as e.g. U.S. president Bush's remark in connection with the War against Terrorism: "If you are not with us, you are against us." In an interview, Beth K. Lamont, a representative of a humanitarian organization, explained the resulting problem that "if you are not waving your flag or professing your patriotism in the accepted way you are suspect" (Lamont in Belz and Hollander). To bring the argument full circle, the over-exposition to this specific kind of patriotism and American flag-mania itself offends other people and cultures and thus creates anti-Americanism.

Of course, this interaction of Americanism and anti-Americanism also works the other way round. Pictures of an anti-American attitude demonstrated by "them" may evoke a pro-American reaction in "us," as the following example will show.

Soon after the attacks on the World Trade Center cheering Arabs were broadcast on the news.[9] The underlying message was that "they" (the "others") celebrate the attacks because they are anti-American. In a rare example of unprofessional camera work, the clip exposes some techniques in the creation of misleading news reports.

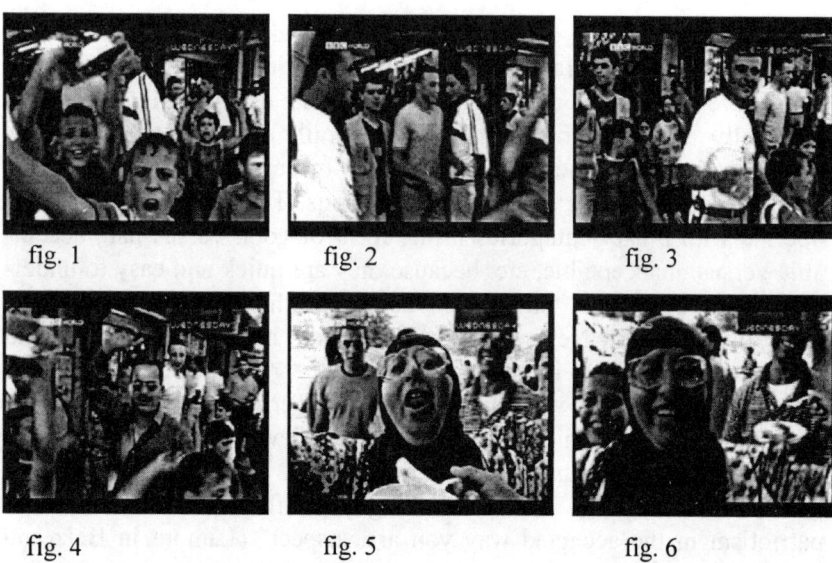

fig. 1   fig. 2   fig. 3
fig. 4   fig. 5   fig. 6

The clip consists of two shots, one showing a cheering crowd (fig. 1 to 4), the other presenting a yelling woman (fig. 5 and 6). A closer analysis of the first shot reveals that there are no more than nine people directly involved. The people in the far back show little interest in the event. Four of the actively involved participants are children (fig. 1). One of them is waving a Jordanian flag. The children are the ones shouting and making noise. The boy in the foreground seems aggressive whereas the others look relaxed. The three adults in the background of fig. 2 seem completely unaffected and calm. They are walking about but do not show any sign of action or involvement. There are two men busy instigating the others: the one in the white T-shirt on the far left in fig. 2 and in the center of fig. 3, and the one wearing sunglasses in fig. 4. They are encouraging the children and making people stay within the camera frame. The second shot of the clip shows one woman in the foreground yelling and three men in the background obviously laughing at her behavior. The boy on the left behind the woman in fig. 6 is the same one waving the flag in the first shot. In the foreground of fig. 5 there is a white plate and a hand with a piece of cake on a fork. The same plate, hand, and cake reappear soon afterwards behind the yelling woman (fig. 6). The sounds uttered by the yelling woman and the cheering crowd are unintelligible and overruled by a voice-over comment of an invisible reporter who says, "some Palestinians are openly delighted over the attacks . . ." (transcribed from the clip).

Various points lead to the conclusion that the clip is an example of a created pseudo-event: Only a few people are actively involved; half of them are children, who are easy to influence. The general interest of all people who are visible in the clip is focused on the camera, which is a sign that the situation was set up. In the context of cheering about the attacks in New York, the piece of cake visible in the second shot does not make sense. It could be the reward offered to the cheering crowd for participating. However, there are no hints visible or audible in the clip that point at the crowd's hostile attitude towards the United States or suggest happiness about the attacks on the World Trade Center. The clip succeeds in misleading the audience only for the context in which it is placed, as a response to the attacks. Without this context and the reporter's explanation, the footage as such does not reveal much. This means that both the set-up and the message of the clip are a media construct. I do not claim that there were no people cheering over the terror attacks of 9/11 in general, but the ones shown in this news clip were motivated by something else.

The broadcast of this poorly edited clip indicates a much larger problem the government and the media industry were confronted with after the attacks: the enemy was invisible. Therefore, clips like the one described were created by the media in order to present the world with what they wanted to see at that moment: someone to hold responsible and someone to hate. Thus, the media constructed this misleading portrayal of anti-Americanism to legitimize pro-Americanism. One could even go so far as to argue that Anti-Americanism as a whole is pushed (if not created) by the media and politics in order to ensure, if not enforce pro-Americanism and thus legitimize military action.

**Conclusion**

A fabric of created pseudo-events and biased news items is manufactured worldwide by the media. Its pattern is American. The freedom to create pseudo-events is the price we pay for the freedom of speech, press, and broadcasting. Being able to analyze and read between the lines of what the media tell us and looking at how they try to manipulate public opinion can help us to understand what is going on at the moment. The hyperreal web that is spun by the media has covered the globe. Spider Woman is indigenous American; her power is not.

**Notes**

[1] Spider Woman is also often referred to as Thought Woman. Navajo children claim that she taught them how to play the string games, a much-enjoyed custom during the wintertime: "They say if you fall into Spider Woman's den she won't let you out unless you can do all these" (qtd. in Toelken 118). The Navajos believe that making these string figures helps them to "think well," not to get into trouble or to get lost (cf. Toelken 124).
[2] The term "spin doctor" has a negative connotation for blurring the expressions "to spin a yarn" and "to doctor something." It describes the political aides "responsible for ensuring that others interpret an event from a particular point of view" (Merriam-Webster). Even though the term is included and defined as such in dictionaries, the existence of spin doctors is usually neglected by the authorities.
[3] In a creative rather than a passive role, the media hold a variety of responsibilities, which are not only political but also ethical in nature. Andrew Belsey outlines the media's dilemma in their position between politics, the media industry and the audience.
[4] This differentiation has opened up an interesting perspective on the cultural function of news and enables a debate about the role, power and responsibility of the media. The ethical implication is not the definition of what is true or false in news broadcasts but deals with the degree of acceptability in the creation of news reports.
[5] This film is itself proof of the media's ability to anticipate events because it came out before the Monika Lewinsky affair.
[6] That this idea can work was illustrated in Orson Welles's renowned 1938 radio adaptation of H. G. Wells's science fiction novel *The War of the Worlds* (1898). People who missed the introduction by the Mercury Theatre and took the radio play for real panicked (cf. Scholes 104-05).
[7] In the second part of Barthes' *Mythologies*, he argues how myths influence, shape, even dictate everyday life. He argues for the necessity of a scientific discourse about mythology, which he places in the field of semiology (cf. 88ff.).

[8] McLuhan was among the first who noted the new technologies' predominant function in the extension of our senses and our social world and summarized it in the form of his widely discussed dictum "the medium is the message" (*Understanding Media* 23).
[9] The clip discussed here is from a BBC World broadcast "This Week" aired on September 15, 2001. The same clip was run on several international networks throughout the week.

## Works Cited

Barthes, Roland. *Mythen des Alltags*. Trans. Helmut Scheffel. Frankfurt: Suhrkamp, 1964.

Baudrillard, Jean. "Simulacra and Simulations." *Jean Baudrillard. Selected Writings*. Ed. Mark Poster. Cambridge: Polity P, 2001. 169-87.

– – –. "The Gulf War Did Not Take Place." *Jean Baudrillard. Selected Writings*. Ed. Mark Poster. Cambridge: Polity P, 2001. 232-53.

BBC World. "This Week." 15 Sept. 2001.

Bell, Martin. "The Journalism of Attachment." *Media Ethics*. Ed. Matthew Kieran. London: Routledge, 1998. 15-22.

Belsey, Andrew. "Journalism and ethics: can they co-exist?" *Media Ethics*. Ed. Matthew Kieran. London: Routledge, 1998. 1-14.

Belz, Corinna, and Neil Hollander. *Other American Voices*. Documentary. ARTE. 8 Sept. 2002.

Boorstin, Daniel J. *The Image or What Happened to the American Dream*. Harmondsworth: Penguin, 1963.

Chomsky, Noam. "Media Control." MIT, March 17, 1991. 7 Sept. 2002. <http://www.zmarg.org/chomsky/talks/9103-media-control.html>.

Day, Julia. "Pentagon hires firm to help with war PR." *Guardian Unlimited*. 26 Oct. 2001. 2 Nov. 2002. <http://media.guardian.co.uk/attack/story/0,1301,580924,00.html>.

Garnham, Nicholas. "The Media and the Public Sphere." *Habermas and the Public Sphere*. Ed. Craig Colhoun. Boston: MIT, 1991. 359-76.

Hampson, Rick. "9/11 didn't change 'everything' – but no one is quite the same." *USA Today* 11 Sept. 2002. 1-2.

Hollander, Paul. *Anti-Americanism. Irrational & Rational.* New Brunswick & London: Transaction Publishers, 1995.

McLuhan, Marshall, and Bruce R. Powers. *The Global Village. Transformations in World Life and Media in the 21st Century.* New York and Oxford: Oxford UP, 1989.

– – –. *Understanding Media: The Extensions of Man.* New York: Signet, 1964.

Merriam-Webster. *Collegiate Dictionary.* 2 Nov. 2002. <www.m-w.com>.

Scholes, Robert, and Eric S. Rabkin. *Science Fiction. History, Science, Vision.* New York: Oxford UP, 1977.

Toelken, Barre. *The Dynamics of Folklore.* Logan: Utah State UP, 1996.

Turnstall, Jeremy. *The Media Are American.* New York: Columbia UP, 1977.

*Wag the Dog.* Dir. Barre Levinson. Perf. Dustin Hoffman, Robert De Niro, and Anne Heche. New Line Studios, 1997.

Wiegerling, Klaus. *Medienethik.* Stuttgart: Metzler, 1998.

# Civilization(s): Rewriting History in Interactive Media

## Markus Rheindorf

The theoretical framework of this paper is broadly that of British cultural studies, with the specific inflection given to it by Lawrence Grossberg. Its perspective is therefore both contextualist and anti-essentialist in the sense that it disavows the notion of stable and inherent meaning and replaces it with the notion of the "articulation" of contextual "conditions of possibility." As a method of studying the contextual meaning and specificity of cultural articulations, this approach can be described as being less concerned with interpreting texts and audiences than with "describing vectors, distances and densities, intersections and interruptions, and the nomadic wandering . . . through this unequally and unstably organized field of tendential forces and struggles" (Grossberg 312). The spatial vocabulary of vectors and lines associated with the notion of articulation derives indirectly from Grossberg's commitment to conjuncturalism. The perspective taken here is equally conjuncturalist insofar as it holds that, while there are no necessary correspondences or relations (between causes and effects, between signs and meanings), there are nevertheless always real, effective correspondences. In formulating this contextualist position, Grossberg rereads Marx's statement that "people make history but in conditions not of their own making," arguing that the links that seem to give a particular text or set of texts a particular effective meaning, that connect it with a particular social group and political position, are forged by people operating within the limits of their real conditions and historically articulated "tendential lines of force." The articulation of any meaning is thus seen as the ongoing construction of unstable (to varying degrees) relations between practices and structures, texts and contexts. This position furthermore fractures the transcendental claim of the sign's function (i.e., the stability of a preconstituted meaning) and posits a notion of the sign as effective precisely insofar as it produces meaning contextually.

Given that the relation between a text and its context is one of articulation, it follows that "[t]he difference between a text and its context, or a practice and a structure, is only a product of the level of abstraction at which one is operating" (Grossberg 221). At a different level, the relation between text and practice therefore parallels that between any effect and its conditions of possibility, because "cultural practices [are] places where multiple trajectories of effects and investment are articulated, as the point of intersection and negotiation of radically different kinds of vectors of determination – including material, affective, libidinal, semiotic, semantic, and so on" (Grossberg 22). Regarding the levels of analysis involved in the present study, actual texts can be said to emerge only as a particular player engages with the program, while the process of playing itself, as well as related phenomena belonging to the domain of fandom, are located at the level of social practices. The stratum of social practices thus mediates, as it were, between textual products and socio-cultural contexts, which it is a part of and yet non-identical with.

Contextual analysis as understood here furthermore entails seeing the significance or "productivity" of any textual practice as "a determined and determining effect of a material context." And while the apparent presence of meaning is not an illusion, since meaning is itself effective within the context, it can never be finished or final, because "it is the product of practices that arrest the potentially unending movement of signifiers" (Grossberg 65). Cultural studies' materialism thus replaces the notion of stable signifiers with that of signifying or discursive practices: these are seen as producing signifiers in apparently stable relationships to one another and in a particular position vis-à-vis the other signifiers.

Bearing all this in mind, the approach taken here begins with the recognition that playing one of the computer games from the *Civilization* series[1] represents not only a set of historically and culturally situated semiotic practices, but also a productive context of texts in its own right. At different levels of abstraction, both these texts and the social practices that produce them are articulations of the broader socio-cultural context that forms the conditions of possibility for their

Civilization(s) 325

existence. In the case of the *Civilization* games, the kind of focus on cultural and historical context called for by Grossberg's theory of articulation has more than merely theoretical implications, not least because the individual game versions differ considerably from each other in their articulation of the "history of mankind." In fact, many of the changes that distinguish *Civilization III*, the latest installment in the series, from earlier game versions can be related to economic and political developments over the past two decades, including but not strictly limited to what the game itself terms "increasing American global dominance."

**The *Civilization* series**

The first *Civilization* computer game was published in the early 1990s and was the first PC game to bring its "creator" immediate recognition and fame. Even today, the *Civilization* series remains the only prominent computer game to bear its creator's name as part of the title and is marketed accordingly as "Sid Meier's *Civilization*."[2] While developed by Firaxis, the *Civilization* franchise is owned and marketed by Infogrames, a software firm that considers itself an "infotainment company." According to the company's website, the game's qualities as an infotainment product are educational as well as entertaining (it is described as "informative" and "exciting") in its portrayal of "historical facts." While the cultural and political implications of making such a claim for a computer game might appear all too obvious, it will not be my line of argument here that there is any inherent danger in the medium of the computer game as such.[3] Rather, it is the specific configurations of possible rewritings of "the history of mankind" that are problematic in the series, and these require both critical distance to and engagement with the games on their own ground.

There are three main areas to my argument which, though treated separately here, need to be seen as interdependent and interrelated in significant ways. The first is the games' basic premise, their *modus operandi*: the rewriting of history by the player. This, I argue, is partially hard-coded into the programs as from a U.S.-American point of view and is in many ways an instance of what is known as American exceptionalism. The second focus of enquiry lies with the deterministic and mechanistic model of civilization/culture that is at the heart of the games. Providing an account of this model of culture from the perspective of cultural studies presents a particularly challenging task, as both "tool" and "object" of analysis are more or less abstract idealizations of the workings of culture. The third field of interest is the ways in which the games, even though they articulate the player as a nearly omnipotent being transcending time, restrict the player's choices within a limited field of predetermined options. These choices are, moreover, conditioned through the transparency of cause-effect relations and the almost complete predictability of effects in the games. While the issues outlined above are pertinent to the entire series of games, the present paper focuses on *Civilization III*, the latest and most complex installment of the series, and will refer to earlier game versions mainly by way of comparison.

## *Civilization III*

To begin with, the self-styled "universe" of *Civilization III* features a customizable game environment, which the player can shape according to his or her wishes in what is referred to in the manual as the "world-setup screen." Although it takes place before the beginning of actual game-play, the world-setup already puts the user/player in a position of virtual omnipotence; powerful enough, at any rate, to shape entire worlds. To be precise, the player is able to choose the relative age of the planet, the size of the landmass, its climate, plus the number of "enemy civilizations" that people it. In addition to these fantastic, computer-generated worlds, there is, however, also "our own lovely gem of a planet" as a playable scenario, "conceived with a combination of accuracy, playability and aesthetic quality." In either case, the civilizations the player can choose to play in *Civilization III* are sixteen in number: America, Aztec, Babylon, China, Egypt, England, France, Germany, Greece, India, Iroquois, Japan, Persia, Rome, Russia, and Zululand.[4] Everything and everyone else, in terms of the binary opposition hard-coded into the game, is "barbarian." This includes Etruscans, Illyrians, Mayans, and other historically significant groups –

all of which figure in the game as mere savages bent only on pillaging and destroying the player's civilization. This logic of exclusion and the resulting binary opposition are the first major steps in the game's rewriting of history, a rewriting in which the player is implicated from the start, as it is he or she who accepts all this, making it "real", as it were, only by repeatedly clicking "OK."[5] The only alternative at this point, really, is to exit the program.

**Rewriting "the history of mankind"**

For some time now, notions of history as always "written by" someone and thus necessarily incomplete, ideological, and reproductive of power relations have gained a foothold in the academic world. Yet, what cultural studies in particular seems to have neglected so far is a look at the popular articulations of this practice of "writing history." These, I would argue, have equally been around for some time. As a matter of fact, people are consciously engaging in various practices that involve a rewriting of history, and they do so in a highly ritualized way every day as part of the games they play. In this respect, I would like to emphasize that cultural studies' commitment to taking the popular side of things as more than simply an "object" of study must entail the distinct possibility that, in any critical engagement with popular culture, the popular is not the only side that can benefit or learn from the other.

The fact that the game's "creators" (and Infogrames' marketing department) are indeed aware of its historiographic practices is indicated by the tongue-in-cheek tag line of the promotional blurb printed on the package of *Civilization III*:

> REWRITE HISTORY . . . WITH THE GREATEST GAME OF ALL TIME!
> From Firaxis Games and Sid Meier, the creative genius behind some of the most critically acclaimed computer games ever produced, comes CIVILIZATION® III. Experience a game of epic proportions. Match wits against the greatest leaders of the world in an all-out quest to build the ultimate empire and rule the world!

Filled with superlatives and exclamations, this short promotional text contains most of the actual ingredients of the game: a rewriting of history, building the ultimate empire as the greatest leader of all time, and ruling the world.

**The dawn of civilization**

The beginning of the game is set at the so-called "dawn of civilization," which the game declares somewhat arbitrarily to be (or have been) in 4,000 B.C. Regardless of which civilization the player chooses, the game begins at this point in time with a message greeting him or her as the leader of the respective civilization and informing the player that "the people have vested absolute power in you." It is no coincidence, then, that the *Civilization* game series belongs to a genre of games also known as "God Games." The result of this universal "dawn of civilization" is that the player is not only able to "found" "America" in 4,000 B.C., but does so as Abraham Lincoln. Despite appearances, however, this idiosyncrasy is only a first indication of what this game has to offer in the way of pleasures – and I do mean pleasures – in turning upside down the commonsensical.

An all-white "America" is thus founded in the distant past, cleanly severed from European history and messy questions of origins. This is when the logic of exclusion operating in the game most obviously takes the form of American exceptionalism. Here is the past that places "American" civilization next to Greek and Roman civilization – in the game's very own hall of fame. And, to make matters even more interesting, *Civilization III* includes more or less detailed descriptions of its sixteen "civilizations" and their respective histories as they supposedly really happened in "our" world. Accessible via the in-game encyclopedia, the so-called "Civilopedia" of the *Civilization* games, the entry under "Americans" gives an account of U.S. history. After characterizing "the Americans" as "expansionist and industrious," the entry gives the familiar story of America's independence from Europe and goes on to say that "[i]n its first century and a half, the country was mainly preoccupied with its own territorial exploration and expansion and with economic growth." It need not be pointed out that this history writes Native American peoples out of the picture entirely, yet another step in cleaning up the most problematic aspects of U.S. history. The story continues as follows:

> American politics became increasingly democratic during the 1820s and 30s. But a matter of freedom would bring the nation to its greatest crisis: the American Civil War. On February 4, 1861 – a month before Abraham Lincoln (1860-1865) could be inaugurated in Washington – six Southern states sent representatives to Montgomery to declare a new independent government. With Jefferson Davis at its head, the Confederate States of America came into being, set up its own bureaus and offices, occupied federal buildings, issued its own money, raised its own taxes, and flew its own flag.
> With the Union preserved, the nation entered a period of unprecedented prosperity after the long conflict and reconstruction.

This is the first part of the history of the United States of America – or simply "America" as the game would have it – as it is presented in *Civilization III*. The odd jumps and gaps in the text – in particular the paragraph break that marks the time and place of the civil war – readily reveal the conspicuous absences.

The "Civilopedia" entry proceeds to tell the story of "American" success: "the United States had become a great power by virtue of its prodigious economic growth since the Civil War; now many thought it ought to begin to act like one. In World War I, and again in World War II, American industrial might and military technology proved decisive." The so-called "debacle of Vietnam, set in the morass of the Cold War" appears in the history book of *Civilization III* only because it "shook America's belief" in itself, causing "a malaise that would not pass for 20 years." Then, "[l]asting but 40 days," the Gulf War happened just in the nick of time, restoring "America's" self-confidence and "was easily won by the U.S.-led coalition at only slight material and human cost." Recent developments, one could argue, have made the irony of these careless words all too clear.

Though not as revealing as the entry on "America," the histories of the other civilizations are also of critical interest – especially in their depiction of war, genocide, and conquest. Thus, of the Aztec empire, the player learns that "its progress was halted in 1519 by the appearance of

Spanish adventurers," and that not much later "the Aztec empire came to an end," as if by itself. The Iroquois nations, though represented as one of the "greatest civilizations," are also described in a peculiar fashion. The "Civilipedia [sic]" provides a relatively detailed history of their military campaigns and ultimate defeat, yet nothing about their culture. They thus figure only as the defeated of the past and the insignificant of the present in the form of current census figures on how many Iroquois are living on reservations today. And, while mentioning World War II could not be avoided altogether in the entry under "Germany," it is alluded to only as "the rise of Hitler," while not a word is included about the atrocities of the holocaust. Hitler, perhaps surprisingly, is described as having come into power "not by popular support" but through "ruthless political intrigue." Indeed, the game's account of German history seems to strive to expunge "the Germans" from any collective guilt as a people and consequently depicts World War II as having been entirely one individual's fault. In fact, it is really "Hitler's War," according to the game's history book. In another entry – this one on Japan, in which one might expect to find at least some mention of World War II in general and of Hiroshima in particular, especially since nuclear missiles are a part of the game environment's virtual arsenal – the text only speaks euphemistically of "the attack on Pearl Harbor and the horrors that followed." On the one hand, the game's rewriting of "real" history thus consistently "suppresses" and "backgrounds," in van Leeuwen's use of the terms, the most traumatic moments in history. On the other hand, however, it fully enables the player to commit genocide on an unprecedented scale within the diegetic world of the game universe.

**The end of history**

Back in the interactive universe of the game, with its *tabula rasa* at the "dawn of civilization," the player becomes situated at the center of the historiographic practice that articulates individuals as the agents of historical change, great leaders whose deaths are usually "turning points" in the history of the respective "civilization." In the histories that can be written by the player, time – pseudo-historical time in this case –

passes strangely. As the game is played in turns, time slows down more and more, as it were, the closer the player gets to the present, as each turn at the beginning equals first 200, then 100, 50, and so on down to two years per turn. Finally, around 1950, each turn consists of a single year. Modernity is thus experienced as much denser than ancient history, more intensely filled with events, development, and "progress." As the manual makes clear, "rapid change is now considered normal." In fact, there can be no better illustration of the game's implicit ideology of linear, technological progress than its own introductory video, showing the development of humanity from the Stone Age to the present in one smooth, gliding camera movement. This movement finally culminates, as does human progress, in the Babel-like structure in which each layer represents a successive stage of technological development. The pinnacle, as it were, in terms of progress and also of the tower visualizing it, is our present age, with a U.S.-American fighter jet representing the ultimate achievement of human civilization.

The "dawn of civilization," as has already been indicated, is fixed in time, but what of the end of the game, the end of history? Unless the game ends with the destruction of the player's civilization, the following ways of winning are possible in *Civilization III*: winning the "Space Race", achieving "Global Domination," being elected "Head of the United Nations," "overwhelming the world with your cultural achievements," or "Conquest," i.e. killing everyone else on the planet. All of these options seem quite straightforward, and yet, why would being elected "Head of the United Nations" have the same (positive) effect as committing multiple genocide? The key, I would argue, is to be found in the game's account of "American" history, which equates being in a position to lead the world with using the U.N. as an instrument for global domination. If these are the game's implicit conditions of becoming "the greatest civilization of all time," political reality seems to have caught up with popular imagination only recently.

**The internal workings of civilization**

As part of its game environment or "universe," *Civilization III* also provides a mathematical model of the internal workings of civilization –

or what cultural studies would call "culture." The in-game manual is less inhibited, of course, than most practitioners of cultural studies would be, in giving a straightforward definition of "civilization" and "culture":

> There is no single driving force behind the urge toward civilization, no one goal toward which every culture strives. There is, instead, a web of forces and objectives that impel and beckon, shaping cultures as they grow. Its five basic impulses are: Exploration, Economics, Knowledge, Conquest, Culture.

As "Exploration" and "Conquest" are both managed through military units in *Civilization III*, and as "Culture" comes into being only through "Knowledge" or science in the game, there are really only three domains to be managed by the player: economics, the military, and science.[6] Knowledge or science, however, is equated simply with new technologies. According to the game manual, "with each new advance, new units and city improvements become available for manufacture." Science thus functions primarily to improve the player's economic and military position.

Of the three domains managed by the player, only that of science is considered here in detail since it includes, in terms of game mechanics, all matters of culture. Science, as has already been mentioned, serves two principal purposes in the *Civilization* games: strengthening the economy and "upgrading" the military. Related to the functionality of science and knowledge is the game's underlying assumption that everything has a price. The player can buy virtually anything in this game instead of obtaining it in a conventional manner: buildings that would take years to complete can be bought in an instant at a price, and so can scientific knowledge, diplomatic alliances, cities, military units, etc. The image that best represents the game's notion of scientific progress is no doubt the schematic referred to as "the knowledge tree": connected by discrete lines, each "advance" is connected to others in a strictly teleological manner. But not only is progress linear in the game, the player also chooses (and thus knows in advance) what to discover next. Thus, the game manual's metaphor of "climbing the technology tree" becomes emblematic of the definition of scientific progress informing the game: "As humankind progressed by fits and starts through the ages, civilizations rose and fell, their success or failure due to what knowledge they acquired and how they employed it." As a consequence, the player is told, "progress is inevitable." Significantly, it is numbers that represent the process of acquiring knowledge, and the "science points" generated by each city drive the player's civilization's "intellectual growth". Since "each new advance costs a certain amount of science," all the player has to do is to accumulate science points. Ironically, the game manual also quotes Abraham Lincoln on scientific progress: "It is in the pursuit of the natural sciences that mankind provides the greatest evidence of his [sic] nobility, of his [sic] spark of the divine." This definition of science as limited to "the natural sciences," apart from any ideological implications it might have, also contributes to the functionality with which knowledge is associated in the *Civilization* games.

Rather than dwell on the implications of the notion of the functionality of knowledge, the following will deal with the ways in which "Culture" appears in the game only as a by-product of so-called science. The effectivity of "Culture" in the *Civilization* games is strikingly similar to that of a waste product, emanating from cities like toxic material and contaminating nearby areas and thus making them part of the player's "empire." In the mechanistic model of culture employed by the game, certain institutions the player can build simply "generate" culture in a strictly numerical sense: a library generates three "culture [sic]" per turn, a cathedral twelve. "What good is all this culture?," the game manual asks rhetorically. "Culture enlarges your borders," is its answer: "It expands the city's culture sphere of influence, your borders, and thus gives you rights to demand that which lies within them." It's all a matter of expansion, ultimately, an expansion that never has to ask itself whether its underlying system is that of colonialism or imperialism. As "Culture" points accumulate in the course of "history," these numbers are used to determine the borders of the player's empire or nation state, and when the value in any area rises above a certain limit, that area automatically becomes part of it. If, for instance, an enemy civilization has a relatively small city next to a very large one belonging to the player, the large city's culture will still spread into the small city and eventually "turn it around." The player is informed of such an event by a message like the following: "Mr.

President, the loyal citizens of Pompeii have overthrown their oppressors and have pledged allegiance to us! They yearn to be part of our culture." Culture in the *Civilization* games is moreover clearly written with a capital "C" as its main sources are buildings such as temples, libraries, and cathedrals. Other significant sources of "Culture" are the "wonders of the world" included in the games.[7] Significantly, construction of these wonders is tied only to certain scientific discoveries, but not to specific places or sites. As a consequence, building "the pyramids" in Washington D.C. can become another idiosyncratic – but also pleasurable – exercise of denying the order and hierarchies of conventional historiography.

But to return to the functional definition that the in-game encyclopedia provides for Culture and its uses: "When a civilization becomes stable and prosperous enough, it can afford to explore the Arts. Though cultural achievements often have little practical value. . . . [Culture] also helps to build a cohesive society that can resist assimilation by an occupying force." Significantly, this definition, while still holding on to the notion of "high culture," seems to claim as an effect of elitist culture the kind of cultural identity that Raymond Williams sought to grasp as "a whole way of life." Paradoxically, the popular, of which the game is itself a part of, is thus written out of history and civilization. The following leaves little doubt as to what kind of "Culture" the game manual is referring to: "The effort you spend on building an enduring cultural identity might seem like a luxury, but without it, you forfeit any chance at a greatness other civilizations will respect." And even though the manual later concedes that "the definition of 'culture' is a slippery one," it ultimately defines culture by virtue of the fact that it "contributes to feelings of nationality, pride of place, and the willingness to resist that which is alien." And, because "a strong culture can impress other nations," the game environment not only allows for the practice of cultural imperialism but actually encourages it as a way of winning the game.

## Transparency, Predictability, and Omnipotence

While all entities and relations in the *Civilization* games are necessarily expressed – at least on the level of programming – in numeric values, the games go well beyond this prerequisite of the medium by making utterly transparent the equation between a given game action and a numeric value, be it "Culture" generated or food harvested. Significantly, the game allows for hardly any element of chance, no element of chaos in the development of mankind. The best will prevail, economically and militarily that is. Of course, such a notion of historical progress – a particularly mechanistic version of "survival of the fittest" – necessarily reflects back on the non-diegetic world. Things are the way they are not so much because they could not have been any other way, but because everyone gets what they deserve based on their scientific, economic, and strategic abilities. This, of course, ultimately can serve to legitimize and naturalize the claim to power of anyone who can wield it.

In the end, it would seem, the control the player has over his or her civilization combines with the total transparency and predictability of effects only to further strengthen the sense of omnipotence evoked by the game environment. As tokens of this transparency one might cite here the fact that when pollution occurs as a result of heavy industry in the game, it is not only easily removed, but the player is "informed of it immediately" and automatically by the game. Another instance of such transparency has already been mentioned in the form of the potent image of the "knowledge tree": teleological and transparent, the progress of mankind can be directed and planned by the seemingly omnipotent player.

## Conditioned choices

All of the above, however, has one principal consequence in the game world of the *Civilization* series. If the player knows in advance what effects each of his or her actions and choices will have, it becomes relatively simple to determine and make what is unequivocally the best choice. Thus, it is mainly through the predictability and transparency of effects that the player's choices may be conditioned and coaxed into a particular direction of pseudo-historical development. A good case in point is the choice of political systems allowed by the game environment. There are six forms of government in *Civilization III*: "Despotism," "The Republic," "Feudalism," "Monarchy," "Democracy", and "Communism."

Each of these options has certain consequences for the player's economic, military, and scientific effectiveness, consequences which the "Civilopedia" lists in the form of a table. When comparing the summaries of these effects to each other, it becomes seemingly easy to decide without a doubt that "Democracy" – and the game developers clearly had U.S. democracy in mind – is quite simply the best form of government (in terms of game values). The in-game definition of "Democracy" reads as follows: "You are elected by the people to rule with their interest at heart. And you are rewarded by increased commerce and production." Remarkably, the manual is quite explicit about the mechanics of conditioning here: the player is rewarded for choosing "Democracy," much more so than with the other forms of government.[8] And yet, the game again displays a rupture, as it were, in its ideological construction and thus invites deconstructive readings of the fact that the government type of "Democracy" becomes available only after "Banking" has been researched by the player.

By way of introducing an unstable element, which functions in the same manner irrespective of the current form of government, the *Civilization* games also simulate "the people." As their omnipotent leader, the player needs to ensure they are happy and do not cause disorder, as this has a devastating effect on the economy. Balancing happiness and "its inverse state, civil disorder," becomes necessary because "the natural trend of citizens' attitude is toward unhappiness . . . as the population of the city grows [and] competition for jobs, commodities, and services increases." Simply enough, the appropriate response to civil disorder advocated by the manual is "restoring order." But this is not done through any change in policy; in fact, this is not even possible. Instead, the player can either send troops to quell unrest, dispense luxuries among the people, or make some citizens entertainers. As with models of knowledge and culture, the ways in which other games model the practice of maintaining hegemonic control over a people would be worth investigating further.

**Alternate universes, open questions**

Of the revealing changes made to previous versions of the game, the most telling ones are perhaps the absences, the erasures of political systems. Significantly, the game manual includes short comments on all the things omitted from version III of *Civilization*, including the following: (1) "Fundamentalism: Government based on religious fanaticism is no longer an option." No further comment on part of the manual. (2) "The Senate: That's right. Republics and Democracies no longer have those pesky Senators refusing to let you go to war and forcing you into unwanted treaties." Again, no further comment. Game reality has been altered to accommodate . . . well, what, exactly?

While I cannot begin to answer this and other questions here, I want to outline possible avenues for further research into the rewriting of history in interactive media that may lead to answers to such questions. It is conceivable, at least on a theoretical level, that there are other ways – less mechanistic and less transparent ways – of modeling civilization, culture, and historical agency in the medium of the computer game. Introducing the notion of genre into the discussion, it should be possible to describe the distinctive ways in which other genres than the "God Game" probably allow the player to rewrite history interactively. On a contextual rather than a textual level of analysis, the discourse of players and fans about these games certainly provides rich material for cultural studies, especially regarding the issue of "realism" in games dealing with historical subject matter. Most importantly, this will allow one to move beyond the kind of primarily textual, semiotic analysis I have provided here, which can never be more than a first step in the direction of understanding the actual uses people make of video and computer games. Do they accept or refuse the position the game seems to invite them into? Are people writing histories in which Native American peoples spread over the entire globe, or ones in which America becomes Communist in the early 20th century? Even more radically, are there widely-available modifications to the game, and if so, what aspects of the programming did the players feel needed to be adapted to their needs and desires? What all these possible avenues call for, however, is a critical engagement with video or computer games as culturally significant phenomena, studying their effectivity beyond the fact of their popularity and apparent ubiquity. As interactive media, video and computer games implicate the player in social and discursive practices in ways that clearly need to be seen as distinct from that of either literature or film, but have so far received little or no attention from within the field of cultural analysis.

**Notes**

[1] For present purposes, the series of *Civilization* games is assumed to furthermore include updates, expansion packs, and other non stand-alone programs published by Infogrames.
[2] The first *Civilization* game was a board game published by Avalon Hill, which Sid Meier adapted rather than "created" for the computer screen. In fact, the term "creator" is often used by the gaming industry in a deliberately ambiguous and misleading way, sometimes referring to a designer, programmer, or "writer." As a consequence of the many different uses of the term, there have more recently been a number of other games, such as *Clive Barker's Undying*, which also bear the name of a person associated with the creation of the game, most commonly the writers of story-boards.
[3] For the purposes of this paper, "medium" is understood primarily as the material and technological properties of a given form of communication, as well as its technical possibilities and restrictions of production, distribution, and reception (cf. Kress and van Leeuwen 22-23). Any medium is thus distinguished from the modes that have become associated with it and which may be seen as the conventionalized uses of the respective medium.
[4] Leaving the core program unchanged, the expansion pack *Civilization III: Play the World* allows players to engage in multiplayer games via LAN or internet, as well as adding another eight civilizations to the game: "the Arabs, the Carthaginians, the Celts, the Koreans, the Mongols, the Spanish, the Ottomans, the Vikings." At least in terms of numbers, it thus manages to slightly shift the focus from "Western" civilization towards a more balanced list of playable civilizations.
[5] It should perhaps be noted that other games, such as the classic *Master of Orion* game series, allow the player to create custom civilizations that can be fashioned according to his or her predilections.

[6] "Conquest," incidentally, is paraphrased as "military persuasion," with the aim "to be the last civilization standing when the dust clears."

[7] These vary in number and definition from one version of the game to the next, and were initially limited to the seven accepted Wonders of the World. In the most recent game version, by contrast, the list of wonders includes such phenomena as Wall Street, The Manhattan Project, and The Cure for Cancer.

[8] Another significant advantage listed by the manual is that "cities of a Democracy are immune to propaganda." Ironically, these ideologically charged games ultimately claim that "Democracy" is free of, and makes its citizens immune to, ideology and propaganda.

## Works Cited

Grossberg, Lawrence. *Bringing It All Back Home: Essays on Cultural Studies.* Durham: Duke UP, 1997.

Kress, Gunther and Theo van Leeuwen. *Multimodal Discourse: The Modes and Media of Contemporary Communication.* London: Arnold, 2001.

Leeuwen, Theo van. "The Representation of Social Actors." *Texts and Practices.* Ed. Carmen R. Caldas-Coulthard and Malcolm Coulthard. London: Routledge, 1996. 32-70.

## Games

*Clive Barker's Undying.* © 2001 by Electronic Arts.

*Master of Orion.* © 1990 by Microprose.

*Master of Orion II.* © 1996 by Microprose.

Sid Meier's Civilization. © 1990 by Microprose.

Sid Meier's Civilization II. © 1996 by Microprose.

Sid Meier's Civilization III. © 2001 by Infogrames.

Sid Meier's Civilization III: Play the World. © 2002 by Infogrames.

# The contributors

**Carmen Birkle** is Associate Professor of American Studies at the University of Mainz and currently teaching as a visiting professor at the University of Vienna. Her publications focus on American women's literature and culture, postcolonialism, ethnic writers, popular culture, and detective fiction. They include *Women's Stories of the Looking Glass: Autobiographical Reflections and Self-Representations in the Poetry of Sylvia Plath, Adrienne Rich, and Audre Lorde* (1996), *Migration – Miscegenation – Transculturation: Writing Multicultural America into the Twentieth Century* (2004), *(Trans)Formations of Cultural Identity in the English-Speaking World* (1998, with J. Achilles) and *Frauen auf der Spur: Kriminalautorinnen aus Deutschland, Großbritannien und den USA* (2001, with S. Matter-Seibel and P. Plummer). She was assistant editor of the journal *Amerikastudien/ American Studies* (1991–2002) and is associate editor of the journal *Feminist Europa* (1998–).

**Günter J. Bischof** is Professor and Executive Director at the Center for Austrian Culture and Commerce at Metropolitan College, University of New Orleans. Founding Co-Editor of "Eisenhower Center Studies of War and Peace" (8 vols.) and *Contemporary Austrian Studies* (10 vols.). His research interests are: Cold War and World War II, U.S.–Austrian relations, prisoners of war, historical memory. Author of *Austria in the First Cold War, 1945-1955* (1999).

**Timothy Conley** is Associate Professor of English and former chair of the American Studies Program at Bradley University in Peoria, Illinois. He has twice been Fulbright Professor of American Literature and American Studies at the University of Vienna and recently completed a Fulbright Professorship at the University of Sarajevo. His publications include studies of 18th-century American literature, Benjamin Franklin, Hector St. John de Crèvecoeur, Faulkner, the discipline of American Literature, and the formation of American Studies. He has edited two books on American Literature curriculum and educational history, and is currently completing a collection of Bosnian Literature in translation.

**Paul Crumbley** is Associate Professor of English and American Studies at Utah State University. He is the author of *Inflections of the Pen: Dash and Voice in Emily Dickinson*, as well as numerous articles on American women writers and the role of wilderness in the formation of American identity. Crumbley is a member of the Executive Board of the Emily Dickinson International Society.

**Markus Heide** teaches American Literature and Cultural Studies at Humboldt-University Berlin and is a post-doc member of the *Graduiertenkolleg* Postcolonial Studies at the University of Munich. Publications include articles on Mexican-American cultural production, 19th- and 20th-century American literature, as well as the forthcoming book *Grenzüberschreibungen: Chicano/a-Erzählliteratur und die Inszenierung von Kulturkontakt*. He is co-editor of *Eating Culture: The Poetics and Politics of Food* (2003).

**Louis J. Kern** is Chair of the History Department at Hofstra University. He teaches courses in cultural history, American literature, film, and popular culture. He is currently working on a study of the roots of a culture of eugenics, grounded in a heterogeneous body of texts ranging from medical texts, popular marital/sex guides, racist tracts, and the literature of sex radicals in the period 1850-1910.

**Verena Klein** is an assistant in the Department of American Studies at the University of Innsbruck. For her thesis on "Literature about Literature: An Analysis of Carol Shields's *Small Ceremonies, Swann* and *The Stone Diaries*" she received the Canadian Studies Award for Young Scholars from the Canadian Studies Center in Innsbruck in May 2002. She is currently pursuing her interest in Canadian literature by working on her doctoral thesis on mother–daughter relationships in Ethel Wilson's work.

**Vincent Kling** is Associate Professor of English and lecturer in German at La Salle University in Philadelphia. He has twice been a guest professor at the University of Vienna, and he spends several months a year in that city. His interests include comparative literature, with emphasis on Austrian literature of the last two centuries, and American literature, with emphasis on the Southern Renaissance, twentieth-century lyric poetry – especially Wallace Stevens – and Eugene O'Neill. His dissertation is on Hofmannsthal, and he has published on Horváth, Doderer, Jonke, and Sebald. Theory of fiction is an additional interest, particularly Georges Perec and the OULIPO movement. Kling is a literary translator and has published renderings of stories by Doderer and Gütersloh.

**Paul Lauter**, Allan K. and Gwendolyn Miles Smith Professor of Literature, Trinity College, Hartford, Connecticut, is Past-president (1994-95) of the American Studies Association (USA) and General Editor of the groundbreaking *Heath Anthology of American Literature*. Lauter was one of the founders of The Feminist Press and its treasurer and an editor for fourteen years. He also held offices in the faculty and staff union at the State University of New York, the American Friends Service Committee, and the U.S. Servicemen's Fund. He worked in freedom schools in Mississippi during the mid-1960s. His recent books include *From Walden Pond to Jurassic Park*, a collection with Ann Fitzgerald on *Class, Culture, and Literature*, and an edition of Thoreau's *Walden* and "Civil Disobedience" in the New Riverside series (for which he serves as general editor). Other projects include a Blackwell companion to American literature, a volume entitled "What is American," and the development of an anthology of American literature for students in Asia.

**Monika Messner** studied English and American Studies and comparative literature at the University of Innsbruck, Austria. Her research interests are contemporary American culture and literature, in particular the American West and American popular culture.

**Greta Olson** is a research fellow at Freiburg University. She was a visiting professor to the North American Studies Program at Bonn University and has also taught at the Universities of Basel, Freiburg, and Innsbruck. She is the author of *Reading Eating Disorders: Writings on Bulimia and Anorexia as Confessions of American Culture* (2003) and the co-editor, with Monika Fludernik, of *In the Grip of the Law: Trials, Prisons and the Space Between* (2004). She has published work on narratology, the 18th-century English novel, Shakespeare's trial scenes, images of the body as a monster in contemporary American women's writing, and on Martin Heidegger's ethics. Forthcoming in American Studies are essays on Alice Sebold, and the obsession with the body in contemporary culture and theory. In English Studies essays on Shakespeare's *Richard III*, criminal bodies in literature and penology, and depictions of women as fetishists are also forthcoming as is an essay on teaching gender studies through creative writing and drama. She is at work on her second book, *Stigmatized Criminals from Shakespeare to Conrad and Frank Norris: Animalistic Representations of Criminals in Literature and the Rise of Biocriminology*.

**Duco van Oostrum** is Lecturer in American Literature at the University of Sheffield. His current research revolves around American sports culture, in particular film and literature. His book project on African American sports literature, film, and autobiography explores in detail African American constructions of subjectivity through ghost-writing and sports aesthetics. Publications associated with this project encompass past and present cultural images of the 1968 Olympics, Ralph Ellison, John Edgar Wideman, cover photographs of *Sports Illustrated*, autobiographies of Mal Whitfield, Bill Russell, Hank Aaron, Michael Jordan, Ali and Foreman, and many others. This interest in (auto)biography and ghost-writing follows on from his monograph on Henry James and Henry Adams, *Male Authors, Female Subjects* (1995). He is also working on a book on 1970s American Culture.

**Roman Puff** is working for the transdisciplinary *Europa-Institut* at the Vienna School of Economics. He is interested in the emergence of the

Modern World following World War I as well as in transatlantic relations – past, present, and future.

**Markus Rheindorf** is a Ph.D. student at the Department of Applied Linguistics at the University of Vienna where he also teaches classes in media and discourse analysis. He is currently a Junior Fellow at the International Research Centre for Cultural Studies in Vienna. His research interests are largely transdisciplinary and include systemic functional linguistics, semiotics, film theory, and cultural studies. He has published a number of articles on popular culture and postmodern theory in relation to such diverse topics as film adaptations of video games, the productivity of pain in mainstream action films, the literary fantastic in comics, and the holistic poetics of Paul Auster.

**Sylvia Schiefer** graduated from the University of Vienna in 1999. The topic of her diploma thesis was *African-American Writers and Traditions of Black Music: James Baldwin*. From 1999 to 2002 she was a high school teacher for English and French. Since 2002 she has worked as an English language trainer for the language institute of the Austrian Armed Forces and the Law Enforcement Academy.

**Claudia Schwarz** is a research assistant and lecturer at the Department of American Studies at the University of Innsbruck, from which she graduated in American and English Studies and Philosophy/Psychology/ Education in 2003. The doctoral thesis she is working on aims at establishing a literary and media-philosophical approach to the "ethics of storytelling" in the various media.

**Andreas Weissenbäck** is a lecturer in the Department of English and American Studies at the University of Vienna and also lectures at the University of Applied Science for International Business Relations in Eisenstadt, Austria. In 1998 he was a visiting scholar at the Institute of Communications Research at the University of Illinois. His research interests include the impact of American consumer culture on Europe, as well as discourse for business purposes. He is also active as a musician with a focus on jazz piano.

## The editors

**Michael Draxlbauer** is Associate Professor at the Department of English and American Studies at the University of Vienna. He has taught courses on American and Canadian literature, Cultural Studies, literary criticism and essay writing. His research interests are Native North American literatures, postcolonialism, New England Puritanism, and American Transcendentalism. In addition to a number of articles, he has published *Das Konzept der "Supreme Fiction" im Spätwerk von Wallace Stevens* (1990) and edited *Remembering the Individual/ Regional/National Past* (1999, with Waldemar Zacharasiewicz), *Sites of Memory and Collective Identities* (2002, with Axel Borsdorf and Waldemar Zacharasiewicz), and *The EmBodyment of American Culture* (2003, with Maureen Devine and Heinz Tschachler). He is currently writing a book on "The Construction of Pocahontas."

**Thomas M. Fröschl** is Associate Professor of Modern History at the University of Vienna. He was visiting professor at the University of Leiden (1998), and at Georgetown University/Washington, D.C. (1999). His academic areas are the intellectual history of the Atlantic world, political and cultural history of the USA, history of Brazil, and the political and cultural history of Central Europe. He has edited *Atlantische Geschichte* (2003) and is currently writing a book on "Die USA in atlantischer Perspektive. 1776 bis zur Gegenwart" (to be published in 2006).

**Astrid M. Fellner** is Assistant Professor at the Department of English and American Studies at the University of Vienna. Her publications include *Articulating Selves: Contemporary Chicana Self-Representation* (2002), a co-edited volume *Body Signs: The Body in Latino/a Cultural Production* (forthcoming Ediciones Nuevo Espacio), and several articles in the fields of U.S. Latino/a literature, Gender Studies, and American Cultural Studies. Currently, she is working on a book about the female body in late-eighteenth-century American literature.

## Wissenschaftliche Paperbacks
Literaturwissenschaft

Thomas Stauder
**Gespräche mit Umberto Eco**
Unter dem Titel *Gespräche mit Umberto Eco* finden sich hier die Texte von vier längeren Interviews mit dem in Mailand lebenden Semiotik-Professor vereint, die zwischen 1989 und 2002 in Italien geführt wurden und die hier zum Teil erstmals in deutscher Übersetzung erscheinen. Auf ein einleitendes Kapitel zum *Namen der Rose* folgen Gespräche über *Das Foucaultsche Pendel, Die Insel des vorigen Tages* und *Baudolino*; den Abschluss bildet ein Gespräch über Stationen von Ecos Biographie, das viele Details enthält, die bisher weder in Italien noch in Deutschland bekannt waren.
Bd. 17, 2004, 176 S., 14,90 €, br.,
ISBN 3-8258-7243-2

## Literatur: Forschung und Wissenschaft

Karl-Heinz Stoll
**Die Interkulturalität afrikanischer Literatur**
Chinua Achebe, Cyprian Ekwensi, Ngũgĩ wa Thiong'o, Wole Soyinka
Die englische Sprache in Afrika, die literarischen Medien Roman und Drama sowie die Themen der afrikanischen Literatur sind Ausdruck kultureller Pluralität. Der Beitrag postkolonialer Literatur zu unserem Orientierungswissen besteht in ihrem Potenzial sprachlicher und inhaltlicher Desorientierung als Voraussetzung einer Emanzipation von eurozentrischen Vorurteilen. Das Buch geht ein auf die englische Sprache als Medium wirtschaftlicher Globalisierung und kultureller Fragmentarisierung. Dann werden anhand der Eigenarten von Sprache, Handlungsführung, Introspektionen und mythologischem Ideengehalt die Werke der vier bedeutendsten schwarzafrikanischen Autoren exemplarisch als „Dazwischen-Literatur" interpretiert. Zielgruppe sind Anglisten, Afrikanisten und alle, die sich für die Rolle von Kultur in unserer globalisierten Welt interessieren.
Bd. 1, 2003, 400 S., 30,90 €, br.,
ISBN 3-8258-6698-x

Jan Jansen; Henk M. J. Maier (eds.)
**Epic Adventures**
Heroic Narrative in the Oral Performance Traditions of Four Continents
The adventures of the 'epic' in modern times are a fascinating topic in themselves. The Romantics claimed that every self-respecting nation should once upon a time have had one, and they set out to reconstruct these epics for political as well as cultural reasons. These epics represented earlier stages in the development of nation-states and in this modern world they were, for a long time, hard to appreciate. The introduction of taperecorders, however, brought the epic back in the lime-light, with a vengeance. It became fashionable for scholars to record long oral narratives, and to present them as long written poems that reflected deeply ingrained ideas. In this process, the idea of the epic was revitalized. This volume presents critical analyses – of epics in Sub-Saharan Africa, the former Soviet Union, South-East Asia, Medieval Europe, and America – about this process of revitalization, sometimes even invention,

**LIT** Verlag Münster – Berlin – Hamburg – London – Wien
Grevener Str./Fresnostr. 2 48159 Münster
Tel.: 0251 – 62 032 22 – Fax: 0251 – 23 19 72
e-Mail: vertrieb@lit-verlag.de – http://www.lit-verlag.de

of epics in particular historical, political and academic contexts.
Bd. 3, 2004, 200 S., 20,90 €, br.,
ISBN 3-8258-6758-7

Leo Truchlar (Hg.)
**One America – Many Americas**
Erkundungen und Verortungen aus historischer, kultureller und literarischer Sicht
Die Frage „Wieviele Amerikas gibt es?" wird in den Beiträgen dieses Tagungsbandes aus historischer, kultureller und literarischer Sicht exemplarisch zu beantworten versucht, und sei es bloß mit vorläufigen Argumenten bzw. gar nur mit neuen, differenzierteren Fragestellungen. Drei Themenbereiche, „Atlantische Perspektiven Europas", „Globale Perspektiven Amerikas" und „Hemisphärische Perspektiven innerhalb der Amerikas", werden ansatzweise sondiert, wobei die jeweiligen Ermittlungen, in der Mehrzahl anhand konkreter Textanalysen, etwa Zeit- und Raumkonfigurationen in europäischer sowie nord- und südamerikanischer Perspektivik, medien- und filmspezifische Diskurse im US-amerikanischen Blickregime oder, im Rückblick auf Herman Melvilles Erzählung „Benito Cereno", das panamerikanische Imaginäre erkunden und verorten. Dabei erweisen sich Bilder und Selbstbilder immer wieder als Rollen-, Klischee- und Trugbilder und können in der Folge als Mittel in einem Aufklärungsprozess verwendet werden, der vor allem und insbesondere jedwede hegemoniale Weltsicht der USA, wie sie nicht nur in verbalen und nonverbalen Entwürfen und Konstrukten disseminiert wird, sondern zusehends für sämtliche Belange der politischen, wirtschaftlichen und gesellschaftlichen Praxis maßgebend ist, radikal in Frage stellt.
Bd. 5, 2004, 192 S., 24,90 €, br.,
ISBN 3-8258-7383-8

**American Studies in Austria**
edited by Univ.Ass. Mag. Dr. Astrid Fellner (University of Vienna), Ass.-Prof. Dr. Klaus Rieser (University of Graz), Dr. Hanna Wallinger (University of Salzburg)

Heinz Tschachler; Maureen Devine; Michael Draxlbauer (Eds.)
**The EmBodyment of American Culture**
American culture has literally become fixated on the body at the same time that the body has emerged as a key term within critical and cultural theory. Contributions thus address the body as a site of the cultural construction of various identities, which are themselves enacted, negotiated, or subverted through bodily practices. Contributions come from literary and cultural studies, film and media studies, history and sociology, and women studies, and are representative of many theoretical positions, hermeneutic, historical, structuralist, feminist, postmodernist. They deal with representations and discursifications of the body in a broad array of texts, in literature, the visual arts, theater, the performing arts, film and mass media, science and technology, as well as in various cultural practices.
Bd. 1, 2003, 224 S., 19,90 €, br.,
ISBN 3-8258-6762-5

LIT Verlag Münster – Berlin – Hamburg – London – Wien
Grevener Str./Fresnostr. 2 48159 Münster
Tel.: 0251 – 62 032 22 – Fax: 0251 – 23 19 72
e-Mail: vertrieb@lit-verlag.de – http://www.lit-verlag.de

## FORECAAST
(Forum for European Contributions to African American Studies)

Maria Diedrich; Carl Pedersen; Justine Tally (eds.)
**Mapping African America**
History, Narrative Formation, and the Production of Knowledge
Bd. 1, 1999, 256 S., 30,90 €, br.,
ISBN 3-8258-3328-3

Stefanie Sievers
**Liberating Narratives**
The Authorization of Black Female Voices in African American Women Writers' Novels of Slavery
Bd. 2, 1999, 232 S., 25,90 €, br.,
ISBN 3-8258-3919-2

Justine Tally
**Paradise Reconsidered**
Toni Morrison's (Hi)stories and Truths
Bd. 3, 1999, 112 S., 17,90 €, br.,
ISBN 3-8258-4204-5

Dorothea Fischer-Hornung; Alison D. Goeller (eds.)
**EmBODYing Liberation**
The Black Body in American Dance
A collection of essays concerning the black body in American dance, *EmBODYing Liberation* serves as an important contribution to the growing field of scholarship in African American dance, in particular the strategies used by individual artists to contest and liberate racialized stagings of the black body. The collection features special essays by Thomas DeFrantz and Brenda Dixon Gottschild, as well as an interview with Isaac Julien.
Bd. 4, 2001, 152 S., 20,90 €, br.,
ISBN 3-8258-4473-0

Patrick B. Miller; Therese Frey Steffen; Elisabeth Schäfer-Wünsche (eds.)
**The Civil Rights Movement Revisited**
Critical Perspectives on the Struggle for Racial Equality in the United States
The crusade for civil rights was a defining episode of 20th century U.S. history, reshaping the constitutional, political, social, and economic life of the nation. This collection of original essays by both European and American scholars includes close analyses of literature and film, historical studies of significant themes and events from the turn-of-the century to the movement years, and assessments of the movement's legacies. Ultimately, the articles help examine the ways civil rights activism, often grounded in the political work of women, has shaped American consciousness and culture until the outset of the 21st century.
Bd. 5, 2001, 224 S., 24,90 €, br.,
ISBN 3-8258-4486-2

Fritz Gysin; Christopher Mulvey (Eds.)
**Black Liberation in the Americas**
The recognition that Africans in the Americas have also been subjects of their destiny rather than merely passive objects of European oppression represents one of the major shifts in twentieth-century mainstream historiography. Yet even in the eighteenth and nineteenth centuries, slave narratives and abolitionist tracts

**LIT** Verlag Münster – Berlin – Hamburg – London – Wien
Grevener Str./Fresnostr. 2 48159 Münster
Tel.: 0251 – 62 03 22 – Fax: 0251 – 23 19 72
e-Mail: vertrieb@lit-verlag.de – http://www.lit-verlag.de

offered testimony to various ways in which Africans struggled against slavery, from outright revolt to day-to-day resistance. In the first decades of the twentieth century, African American historians like Carter G. Woodson and W. E. B. Du Bois started to articulate a vision of African American history that emphasized survival and resistance rather than victimization and oppression. This volume seeks to address these and other issues in black liberation from interdisciplinary and comparative perspectives, focusing on such issues as slave revolts, day-to-day resistance, abolitionist movements, maroon societies, the historiography of resistance, the literature of resistance, black liberation movements in the twentieth century, and black liberation and post colonial theory. The chapters span the disciplines of history, literature, anthropology, folklore, film, music, architecture, and art, drawing on the black experience of liberation in the United States, the Caribbean, and Latin America.
Bd. 6, 2001, 280 S., 24,90 €, br.,
ISBN 3-8258-5137-0

Justine Tally
**The Story of *Jazz***
Toni Morrison's Dialogic Imagination
Ever since its publication in 1992, *Jazz*, probably Toni Morrison's most difficult novel to date, has elicited a wide array of critical response. Many of these analyses, while both thoughtful and thought-provoking, have provided only partial or inherently inconclusive interpretations. The title, and certain of the author's own pronouncements, have led other critics to focus on the music itself, both as medium and aesthetic support for the narration.
Bd. 7, 2001, 168 S., 20,90 €, br.,
ISBN 3-8258-5364-0

Mar Gallego
**Passing Novels in the Harlem Renaissance**
Identity Politics and Textual Strategies
*Passing Novels in the Harlem Renaissance* offers an insightful study of the significance of passing novels for the literary and intellectual debate of the Harlem Renaissance. Mar Gallego effectively uncovers the presence of a subversive component in five of these novels (by James Weldon Johnson, George Schuyler, Nella Larsen, and Jessie Fauset), turning them into useful tools to explore the passing phenomenon in all its richness and complexity. Her compelling study intends to contribute to the ongoing revision of the parameters conventionally employed to analyze passing novels by drawing attention to a great variety of textual strategies such as double consciousness, parody, and multiple generic covers. Examining the hybrid nature of these texts, Gallego skillfully highlights their radical critique of the status quo and their celebration of a distinct African American identity. "*Passing Novels in the Harlem Renaissance* is an impressive work of scholarship and interpretation. It is well researched and stimulating to read." Hanna Wallinger, University of Salzburg "Mar Gallego draws our renewed attention to the uses and subversions of the trope of passing that have characterized the African American novelistic tradition also in the twentieth century." Giulia Fabi, University of Ferrara "Mar Gallego's

**LIT** Verlag Münster – Berlin – Hamburg – London – Wien
Grevener Str./Fresnostr. 2 48159 Münster
Tel.: 0251 – 62 03 22 – Fax: 0251 – 23 19 72
e-Mail: vertrieb@lit-verlag.de – http://www.lit-verlag.de

thorough scholarship now provides us with a new, in-depth and refreshing reading of texts we thought we already knew something about. A provocative text and a welcome addition to the field!"
Justine Tally, University of La Laguna
Bd. 8, 2003, 224 S., 24,90 €, br.,
ISBN 3-8258-5842-1

Paola Boi; Sabine Broeck (Eds.)
**CrossRoutes – The Meanings of "Race" for the 21st Century**
This collection reflects the still urgent project of historical recuperation, as well as an examination of literary representations and other cultural manifestations of the Black Diaspora. Disciplinary work within the boundaries of African American Studies has been enhanced by more general considerations of the history of "race" and racism in globalized contexts. The articles assembled here reflect recent empirical research as well as challenging theoretical considerations. Contributions address particular formations of racialized modernity owed to the impact of the Atlantic slave trade and slavery, and thus broaden the approach to the Middle Passage, to improve our understanding of it as a constitutive transatlantic phenomenon in the widest possible sense.
Bd. 9, 2003, 272 S., 25,90 €, br.,
ISBN 3-8258-6651-3

Sylvia Mayer (ed.)
**Restoring the Connection to the Natural World**
Essays on the African American Environmental Imagination
Since its emergence in the second half of the nineteenth century American environmentalism had predominantly been a white, middle-class pursuit, preoccupied with notions of wilderness and wildlife preservation. Only fairly recently, with the advent of the environmental justice movement in the 1980s, has American environmentalism broadened its definition of "environment" to include the concerns relevant to a community's way of living. Especially the concerns of poor urban communities of color, which have been exposed to environmental hazards disproportionately, have entered the political agenda.
Bd. 10, 2003, 208 S., 20,90 €, br.,
ISBN 3-8258-6732-3

Kimberley Phillips; Hermine Pinson; Lorenzo Thomas; Hanna Wallinger (eds.)
**Critical Voicings of Black Liberation**
Resistance and Representations in the Americas
The contributions to "Critical Voices of Black Liberation in the Americas" originated from the 1999 CAAR Conference in Münster and from conferences held in the US in 2000 and 2001. More than half of the eleven essays consider black performances on stage, in sound, and on film; the remaining essays explore slavery, African American literature, and nineteenth-century black educators. These exciting essays creatively examine artistic and/or political articulation of black liberation as the construction of a new critical and signifyin(g) voice. This liberated and critical voice asserts itself as much as a communal expression of black subjectivities as it is an articulation of the black self.
Bd. 11, 2003, 192 S., 20,90 €, br.,
ISBN 3-8258-6739-0

LIT Verlag Münster – Berlin – Hamburg – London – Wien
Grevener Str./Fresnostr. 2 48159 Münster
Tel.: 0251 – 62 032 22 – Fax: 0251 – 23 19 72
e-Mail: vertrieb@lit-verlag.de – http://www.lit-verlag.de

Ana María Manzanas; Jesús Benito
**Intercultural Mediations**
Hybridity and Mimesis in American Literatures
Intercultural Mediations proposes a study of the multiple crossings between and among the different literary traditions of the United States. The volume draws upon two main theoretical sources, namely postcolonial theory and American Border Studies, and aims to articulate a model of the hybrid, postcolonial and liminal nature of writing in the US. Ana M$^a$ Manzanas and Jesús Benito explore the nature of the ëthnicÖthers' appropriation, dialogization and Subversion of the Euroamerican authoritative discourse – embodied in what the authors call the Book of the West – as well as the inscription of cultural difference on the white page.
Bd. 12, 2003, 224 S., 25,90 €, br.,
ISBN 3-8258-6738-2

Joanne M. Braxton;
Maria I. Diedrich (Eds.)
**Monuments of the Black Atlantic: Slavery and Memory**
With Aldon Nielson, the editors of this volume agree that "the middle passage may be the great repressed signifier of American historical consciousness." The essays collected here illustrate that the repressed memory of crossing lives not only in the academy, in oral traditions, and in the stone walls of slave fortresses but in the liturgy as well as the spiritual and religious practices throughout the African Diaspora. Descendants of African slaves living in the wide Diaspora are bearers of an "unforgetful strength" that endures and endures, manifesting itself in every aspect of culture. Black writers, artists and musicians in the New World have tested the limits of cultural memory, finding in it the inspiration to "speak the unspeakable."
Bd. 13, 2004, 168 S., 24,90 €, br.,
ISBN 3-8258-7230-0

Maria I. Diedrich; Theron D. Cook; Flip Lindo (Eds.)
**Crossing Boundaries**
African American Inner City and European Migrant Youth
Upon walking U.S. inner-city streets you sooner or later come upon groups of black kids wearing prison-style outfits; there is a boom box, and rap music. And inevitably you will hear the N-word. Upon entering a district housing migrants in any European city you will encounter almost identical scenes – youngsters dressed in prison style, the boom box, rap. Only most of the kids are of a "white" or olive complexion. They call themselves "Wiggers", "white Niggers" or "Black albinos."
Bd. 14, 2004, 200 S., 24,90 €, br.,
ISBN 3-8258-7231-9

# Erlanger Studien zur Anglistik und Amerikanistik
hrsg. von Rudolf Freiburg
und Dieter Meindl

Rudolf Freiburg; Jan Schnitker (Hg.)
**"Do you consider yourself a postmodern author?"**
Interviews with Contemporary English Writers
Bd. 1, 1999, 248 S., 20,90 €, br.,
ISBN 3-8258-4395-5

L**IT** Verlag Münster – Berlin – Hamburg – London – Wien
Grevener Str./Fresnostr. 2 48159 Münster
Tel.: 0251 – 62 032 22 – Fax: 0251 – 23 19 72
e-Mail: vertrieb@lit-verlag.de – http://www.lit-verlag.de

Hannah Jacobmeyer
**Märchen und Romanzen in der zeitgenössischen englischen Literatur**
Im Zentrum einer vielfach konstatierten Renaissance des "Wunderbaren" in der Kultur des ausgehenden 20. Jahrhunderts stehen die Formen und Strukturen von Märchen und Romanze. Gelten sie uns einerseits als Merkmale einer prämodernen Narrativik, so sind sie andererseits zu Konstanten von Literatur geworden, die sich durch die Jahrhunderte bis in die sogenannte postmoderne Literatur hinein nachweisen lassen. Anhand ausgewählter zeitgenössischer Texte der englischen Literatur zeigt die Autorin, wie Märchen und Romanzen fortleben - aber auch, wo sie sich überschneiden und auf welche Weise sie in eine endlose, intertextuelle "Echokammer" eingebunden werden. Romanzenmuster erlauben zudem, Einsicht in die Gemeinsamkeiten hoher und "trivialer" Literatur zu nehmen. Autoren der detailliert analysierten Märchen und Romanzen sind u. a. Salman Rushdie, A. S. Byatt, Graham Swift, Angela Carter und Barbara Cartland.
Bd. 2, 2000, 224 S., 35,90 €, br.,
ISBN 3-8258-4686-5

Dieter Meindl
**North American Encounters**
Essays in U.S. and English and French Canadian Literature and Culture
These essays (in English except for four items in German and French) provide an intercultural perspective. They deal with such diverse aspects of North American (including Québécois) literature as "Kanadas Verhältnis zu den USA im Spiegel seiner Literatur," "Canada and American Slavery", the Acadian theme in "Longfellow et Antonine Maillet" and "The Western Love Code: Faulkner, Hébert, Hemingway, and Ondaatje." The continental context also pervades treatments of novels (featuring Indian wars, sentimentalism, the West, and modern *pícaros*), story cycles (e.g., Atwood's), and the long poem (Kroetsch).
Bd. 3, 2002, 184 S., 19,90 €, br.,
ISBN 3-8258-6110-4

Aglaja Frodl
**Das Selbst im Stil**
Die Autobiographien von Muriel Spark und Doris Lessing
Für die Autobiographie hat die poststrukturalistische Annahme einer weltschaffenden Funktion von Sprache weitreichende Folgen: Sie stellt in Frage, daß ein vor jedem Schreiben vorhandenes Selbst in einer Autobiographie beschrieben werden kann, da jeder sprachliche Akt immer nur auf Sprache zurückverweise und so das autobiographische Ich durch das Schreiben erst geschaffen werde. Dagegen entwickelt die vorliegende Studie das theoretische Modell eines „Selbst im Stil", das lebensweltliches und in der Autobiographie erst geschaffenes Selbst über den Stil verbindet und den Verlust des Selbst in Sprache widerlegt. Dieses Modell des Selbst im Stil bildet die Basis der Analyse zweier zeitgenössischer Autobiographien: Muriel Sparks *Curriculum Vitae* und Doris Lessings Zweiteiler *Under My Skin / Walking in the Shade*.
Bd. 4, 2004, 296 S., 41,00 €, br.,
ISBN 3-8258-7893-7

LIT Verlag Münster – Berlin – Hamburg – London – Wien
Grevener Str./Fresnostr. 2 48159 Münster
Tel.: 0251 – 62 032 22 – Fax: 0251 – 23 19 72
e-Mail: vertrieb@lit-verlag.de – http://www.lit-verlag.de